A DICTIONARY
OF JAPANESE
IDIOMS

William de Lange

Edited by
Hiromi Miyagi-Lusthaus

FLOATING
WORLD
EDITIONS

First edition, 2005

Published by **Floating World Editions**
26 Jack Corner Road, Warren, CT 06777
floatingworldeditions.com

ISBN 1-891640-24-0

Printed and bound in the U.S.A.

Library of Congress Cataloging-in-Publication Data available upon request.

Preface

Idioms are perhaps the most difficult aspect of a foreign language for a student to master. Indeed, even the most advanced speakers of a foreign language may occasionally get the idiom wrong. Thus, politicians, artists, and even writers entertaining foreign audiences, may resort to a figure of speech that seems appropriate in the context of their own language, but will only be the cause of puzzlement, hilarity, or even embarrassment when rendered into the language of their hosts. This is because idioms are so firmly rooted in the culture, tradition, beliefs, and habits of a people.

   This applies as well if not more so when rendering Japanese into English. There are profound differences between the cultures of the Far East and the West, and such differences are often directly reflected in the makeup of an idiom. To those familiar with Japan's long feudal history, it will come as no surprise that many of its idiomatic expressions derive from a martial context. Two examples that draw directly on the Japanese art of fencing are the expressions 鍔を割る (to smash a hand guard) and 鐺が詰まる (to have the tip of one's sheath obstructed—and thus be unable to draw one's sword). Though both have gone out of fashion, the former may still used to describe a desperate fight or, more figuratively, a fierce competition, and the latter to describe someone who is in financial trouble or in dire straits. Another idiom that has its roots in Japan's feudal history is the expression 鉾を向ける (to direct one's halberd at someone), which now means to attack someone verbally, as in an argument. Other idioms have their roots in more peaceful pastimes, such as the drinking of tea. Though shared by other nations, in Japan, where it has become a ritual in its own right, the drinking of tea has spawned such expressions as 茶を言う (to talk tea), which means to talk nonsense. Another Japanese idiom related to tea is お茶を濁す (to make the tea turbid), which can be used either to indicate that something is done in a halfhearted way or, to use the English equivalent, when someone is "beating about the bush." Even the absence of certain idioms in a language can reveal a lot about those who speak it. Unlike, for instance, the English, Dutch, and Hispanic languages, which are spoken by peoples who have a longstanding seafaring tradition, for an island people, the Japanese have remarkably few idioms that derive from a nautical context.

   The largest number of Japanese idioms involve parts of the human body, perhaps more so than in any other language. The head, the ears, the eyes, the nose, the mouth, the chin, the jaw, the neck, the arms, the elbows, the hands, the fingers, the nails, the chest, the heart, the liver, the stomach, the veins, the navel, the groin, the legs, the knees, the heels, indeed the body itself, whether in the form of 体, 体 or 身, are at the center of the large majority of Japanese idioms.

Entries

In compiling the main entries for this dictionary a few basic principles have been observed. Care has been taken to avoid the unnecessary inclusion of synonymous entries. There are in Japanese, as in Chinese, a large number of single and compound nouns that are exceedingly close in meaning. Words such as 恩 and 恩義 (a favor) or 刑 and 刑罰 (punishment), essentially have the same meaning. Although they may differ in nuance or in the specific context or sentence structure in which they are used, such synonyms tend to combine with the same verbs to create identical idiomatic expressions. Consequently, it is pointless to include different versions of such synonyms here. As a rule, preference has been given to nouns that consist of just one Chinese character, simply because they feature in a larger number of idiomatic expressions. Needless to say that in those cases where the various synonyms of a noun *do* combine with one or more completely different verbs to create new or different idiomatic expressions, such nouns have been included among the main entries.

At first glance, the reader will notice that a considerable number of sub-entries in this dictionary are not purely idiomatic, that is, their meaning follows logically from the sum of their constituent parts, and in many cases their constituent parts can simply be replaced by another word similar in meaning. Most of the sub-entries, however, are sufficiently unpredictable to pose a stumbling block to the foreign student. Thus obvious and straightforward noun-verb combinations such as 歌を歌う (sing a song) or 金で買う (buy with money) have been left out, but an expression such as 金を掛ける (invest money), has been included, simply to bring it to the attention of the foreign student and to distinguish it from the homonymous expression 金を賭ける (bet money). Indeed, the choice for many of the verbs that occur in strictly non-idiomatic expressions are far from logical and at times even bewildering. One only has to think of instances such as 果実を結ぶ (bear fruit), 富が落ちる (win a prize in a lottery), 記事を差し止める (ban a newspaper article), or 異を差し挟む (hold uncommon views), to realize that, especially for the beginning student, the inclusion of such expressions is essential.

Particles

Another major stumbling block for foreign students lies in the difficulty of choosing the right postpositional particle: が, で, と, に, は, へ, or を (助詞). Often a student will be quite sure as to which verb combines with which noun, but to choose the right particle to join them together is often frustratingly difficult. Perhaps the easiest aspect in the context of the idioms presented in this book is the distinction between the particles が and を; the former being used in combination with intransitive verbs (自動詞), as in 気が抜ける, the latter in combination with transitive verbs (他動詞), such as 気を抜く.

Nothing, however, prepares the student fully for other combinations, which seem quite arbitrary and offer no clue as to which particle they require. Which particle, for instance, joins the noun 山 (mountain) with the verb 登る (climb) to express in Japanese the phrase "climb a mountain," を or に? (the latter). And which particle combines 人 (person) with 成る (become) to express the phrase "to grow up," or "come to oneself," に or と? (the latter). To complicate matters, the use of a different particle may even radically change the meaning of an expression, such as in 顔に出す (show one's emotions) and 顔を出す (show up), or as in 鍵に掛ける (deceive someone) and 鍵を掛ける (lock something up). Given the important role of the particle in the meaning of an idiom, all the idioms listed in this dictionary are arranged under the particle by which the noun and verb are combined: が , で , と , に , へ , or を .

Senses

Another difficulty with Japanese idiomatic expressions is the many senses that a single expression may cover. In many cases the two given senses derive simply from the difference between the literal and figurative meaning of an expression, as in 垢を抜く which in its literal sense means to "wash off the dirt" and in its figurative sense means to "clear one's name." In other cases senses may even seem to contradict each other, such as in (人を) 自由にする, which may either mean to "set someone free," or to "have someone at one's mercy." Another example is 幕を切る, which can either mean to "start on something" or to "bring something to an end." In these cases, only the context in which the expression occurs will solve the paradox. Then there are a number of expressions that have a bewilderingly large number of senses. Expressions such as 手を入れる, for example, which, depending on the context, may either mean to "touch something up," to "sound someone out," to "find a means," or to "make a raid."

Here, too, the sense that applies is usually suggested by the context, although only a full grasp of all the nuances will lead to a correct interpretation.

In most cases, there is no profound distinction between the basic senses of the intransitive and transitive form of an idiom. Usually, there is a slight difference in intentionality, the intransitive form having a more passive tone, while the transitive form has a more active tone. However, idioms being what they are, here too, there may be considerable differences in meaning from case to case, while certain senses may only derive from either the intransitive or the transitive form. A case in point is the earlier mentioned idioms 気が抜ける and 気を抜く which have not one sense in common while the former has the additional meaning of to "lose flavor," "go flat," or "go stale."

Patterns

Luckily, there is some consistency in the way in which some verbs combine with certain nouns. Think, for instance, of the verbs 上がる (rise) or 貸す (lend) and the nouns 腕 (arm) and 手 (hand). One of the aims of this dictionary is to help the foreign reader to develop a feeling for such patterns of usage. Thus, as one grows familiar with the makeup of Japanese idioms, one will find that verbs such as 陥る frequently combine with nouns denoting trouble, difficulty or any kind of situation one can get into or fall into. Thus, the verb 抱く often combines with nouns denoting doubt, suspicion, and other emotions that can be entertained, harbored, or cherished. And thus the verb 背く tends to combine well with nouns denoting rule, custom, morality, and other things that can be violated or contravened. There is, however, no hard and fast rule, as the same verbs will combine with far less obvious nouns, as in 羽目に陥る (be in a quandary), 膝を抱く (implore someone), or 名に背く (belie one's name).

When these many and often difficult hurdles have finally been overcome, the student can turn his or her full attention to the thousands of truly idiomatic expressions that have a meaning completely removed from the literal meanings of their constituent parts. Idioms such as 鯖を読む (cheat in counting) or 鰹節に使う (make a cat's paw of someone), the application of which seems to bear no relation to the individual meanings of their constituent parts. These are the most difficult to master, as the key to their meaning and usage lies deeply buried in old and, to the student, alien customs and traditions. They are quintessentially Japanese and, as such, are a source of joy to those who have mastered them, as they will have brought them yet a step closer to the essence of the people and culture that have spawned them.

Symbols

Where relevant, different senses of meaning for each entry are indicated by the symbols ❶ , ❷ , ❸ , etc. The senses are generally listed with the sense used most frequently appearing first.

Other symbols used throughout this dictionary are listed with their meanings below. Please note that the usage of the symbols differs slightly for the main entries, the sub-entries, and the sample phrases.

Main entries:	Sub-entries	Sample phrases
Ⓐ archaic	Ⓐ archaic	① idiomatic equivalent
Ⓗ historic	Ⓞ obsolete	Ⓐ abstract equivalent
Ⓓ dialect	Ⓓ dialect	Ⓛ literal equivalent
Ⓔ elegant	Ⓔ elegant	Ⓔ elegant equivalent
Ⓒ colloquial	Ⓒ colloquial	Ⓒ colloquial equivalent
Ⓒ vulgar	Ⓥ vulgar	Ⓥ vulgar equivalent
Ⓢ slang	Ⓢ slang	Ⓢ slang equivalent

ア

愛 love

に Ⓐ ～に愛持つ be blinded by love. ～に溢れる overflow with love. ～に溺れる dote on *sb*; Ⓒ be mad about *sb*. ～に答える requite *sb's* love; love *sb* in return. ～に背く betray *one's/sb's* love. ～に絆される be a slave of love; be tied to *sb* by love. ～に報いる return *sb's* love; requite *sb's* love.

を ～を受ける be the object of *sb's* love. ～を受け入れる accept *sb's* love. ～を失う lose *sb's* love. ～を打ち明ける Ⓔ confess (one's) love. ～を奪う Ⓔ steal (one's) love away. ～を得る win *sb's* love; gain *sb's* love. ～を割く suppress one's feelings of love; abandon one's feelings of love; Ⓔ forsake *sb's* love. ～を囁き合う whisper words of love. ～を示す express (one's) love; demonstrate one's love. ～を誓い合う promise to love each other; Ⓔ exchange tender vows. ～を告げる declare (one's) love; Ⓔ testify to one's feelings. ～を報いる return *sb's* love; requite *sb's* love; love *sb* back. ～を持つ be charming; be attractive.

愛嬌 charms; winsomeness

が ～が有る be attractive; be charming; be endearing; be cute. ～が付く become lovable; gain in charm; Ⓔ grow winsome. ～が零れる be overflowing with smiles.

を ～を売る sell one's favors; Ⓔ traffic in one's charms; Ⓘ curry favor with *sb*. ～を呉れる [*kabuki*] delight the crowds. ～を零す ❶ be alluring; be seductive. ❷ alienate *sb*. ～を振り巻く please everyone; spread one's charms around; be all smiles; Ⓒ Ⓘ turn on the charm.

愛顧 patronage; favor

を ～を受ける receive *sb's* favors; be patronized. ～を失う lose favor with *sb*; Ⓘ fall from grace. ～を乞う solicit *sb's* patronage; ask for *sb's* favor.

愛情 affection; love

に ～に飢える be starved for love; be deprived of affection. ～に溺れる be infatuated with *sb*. ～に報いる requite *sb's* love.

を ～を抱く hold *sb* in affection. ～を得る gain *sb's* affection; win *sb's* love. ～を捧げる give one's love to *sb*; be devoted to *sb*. ～を注ぐ shower *sb* with affection; Ⓔ pour one's affection on *sb*. ～を持つ feel affection toward *sb*. ～を求める seek *sb's* affection; crave *sb's* affection.

愛想 friendliness; amiability

が ～が尽きる despair of *sb*; be disgusted with *sb*; be through with *sb*; Ⓒ be fed up with *sb*.

を ～を言う pay *sb* a compliment. ～を尽かす despair of *sb*; be disgusted with *sb*; be exasperated

1

with *sb*; © be fed up with *sb*. 〜を
する give *sb* a cordial reception; be
hospitable; receive *sb* warmly.

間 an interval; a space ⬥ 間
[に] 〜に立つ mediate between. 〜
に入る mediate between.
[へ] 〜へ入る mediate between.
[を] 〜を置く leave an interval. 〜を
裂く estrange *sb* from *sb* else. 〜を
塞く drive two people apart. 〜を
詰める leave no space.

相槌 Ⓗ alternate hammering
[を] 〜を打つ ◎ ❶ hammer (a sword)
alternately. © ❷ make verbal
responses (to smoothen the conversation); echo *sb's* words; repeat *sb's*
sentiments; ① chime in with *sb*.

合間 an interval
[を] 〜を縫う use the spare moments.

青息 distress
[を] 〜を吹く sigh with worry; be in
distress; © be at one's last gasp.

青筋 a blue vein
[を] 〜を立てる turn purple with rage.
〜を張る turn purple with rage.

煽ち a gust of wind
[に] Ⓐ 〜に乗る be taken in by *sb*;
be led astray.

障泥 a saddle flap
[を] ⊕ 〜を打つ spur *sb* on; egg *sb*
on; encourage *sb*.

垢 dirt; filth; grime
[が] 〜が付く become dirty; become
soiled. 〜が出る exude dirt. 〜が抜
ける ❶ become sophisticated.
❷ clear one's name; be cleared of
suspicion.
[を] 〜を落とす wash off the dirt;
rinse *sth* out; clean *sth*. 〜を抜く
❶ wash off the dirt. ❷ clear one's
name; be cleared of suspicion; be
vindicated.

赤字 a deficit; red figures
[に] 〜に陥る ① fall into the red;
① go in the red. 〜になる suffer a
loss; ① go in the red.
[を] 〜を埋める make up a loss;
cover a deficit. 〜を出す run up a
deficit; ① go in the red.

赤腹 a brown thrush; a dace
[を] Ⓐ 〜を垂れる tell a lie.

明かり a light; a lamp; light
[が] Ⓐ 〜が立つ be vindicated; prove
sth to be groundless; be cleared of
suspicion.
[を] Ⓐ 〜を走る be evident; be
obvious; be clear to all.

秋 autumn; (the) fall
[を] ◎ 〜を吹かす love starts to
cool.

秋風 the autumn wind
[が] 〜が立つ love starts to cool.
[を] ◎ 〜を吹かす love starts to
cool; fall out of love.

諦め resignation; acceptance
〔が〕 ～が付く be reconciled; come to terms with; resign oneself to *sth*.

空家 a vacant house
〔を〕 ～を叩く ❶ be ignored in spite of one's efforts; make futile efforts; exert oneself to no purpose. ⒶⒷ ❷ call in vain.

悪 evil; wickedness
〔に〕 ～に与する be a party to vice. ～に誘う entice *sb* to vice; tempt *sb*. ～に染まる sink into vice; Ⓒ be steeped in vice. ～に陥る fall into evil ways. ～に走る take to crime. ～に耽る Ⓒ abandon oneself to evil; Ⓒ be given to evil ways. ～に負ける yield to evil; be conquered by evil.
〔を〕 ～を一掃する root out evil. ～を重ねる repeat malpractices. ～を滅ぼす overthrow evil.

灰汁 lye; ash; harshness
〔が〕 ～が抜ける become polished; become refined; be free from vulgarity.
〔を〕 ～を去る ❶ become polished; become refined; Ⓒ be free from vulgarity. Ⓒ ❷ draw out the harshness; Ⓒ skim off the scum. ～を抜く draw out the harshness; Ⓒ skim off the scum.

悪意 malice; evil intent; ill will
〔に〕 ～に取る take *sth* amiss; take *sth* the wrong way; Ⓒ put a bad construction on *sth*.

悪事 an evil deed; vice; a crime
〔を〕 ～を抱く harbor ill will (against *sb*); bear a grudge against *sb*.

悪事 an evil deed; vice; a crime
〔に〕 ～に耽る indulge in vice; give oneself over to evil.
〔を〕 ～を行う do evil; practice evil. ～を重ねる commit one crime after another. ～を企む plot evil; plan a crime. ～を働く do evil; work evil; commit a crime.

悪態 abuse; foul language
〔を〕 ～を吐く insult *sb*; abuse *sb*; call *sb* names; ① fling dirt at *sb*.

欠伸 a yawn; yawning
〔を〕 ～を隠す hide a yawn (behind one's hand). ～を噛み殺す stifle a yawn; choke down a yawn. ～を移す infect *sb* with one's yawning. ～をさせる be boring; make *sb* yawn; Ⓒ give *sb* the gapes.

胡座
〔を〕 ～を掻く ❶ sit cross-legged. ❷ ① rest on one's laurels.

朱 red; cinnabar; blood ▶朱
〔に〕 ～に染まる be smeared with blood; Ⓒ welter in blood. ～に成る ❶ dye *sth* red. ❷ be smeared with blood; be covered in blood.

顎 the chin; the jaw
〔が〕 ～が奪われる be stranded; be tied up. ◎ ～が多い be talkative; Ⓒ be loquacious; Ⓒ be a chatterbox;

3

① talk people's head off. 〜が落ちる be delicious. 〜が食い違う be frustrated; be disappointed. 〜が草臥れる get tired of talking. Ⓐ 〜が怖い be argumentative; be glib-tongued. 〜が出る be exhausted; become tired out; Ⓢ be knackered. 〜が外れる ❶ have one's jaw dislocated. ❷ have fits of laughter; Ⓒ Ⓘ fall over laughing; Ⓒ Ⓘ kill oneself laughing. 〜が干上がる suffer loss of income; lose one's means of livelihood.

Ⓒ 〜で使う ❶ deceive sb; Ⓘ take sb in; Ⓒ Ⓘ lead sb by the nose. ❷ boss sb around; Ⓘ have sb at one's beck and call; Ⓘ wrap sb round one's little finger.

Ⓦ 〜を刳る Ⓘ turn up one's nose. 〜を出す be exhausted; become tired out; Ⓢ be knackered. 〜を撫でる pride oneself on sth; be elated. 〜を外す have fits of laughter; Ⓒ Ⓘ fall over laughing; Ⓒ Ⓘ kill oneself laughing. 〜を引く put on a brave face. Ⓞ 〜を養う make a living; support oneself; Ⓔ earn one's daily bread.

足 a foot; a leg

Ⓖ Ⓐ 〜が上がる lose one's job. 〜が重い have leaden feet; be disinclined (to visit sb). 〜が軽い have light feet; be light-footed. Ⓐ 〜が近い visit each other frequently; see much of each other. 〜が付く be traced; be tracked down; be found out. 〜が

強い ❶ [nautical] be a fast sailor. ❷ keep well; last a long time. 〜が出る ❶ exceed the budget; Ⓘ break the bank. ❷ have one's faults exposed; Ⓘ show the cloven hoof; Ⓒ Ⓘ show oneself up. 〜が遠い visit each other infrequently; see little of each other. 〜が鈍る be less eager to; lose enthusiasm for sth. 〜が早い ❶ be quick on one's feet. ❷ go bad quickly; be perishable. 〜が向く head for (a place); go somewhere; Ⓔ turn one's steps toward (a place). 〜が弱い ❶ have a poor leg; be a bad walker. ❷ [nautical] be a slow sailer. ❸ go bad quickly; be perishable.

Ⓦ 〜を洗う ❶ give up (one's bad habits); make a new start. ❷ be through with sb; Ⓘ wash one's hands of (a matter). 〜を痛める injure one's leg. 〜を入れる set foot in (a place). 〜を奪う strand sb; deprive sb of transportation. 〜を屈める bend one's legs. 〜を固める secure a foothold. 〜を組む cross one's legs; sit with crossed legs. 〜を掬う trip sb up; sweep sb's legs from under him/her. 〜を揃える keep pace with sb; walk in step. 〜を出す ❶ be short of money; Ⓘ go in the red. ❷ betray oneself; reveal one's true character; Ⓘ show one's true colors; Ⓘ show the cloven hoof. 〜を解く unwind one's legs. 〜を止める stop in one's tracks; force sb to stay. 〜を取られる lose one's footing. 〜を

抜く extricate oneself (from an awkward situation). 〜を延ばす ❶ stretch one's legs; make oneself at home. ❷ extend one's journey; go farther. 〜を運ぶ call on *sb*; pay *sb* a visit; visit a place. 〜を早める quicken one's pace. 〜を払う trip *sb* up; sweep *sb's* legs from under him/her. 〜を引っ張る stand in *sb's* way; drag *sb* down. 〜を踏み入れる give *sth* a try; get involved in *sth*; ⓘ have a shot at *sth*. 〜を踏み換える change foot. 〜を踏む ⓔ step on *sb's* foot. 〜を向ける ❶ head for (a place); go somewhere; ⓔ turn one's steps toward (a place). ❷ contemplate *sth*; consider *sth*. 〜を緩める slacken one's pace.

味 taste; flavor; savor

[が] 〜が変わる the taste changes; turn sour; go stale. 〜が抜ける lose flavor. 〜が分かる ❶ be a gourmet. ❷ have experience of *sth*; know *sth* by experience.

[を] 〜を覚える ❶ remember the taste. ❷ have experience of *sth*. 〜を聞く try *sth*; taste *sth*. 〜を占める take a liking to *sth*; ⓔ get a taste for *sth*. 〜を知る ❶ know the taste of *sth*; ❷ have experience of *sth*; know *sth* by experience. ⓥ ⓢ ❸ (女の) know a woman; have slept with a woman; ⓔ have carnal knowledge of a woman. 〜を付ける flavor (food); season (food). 〜を見る try the taste of *sth*; taste *sth*; sample (food).

足並 a pace; a step

[が] 〜が揃う fall into step; fall into line; ⓔ act in concert. 〜が乱れる fall out of step; fall apart.

[を] 〜を揃える fall into step; ⓔ act in concert. 〜を乱す be out of tune; be in disarray.

仇 a foe; an enemy

[を] 〜を討つ avenge *sb*; take revenge for *sb*; ⓘ settle old scores (with *sb*); ⓘ square accounts with *sb*. 〜を返す revenge oneself on *sb*. 〜をする do *sb* harm; do *sb* a disservice. 〜を為す ❶ make enemies; harm *sb*; ⓘ create bad blood. ❷ hold a grudge against *sb*; ⓔ harbor a private malice; ⓘ have a chip on one's shoulder.

頭 the head; the brain ♦ 頭 ♦ 頭

[が] ◎ 〜が荒い be short of breath; breathe hard. 〜が良い be clear-headed; be clever; be bright. 〜が痛む ❶ have a headache. ❷ worry about *sb*/*sth*; fret over *sb*/*sth*. 〜が要る require brains. 〜が重い have a headache. 〜が固い have fixed ideas; be inflexible; be set in one's ways; ⓘ be dyed in the wool. 〜が固まる become fixed in one's ideas. 〜が切れる be clear-headed; be a quick thinker; be quick on one's feet; ⓢ ⓘ be on the ball. 〜が臭い have smelly hair. ◎ 〜が苦しい be suffocating; ⓔ be stuffy. 〜が下がる ❶ bow one's head (in greeting); bow to one;

Ⓛ take off one's hat to *sb* ❷ admire *sb*; be impressed by *sb*; Ⓘ take off one's hat to *sb*. ～が鋭(するど)い be sharp-witted. ～が高(たか)い be arrogant; be haughty; be proud; have an over-bearing attitude. ～が違(ちが)う have a different mind. ◎ ～が長(なが)い have a long breath; keep well. ～が鈍(にぶ)い be dull-witted. ～が働(はたら)く have the presence of mind (to); have the sense (to). ～が低(ひく)い be courteous; be humble; Ⓘ keep a low profile. ～が古(ふる)い have outdated ideas. ～が悪(わる)い be slow-witted; be muddle-headed; Ⓒ be brainless.

[に] ～に入(い)れる learn *sth* by heart. ～に浮(う)かぶ come to mind; occur to one. ～に描(えが)く picture (a situation); envisage (a scene). ～に置(お)く take *sth* into consideration; bear *sth* in mind; Ⓘ take *sth* on board. ～に来(く)る Ⓒ ❶ get mad; lose one's temper; be vexed by *sth*; Ⓢ Ⓘ blow a fuse. ❷ Ⓘ go to one's head; Ⓘ lose one's head; Ⓢ Ⓘ lose one's marbles; Ⓢ freak out. ❸ become nervous; fret over *sth*. ～に閃(ひらめ)く flash across one's mind.

[へ] ～へ来(く)る ❶ Ⓘ lose one's head Ⓢ Ⓘ lose one's marbles; Ⓢ freak out. ❷ become nervous; worry over *sth*; fret over *sth*.

[を] ～を上(あ)げる show oneself. ～を痛(いた)める worry about *sth*; fret over *sth*. ～を抑(おさ)える keep *sb* under control; Ⓘ keep *sb* under one's thumb; hold *sb* down. ～を抱(かか)える ❶ think hard about *sth*; Ⓒ Ⓘ rack one's brains. ❷ be at a loss (about what to do); Ⓘ be at one's wits' end; Ⓘ be all at sea. ～を掻(か)く scratch one's head. ～を下(さ)げる ❶ bow one's head (in greeting); bow to one. ❷ give up; give in. ～を搾(しぼ)る think hard about *sth*; Ⓒ Ⓘ rack one's brains. ～を垂(た)れる ❶ drop one's head. ❷ be discouraged; lose heart. ～を使(つか)う use one's brains; Ⓢ Ⓘ use one's loaf. ～を突(と)っ込(こ)む ❶ thrust one's head (into). ❷ take part in *sth*; Ⓒ dabble in *sth*. ～を撫(な)でる pat *sb* on the head. ～を悩(なや)ませる be worried about *sth*. ～を撥(は)ねる ❶ cut off *sb's* head. ❷ extort money from *sb*; take a percentage. ～を捻(ひね)る think hard about *sth*; Ⓒ Ⓘ rack one's brains. ～を冷(ひ)やす settle down; calm down; Ⓐ cool down. ～を解(ほぐ)す Ⓘ clear one's head. ～を丸(まる)める become a Buddhist priest; take the tonsure. ～を擡(もた)げる ❶ gain power; Ⓘ be in the ascendant. ❷ come to mind; gain hold; come to the fore.

辺(あた)り the vicinity; surroundings

[を] ～を構(かま)う have regard for those around one. ～を見(み)回(まわ)す look around. ～を払(はら)う ❶ keep people at bay; drive the crowd away. ◎ ❷ be overbearing; overshadow others.

圧迫(あっぱく) pressure; oppression

[を] ～を受(う)ける be under pressure; be pressed. ～を加(くわ)える put pressure on *sb*; bring pressure to bear on *sb*; Ⓘ turn the screws on. ～を続(つづ)ける keep up the pressure. ～を強(つよ)める intensify the pressure; raise the stakes. ～を除(のぞ)く take off the pressure.

当(あ)てずっぽう [S] **a random guess**

[を] Ⓢ ～を言(い)う have a guess; guess at *sth*; Ⓘ try a shot in the dark.

後(あと) the back; the future

[に] ～になる fall behind. ～に引(ひ)けない refuse to yield; Ⓘ hold the line.

[で] ～で引(ひ)く turn back.

[へ] ～へ回(まわ)す postpone *sth*; put *sth* of; lay *sth* aside; Ⓘ put *sth* on ice.

[を] ～を立(た)てる re-establish an extinct family. ～を継(つ)ぐ succeed *sb*; step into *sb's* shoes. ～を弔(とむら)う perform religious rites for the repose of *sb's* soul. ～を濁(にご)す leave a bad impression. ～を引(ひ)く be unable to stop; find it hard to quit; grow on one.

跡(あと) a mark; a stain; a trace

[が] ～が絶(た)える disappear without a trace; leave no trace; become extinct; go out of existence; die out. ～が付(つ)く leave traces.

[に] ～に習(なら)う follow a precedent.

[で] Ⓞ ～で座(すわ)る succeed *sb*; Ⓘ step into *sb's* shoes.

[を] ～を追(お)う ❶ trail *sb*; run after *sb*; Ⓘ follow up the scent. ❷ follow *sb* in death. ～を隠(かく)すconceal one's whereabouts. ～を晦(くら)ます conceal one's whereabouts; Ⓘ erase one's steps; Ⓘ cover up one's tracks. ～を絶(た)つ be exterminated; be wiped out; put an end to *sth*; wipe out; disappear without a trace. ～を辿(たど)る trace *sb*; follow up a lead. Ⓞ ～を垂(た)る set an example. ～を付(つ)ける trace *sb*; trail *sb*; track *sb* down. ～を取(と)る succeed *sb*; step into *sb's* shoes. ～を残(のこ)す leave traces. ～を踏(ふ)む step in *sb's* footsteps. ～を守(まも)る continue a (family) tradition; take charge of the house.

後釜(あとがま) [S] **a successor**

[に] Ⓢ ～に座(すわ)る succeed sb; replace *sb*; Ⓘ step into *sb's* shoes. Ⓢ ～に据(す)える install *sb* in another's place.

後知恵(あとじえ) [S] **wisdom after the event**

[を] Ⓢ ～を動(うご)かす use the wisdom of hindsight; second-guess.

後始末(あとしまつ) settlement; clearance

[を] ～を付(つ)ける round (a matter) off; settle (an affair); put an end to *sth*; bring *sth* to a close.

後棒(あとぼう) a palanquin's hind bearer

[を] ～を担(かつ)ぐ ❶ bear a palanquin. ❷ be involved in an intrigue; Ⓔ be party to a conspiracy; Ⓘ have a hand in a plot; Ⓢ Ⓘ be in cahoots.

穴(あな) a hole; a burrow; a gap ➧ 穴(けつ)

[を] ～を開(あ)ける ❶ make a hole. ❷ cause a deficit; Ⓘ go in the red. ❸ lose time; get behind (on schedule). ～を埋(う)める ❶ fill up a hole.

❷ make up a loss. ❸ be supplied with *sth*. 〜を捜す find fault with *sb*; carp at *sb's* faults. 〜を掘る dig a hole.

油 oil
囲 〜が切れる ❶ run out of oil. ❷ lose energy; ⓒ ① run out of steam. 〜が乗る ❶ put on fat. ❷ be interested in *sth*. ❸ be at the height of one's skill; ⓔ be at the zenith of power.
囲 〜を売る ❶ sell oil. ❷ idle one's time away; ⓒ dawdle away one's time; ⓢ loaf around. Ⓐ 〜を掛ける incite *sb* to action; wheedle *sb* into doing *sth*. 〜を差す encourage *sb*; egg *sb* on. 〜を絞る ❶ extract oil from *sth*. ❷ take *sb* to task; ⓒ tell *sb* off; ① haul *sb* over the coals. (火に)〜を注ぐ ① pour oil (on the flames); ① add fuel to the fire; fuel *sb's* anger. 〜を付ける put oil on *sth*; anoint *sb*. 〜を採る ❶ extract oil. ❷ reprimand *sb*; ① haul *sb* over the coals. ❸ skimp one's work; ⓢ ① skate on the job.

阿呆 a fool; a simpleton; an ass
囲 Ⓐ 〜を尽くす play the fool.

網 a net; a dragnet; a net trap
囲 Ⓐ 〜が上がる resolve a situation; reveal (*sth* hidden). 〜が下りる be brought to justice; be sentenced.
囲 (法の)〜に掛かる be caught in the meshes (of the law); fall into the clutches (of the law). (法の)〜に漏れる escape from the clutches (of the law); slip through the meshes (of the law).
囲 〜を打つ throw a net; cast a net. 〜を張る ❶ pitch a net; lay a net. ❷ set a trap. 〜を広げる spread a net.

過ち a mistake; an error
囲 〜に陥る fall into bad ways.
囲 〜を犯す ❶ make a mistake; commit an error; ⓒ ① drop the ball. ⓔ ❷ have an extramarital affair; ⓔ commit adultery. 〜を悟る be convinced of one's error; see one's mistake. 〜を正す correct one's mistake; put right an error. 〜を認める acknowledge one's error; recognize one's mistake. 〜を詫びる apologize for one's mistake.

粗 fish bones; a fault
囲 〜を捜す find fault with *sb*; carp at *sb's* faults. 〜を拾う find fault with *sb*; carp at *sb's* faults. 〜を穿る be critical of *sb's* faults; pick at *sb's* faults; ① split hairs.

新 ⓢ brand-new; fresh
囲 ⓢ 〜で買う buy *sth* brand-new.

泡 bubbles; foam; scum
囲 〜となる come to nothing; ① go up in smoke.
囲 ⓢ 〜を食う be confused; be flurried; be taken aback. 〜を立てる make foam; create bubbles. 〜

を吹く froth at the mouth; blow bubbles.

哀れ sorrow; grief; pathos

を ～を訴える plead for mercy; appeal for *sb's* mercy. ～をそそる excite one's pity. ～を増す deepen one's sorrow; add to one's loneliness. ～を催す be moved to pity; be touched with compassion.

哀れみ compassion; pity

を ～を掛ける treat *sb* with compassion; take pity on *sb*. ～を請う ❶ beg for mercy; appeal for *sb's* pity. ❷ beg for alms.

案 an idea; a plan; a scheme

に ～に落つ go according to plan; prove a success; work out well.

を ～を立てる work out a plan. ～を出す present a plan; launch an idea. ～を作る make a plan; hatch an idea; draw up a plan. ～を練る elaborate on a plan; scrutinize a scheme. ～を述べる present one's plan; explain an idea; give one's opinion.

暗礁 a hidden reef

に ～に乗り上げる ❶ strike a hidden rock; be stranded on a hidden reef; run aground. ❷ be deadlocked; ⓒ ① hit a snag.

安否 safety; one's welfare

を ～を尋ねる inquire after *sb's* health; find out how *sb* is doing.

按摩 a massage; a masseur

を ～をする give *sb* a massage. ～を取る have a massage; call in a masseur.

イ

意 a mind; a will; heart; sense

が Ⓔ ～が有る have a mind to do *sth*; be inclined to do *sth*.

と ⓞ ～と為す mind about *sth*; give heed to *sth*; ① take *sth* to heart.

に Ⓐ ～に中たる meet one's/*sb's* expectations. ～に介する worry about; care about; give heed to *sth*. ～に適う be agreeable; be pleasing. ～に従う do as *sb* says; Ⓔ yield to *sb's* wishes. ～に染む be willing; be inclined to. ～に任す leave *sth* to *sb's* discretion. ～に満たす satisfy one; be satisfactory.

を ～を表わす show one's approval; Ⓔ voice one's satisfaction. Ⓔ ～を安じる feel at ease; be at ease. Ⓐ ～を致す express one's thoughts. ～を受ける do as *sb* says; Ⓔ comply with *sb's* wishes. ～を得る be satisfactory; meet one's approval; have one's way. ～を酌む take *sb's* thoughts into consideration; bear *sth* in mind; ① take *sth* on board. ～を決する make up one's mind ～を探る sound *sb's* mind. ～を注ぐ make an effort; pay attention to. ～を体する Ⓔ be in compliance with *sb's* wishes. ～を通じる ❶ make oneself understood; make

9

one's intentions known. ❷ contact *sb* secretly; make secret overtures. ～を尽くす express oneself carefully. ～を唱える voice one's disapproval; raise an objection; Ⓔ take exception to *sth*. ～を曲げる force oneself (to do *sth*). Ⓐ ～を迎える humor *sb*; Ⓔ ingratiate oneself with *sb*; Ⓘ curry favor with *sb*. ～を用いる take care with *sth*; pay attention to *sth*.

威 dignity; authority; influence

[を] ～を借りる shelter under *sb's* influence; Ⓘ ride on *sb's* coat-tails. ～を示す display one's power. ～を振るう wield power; exercise influence.

異 uncommonness; strangeness

[を] ～を差し挟む hold uncommon views; Ⓔ assert a heterodox opinion. ～を立てる do *sth* uncommon; Ⓔ depart from convention.

帷 [E] a curtain; hangings

[を] Ⓐ Ⓔ ～を下す open a private school.

言い掛かり a false charge

[を] ～を付ける accuse *sb* falsely; trump up charges.

家 a house; a household; home

[に] ～に杖突く be fifty years old.

[を] Ⓐ ～を明ける vacate a house; stay away from home. ～を出ず ❶ leave home; go out into the world; enter the real world. ❷ become a Buddhist priest; take the tonsure; enter a Buddhist monastery. ～を失う become homeless. ～を興す ❶ make one's fortune. Ⓗ ❷ found a clan. Ⓔ ～を傾ける exhaust one's family fortune; be bankrupted. ～を構える Ⓔ take up one's abode. ～を知る become the head of a household. ～を建てる build a house. ～を飛び出す run away from home. ～を持つ own a house.

家路 [E] one's way home

[に] ～につく make one's way home.

[を] Ⓔ ～を辿る return home; Ⓔ wend one's way home.

意外 unexpected; unforeseen

[に] ～に驚く be astonished; be surprised at *sth*. ～に思う think *sth* strange; think *sth* odd; be surprised; be taken aback.

鋳型 a mold

[に] ～に注ぎ込む pour (metal) into a mold; cast iron. ～に嵌める mold *sb/sth* to the same example.

[を] ～を取る cast a mold. ～を放す strip a mold.

怒り anger; a rage; wrath

[が] ～が解ける relent toward *sb*; calm down; Ⓐ cool down.

[に] ～に触れる arouse *sb's* anger; offend *sb*; Ⓔ incur *sb's* anger. ～に任せる lose one's temper; give way to anger; ⓒ be borne away with anger. ～に燃える be irate; burn with anger; ⓒ be consumed with rage.

を ～を遷す vent one's anger on *sb*; ⓒ ① take it out on *sb*. ～を抑える restrain one's anger; ⓒ suppress one's wrath. ～を買う arouse *sb's* anger; make *sb* angry. ～を静める calm oneself down; ⓒ quell one's anger; ⓒ appease one's anger. ～を遷す lash out against *sb*; ⓒ vent one's anger. ～を宥める calm *sb's* anger; calm *sb* down; ⓒ appease *sb's* anger. ～ぶちまける fly into a rage; ⓒ open the flood gates of wrath; ⓒ ① fly off the handle. ～を招く invite *sb's* anger; trigger *sb's* anger; ⓒ incur *sb's* wrath. ～を漏らす betray one's anger; vent one's anger; ⓒ ① let off steam.

錨 an anchor

が ～がずれる the anchor drags.

を ～を上げる raise anchor; weigh anchor. ～を打つ ❶ the anchor finds bottom. ⓒ ❷ establish oneself; find one's footing. ～を下ろす ❶ drop anchor; let go the anchor; cast anchor; lie at anchor. ❷ sit down; squat on one's haunches. ～を切る ❶ cut loose the anchor. ⓒ ❷ become independent; ① cut the cord. ～を引きずる drag one's anchor. ～を巻く weigh anchor.

息 one's breath; breathing

が ～が合う be in harmony; be in tune. ～が上がる have difficulty in breathing. ～が掛かる be under *sb's* patronage; be backed up by *sb*; enjoy *sb* 's interest. ～が通う touch *sb's* heart; ⓒ call forth a response in *sb's* heart; ① strike a sympathetic cord. ～が切れる be out of breath; run out of steam; ebb away. ～が絶える pass away; ⓒ ① breathe one's last. ～が続く ① have a long wind. ～が詰まる ❶ be suffocated; be stifled. ❷ be very nervous; ① be on tenterhooks. ～が弾む be out of breath. ⒟ ～が短い have a short temper; be hot-tempered; be touchy.

を ～を入れる take a breath. ～を切らす be out of breath; lose one's breath. ～を凝らす hold one's breath; ⓒ do *sth* with bated breath. ～を殺す hold one's breath: ⓒ anticipate *sth* with bated breath. ～を吸う take a deep breath. ～を吐く ❶ draw breath; take breath; breathe a sigh of relief. ❷ make a living; support oneself (on a pittance). ～を継ぐ ❶ gather breath. ❷ take a short rest. ～を詰める hold one's breath. ～を止める strangle *sb*; choke *sb*. ～を抜く ❶ take a breath. ❷ give a sigh of relief; be able to breathe again. ❸ feel relieved; be reassured; be put at ease. Ⓐ ～を延ぶ ❶ give a sigh of relief; be able to breathe again. ❷ feel relieved; be reassured; be put at ease. ～を呑む ❶ swallow one's breath. ❷ be astonished; gasp in amazement. ～を弾

ませる ❶ gasp for breath; pant for breath. ❷ be excited; be flustered. ◎〜を張る take a deep breath. 潜める gather breath; catch one's breath. 〜を引き取る pass away; ⓔ① breathe one's last. 〜を引く ❶ draw breath; breathe in. ◎❷ suffer from asthma. 〜を吹き返す revive (the economy); come back to life. 〜を吹き込む breathe new life into (a project).

異議 objection; a protest

が 〜が有る take exception to *sth*; have an objection.

を 〜を差し挟む make a protest; lodge a complaint. 〜を唱える voice one's disapproval; raise an objection; ⓔ take exception to *sth*. 〜を申し立てる lodge a complaint; voice an objection.

生き血 blood of a living being

を 〜を搾る sacrifice others for one's own ends. 〜を吸う suck the lifeblood out of *sb/sth*. 〜を啜る sacrifice others for one's own ends.

委曲 details

を ⓔ 〜を尽くす explain *sth* in detail; ⓔ elaborate on *sth*.

意見 an opinion; a view

が 〜が合う be like-minded; get along well; ⓔ be congenial to one; ① see eye to eye; ⓒ① hit it off. 〜が食い違う have conflicting views (on a matter).

に 〜に従う yield to *sb's* opinion.

を 〜を改める modify one's opinion. 〜を言う give one's opinion; speak one's piece. 〜を抱く cherish an idea, entertain an opinion. 〜を入れる accept *sb's* opinion. 〜を受け入れる accept *sb's* opinion. 〜を聞く ask *sb's* opinion. 〜を決める form an opinion. ⓔ 〜を懲する consult *sb*; ask for *sb's* advice; seek *sb's* opinion; ⓔ take counsel with *sb*. 〜を探る sound *sb* out; feel *sb* out. 〜を確かめる ascertain *sb's* opinion; make sure of *sb's* view. 〜を尋ねる ask *sb's* opinion. 〜を戦わす debate each other's opinions. 〜を叩く sound *sb* out; feel *sb* out; ① feel *sb's* pulse. 〜を立てる form an opinion; come to hold a viewpoint. 〜を通す gain one's point; carry one's point. 〜を唱える advocate an opinion. 〜を述べる state one's opinion; express one's views. 〜を持つ have an opinion. 〜を求める seek *sb's* opinion.

威厳 dignity; gravity; august

に 〜に関わる reflect on one's dignity; be below one's dignity.

を 〜を冒す insult *sb's* dignity; ⓔ affront *sb's* dignity. 〜を落とす damage one's/*sb's* dignity. 〜を示す show dignity; display dignity; be august. 〜を保つ maintain one's dignity; keep up one's state; ⓢ keep one's cool. 〜を作る be on one's dignity; get on one's dignity.

意向 intention; inclination

を ～を探る sound *sb* out; feel *sb* out. ～を確かめる ascertain *sb's* intentions; make sure of *sb's* intentions. ～を質す inquire after *sb's* intentions; ask *sb's* intention. ～を漏らす reveal one's intentions; ⓒ disclose one's intentions.

意志 will; volition

が ～が通じる be well understood; make oneself understood.

に ～に屈する yield to *sb*; give in to *sb's* wishes; ⓒ bend to *sb's* will. ～に従う obey *sb's* will. ～に反する be against one's will.

を ～を働かせる exercise one's will. ～を曲げる yield to *sb*; give in to *sb's* wishes; ⓒ bend to *sb's* will.

意思 an intention; a mind

に ～に沿う go along with *sb's* wishes; comply with *sb's* wishes. ～に背く go against *sb's* wishes; be contrary to *sb's* intentions.

を ～を変える change one's mind. ～を通じる make oneself understood; get one's across one's intentions. ～を洩らす reveal one's intentions; express one's intentions.

意地 temper; disposition

が ～が有る have a strong will; have pride. ～が汚い be greedy; be mean; ⓒ be avaricious. ～が悪い be malicious; be ill-natured.

に ～に掛かる refuse to give in; be obstinate; be stubborn. ～になる

refuse to give in; be obstinate; be stubborn.

を ～を通す have one's own way; do as one wants. ～を張る refuse to give in; persevere in one's ideas; hold on; ⓒ ① dig in one's heels.

意識 consciousness; awareness

に ～に上せる become conscious of; grow aware of.

を ～を失う lose consciousness; pass out; ⓒ black out.

威信 Ⓔ prestige; dignity

に ⓒ ～に係わる affect one's prestige. ⓒ ～を保つ maintain one's dignity; keep up one's state; ⓢ keep one's cool. ⓒ ～を傷つける injure *sb's* prestige; mar *sb's* reputation.

を ⓒ ～を保つ maintain one's dignity; keep up one's state; ⓢ keep one's cool.

椅子 a chair; a post; a position

を ～を失う lose one's post; ⓒ ① be thrown out of the saddle. ～を占める occupy a post; hold a post. ～を勤める offer *sb* a chair. ～を保つ occupy a post; ⓒ ① be in the saddle. ～を並べる set chairs. ～を狙う have one's eye on a post; covet a post. ～を張る upholster a chair.

板 a board; a plank; a plate

で ～で囲う board (a place) up. ～で塞ぐ board (a window) up.

に ～に付く be at home in (a subject); get used to *sth*; ⓒ be well

13

versed in (a subject). ⓒ ～に載せる put a play on the stage. ⓔ ～に上す publish (a book); issue a book.

一道 ⓔ one road; an art
に ⓔ ～に秀でる excel in an art.

一命 a life; a single order
が ～が危ない be in grave danger; ⓔ be in peril of one's life.
に ～に関わる be a matter of life and death; be lethal; be deadly. ～に賭けて...する do *sth* at the risk of one's life; stake one's life on *sth*.
を ～を失う lose one's life. ～を賭ける risk one's life; hazard one's life; ⓔ put one's life at stake. ～を下す give a single order. ～を捧げる devote one's life (to a cause). ～を救う rescue *sb*; save *sb's* life. ～を捨てる throw away one's life; give up one's life. ～を助ける rescue *sb*; save *sb's* life. ～を繋ぐ stay alive; keep on living; eke out a living. ～を賭する risk one's life; ⓔ hazard one's life. ～を取り留める escape with one's life; be saved from death; ① have a close call. ～を投げ打つ lay down one's life (for a cause); pay for *sth* with one's life.

一翼 one wing
を ～を担う play a part in *sth*; contribute to *sth*; have a share in *sth*; have a stake in *sth*.

一家 a house(hold); a family
を ～を治める manage a household.

～を構える make a home of one's own; keep house. ～を立てる set up house; start housekeeping. ～を成す develop one's own style; establish oneself.

一矢 ⓔ an arrow
を ⓔ ～を報いる ❶ shoot back; return fire. ❷ fight back; retaliate. ❸ talk back; ⓔ rebut (a charge).

一生 a lifetime; one's life
を ～を誤る make a failure of one's life; ruin one's life; ⓔ wreck one's chances in life. ～を得る be saved. ～を終える pass away; reach the end of one's life. ～を送る spend one's life; go through life. ～を賭ける risk one's life; stake one's life. ～を捧げる devote one's life to (a cause); give one's life to (a cause).

一笑 a laugh; a smile
に ⓔ ～に付し去る laugh *sb* down; dismiss *sth* with a laugh. ～に付す laugh *sb* down; dismiss *sth* with a laugh.
を ～を買う be laughed at; be scorned; ⓔ invite ridicule.

一世 a generation; an age
を ～を驚かす startle the world; create a sensation; ① make a stir. ～を風靡する dominate one's age; ⓔ take the world by storm.

一石 one stone
を ～を投じる cause excitement;

be much talked about; ⓓ make a stir; ⓔ give rise to a controversy.

一戦 a battle; an engagement
を ～を交える exchange fire; fight a battle; ⓔ engage an enemy.

一線 one line
を ～を画する draw a clear line; make a sharp distinction (between).

一歩 one step
を ～を退く take a step backward; retrace one step; take a step backward. ～を進む advance a step; take a step forward. ～を誤る take a wrong step; make a wrong move. ～を進める go one step farther; carry *sth* a step forwards. ～を譲る recede one step; yield a step; ⓔ concede a point.

一本 one; a piece; a roll
に ～にする line up; unify *sth*; standardize *sth*. ⓒ ～になる become a fully fledged *geisha*.
を ～を取られる be beaten. ⓓ ～を補う buy a book. ～を参る give *sb* a blow; upset *sb*; baffle *sb*; ⓔ ⓘ put *sb* out of countenance.

糸 thread; yarn; filament
を ～を繰る reel thread. ～を手繰る [fishing] haul in the line; draw up the line. ～を垂れる cast a line; fish; angle. ～を紡ぐ spin thread; spin yarn. ～を通す thread a needle. ～を解く unravel thread.

～を抜く take out the stitches. ～を伸ばす [fishing] let out a line. ～を引く ❶ pull a rope. ❷ manipulate (a situation); ⓘ pull the strings; ⓘ work the wires. ～を巻く quill. ～を縒る twist thread.

意図 an intent; a design; an aim
を ～を隠す hide one's intentions; ⓘ cover one's tracks. ～を挫く frustrate *sb's* plans; thwart *sb's* aims. ～を見抜く see through *sb's* plot; penetrate *sb's* mind.

糸口 a beginning; a start; a clue
と ～となる lead to (a success); become the first step (to success).
を ～を失う lose the clue. ～を得る find a clue; have a key to (a problem). ～を捜す look for a clue; search for a key (to a problem). ～を掴む find a clue; have a key to (a problem). ～を開く pave the way (for *sb/sth*); make a beginning.

暇 leisure; spare time ▶ 暇
が ～が出る ❶ be dismissed; ⓔ be relieved of one's post; ⓢ ⓘ get the sack. ❷ get time off; have time off. ❸ be divorced.
に ～になる be dismissed; ⓔ be relieved of one's post; ⓢ ⓘ get the sack.
を ～を乞う ❶ ask for a vacation; ask for time off. ❷ ask to be relieved of one's post. ❸ take one's leave; ⓔ bid *sb* farewell. ～を出す ❶ dismiss *sb*; discharge *sb*; ⓒ fire *sb*;

ⓢ ① give *sb* the sack; ⓒ ① send *sb* packing. ❷ give *sb* time off. ❸ get divorced (from one's wife); get separated. 〜を告げる say goodbye; take one's leave; ⓔ bid *sb* farewell. 〜を取る ❶ resign from one's post; tender one's resignation. ❷ take time off; have a vacation. ❸ get divorced (from one's husband); get separated. 〜を願う ❶ ask for a vacation; ask for time off. ❷ take one's leave; ⓔ bid *sb* farewell. 〜を遣る ❶ dismiss *sb*; discharge *sb*; ⓒ fire *sb*; ⓢ ① give *sb* the sack. ❷ get divorced (from one's wife).

命 life

|が| 〜が危ない be in grave danger; ⓒ be in peril of one's life. 〜が助かる be saved; escape death; survive. 〜が長い have a long life; be long-lived. 〜が延びる take on a new life; ⓔ ① get a new lease of life. 〜が短い have a short life; be short-lived.

|と| 〜と頼む rely on *sth* with one's life; ⓔ regard *sth* as the wellspring of one's life.

|に| 〜に換える value *sth* as much as one's own life; do *sth* in the face of death. 〜に関わる be a matter of life and death. 〜に賭けて…する do *sth* at the risk of one's life; stake one's life on *sth*. 〜に向かう be life-staking; be perilous.

|を| 〜を預ける put one's life in *sb's* hands; entrust one life to *sb*. 〜を失う lose one's life. 〜を打ち込む put one's heart and soul into *sth*. 〜を得る gain life; have life. 〜を惜しむ value life (above *sth* else). ⓔ hold one's life dear. 〜を落とす pass away. 〜を賭ける risk one's life; hazard one's life; ⓔ put one's life at stake. 〜を削る shorten one's life; ① drive a nail into one's coffin. 〜を支える support life. 〜を捧げる devote one's life (to a cause). 〜を捨てる throw away one's life; give up one's life. 〜を託する put one's life in *sb's* hands; entrust one life to *sb*. 〜を保つ stay alive; keep on living; maintain life; ⓔ preserve life. 〜を縮める shorten one's life; ① drive a nail into one's coffin. 〜を継ぐ eke out a living; stay alive; keep on living. 〜を繋ぐ eke out a living; stay alive; keep on living. 〜を尊ぶ value life; hold life dear. 〜を取られる pay with one's life. 〜を取る take *sb's* life; kill *sb*. 〜を投げ打つ throw away one's life; give up one's life. 〜を投げ出す risk one's life; hazard one's life; ⓔ put one's life at stake. 〜を狙う seek after *sb's* life; ⓔ have a design on *sb's* life. 〜を拾う escape with one's life; get out alive; get away unscathed. 〜を譲る sacrifice one's life.

祈り prayers; a supplication

|が| 〜が叶う have one's prayers answered.

|を| 〜を捧げる offer up a prayer; say a prayer. 〜をする say a prayer.

茨 brambles; thorny shrubs

を Ⓔ ～を負う do penance; take the responsibility for the crimes of others. ～を開く ❶ make one's way through brambles. ❷ reclaim waste land; cultivate land; open up land.

今 now; the present

を ～を時めく be at the height of one's powers; enjoy great fame and influence.

意味 meaning; significance

を ～を失う lose its meaning. ～を掴む grasp the meaning. ～を伝える convey the meaning. ～を取る understand *sth*; comprehend *sth*. ～を為す make sense of *sth*; stand to reason.

嫌気 aversion; dislike; disgust

が ～が差す feel a repugnance for; be tired of; Ⓒ get sick (and tired) of *sb/sth*.

を ～を起こす cause *sb* to dislike *sb/sth*; make *sb* sick of *sth*; Ⓒ put *sb* out of conceit with *sb/sth*.

色 a color; a hue; love; lust

が ～が褪せる ❶ a color fades; lose color; turn pale. ❷ lose attractiveness. ～が薄い have a light color. ～が濃い have a deep color.

に ～に溺れる be addicted to sensual pleasures; be a slave to lust. ～に出る show one's emotions; betray one's feelings.

を ～を漁る dangle after women;

go in for sensual pleasures. ～を失う ❶ lose color; turn pale. ❷ get worked up; Ⓒ lose one's composure. ～を売る prostitute oneself; Ⓒ sell one's favors. ～を変える change color; turn pale; go pale. ～を好む be amorous; be sensual; be lustful; be lascivious. ～を損ず be upset; be mad; get angry. ～を正す look stern; Ⓒ put on a grave face. ～を作る make oneself up; put on make-up. ～を付ける ❶ color *sth*; paint *sth*. ❷ lay on the colors; embellish *sth*. ❸ make a concession; Ⓒ throw in *sth* extra. Ⓔ ～を作す turn red with anger; Ⓒ flare up; Ⓢ lose it. ～を抜く decolorize *sth*; remove the color from *sth*; bleach *sth*. ～を塗る ❶ color *sth*; paint *sth*. ❷ lay on the colors; embellish *sth*. Ⓞ ～を粥ぐ prostitute oneself; Ⓒ sell one's favors. ～を持つ have a lover; have a sweetheart.

韻 a rhyme

を ～を合わせる rhyme the lines. ～を押す rhyme with *sth*. ～を踏む rhyme with *sth*.

陰 Ⓔ shade; the hidden ⇒ 陰

に Ⓒ ～に籠る ❶ be pent up; hide one's resentment. ❷ be gloomy; feel dejected; be cast down; be in low spirits; Ⓒ Ⓘ have the blues.

淫 Ⓔ license; indulgence

を Ⓔ ～を好む be licentious.

陰影 Ｅ shadow; gloom

に Ｅ 〜に富む be full of nuances; be profound; Ｃ be deep.

を Ｅ 〜を付ける shade (a picture). Ｅ 〜を投じる cast shadows; cast a gloom over *sth*.

咽喉 the throat

を Ｅ 〜を扼する Ｉ have the upper hand over *sb*; Ｉ hold all the cards; Ｃ Ｉ have the drop on *sb*.

印綬 Ｈ an official seal

を 〜を帯びる be appointed to a post; hold a position. 〜を解く release *sb* from office.

印象 an impression

を 〜を与える make an impression; impress *sb*; have an impression on *sb*. 〜を残す leave a good/bad impression; leave one's mark. 〜を述べる voice one's impression; express one's views. 〜を深める deepen an impression.

引導 Ｅ the last words

を Ｅ 〜を渡す address the last words to a deceased person; give *sb* his/her notice; put *sb* to death; Ｅ send *sb* to glory.

因縁 cause and occasion; karma

を 〜を付ける find a pretext to pick a fight; accuse *sb* falsely.

陰謀 a plot; a conspiracy

に 〜に加わる join in a conspiracy; be implicated in a plot. 〜に巻き込まれる be entangled in a plot.

を 〜を暴く expose a plot; reveal a plot; Ｉ blow the gaff on *sb*. 〜を嗅ぎ付ける scent a plot. 〜を企てる conspire against *sb*; lay a plot. 〜を企む conspire against *sb*; lay a plot. 〜を幇助する abet a plot. 〜を回らす weave a plot. 〜を巡らす devise a plot; plot against *sb*.

ウ

伺い a call; a visit; an inquiry

を 〜を立てる inquire of *sb*; ask *sb* for instructions; invoke an oracle.

浮き名 Ｅ a romance; a scandal

を Ｅ 〜を立てる cause a scandal; Ｃ Ｉ become the talk of the town; be talked about. Ｅ 〜を流す cause a scandal; Ｃ Ｉ become the talk of the town; be talked about.

憂き日 Ｅ a wretched life

を Ｅ 〜を送る lead a miserable existence; have a wretched life.

憂き身 Ｅ hardships

を Ｅ 〜を窶す devote oneself to *sth*; be absorbed in *sth*; pine for (*sb's* love).

憂き目 hardships; hard times

を 〜を見る have a hard time; suffer great hardships; Ｅ have trials and tribulations; Ｉ come to grief.

う

浮き世 the (fleeting) world; life
を ～を捨てる renounce the world; turn one's back on life. ◎ ～を立つ earn one's living; make one's way through the world.

牛 cattle; a cow; a bull; a steer
に ◎ ～に喰らわる be deceived; ① be taken in; ◎ be duped. ～を飼う keep cows; raise cattle.

後ろ the back; the rear
に ～に隠れる hide behind *sb/sth*. ～に忍び寄る sneak up on *sb* from behind. ～に回る move behind *sb/sth*.
へ ～へ忍び寄る sneak up on *sb* from behind. ～へ回る move behind *sth*.
を ⓐ ～を切る vanish; disappear; ① erase one's steps; ① cover up one's tracks. ～を見せる run away; reveal one's weakness; ① show one's heels. ～を見る look over one's shoulders; look behind one. ～を向く ① turn on one's heels.

嘘 a lie; an untruth; a falsehood
で ～で固める back (one's story) up with lies; ◎ be a pack of lies.
を ～を言いふらす circulate a lie. ～を教える misinform *sb*; tell *sb* a lie ～をつく tell a lie. ～を面責する reprove *sb* for telling a lie; ① give *sb* the lie.

疑い doubt; suspicion
を ～を抱く have doubts; entertain suspicions. ～を入れる be open to doubt; offer room for doubt. ～を受ける be under suspicion; ◎ incur suspicion. ～を起こす begin to doubt. ～を掛ける cast suspicion on *sb/sth*; attach suspicion to *sb/sth*. ～を挟む raise questions about *sb/sth*; throw doubt on *sb/sth*; cast doubt upon *sb/sth*. ～を解く dissipate doubts; allay suspicion; clear oneself of suspicion ～を晴らす dispel doubts; allay suspicion; clear oneself of suspicion. ～を招く invite suspicion; ◎ incur suspicion. ～を持つ have doubts; ◎ entertain suspicions.

内 the inside; the interior; home
に ～にいる be at home; be in. ～に帰る return home. ～に閉じ籠る stay at home; shut oneself up. ～に入る ❶ enter a house. ❷ be a number of a family; belong to a family.
を ～を空ける stay out; stay away from home. ～を治める rule over a people; ◎ conduct the affairs of state. ～を出る leave home; go out.

団扇 a (round) fan
を ～を使う use a fan; fan oneself; cool oneself. ～を上げる decide in favor of *sb*; declare *sb* the winner.

現 alive; awake; conscious
を ～を抜かす be engrossed in *sth*; abandon oneself to *sb*; be besotted by *sb*; ◎ be mad about *sb/sth*.

討手 Ⓐ a punitive force

Ⓦ ～を差し向ける send a punitive force against *sb*.

鬱憤 resentment; rancor; wrath

Ⓦ ～を押える control one's anger; hide one's resentment. ～を晴らす vent one's anger; ⓒ satisfy one's resentment. ～を漏らす betray one's anger; vent one's anger; ⓒ ① let off steam.

腕 the arm; the wrist; skill

Ⓖ ～が上がる get better at *sth*; acquire more skill; (be able to) drink more. ～が有る have skill; ① be a good hand. ～が利く be skilled; be capable; ⓒ ① be a dab hand at *sth*. ～が冴える get better at *sth*; acquire more skill. ～が立つ be able; be skillful. ～が鳴る be eager to do *sth*; itch for action; be rearing to go

Ⓝ ～に縋る lean on *sb's* arm.

Ⓦ ～を上げる improve one's skill; (be able to) drink more. ～を買う esteem *sb's* ability; value *sb's* skills. ～を挫く sprain one's arm. ～を組む fold one's arms; lock arms with *sb*. ～を拱く stand by idly; remain an onlooker; ① sit on the fence. ～を摩る be eager to show one's skill. ～を試す try one's hand; put one's skill to the test. ～を鳴らす gain recognition; win reputation. ～を伸ばす ❶ stretch out one's arm; reach out. ❷ develop one's skill to the full. ⓪ ～を引

く make a solemn vow; make a blood-oath. ⓔ ～を撫す be eager to show one's skill. ～を揮う display one's skill. ～を捲る ① roll up one's sleeves. ～を磨く polish one's skills; brush up one's skills. ～を見せる display one's skill; show one's ability.

産声 the cry of a newborn

Ⓦ ～を上げる ❶ be born; ⓒ utter one's first cry. ❷ come into being; ⓒ see the light of day.

馬 a horse; a pony

Ⓖ ～が合う be like-minded; get along well; ⓒ be congenial to one; ① see eye to eye; ⓒ ① hit it off.

Ⓝ ～に乗る mount a horse; ride a horse. ～に跨る sit astride a horse.

Ⓦ ～を急がす spur on a horse. ～を飼う keep a horse; rear a horse. ～を換える change horses. ～を繋ぐ hitch a horse. ～を止める check one's horse. ～を慣らす train a horse; break in a horse. ～を乗り潰す ride a horse down. ～を走らす gallop one's horse; course one's horse. ～を放す unhitch a horse. ～を引く ❶ lead a horse. ❷ be followed by a bill collector. ～を雇う hire a horse.

裏 the reverse; the other side ▶ 裏

Ⓗ ～へ回る ❶ go to the rear (of a building); go round to the back. ❷ do *sth* in secret; do *sth* by stealth; ⓢ do *sth* on the sly.

う

[を] ◎ 〜を言う be ironical; be sardonic. 〜を行く baffle sb; outwit sb; outsmart sb. 〜を返す ❶ turn sth over; turn sth inside out; turn sth upside down. ❷ do sth a second time; repeat an action. ❸ flatten the tip of a protruding nail. ❹ give (a wall) a coating. ◎ ❺ visit the same prostitute twice. 〜をかく ❶ baffle sb; outwit sb; outsmart sb. ◎ ❷ drive a spear through sb; run sb through; impale sb on one's sword. 〜を掛ける turn (a record) over; play the reverse side of a record. (法律の)〜を潜る slip through the meshes of the law. 〜を付ける line a coat. 〜を取る verify (a story); ⓒ ascertain the truth. 〜を封す seal a letter. 〜を見透かす see through sb 's schemes. 〜を行く baffle sb; outwit sb; outsmart sb.

恨み a grudge; resentment

[が] 〜が有る hold a grudge against sb; ⓔ harbor a private malice; ⓘ have a chip on one's shoulder. 〜が解ける satisfy one's grudge; get back at sb.

[に] 〜に思う feel bitter toward sb; ⓘ keep a score on wrongs; ⓘ have a chip on one's shoulder.

[を] 〜を言う reproach sb. 〜を抱く hold a grudge against sb; ⓔ harbor a private malice; ⓒ have it in for sb; ⓘ have a chip on one's shoulder. 〜を買う cause sb to hold a grudge against one; make an

enemy of sb; ⓘ create bad blood; ⓔ incur sb's enmity. 〜を飲む repress one's anger; swallow one's words; pocket an insult. 〜を晴らす vent one's spite; take revenge upon sb; ⓘ settle old scores with sb; ⓘ square accounts with sb. 〜を招く earn sb's enmity; ⓘ create bad blood. 〜を持つ hold a grudge against sb; ⓔ harbor a private malice; ⓒ have it in for sb; ⓘ have a chip on one's shoulder. 〜を忘れる forget one's grudges; let bygones be bygones.

裏目 the reverse side

[に] 〜に出る produce the opposite result; go against one; backfire.

噂 a rumor; a report; gossip

[が] 〜が立つ a rumor spreads.

[に] 〜に聞く hear sth by rumor; ⓒ get wind of sth; ⓘ hear sth on the grapevine. 〜に上る be talked about; ⓒ ⓘ become the talk of the town; ⓒ ⓘ go the rounds.

[を] 〜をする gossip about sb/sth; ⓒ spread tales about sb/sth. 〜を立てる start a rumor; spread a rumor. 〜を流す start a rumor; spread a rumor. 〜を広める spread a rumor; circulate a story. 〜を揉み消す kill a rumor; stifle a rumor.

上手 the upper part; upstream

[に] 〜に出る outdo sb; gain the lead; ⓘ gain the upper hand.

[を] 〜を行く be superior to sb. 〜を

21

持(も)つ [*shōgi*] occupy the superior side of the board.

上辺(うわべ) **the exterior; the outside**
[を] ～を飾(かざ)る gloss over a mistakes; Ⓘ keep up appearances. ～を繕(つくろ)う save appearances; Ⓘ save one's face.

上前(うわまえ) [H] **the outer skirt**
[を] ～を跳(は)ねる take a percentage; Ⓒ take a rake-off.

運(うん) **destiny; fate; fortune**
[が] ～が尽(つ)きる meet one's doom; run out of luck; be at the end of one's luck. ～が蹲(つくば)う meet one's doom; run out of luck. ～が強(つよ)い have luck on one's side; be fortunate. ～が開(ひら)く be in luck's way; be favored by fortune. ～が向(む)く be in luck's way; Ⓔ be favored by fortune. ～が良(よ)い be fortunate; be lucky; be auspicious. ～が悪(わる)い be unfortunate; be unlucky; be inauspicious.
[に] ～に任(まか)せる trust to chance; Ⓔ trust to Providence. ～に恵(めぐ)まれる be fortunate; be lucky; Ⓔ be favored by fortune.
[を] ～を試(ため)す take chances; try one's luck. ～を開(ひら)く create one's own luck; Ⓘ sieze the day.

運勢(うんせい) **one's star; one's fortune**
[が] ～が衰(おとろ)える fortunes are waning.
[を] ～を見(み)る tell *sb's* fortune.

蘊蓄(うんちく) [E] **one's stock of knowledge**
[を] Ⓔ ～を傾(かたむ)ける pour all one's learning into (one's work); freely draw on one's profound learning.

蘊能(うんのう) [E] **principles; doctrine**
[を] Ⓔ ～を窮(きわ)める master the secrets of (an ancient craft); be initiated in the mysteries of (an art).

雲表(うんぴょう) [E] **"above the clouds"**
[に] Ⓔ ～に聳(そび)える soar above the clouds; tower above the clouds.

運命(うんめい) **destiny; fate; fortune**
[と] ～と諦(あきら)める resign oneself to one's fate. ～と戦(たたか)う fight one's fate; Ⓔ strive against fate.
[に] ～に甘(あま)んじる resign oneself to one's fate; submit to fate. ～に任(まか)せる leave *sb* to his/her fate; abandon oneself to fate. ～に弄(もてあそ)ばれる be the sport of fortune; Ⓘ drop in the lap of fate.
[を] ～を託(かこ)つ howl at one's fate; Ⓔ bewail one's predicament. ～を決(けっ)する seal one's/*sb's* fate. ～を作(つく)る mold one's destiny; carve out one's fate. ～を共(とも)にする join fortunes with *sb*; Ⓘ throw in one's lot.

エ

鋭意(えいい) **eagerness; diligence**
[に] ～に当(あ)たる apply oneself to (one's work); devote oneself (to a cause). ～に従(したが)う apply oneself to (one's work); devote oneself (to a cause).

影響 influence; effect

に ～に働かされる be susceptible to an influence.

を ～を与える exert an influence over. ～を受ける be influenced by; be affected by. ～を及ぼす exert influence; have an effect.

英風 E lofty virtues

を © ～を慕う admire sb; look up to sb; have a high regard for sb.

永別 E the last parting

を © ～を告げる say one's last goodbye; take leave of sb; © bid one's last farewell.

易 fortune-telling; divination

を ～を立てる tell sb's fortune; cast a horoscope. ～を見る tell sb's fortune; © cast a horoscope.

枝 a branch; a bough; a limb

に ～に分かれる ❶ © branch out. ❷ Ⓐ branch out; spread into branches; branch off.

を ～を折る break off a branch. ～を下ろす prune a tree; lop off branches. ～を切る prune a tree; lop off branches. ～を出す shoot out branches. Ⓐ ～を交す have an intimate relationship with sb. ～を挿げる be argumentative; ① split hairs. Ⓐ ～を鳴らさず be at peace. ～を払う prune a tree; lop off branches. ～を広げる ❶ © branch out. ❷ Ⓐ branch out; spread into branches; branch off.

襟 the neck; a collar; a neckband

に ～に付く flatter sb; ① curry favor with sb.

を ～を正す ❶ adjust one's dress; straighten oneself. ❷ be awed; © stand in awe. ～を立てる turn up one's collar. ～を掴む seize sb by the collar; collar sb.

縁 a relation; a connection ▶ 縁

が ～が切れる be cut off; get separated; be disowned.

に Ⓐ ～に付く marry a man; get married. Ⓐ ～に付ける give one's daughter in marriage; marry one's daughter off. ～に繋がる be related to; be connected with. ～に引かされる be drawn together.

を ～を切る ❶ break off relations; © sever one's connections with sb. ❷ disown sb; disinherit sb; ① cut sb off without a penny. ❸ divorce sb; get separated; © secure a divorce; © split up. ～を断つ ❶ break off relations; © sever one's connections with sb. ❷ disown sb; disinherit sb; ① cut sb off without a penny. ❸ divorce sb; get divorced; get separated; © secure a divorce; © split up. ～を辿る hunt up one's connections. Ⓐ ～を離る live an ascetic life. ～を結ぶ form a connection with; marry sb; © ① tie the knot.

宴 E a banquet; a feast; a party

に © ～に列する attend a banquet; be present at a dinner.

を ⑥ 〜を張る hold a banquet; give a dinner; ⓒ throw a party.

縁起 the history; the origin
を 〜を祝う wish *sb* good luck; welcome a sign of good luck. 〜を担ぐ be superstitious; believe in omens. 〜を直す change one's fortune.

怨言 ⑥ bitter remarks
を ⓒ 〜を放つ mutter words of discontent; voice one's misgivings.

冤罪 ⑥ a false charge
に ⓒ 〜に泣く be falsely charged; be accused wrongly.
を ⓒ 〜を雪ぐ exonerate oneself; clear oneself of a false charge; ⓒ vindicate oneself. ⑥ 〜を被る be falsely charged; be accused wrongly.

援助 assistance; aid
を 〜を仰ぐ look for help. 〜を与える give aid; ⓒ render assistance. 〜を得る receive aid; get assistance. 〜を約する promise help; ⓒ pledge one's assistance.

宴席 ⑥ a seat in a dining hall
に ⓒ 〜に侍る wait at a banquet. ⓒ 〜に列する attend a banquet; be present at a dinner.
を ⓒ 〜を設ける hold a banquet.

遠島 ⑪ a distant island
を 〜を申し付ける banish *sb* to a distant island; send *sb* into exile.

遠慮 reserve; forethought
が 〜が有る have forethought; be farsighted.
を 〜を欠く lack forethought; lack restraint. 〜を捨てる throw off restraint. 〜を忘れる forget one's reserve; break through reserve.

オ

尾 a tail; a brush; a train
が 〜が出る be exposed; come to light. ⓐ 〜が掛かる be in hot pursuit; chase *sb*. ⓐ 〜が見える be exposed; come to light.
に 〜に付く echo *sb's* words; parrot *sb*; ⓒ copycat *sb*.
を ⓐ 〜を滑る be dispirited. 〜を出す expose oneself; betray oneself. 〜を引く leave traces; have a lasting effect; linger on. 〜を振る ❶ wag its tail; whisk its tail. ❷ try to please (a superior); ingratiate oneself with *sb*. 〜を巻く ❶ loop its tail. ❷ sneak away; ① beat a retreat. 〜を見せる expose oneself; betray oneself.

老い old age; the aged
を 〜を労る tend to the old; look after the elderly. 〜を送る live out the rest of one's days. 〜を養う live out the last days of one's life.

王 a king; a monarch
を 〜を立てる put a king on the throne; enthrone a king. 〜を詰める

[*shōgi*] checkmate the king. 〜を廃する depose a king; dethrone a king.

王位 the throne; the crown
に 〜に在る be on the throne; hold the throne. 〜に就く take the throne; ⓔ accede to the throne. 〜に登る mount the throne; ⓔ ascend the throne; ⓔ accede to the throne.

を 〜を争う contend for the throne. 〜を失う ⓔ forfeit one's crown. 〜を奪う usurp the throne. 〜を捨てる abdicate; resign the kingship. 〜を継ぐ succeed to the throne. 〜を譲る abdicate in *sb's* favor; make over the throne to *sb*.

扇 a (folding) fan
を ⓔ 〜を請く master the secrets of (an ancient craft); be initiated in the mysteries of (an art). 〜を翳す shade one's eyes with a fan. 〜を使う fan oneself. 〜を鳴らす beckon *sb*.

横死 an untimely death
を 〜を遂げる die a violent death.

横柄 arrogance; haughtiness
に 〜に扱う treat *sb* with disdain. 〜に構える assume an attitude of superiority. 〜に振る舞う behave arrogantly; act haughtily.

を Ⓐ 〜を捌く behave haughtily; ⓒ lord it over *sb*.

大風呂敷 bragging; boasting
を 〜を拡げる boast about *sth*;

brag about *sth*; ⓒ ① blow one's own horn (trumpet); ① talk big.

大骨 big bones; large bones
を 〜を折る ❶ take great pains to do *sth*; make strenuous efforts. ❷ go to a lot of trouble; suffer extreme hardships.

大目 extra; surplus; ample
に 〜に見る condone *sth*; pass over *sth*; overlook *sth*; let *sth* pass; let *sb* off (lightly); ⓢ ① give *sb* a break.

お株 one's forte; a favorite trick
を Ⓐ 〜を言う repeat oneself; ① harp on the same string. 〜を奪われる be outdone in one's own forte; ① be beaten at one's own game.

お釜 a pot; a kettle
が ⓞ 〜が割れる ❶ be divorced; a family breaks up. ❷ go to ruin; be a failure; ⓒ make a mess of *sth*.

に ⓞ 〜に掛ける deride one's superior(s); scoff at one's superior(s); make a fool of one's boss.

を ⓞ 〜を興す increase the family fortune; cause one's house to flourish. ⓞ ⓥ 〜を掘る practice sodomy.

沖 the offing; the open sea
に 〜にいる ① be out at sea; ① be in the offing. 〜に出る gain an offing; stand out to sea.

を Ⓐ 〜を泳ぐ indulge in lewd pleasures. 〜を漕ぐ ❶ excel in *sth*.

❷ indulge in lewd pleasures. Ⓐ ～を越える ❶ excel in *sth*. ❷ go too far; carry things too far. ～を眺める gaze out across the sea.

燠 embers; live coals
図 ～を掻き立てる stoke embers; stir the coals.

置網 Ⓔ standing nets
図 Ⓐ Ⓔ ～を言う talk prematurely; talk rashly; tempt providence.

掟 a rule; a law; a regulation
回 ～に従う comply with the rules; obey the law. ～に背く violate a law. ～による be according to law. 図 ～を定める lay down the law; establish a rule. ～を守る observe the law; Ⓒ stick to the rules. ～を破る break the law; violate the rules.

遅れ a delay; a time lag
図 ～を取る be beaten; be routed. ～を取り戻す catch up with *sb*; work off arrears. ～を見せる be intimidated by *sb*; shrink from *sth*; recoil from *sth*; wince at *sth*.

朸 a (merchant's) carrying pole
図 Ⓐ ～を折る suffer a devastating financial loss; be bankrupted.

抑え weight; pressure; control
がⅠ ～が利く have *sth* under control; be in control; be under control; Ⓢ Ⓘ call the shots.

押し a push; a weight; audacity
がⅠ ～が利く have influence; be influential; Ⓘ carry weight. ～が強い be pushing; be aggressive; Ⓒ be pushy.
図 ～をする put pressure on *sb*/*sth*; put *sb*/*sth* under pressure.

教え teachings; a lesson
図 ～を仰ぐ ask for instruction; Ⓔ seek instruction. ～を受ける be taught; study under *sb*.

汚職 corruption; graft; bribery
図 ～を一掃する root out corruption; wipe out corruption. ～を生む breed corruption.

汚辱 disgrace; ignominy
図 ～を加える cast a slur on *sb*; Ⓒ Ⓘ sling mud at *sb*. ～を被る be subjected to slander. ～を忍ぶ endure ignominy; Ⓘ eat humble pie.

白粉 toilet powder; face paint
図 ～を遣う use powder. ～を付ける powder one's face; paint one's face. ～を塗り立てる powder one's face thickly; make a heavy toilet; paint one's face thickly.

恐れ fear; dread; terror; horror
がⅠ ～が有る be in danger of; run the risk of.
図 ～を抱く be filled with fear; be afraid of. ～を為す be scared; be frightened.

26

落(お)ち a slip; the point (of a joke)

[が] ～が有(あ)る contain an omission. ～が来(く)る win esteem; be cheered; be lauded; be applauded. ～が分(わ)かる understand the gist (of a joke); Ⓒ Ⓘ get the point; Ⓢ Ⓘ get it.

[を] ～を取(と)る win esteem; be lauded; be lauded; be applauded. (人(ひと)の)～を拾(ひろ)う pick up *sb's* mistake; make good *sb's* omission.

落(お)ち着(つ)き composure; serenity

[を] ～を失(うしな)う get worked up; Ⓔ lose one's composure; be thrown off one's balance. ～を取(と)り戻(もど)す regain one's presence of mind; Ⓔ recover one's composure.

乙(おつ) [S] strange; odd; queer

[に] Ⓢ ～に絡(から)む make witty remarks about *sb*; make fun of *sb*.

[を] Ⓢ ～を澄(す)ます strike an affectedly serene pose; Ⓘ put on airs.

音(おと) a sound; a noise; a report

[が] ～がする hear a noise.

[に] ～に聞(き)く be famous; be well known; be notorious.

[を] ～を消(け)す stifle the noise; absorb the sound. ～を出(だ)す produce a sound. ～を立(た)てる make a noise.

頤(おとがい) [E] the chin; the mentum

[が] Ⓔ ～が落(お)ちる ❶ be delicious. ❷ shiver with cold.

[を] Ⓔ ～を利(き)く wag one's tongue; babble. Ⓔ ～を叩(たた)く wag one's tongue; babble. Ⓔ ～を解(と)く make *sb* laugh; Ⓘ set the table roaring. Ⓔ ～を鳴(な)らす wag one's tongue; babble. Ⓔ ～を吐(は)く say bad things about *sb*; abuse *sb*; speak ill of *sb*; bad-mouth *sb*; Ⓢ slur *sb*. Ⓔ ～を放(はな)つ roar with laughter. Ⓔ ～を開(ひら)く be talkative; Ⓔ be loquacious; Ⓒ be a chatterbox; Ⓘ talk people's head off. Ⓔ ～を養(やしな)う make a living; support oneself; Ⓔ earn one's daily bread.

男(おとこ) a man; a male; menfolk

[が] ～が廃(すた)る lose one's honor; be ashamed of oneself. ～が立(た)つ have one's honor satisgied; have one's own way; Ⓘ save one's face.

[に] ～にする make a man out of *sb*. ～に成(な)す celebrate a child's coming of age. ～に成(な)る ❶ become a man. ❷ return to secular life; renounce the cloth.

[を] ～を上(あ)げる build up one's image; rise in public estimation. ～を売(う)る widen one's reputation; win fame. ～を拵(こしら)える find a lover; desert one's husband; Ⓒ carry on with a man. ～を下(さ)げる fall in public estimation; be disgraced; Ⓘ lose face. ～を知(し)る know a man; have slept with a man; Ⓔ have carnal knowledge of a man. ～を立(た)てる satisfy one's honor; Ⓘ save one's face. ～を作(つく)る ❶ build up one's character. ❷ find oneself a man; find a lover. ～を振(ふ)り捨(す)てる desert a man for *sb* else; jilt one's lover. ～を磨(みが)く ❶ build up one's character. ❷ attempt to preserve one's honor. 〜を見せる show one's manliness. 〜を持つ have a husband; have a lover; be married.

音骨 a voice; a sound
[を] 〜を立てる raise one's voice.

囮 a decoy; a lure; a bait
[に] 〜に使う use *sth* as a decoy.

斧 an axe; a hatchet
[を] 〜を入れる reclaim wasteland; open up wasteland; cut down woods; ⓒ put (virgin land) to the plow. 〜を加える take an axe to (a tree). ◎ 〜を投ぐ resolve to take up learning.

己 oneself; myself
[に] 〜に克つ conquer oneself.
[を] 〜を知る know oneself. 〜を捨てる rise above oneself. 〜を枉ぐ act against oneself; ⓒ compromise one's principles.

帯 a belt; a sash; a girdle
[を] 〜を締める tie a girdle; put on a sash. 〜を解く ❶ ungirdle oneself; undo a sash. ❷ take a rest. 〜を結ぶ tie a sash. 〜を緩める feel relieved; feel relaxed.

尾鰭 tail and fin
[が] 〜が有る have dignity; have presence.
[を] 〜を付ける resort to hyperbole; embellish a story; ⓘ stretch the facts; ⓘ embroider the truth; ⓘ paint *sth* in high colors; ⓢ ⓘ lay it on thick.

お祭り E a festival; a fete
[が] ◎ ⓥ ⓢ 〜が渡る have sexual intercourse; sleep with each other.

汚名 a stigma; a slur; a taint
[を] 〜を被る have one's good name stained; be stigmatized. 〜を濯ぐ clear one's name; live down one's reputation.

思い a thought; feelings
[が] 〜が届く get one's ideas across. 〜が積もる have mixed feelings. 〜が残る have a lingering regret.
[に] 〜に掛ける be troubled by *sth*; ⓘ weigh on one's mind.
[を] ◎ 〜を致す take *sth* into consideration; give thought to; ⓘ take *sth* on board. 〜を掛ける give one's heart to; take a fancy to. 〜を砕く ❶ worry about *sth*; fret over *sth*; ⓒ ⓘ rack one's brains. ❷ have a hard time; suffer great hardships. 〜を焦がす pine for *sb*; languish for. 〜を凝らす apply one's mind to *sth*; think hard about *sth*; ⓒ ⓘ rack one's brains. 〜を遂げる achieve one's aims; satisfy one's desire. 〜を残す pass away with regrets. 〜を馳せる think about (home); long for; pine for. 〜を晴らす ❶ relieve one's mind. ❷ accomplish one's aim; see one's dream through. ❸ settle old scores;

revenge oneself on *sb*; ⓔ wreak one's wrath; ⓘ get one's own back. ～を潜める ponder on *sth*; think deeply. ～を巡らす turn *sth* over in one's mind. ～を寄せる lose one's heart to *sb*; fall in love with *sb*; give one's heart to *sb*; take a fancy to *sb*; set one's heart on *sb*.

重き weight; dignity

ⓦ ～を置く lay stress on *sth*; emphasize *sth*; attach importance to *sth*. ～を加える gain in significance. ～を為す ❶ be held in high esteem; be thought of highly. ❷ have authority; ⓘ carry weight.

表 the surface; the exterior

ⓗ ～へ出る go out of doors.
ⓓ ～で遊ぶ play outdoors.
ⓦ ～を飾る save appearances; ⓘ keep up appearances. ～を出す face upwards; face outward. ～を張る ⓘ keep up appearances.

面 the (sur)face ⇒ 面 ⇒ 面

ⓝ ～に負く be intimidated by *sb*; become afraid of *sb*.
ⓦ ～を合わす meet face to face. ～を冒す defy *sb*; ⓔ reprove *sb* to his/her face; ⓒ tell *sb* off. ～を起こす ❶ look up; raise one's head. ❷ gain honor; get credit for *sth*. ～を変える change color; turn pale; lose color. ～を汚す injure *sb's* dignity; cause *sb* to lose face; ⓔ blight *sb's* honor. ～を曝す ❶ show oneself; appear in public;

step into the public eye. ❷ disgrace oneself in public; bring shame on oneself. ～を伏す ❶ drop one's head in one's hands; hang one's head. ❷ be embarrassed; ⓘ lose face. ～を向ける ❶ turn to face *sb*; face *sb*. ❷ offer resistance; stand against *sb*; oppose *sb*. ～を和らげる soften one's expression; look benign. ～を汚す disgrace *sb*; humiliate *sb*; ⓘ take *sb* down a peg.

重荷 a heavy burden

ⓦ ～を下ろす unburden oneself. ～を負わせる burden *sb*. ～を担う shoulder a burden. (心の)～を除く take a load off one's mind.

終わり an end; a close; a finish

ⓦ ～を告げる come to an end; mark the end of *sth*; ⓒ ⓘ wind *sth* up. ⓐ ～を取る die; pass away; ⓔ ⓘ breathe one's last. ～を全うする end well; come to a good end; make a happy ending of *sth*.

恩 a favor; an obligation

ⓝ ～に受ける be indebted to *sb*; be obliged to *sb*; owe *sb* a favor. ～に掛ける make *sb* feel obliged; expect a favor in return. ～に着せる make *sb* feel obliged; expect a favor in return. ～に着る feel deeply indebted toward *sb*; be deeply grateful to *sb*. ～に報いる return a favor; repay *sb* for received favors.

を ～を知る have a sense of gratitude; be sensible to kindness. ～を売る try to win *sb's* favors. ～を返す repay *sb* a favor; return a favor. ～を感じる feel indebted; have a sense of obligation. ～を着せる make *sb* feel obliged; expect a favor in return. ⓒ ～を着る feel deeply indebted toward *sb*. ～を蒙る receive favors; enjoy *sb's* patronage. ～を知る be grateful (to *sb*). ～を報ずる repay kindness; return a favor. ～を施す do *sb* a favor; oblige *sb*. ～を忘れる be ungrateful; forget one's obligations.

音頭 leading (in singing)

を ～を取る ❶ lead a chorus; lead the song. ❷ take the lead; call the tune; ⓒ play the first fiddle.

女 a woman; womenfolk

に ～になる become a woman.
を ～を囲う keep a woman. ～を知る know a woman; have slept with a woman; ⓒ have carnal knowledge of a woman. ～を拵える find a lover; desert one's wife; ⓒ carry on with a woman. ～を弄ぶ make a plaything of a woman.

カ

我 oneself; the self; I ♦我

が ～が折れる give in to *sb's* demand; drop one's stubborn attitude. ～が張る refuse to give in; be obstinate; be stubborn.
に ⒶⒶに成る ❶ act willfully; have one's way. ❷ give oneself airs; be pompous; ⓒ be ostentatious; ⒟ put on airs; ⓢ ⓘ be stuck-up.
を ～を折る yield to *sb's* will; give in. ～を殺す suppress one's ego; efface oneself. ～を出す reveal one's true self. ～を立てる be self-willed; assert oneself; ⓒ ⓘ stick to one's colors. ～を通す have one's own way. ～を張る cling to; hold fast to; persist in; assert oneself.

会 a meeting; a party

に ～に加える attend a meeting; participate in a meeting; join a party. ～に付する submit (an issue) to conference; bring (a matter) before the council. ⓔ ～に召す summon *sb* to council. ～に列する take part in a conference; attend a meeting.
を ～を操る manipulate a meeting. ～を閉じる close a meeting. ～を始める be in conference. ～を開く hold a meeting; sit in council. ～を催す convene a meeting; hold a meeting; give a party.

貝 a shellfish

を Ⓐ ～を作る be close to tears; be ready to cry; be almost in tears. ～を拾う gather shellfish. ～を吹き鳴らす blow on a shell. ～を伏す pile *sth* up; herd *sth* together; hoard *sth*. ～を掘る dig up shellfish.

戒 a (Buddhist) commandment

[を] ～を受ける become a Buddhist priest; take the tonsure. ～を授ける give *sb* the Buddhist commandments; ordain *sb* to the priesthood. ～を守る observe the Buddhist commandments.

櫂 an oar; a paddle

[が] Ⓐ ～が回る live a life of leisure; Ⓒ be well off.

[を] ～を納める lay in the oars; boat an oar; Ⓔ ship the oars. ～を漕ぐ pull an oar. ～を揃える keep stroke (in rowing). ～を立てる up the paddles (in salute). ～を外す take out the oars; Ⓔ unship the oars. ～を嵌める lay in the oars; boat an oar; Ⓔ ship the oars.

骸 a skeleton

[を] Ⓐ ～を乞う tender one's resignation; Ⓔ beg to be relieved of one's post.

甲斐 an effect; a result

[が] ～が有る be worthwhile; be rewarding; be worth doing.

害 injury; hurt; harm; damage

[を] ～を与える damage *sth*; do injury to *sb*/*sth*; work evil on *sb*. ～を受ける ❶ suffer damage; be injured; be damaged; suffer a loss. ❷ be injured; be hurt. ～を及ぼす cause injury to *sb*/*sth*. ～を加える inflict injury on *sb*; injure *sb*. ～を被る suffer damage; be damaged; be affected (negatively). ～を避ける avoid being injured; keep out of harm's way.

我意 self-will

[を] ～を通す have one's own way. ～を張る assert oneself; be self-willed; Ⓒ stick to one's own opinion.

凱歌 Ⓔ a triumphal song

[を] Ⓒ ～を揚げる be victorious; win a victory; Ⓔ ～を奏する sing in triumph; crow over the enemy.

骸骨 a skeleton

[を] Ⓐ ～を乞う beg to be relieved of one's post; Ⓔ tender one's resignation.

解釈 an interpretation

[を] ～を誤る have a false idea of *sth*; Ⓒ ⓘ hold the wrong end of the stick; Ⓒ ⓘ get the boot on the wrong leg. ～を下す put an interpretation on *sth*.

外聞 reputation; honor

[が] ～が立つ preserve one's honor; be saved from disgrace.

[を] ～を失う be disgraced; Ⓔ bring disgrace upon oneself; ⓘ lose face. ～を欠く be embarrassed; Ⓔ ⓘ be put out of countenance. ～を繕う save appearances; ⓘ keep up appearances.

顔 a face; looks; features

[が] ～が合う ❶ meet face to face.

31

❷ run into *sb*; come across *sb*. ❸ [sports] compete with *sb*; play a match. 〜が厚い be impudent; be cheeky. 〜が売れる ❶ be popular; be widely known. ❷ have influence; have authority. 〜が利く be influential; have authority. 〜が揃う have full attendance; come together. 〜が立つ save one's honor; maintain one's dignity; keep up one's state; ⓢ keep one's cool. 〜が潰れる be disgraced; ⓘ lose face. 〜が広い be widely known; have wide connections; ⓒ get around. 〜が汚れる be disgraced; ⓔ bring disgrace upon oneself; ⓘ lose face. 〜が悪い ❶ be untrustworthy; be unreliable. ❷ be ugly; be bad-looking.

に 〜に免ずる let *sb* off (so as to preserve face); (do *sth*) for *sb's* sake. 〜に出す show one's emotions; betray one's feelings.

を 〜を赤らめる go red in the face; blush; be ashamed. 〜を上げる look up; raise one's head. 〜を合わせる meet face to face. 〜を洗う wash one's face. 〜を打つ strike *sb* in the face. 〜を売る make oneself known; gain influence. 〜を犯す defy *sb*; ⓔ reprove *sb* to his/her face. 〜を覚える remember *sb's* face; recognize *sb's* face. 〜を貸す assist *sb* (to help them gain standing); lend oneself for *sth*; meet *sb's* wishes. 〜を利かす use one's influence; ⓘ pull the strings. 〜を曇らす make a dark face; ⓔ cloud one's face. 〜を顰める make grimaces; make a wry face; ⓒ wrinkle one's face. 〜をする ❶ ⓘ pull a face. ❷ do one's makeup; powder one's face. 〜を背ける turn aside; look away. 〜を染める ❶ paint one's face; apply makeup. ❷ blush; be ashamed. 〜を出す ❶ make one's appearance; attend (a meeting); show up. ❷ pay *sb* a visit; ⓘ pay one's respects; visit *sb*. 〜を立てる ⓘ save *sb's* face; back *sb* up; ⓔ ⓘ keep *sb* in countenance. 〜を作る ❶ ⓘ make a face (forcefully). ❷ put on one's makeup; powder one's face. 〜を繋ぐ ❶ introduce *sb* to *sb* else. ❷ maintain contacts; keep up one's contacts. 〜を潰す injure *sb's* dignity; cause *sb* to lose face; ⓔ blight *sb's* honor. 〜を直す ❶ regain one's presence of mind; ⓒ recover one's composure; ⓘ pull oneself together. ❷ redo one's makeup. 〜を拭う ❶ wipe one's face; ❷ bear the shame; endure ignominy. 〜を伏せる hang one's head; drop one's head in one's hands. Ⓐ 〜を踏む injure *sb's* dignity; cause *sb* to lose face; ⓔ blight *sb's* honor. 〜を振る ❶ shake one's head (in denial). ❷ turn one's face away. ❸ refuse an offer; turn down a request. 〜を綻ばす break into a smile; have a beaming face. 〜を見せる make one's appearance; show up; visit *sb*; attend (a meeting). 〜を向ける

turn to face *sb*. 〜を和らげる soften one's expression; look benign. 〜を汚す disgrace *sb*; humiliate *sb*; ① take *sb* down a peg.

顔色 complexion; countenance

が 〜が良い have good color; look fine. 〜が変わる go pale; lose color. 〜が黒い have a dark complexion. 〜が白い have a fair complexion. 〜が悪い have no color; look pale; look unwell.

で 〜で察する read *sb's* thoughts; tell *sth* by *sb's* expression.

に 〜に出す betray one's emotions; show one's feelings.

を 〜を窺う gauge *sb's* feelings; sound *sb* out; ⓒ check *sb's* mood; ⓔ consult *sb's* pleasure. 〜を失う lose color; go pale; ⓔ turn livid. 〜を犯す defy *sb*; ⓔ reprove *sb* to his/her face. 〜を変える change color; turn pale; lose color. 〜を正す compose oneself; make a straight face. 〜を和らげる relax one's expression. 〜を読む read *sb's* expression.

踵 the heel ▶踵

を ⓐ 〜を狙う take advantage of *sb's* condition; ① aim below the belt. 〜を踏む follow on *sb's* heels; follow *sb* closely; ① breathe down *sb's* neck.

垣 a fence; a railing; a hedge

に ⓐ 〜に鬩ぐ have a private dispute; quarrel among each other.

を 〜を廻らす enclose (a garden) with a fence. 〜を結う put up a fence; fence (a place) off.

鍵 a key; a hook; a clue

に ⓞ 〜に掛かる be deceived; ① be taken in; ⓒ ⓞ be led by the nose. ⓞ 〜に掛ける deceive *sb*; ① take *sb* in; ⓒ ① lead *sb* by the nose. ⓞ 〜になる become partners in crime.

を 〜を開ける unlock (a door); open a lock with a key. 〜を掛ける lock *sth* up; turn a key on *sth*. 〜を握る have a solution; ⓐ hold the key to (a secret/problem). 〜を回す turn the key.

陰 the back; the dark ▶陰

で 〜で笑う laugh behind *sb's* back; ⓒ poke fun at *sb*.

に 〜に隠す take *sb* in protection; place *sb*/*sth* under one's protection. 〜に隠れる hide in the shade; hide behind *sth*. 〜に潜む be concealed; lay hidden; lurk in the dark. 〜に回る do *sth* behind *sb's* back.

へ 〜へ回る do *sth* behind *sb's* back.

を ⓐ 〜を頼む ask for *sb's* help; rely on *sb*. 〜を付ける shade (a picture).

影 light; a reflection; a sign

が 〜が薄い ❶ be in eclipse; be insignificant; ① be on the way out. ❷ be on the verge of death; ① be at death's door. 〜が映る throw a shadow; cast a reflection; be silhouetted. 〜が射す ❶ catch a

glimpse of *sb*; appear suddenly.
❷ cast a shadow. ❸ be illuminated.
❹ show symptoms (of a disease).
囮 ⓪ ～を致す hide oneself; go into
hiding; ① lie low; ① go to ground.
Ⓐ ～を搏つ find no response; beat
the air; ① draw a blank. ～を映す
reflect an image; mirror a reflection. ～を追う chase a phantom.
～を落とす ❶ cast a shadow on
sth. ❷ be a blight on (one's
honor). ❸ throw light upon *sth*;
illuminate *sth*. ～を隠す hide
oneself; go into hiding; ① lie low;
① go to ground. ～を投げる cast a
shadow on *sth*; throw a shadow on
sth. ～を潜める conceal oneself;
disappear from sight; lay hidden;
① lie low. ～を踏む cast a shadow;
throw a shadow.

過去 the past; bygone days
囮 ～に生きる live in the past. ～
に遡る be retroactive; go back in
time. ～に葬る put *sth* behind one;
bury *sth* in the past; let bygones
be bygones.
囮 ～を思う think of the past. ～を
顧みる reflect on the past. ～を振
り返る look back upon the past.

傘 an umbrella
囮 ⓪ ～に乗る ❶ hide under *sb's*
umbrella. ❷ become (too) excited;
① get carried away.
囮 ～をさす put up an umbrella. ～
を窄める close an umbrella. ～を拡
げる open an umbrella.

笠 a bamboo hat; a lamp shade
囮 (人を)～に着る hide behind
(*sb's* authority); do *sth* under *sb's*
aegis; ① ride on *sb's* coattails.
囮 Ⓐ ～を揚ぐ raise one's hat in
surrender; ① throw in the towel.

嵩 bulk; quantity; volume; size
囮 ～が張る be voluminous; be
unwieldy; be bulky.
囮 ～に懸かる ❶ (ab)use one's
superior position; follow up one's
advantage over *sb*; take advantage
of the circumstances. ❷ be high-
handed; be overbearing; Ⓔ lord it
over *sb*. ～に懸ける spur oneself
on; brace oneself up. ～に回る
attain superiority (over *sb*); ① gain
the upper hand over *sb*.
囮 ～を懸く ❶ abuse one's superior
position; follow up one's advantage
over *sb*; take advantage of the circumstances. ❷ exaggerate; Ⓔ indulge
in hyperbole; ① stretch the facts;
Ⓢ ① pile it on; Ⓢ ① lay it on thick.
⓪ ～を着す exaggerate; Ⓔ indulge
in hyperbole; ① stretch the facts;
Ⓢ ① pile it on; Ⓢ ① lay it on thick.

風上 the windward
囮 ～に出る get to the windward
of (another boat). ～に向かう face
to windward. ～に向ける beat to
windward.

風下 the leeward
囮 ～にあう lie leeward. ～に当た
る face leeward.

舵(かじ) a rudder; a helm

[を] ～を取(と)る ❶ steer (a ship); Ⓛ be at the helm. ❷ be in control; Ⓐ be at the helm (of a company); Ⓢ Ⓘ call the shots. ❸ humor *sb*; ingratiate oneself with *sb*; Ⓘ curry favor with *sb*. ～を誤(あやま)る steer (a ship) in the wrong direction.

火事(かじ) a fire; a conflagration

[で] ～で焼(や)ける be burnt in a fire.
[に] ～に遭(あ)う be in a fire.
[を] ～を消(け)す put out a fire. ～を出(だ)す start a fire.

過失(かしつ) an error; a blunder; a fault

[を] ～を改(あらた)める correct a mistake. ～を犯(おか)す commit an error; make a mistake; Ⓒ Ⓘ drop the ball. ～を認(みと)める acknowledge one's mistake.

果実(かじつ) fruit

[を] ～を結(むす)ぶ bear fruit.

頭(かしら) the head; a leader ▶頭(あたま) ▶頭(ず)

[が] Ⓞ ～が打(う)つ have a severe headache; Ⓒ have a splitting headache.
[に] ～に立(た)つ take the lead; stand at the head.
[を] ～を下(お)ろす ❶ shave one's head. ❷ become a Buddhist priest; take the tonsure.

数(かず) a number

[が] ～が少(すく)ない be few in number. ～が増(ふ)える grow in number. ～が減る fall in number.
[で] ～でこなす make profit by selling *sth* in large quantities.
[に] ～に入(い)れる include in the number; take into account.
[を] ～を覚(おぼ)える keep count of. ～を数(かぞ)える take count of. ～を揃(そろ)える complete the number. ～を尽(つ)くす be in abundance. ～を増(ま)す increase the number.

掠(かす)り [S] a rake-off; a kickback

[を] Ⓐ Ⓢ ～を食(く)う be forced to pay a percentage; Ⓒ pay *sb* a rake-off. Ⓢ ～を取(と)る take a percentage; Ⓒ take a rake-off.

風(かぜ) a wind; a breeze; a draft

[が] ～が変(が)わる ❶ the wind changes. ❷ have a change of mood.
[に] ～に当(あ)たる expose oneself to the wind. ～に戦(そよ)ぐ rustle in the wind; Ⓔ be stirred by the wind. ～に付(つ)く come before the wind. ～になびく bend before the wind; yield to the wind. ～に乗(の)る come before the wind. ～に運(はこ)ばれる be carried forward by the wind; Ⓔ be windborne. ～に翻(ひるがえ)る wave in the wind; flutter in the wind. ～が悪(わる)い ❶ [nautical] have a poor wind. ❷ have the tide against one; face an uphill struggle.
[を] ～を入(い)れる ventilate; let air into. ～を追(お)う make haste. ～を切(き)る ❶ go against the wind. ❷ work vigorously; Ⓒ be full of go. ～を掴(つか)む say impossible things; Ⓒ talk rubbish. ～を繋(つな)ぐ say impossible

か

things; talk rubbish. ～を通す admit fresh air into (a room). ～を捕える clutch air. (帆が)～を孕む fill with wind; swell with the wind. ～を吹かす give oneself airs; Ⓘ put on airs; Ⓢ Ⓘ be stuck-up. ◎ ～を結ぶ say impossible things; © talk rubbish.

風邪 a cold; the common cold

[を] ～を移す pass on a cold. ～を引く catch a cold.

方 a manner; a side; a person

[が] ～が付く be settled; be brought to a conclusion.

[を] ～を付ける settle *sth*; reach an agreement.

肩 the shoulder

[が] ～が良い [sports] have a good throw. ～が怒る ❶ become worked up. ❷ have square shoulders. ❸ have a stiff neck. ～が薄い look down and out; look disheveled; look seedy. ～が利く have strong shoulders; be powerful. ～が凝る ❶ have stiff shoulders; have a stiff neck. ❷ be ill at ease; feel uncomfortable. ◎ ～が窄る feel inferior; feel small. ～が狭い be ashamed; Ⓔ Ⓘ lose countenance. Ⓐ ～が閊える have stiff shoulders; have a stiff neck. ～が抜ける feel relieved; fulfill one's duty. ～が張る ❶ have stiff shoulders. ❷ feel constrained; be tense. Ⓐ ～が良い be fortunate; be lucky. Ⓐ ～ が 悪 い be unfortunate be unlucky.

[で] ～で笑う shake with laughter; ridicule *sb*; make fun of *sb*.

[に] ～に掛かる be charged with (a responsibility). ～に担ぐ bear a burden; carry *sth* on one's shoulders; shoulder *sth*. ～にする bear a burden; carry *sth* on one's shoulders; shoulder *sth*. ～に乗せる lift *sth* on one's shoulders.

[を] ～を怒らせる ❶ square one's shoulders. ❷ get worked up. ～を入れる ❶ put one's shoulders under *sth*. ❷ back *sb*/*sth* up; patronize *sb*. ～を落とす ❶ drop one's shoulders. ❷ feel dejected; lose courage. ～を変える ❶ shift (a burden) from one shoulder to the other. ❷ take turns. ～を貸す Ⓘ give *sb* a shoulder; assist *sb*. ～を越す ❶ surpass *sb*; outstrip *sb*. ❷ exceed a limit; overstep the bounds. ～を竦める shrug one's shoulders. ～を窄める shrug one's shoulders. ～を聳やかす swell with pride. ～を叩く ❶ massage one's shoulders. ❷ tap *sb* on the shoulder. ❸ urge *sb* to resign. ～を並べる ❶ stand in line; walk in file; be shoulder to shoulder. ❷ be on a par with *sb*; rank with *sb*; be equal to *sb*. Ⓐ (人から)～を抜く escape one's responsibility; unburden oneself; relieve oneself of a responsibility. ～を脱ぐ ❶ bare one's shoulder(s). ❷ give *sb* a shoulder; assist *sb*. ～を張る open one's shoulders. ～を解す ❶ relax one's shoulders. ❷ feel relieved; feel relaxed. ～を持つ

support *sb*; side with *sb*; stand by *sb*; show partiality to *sb*.

型（かた） a model; a mould; a pattern

[に] ～に嵌（は）まる be set in a model; be unconventional; run to a pattern; fall into a rut. ～に嵌（は）める Ⓐ force *sb* into a pattern; make *sb* conform.

[を] ～を破（やぶ）る break with tradition; go against convention.

形（かた） shape; a pledge ➧ 形（かたち）

[が] ～が崩（くず）れる go out of shape; lose shape.

[に] ～に取（と）る keep *sth* as security; receive *sth* as security.

片（かた） settlement; disposal

[が] ～が付（つ）く be settled; come to a close; be disposed of.

[を] ～を付（つ）ける ❶ settle a matter; set things in order. ❷ finish one's work; bring (a project) to a close. ❸ pay off (one's debts).

片意地（かたいじ） stubbornness; obstinacy

[を] ～を張（は）る refuse to give in; be obstinate; be stubborn.

固唾（かたず） [E] saliva

[を] ～を呑（の）む hold one's breath; catch one's breath; be intensely anxious.

形（かたち） a form; a shape; a figure ➧ 形（かた）

[が] ～が崩（くず）れる go out of shape; lose shape. ～が出来（でき）る ❶ take shape; acquire a form. ❷ become an adult; Ⓘ come of age.

[を] ～を与（あた）える give shape to. ～を改（あらた）める sit up straight; straighten oneself. ～を変（か）える take another form; disguise oneself. ～を正（ただ）す sit up straight; straighten oneself. ～を繕（つくろ）う save appearances; Ⓘ keep up appearances. ～を取（と）る take (a certain) form.

刀（かたな） a sword

[を] ～を納（おさ）める sheathe a sword. ～を試（ため）す try a (new) sword. ～を抜（ぬ）く draw a sword. ～を振（ふ）り上（あ）げる raise a sword. ～を振（ふ）り回（まわ）す brandish a sword.

片棒（かたぼう） a palanquin bearer

[を] ～を担（かつ）ぐ be involved in an intrigue; Ⓔ be a party to a conspiracy; Ⓘ have a hand in a plot; Ⓢ Ⓘ be in cahoots.

肩身（かたみ） public honor

[が] Ⓐ ～が窄（すぼ）る feel inferior; feel small. ～が狭（せま）い feel inferior; be ashamed. ～が広（ひろ）い stand tall; feel at ease.

[を] ～を窄（すぼ）める fear the public gaze; Ⓔ shrink from the public eye.

片目（かため） one eye

[が] ～が明（あ）く learn to read a bit.

[で] ～で見（み）る look with one eye.

[を] ～を潰（つぶ）す lose one eye; lose the sight in one eye; become blind in one eye.

勝ち a victory; a conquest

に ～に乗る follow up a victory.
を ～を得る gain a victory; carry/win the day. ～を占める gain a victory; carry/win the day. ～を拾う gain an unexpected victory. ～を譲る give *sb* a game; ⓘ yield one's palm.

価値 value; worth; merit

が ～がある be of value; be worthwhile.
を ～を失う lose value. ～を落とす drop the value (of); depreciate the value (of *sth*). ～を損じる impair the value (of *sth*). ～を高める heighten the value (of *sth*). ～を認める recognize the value (of *sth*).

活 live; living; resuscitation

を ～を入れる ❶ resuscitate *sb*; bring *sb* round. ❷ encourage *sb*; rally *sb's* strength; ⓢ buck *sb* up.

渇 Ⓔ thirst

を Ⓔ ～を癒す quench one's thirst. Ⓔ ～を訴える complain of thirst. Ⓔ ～を覚える feel thirsty.

鰹節 dried bonito

に Ⓐ ～にする use *sth* as a pretext. Ⓐ ～に使う involve *sb* in (one's excuses); ⓘ make a cat's paw of *sb*; ⓘ make a scapegoat of *sb*.

活気 vigor; spirit; zest

が ～がある be lively. ～が付く become animated; liven up.

に ～に富む be full of life. ～に満ちる brim with life.
を ～を失う lose vigor. ～を帯びる pick up vigor. ～を添える put life into *sth*; give life to *sth*. Ⓔ ～を呈する display vigor.

客気 Ⓔ youthful ardor; rashness

に Ⓔ ～に駆られる be carried away by youthful ardor; act on impulse.

格好 shape; form; appearances

が ～が崩れる get out of shape; look worse.
を ～を付ける give shape to *sth*; add style to one's appearance; try to look good.

喝采 applause; an ovation

を ～を受ける receive an ovation. ～を博する win applause; receive an ovation.

勝手 one's own way; willfulness

が ～が違う be out of one's element; ⓘ be not in one's line. ～が分かる be familiar with; know how to do; ⓘ know the ropes.
に ～に合う suit one's fancy. ～に変える take (great) liberties with. ～にする do as one pleases; have one's own way. ～に使う appropriate *sb's* things for one's own use; make free use of *sb's* things. ⓞ ～に付く do as one pleases; have one's own way. ～に振る舞う act in a willful manner; behave selfishly.

图 〜を知る be familiar with *sth*; know how to do *sth*; ① know the ropes; ⓒ get the knack of *sth*. 〜を飲み込む grasp the situation; ⓒ get the hang of *sth*. 〜を計る be self-seeking. 〜を許す ① give *sb* a free hand; ① give *sb* plenty of rope.

角 a corner; an edge ▶ 角

画 〜が立つ arouse bitterness; cause offense; aggravate *sb*; have a rough going. 〜が取れる ❶ round off one's rough edges; become sociable; become affable. ❷ be sophisticated; be refined; be polished.

图 ⓐ 〜を入る look angry. 〜を落とす round off the corners. 〜を立てる speak harshly; make matters worse; ⓒ aggravate a situation. 〜を取る mellow out; round off the rough corners; ⓒ soften up. 〜を曲がる turn a corner.

門 a door; a gate ▶ 門

画 (お)〜が違う ❶ go to the wrong place; visit the wrong person. ❷ accuse the wrong person; ⓒ ① bark up the wrong tree.

图 ⓐ 〜を出ず ❶ leave home; go out into the world; enter the real world. ❷ become a Buddhist priest; take the tonsure; enter a Buddhist monastery. 〜を売る sell *sth* from door to door; set up shop. ⓐ 〜を広ぐ increase the number of one's family. ⓐ 〜を塞ぐ feel awkward to visit *sb*; have leaden feet.

悲しみ sorrow; sadness; grief

图 〜に暮れる give way to grief. 〜に沈む be overwhelmed with sorrow; be lost in sorrow. 〜に堪える bear the sorrow.

图 〜を和らげる lessen the sorrow; alleviate one's sorrow; ⓔ blunt the edge of sorrow.

金棒 an iron rod

图 〜を引く spread scandal; stir up rumors; go about gossiping.

金 money; wealth; riches

画 〜が唸る be rolling in money; wallow in money. 〜が掛かる require (a lot of) money. 〜が切れる run out of money. 〜が溜まる have some money saved. 〜が出来る grow rich; make money. 〜が入る come into money.

囮 〜で釣る bait *sb* with money.

囝 〜と転ぶ be swayed by money.

囵 〜に飽かす use one's money freely; lavish money on *sth*. 〜に転ぶ be swayed by money. 〜に付く ingratiate oneself with the rich; ① curry favor with the rich; flirt with wealth. 〜になる be profitable; make money.

图 〜を扱う handle money. 〜を得る earn money; obtain money; gain (access to) money. 〜を送る send money; remit money. 〜を掛ける spend money; invest money. 〜を賭ける bet money (on *sth*); stake money on (a race). 〜を返す repay money; give back money. 〜を貸す

lend money. 〜を借りる borrow money. ◎ 〜を切る break (into small) money; change money. Ⓢ 〜を食う be expensive; eat money. 〜を崩す break (into small) money; change money. 〜を工面する raise money. 〜を拵える raise money. 〜を死蔵する lock money away. ◎ 〜を摩る lose one's money (in speculation). 〜をせびる pester *sb* for money; extort money from *sb*. 〜を出す give money; hand out money; furnish the money. 〜を溜める save money; hoard money. 〜を使う use money; spend money. 〜を投じる throw money at (a project); sink money into (a project). 〜を取る charge money; take money. 〜を握らせる bribe *sb* with money; Ⓒ Ⓘ grease *sb's* palm. 〜を寝かす Ⓐ sit on one's money. 〜を残す have surplus money; leave money to *sb*. 〜を払う pay money. 〜を散蒔く be a spendthrift; Ⓒ fling money about. 〜を回す circulate capital; invest money; finance (a project).

鐘 a bell; a gong

[を] Ⓐ 〜を打つ ❶ make a promise; make a vow. ❷ give something up; quit halfway. 〜をつく strike a bell; toll a bell. 〜を鳴らす ring a bell.

過半数 more than half

[を] 〜を得る obtain a majority; win a majority. 〜を占める hold a majority.

黴 mold; mildew; must

[が] 〜が生える ❶ go moldy; go stale. ❷ go out of fashion, become outdated; become old-fashioned.

[を] 〜を取り除く remove the mold; get the mold off *sth*. 〜を防ぐ keep *sth* from getting moldy.

株 stocks; shares; a stump

[が] 〜が上がる ❶ one's stock rises. ❷ rise in public esteem; gain status; Ⓔ be in the ascendant.

[を] 〜を奪う beat *sb* at his/her own game; outdo *sb* in his/her own forte. 〜を売る sell one's assets. 〜を買う buy shares; invest in stocks. 〜を取る beat *sb* at his/her own game; outdo *sb* in his/her own forte. 〜を持つ hold shares (in a company). 〜を譲る transfer the goodwill (of an enterprise).

兜 a (military) helmet

[を] 〜を脱ぐ ❶ take off one's helmet; remove one's helmet. ❷ admit defeat; give *sb* best; give up; Ⓘ take off one's hat to *sb*.

壁 a wall; a barrier

[で] 〜で囲む wall (a place) off.

[と] ◎ 〜と見る ridicule *sb*; Ⓔ hold *sb* in contempt; despise *sb*; look down on *sb*.

[に] ◎ 〜にする ridicule *sb*; despise *sb*; look down on *sb*; Ⓔ hold *sb* in contempt. 〜に突き当たる face unsurmountable difficulties; Ⓘ run into a stone wall; Ⓒ Ⓘ hit a snag.

～にぶつかる be bogged down; have difficulties; ⓘ run into a stone wall.

を ◎ ～を背負う squat against a wall; sit against a wall. ～を塗る plaster a wall. ～を破る tear down a wall; break through a wall.

釜 a pot; a kettle; a cauldron

を Ⓐ Ⓥ ～を抜く practice sodomy. Ⓥ ～を掘る practice sodomy.

鎌 a sickle; a scythe; a hook

が ◎ ～が切れる go well; yield results.

を ～を掛ける ❶ put an enticing question; ask a leading question. ❷ entice sb to speak; draw sb out; pump out a secret.

竈 a kitchen range; a furnace

が ～が賑わう live the good life.

に Ⓐ ～に媚ぶ ❶ flatter the cook; ⓘ curry favor with the cook. ❷ ingratiate oneself with the men behind the scene. Ⓐ ～に跨がる surpass one's parents.

を ◎ ～を起す increase the family fortune; cause one's house to flourish. ◎ ～を覆す lose one fortune; ⓢ go bust. ◎ ～を占める run a household. ◎ ～を立てる set up a house; start housekeeping. ◎ ～を持つ possess a fortune. ◎ ～を破る be ruined; go bankrupt; Ⓔ dissipate one's fortune. ◎ ～を分る set up a branch family; keep a separate house.

神 a god; a goddess; a deity ◆神

に ～に祈る pray to God/the gods. ～に捧げる dedicate to God/the gods; make offerings to God/the gods. ～になる be elevated to godhood. ～に祭る deify sb; enshrine sb; apotheosize sb.

を ～を敬う be pious; revere God/the gods. ～を畏れる fear God/the gods. ～を信じる believe in God/the gods. ～を祭る worship God/the gods.

紙 paper

に ～に書く write on paper. ～に包む wrap sth in paper.

を ～を畳む unfold a sheet of paper. ～を伸ばす flatten crumpled paper. ～を張る paper a wall; paste paper on sth. ～を広げる unfold a sheet of paper.

髪 hair; hairdo; locks

が ～が抜ける lose one's hair.

を ～を編む braid one's hair. ～を下ろす ❶ shave one's head. ❷ become a Buddhist priest; take the tonsure. ～を刈る have one's hair cut. Ⓔ ～を梳る comb one's hair. Ⓢ ～を梳く comb one's hair. ～を束ねる bind one's hair. ～縮らす curl one's hair. ～を解く let down one's hair; take down one's hair. ～を直す tidy one's hair. ～を撫でる caress sb's hair; stroke sb's hair. ～を伸ばす let one's hair grow long. ～を乱す rumple one's hair; tousle one's hair. ～を毟る tear one's

か

hair; rend one's hair. 〜を分ける split one's hair. 〜を結う dress one's hair.

裃 Ⓗ a *kamishimo* [garment]
を 〜を着る be ceremonious; be formal. 〜を脱ぐ be relaxed; be unceremonious.

雷 thunder; a thunderbolt
が 〜が落ちる ❶ be struck by lightning. ❷ be scolded; be told off; be given a dressing-down.
を 〜を落とす scold *sb*; tell *sb* off; ⓘ haul *sb* over the coals.

鴨 a (wild) duck; a drake
に Ⓒ 〜にする target *sb*; victimize *sb*.

空 emptiness; vacancy ▶ 空 ▶ 空
に 〜にする empty (a box). 〜になる become empty; be emptied.
を Ⓐ 〜を踏む be disappointed (in one's hopes); be frustrated; prove a disappointment.

殻 a husk; a hull; a shell
を Ⓐ 〜を言う exaggerate; stretch the facts; Ⓔ indulge in hyperbole; Ⓢ ⓘ pile it on; Ⓢ ⓘ lay it on thick. 〜を破る Ⓐ break out of one's shell; shake off one's inhibitions.

体 the body; physique ▶ 体
が 〜が空く have time to oneself; be free; be vacant; have time on one's hands. 〜が続く keep going strong; be in good health; Ⓔ be in good fettle. 〜が強い have a strong constitution. 〜が太る gain weight; put on weight. 〜が弱る become weak; be run down. 〜が痩せる lose weight; lose flesh. 〜が弱い have a weak constitution. 〜が弱る become weak; be run down.
で 〜で覚える know *sth* through experience; learn from experience; (learn to) do *sth* by instinct.
に 〜に合う ❶ fit (one's body) well. ❷ agree with one. 〜に障る be harmful to one's health; injure one's health.
を 〜を惜しむ spare oneself (the trouble); be idle; be lazy. 〜を固める be settled down. 〜を壊す impair one's health; ruin one's health; lose one's health; make oneself ill. 〜を沈める go down in the world; Ⓔ fall into reduced circumstances; Ⓢ ⓘ go to the dogs. 〜を調べる go through *sb's* pockets; search *sb*. 〜を作る build up one's body. 〜を張る ❶ do *sth* at the risk of one's life; devote oneself to (a cause); throw oneself into *sth* heart and soul. ❷ prostitute oneself; sell one's body. 〜を休める rest one's body; have a rest; give oneself a rest. 〜を悪くする injure one's health.

川 a river; a stream; a rivulet
が Ⓐ 〜が明く a river is cleared. Ⓐ 〜が止まる a river too high to wade across.

〈を〉〜を下る go down a river. 〜を遡る go up a river. 〜を渡る cross a river; wade across a stream.

皮 the skin; a hide; a pelt; a fur
〈を〉〜を被る play the hypocrite; feign innocence. 〜を殺ぐ pare leather. 〜を鞣す tan hide. 〜を剥ぐ skin (an animal, a tree). 〜を剥く peel off the skin.

巻 a volume; a reel; a tome
〈を〉〜を追う read a book volume by volume. 〈ⓞ〉〜を掩う close a book; finish reading a book.

勘 an intuition; a hunch
〈が〉〜が付く have a general idea.
〈で〉〜で分かる know *sth* by intuition; ⓒ have a hunch; ⓘ feel *sth* in one's bones.
〈を〉〜を覆す reconsider the facts. 〜を働かす use one's intuition; ⓒ ⓘ play one's hunch.

歓 Ⓔ delight; pleasure; joy
〈を〉ⓔ〜を尽す make merry; have a good time.

燗 heated *sake*
〈が〉〜が通る *sake* with exactly the right temperature.
〈を〉〜をする warm up *sake* in a bottle. 〜を付ける warm up sake in a bottle.

癇 a quick temper; mettle
〈が〉〜が高ぶる lose one's temper;

become irate; ⓢ ⓘ blow a fuse. 〜が立つ lose one's temper; ⓒ ⓘ fly off the handle; ⓢ ⓘ blow a fuse.
〈に〉〜に障る irritate one; cut one to the quick; ⓘ rub one the wrong way; ⓒ get on one's nerves.
〈を〉〜を起こす lose one's temper; become irate; ⓒ ⓘ fly off the handle; ⓢ ⓘ blow a fuse.

寛 Ⓔ leniency; generosity
〈に〉ⓔ〜に過ぎる be too lenient; be too generous.

閑 Ⓔ leisure; time off
〈を〉ⓔ〜を得る have time to oneself; be free; be vacant; ⓘ have time on one's hands. ⓔ〜を盗む steal time (to do *sth*)

冠 Ⓔ a crown; a coronet ▶ 冠
〈を〉Ⓐ Ⓔ〜を掛く resign from one's post; ⓔ tender one's resignation.

款 Ⓔ an article; goodwill
〈を〉ⓔ〜を通じる make friends with *sb*; ⓔ enter into friendly relations with *sb*; make secret overtures (to the enemy).

官 Ⓔ government; high office
〈に〉ⓔ〜に就く enter government service; take office.
〈を〉ⓔ〜を辞する leave office; step down from public service.

感 Ⓔ a feeling ; a sensation
〈に〉ⓔ〜に堪える show deep signs

of emotion; be deeply impressed.

[を] Ⓔ 〜を与える strike *sb* (as); leave an impression.

願 a prayer; a wish; a vow

[が] 〜が叶う have one's prayer answered.

[に] Ⓐ 〜に懸ける ❶ worry over *sth*; fret about *sth*. ❷ be haunted by; prey on one's mind. ❸ offer a prayer; make a vow.

[を] ◎ 〜を起こす offer a prayer; make a vow. 〜を懸ける offer a prayer; make a vow. 〜を立てる offer a prayer; make a vow. 〜を解く revoke a vow.

眼 Ⓢ the eye; eyesight

[を] Ⓢ 〜を付ける glare at *sb* (with envy); stare at *sb* (suspiciously); Ⓔ fasten one's eyes on *sb*.

干戈 Ⓔ arms; weapons

[に] ◎ Ⓔ 〜に訴える resort to arms.

[を] Ⓐ Ⓔ 〜を動かす open hostilities; take up arms against *sb*. Ⓐ Ⓔ 〜を納める lay down arms. Ⓐ Ⓔ 〜を交える open hostilities; go to war; cross swords with *sb*; fight each other.

考え thought; ideas; a notion

[が] 〜が有る have an idea. 〜が浮かぶ come to mind; occur to one. 〜が固まる an idea takes shape. 〜が変わる change one's mind. 〜がつく form an opinion.

[に] 〜に入れる take *sth* into consideration; bear *sth* in mind;

① take *sth* on board. 〜に沈む be lost in thought. 〜に耽る be deep in thought.

[を] 〜を改める revise one's thinking. 〜を抱く entertain a thought. 〜を起こす get an idea. 〜を決める make up one's mind; ① take *sth* into one's head. 〜を捨てる relinquish a thought; drop an idea. 〜を伝える convey one's thoughts. 〜を盗む steal *sb's* idea. 〜を述べる express one's views; speak one's mind. 〜を纏める collect one's thoughts. 〜を持つ entertain a thought.

感覚 sensation; sense; feeling

[に] 〜に訴える appeal to the senses.

[を] 〜を失う lose feeling (in one's limbs); become past feeling.

寒気 cold weather; the cold

[が] 〜が増す grow cold.

[に] 〜に堪える bear the cold; stand the cold. 〜に負ける yield to the cold.

[を] 〜を凌ぐ ward off the cold. 〜を冒す brave the cold.

感興 interest; inspiration; fun

[が] 〜が湧く become interested in *sth*; warm up to (an idea).

[を] 〜を誘う arouse *sb's* interest. 〜を殺ぐ spoil the fun; dampen *sb's* enthusiasm. 〜をそそる excite *sb's* interest. 〜を求める seek new sensations; seek pleasure.

関係 a relation; a relationship

⟨が⟩〜がある ❶ be related; ⓒ have something to do with *sb/sth*. ⓒ ❷ have a sexual relation with *sb*. ⟨を⟩〜を促進する promote relations. 〜を改善する improve relations. 〜を断つ cut one's ties with *sb*; break off relations; ⓔ sever one's connections with *sb*. 〜を続ける sustain a relation. 〜を結ぶ establish a connection with. 〜を持つ entertain relations with.

間隙 a gap; an aperture

⟨に⟩〜に乗じる take advantage of an unguarded moment; catch *sb* off guard.
⟨を⟩〜を埋める stop a gap; bridge a divide. 〜を生じる fall out with *sb*. 〜を縫う slip through a gap; pass between two obstacles.

勧告 advice; counsel

⟨に⟩〜に従う take *sb's* advice.
⟨を⟩〜を受ける take *sb's* advice.

感じ feelings; sense

⟨が⟩〜がする have a feeling.
⟨を⟩〜を与える produce a feeling.

感謝 gratitude; appreciation

⟨に⟩〜に値する be worthy of one's appreciation; deserve one's thanks.
⟨を⟩〜を受ける receive thanks. 〜を捧げる offer thanks; give thanks.

慣習 tradition; custom; habit

⟨を⟩〜を捨てる do away with tradition. 〜を守る uphold a tradition; keep a tradition alive. 〜を破る break with tradition.

干渉 interference; meddling

⟨を⟩〜を受ける be interfered with. 〜をする meddle in *sb's* affairs. 〜を招く invite interference.

感情 feelings; emotions

⟨が⟩〜が薄らぐ calm down; ⓐ cool down. 〜が籠る be impassioned; be full of emotion. 〜が高まる get excited; let one's feelings run high. 〜が燃え上がる get passionate over *sth*; let emotions flare up.
⟨に⟩〜に訴える appeal to *sb's* sentiments. 〜に駆られる do *sth* on the impulse of the moment; be driven by emotions. 〜に走る give way to one's emotions. 〜に任せる give vent to one's emotions. 〜に負ける let one's emotions get the better of one; be swayed by emotions.
⟨を⟩〜を表わす express one's feelings. 〜を偽る feign one's feelings. 〜を動かす work up one's/*sb's* feelings. 〜を押える contain one's passions; suppress one's feelings. ⓔ 〜を害する hurt one's/*sb's* feelings. 〜を隠す hide one's feelings; ① keep a straight face. 〜を込める do *sth* with feeling; ① put one's heart into *sth*. 〜を刺激する excite one's/*sb's* emotions; stir one's/*sb's* feelings. 〜を和らげる appease *sb*; ⓔ pacify one's/*sb's* sentiments.

45

勘定 かんじょう counting; reckoning

[が] 〜が合う the accounts tally. 〜が嵩む run up bills.

[に] 〜に入れる count sth in; take sth into account. 〜に組み入れる place to sb's account. 〜に付ける charge sb's account. 〜に入る count.

[を] 〜を締め切る close accounts. 〜を締める add up accounts. 〜をする settle one's accounts; foot the bill. 〜を溜める run up bills. 〜を付ける pay money; foot the bill. 〜を取る collect a bill. 〜を延ばす postpone one's payment. 〜を払う pay money; foot the bill. 〜を引き合わせる check account.

関心 かんしん concern; interest

[が] 〜が薄らぐ interest wanes; lose interest.

[を] 〜を抱く have an interest in sth. 〜を示す show concern; display interest. 〜を引く draw one's/sb's interest; arouse concern; capture sb's interest. 〜を持つ be interested; be concerned; take notice. 〜を寄せる give thought to; take an interest in.

歓心 かんしん favor; good will; approval

[を] 〜を買う ingratiate oneself with sb; win sb's heart; ⓘ curry favor with sb.

肝胆 かんたん Ⓔ the liver and gallbladder

[を] Ⓐ Ⓔ 〜を出す show one's good faith toward sb; do sth with devotion. Ⓐ Ⓔ 〜を傾ける unbosom oneself; ⓘ pour out one's heart to sb. Ⓐ Ⓔ 〜を砕く devote oneself to sth. Ⓐ Ⓔ 〜を吐く reveal one's real intentions; ⓘ put one's cards on the table. Ⓐ Ⓔ 〜を披く unbosom oneself; ⓘ pour out one's heart to sb.

看板 かんばん a signboard; a sign

[が] 〜が泣く be not true to one's name; be not worthy of one's reputation.

[を] 〜を下ろす close down (a shop). 〜を出す put up a sign. 〜を塗り替える ❶ repaint a signboard. ❷ change one's policy; change occupation; Ⓐ change one's colors.

冠 かんむり a crown; a coronet ▶冠 かん

[を] Ⓐ 〜を掛く step down from office; Ⓑ retire from public office; leave government service. 〜を被せる crown sb. 〜を加える ❶ crown sb. ❷ celebrate one's coming of age. 〜を着ける put a crown on one's head; wear a crown. Ⓐ 〜を弾く prepare for public office. 〜を曲げる be offended; take offense at sth; Ⓒ Ⓐ get sour.

歓楽 かんらく pleasure; merriment; mirth

[に] 〜に酔う indulge in pleasure.

[を] 〜を追う pursue (a life of) pleasure. 〜を尽くす give oneself up to pleasure. 〜を求める seek pleasure.

慣例 かんれい custom; normal practice

[に] 〜に従う conform to the

custom; follow normal practice; ① fall into line. 〜に背く go against normal practice. 〜による be according to custom.

を 〜を残す set a precedent. 〜を廃する abandon normal practice; do away with custom. 〜を破る violate custom; break with custom.

キ

気 spirit; a mind; a heart

が 〜が合う be like-minded; get along well; ⓔ be congenial to one; ① see eye to eye; ◎ ① hit it off. 〜が焦る be impatient. 〜が荒い be quarrelsome; be ill-tempered. 〜が改まる be braced up; feel renewed; feel refreshed. 〜がある have a mind to; be interested in; be ready to (take sth up). 〜が良い be good-natured; be generous. 〜が行く be attentive. ◎ 〜が痛む ❶ fret over sth; worry about sth. ❷ feel inferior; feel small. 〜が入る ❶ fret over sth; worry about sth. ❷ be impassioned; be full of emotion. ◎ 〜が煎れる be anxious; be nervous; be upset; be nettled. 〜が多い ❶ be fickle; be flighty. ❷ be inconstant; be unfaithful. 〜が大きい be broad-minded; be large-hearted; be generous. 〜が後れる lose one's nerve; be daunted by; become diffident. 〜が置ける feel ill at ease. ◎ 〜が落つ be disappointed; feel discouraged; be dejected; lose

heart; lose courage. 〜が重い be downcast; be in low spirits. 〜が折れる be discouraged; lose heart. 〜が勝つ be strong-willed; be opinionated; ⓢ be hard-nosed. 〜が軽い be cheerful; be sociable; be easy to get on with. 〜が変わる change one's mind; have a change of heart. 〜が利く ❶ be clever; be sensible. ❷ be tactful; be thoughtful; be smart; ⓢ ① be on the ball. ❸ be chic; be fashionable; ◎ be hip; ⓢ be cool. 〜が腐る be dejected; feel depressed; ◎ feel blue. 〜が挫ける be discouraged; lose heart. 〜が狂う lose one's mind; go mad; ⓢ go crazy; ⓢ ① lose one's marbles. 〜が冴える be cheerful; have a sunny disposition. 〜が差す feel guilty; ① feel the pricks of conscience. 〜が静まる calm down; settle down; ⓔ regain one's composure. 〜が沈む be depressed; be in low spirits; feel gloomy. 〜が進む feel like doing sth; be in the mood (to do sth); ⓔ be in the right frame of mind. 〜が済む be satisfied; be appeased; feel content. 〜がする get a certain notion; feel as if; believe that. 〜が座る feel relieved; be at ease. 〜が急く be impatient; be anxious; be in a hurry; be eager; ① chafe at the bit. 〜が殺がれる lose enthusiasm; be dampened in spirit. 〜が外れる be distracted; fail to pay attention. 〜が高い be high-handed; be haughty. 〜が立つ

be upset; be agitated; be on edge; be wrought up. ～が小(ちい)さい be timid; be faint-hearted; be cautious. ～が違(ちが)う be out of one's mind; be mad; Ⓢ be crazy. ～が散(ち)る be distracted; lose one's concentration; Ⓢ lose it. ～が支(つか)える be distraught; be dejected; feel depressed. ～が尽(つ)きる ❶ lose spirit; run out of energy; Ⓔ become enervated; Ⓔ lose one's zest for life. ❷ be bored; feel weary. ❸ feel wretched; be out of sorts. ～が付(つ)く ❶ notice *sth*; be aware of *sth*; dawn on one. ❷ be attentive; thoughtful; be considerate. ❸ regain consciousness; Ⓘ come to; Ⓘ come round. ～が詰(つ)まる feel oppressed; feel uncomfortable; be ill at ease. ～が強(つよ)い be bold; be daring; be strong-willed. ～が出(で)る feel like doing *sth*; be in the mood (to do *sth*); Ⓔ be in the right frame of mind. ～が通(とお)る be worldly-wise; know the world; be street-wise. ～が咎(とが)める have a guilty conscience; feel guilty; be sorry. ～が閉(と)じる be depressed; be gloomy; feel dejected; be cast down; be in low spirits; Ⓒ Ⓘ have the blues. ～が直(なお)る recover one's spirit. ～が長(なが)い be patient; be self-composed; Ⓒ be laid-back. ～が抜(ぬ)ける ❶ lose consciousness; pass out; Ⓒ black out. ❷ be let down; be frustrated. ❸ lose flavor; go flat; go stale. ～が練(ね)れる have a good temper; be gentle; be patient. ～が上(のぼ)る ❶ have a rush of blood to the head; feel dizzy. ❷ go mad; lose one's senses; Ⓢ Ⓘ lose one's marbles. ～が乗(の)る take interest in *sth*; be excited by *sth*; Ⓢ Ⓘ be on a roll. ～が入(はい)る get into *sth*; put one's mind to *sth*. ～が弾(はず)む be in high spirits; get excited; have a light heart; be merry. ～が早(はや)い ❶ be hasty; be rash. ❷ have a quick temper; be short-tempered. ～が逸(はや)る be hasty; be impatient; be rash. ～が張(は)り詰(つ)める be on the alert; Ⓘ be on tenterhooks. ～が張(は)る strain one's nerves; be tense; be under stress; be anxious. ～が晴(は)れる feel relieved; be cheered up. ～が引(ひ)き締(し)める feel bolstered (by *sth*). ～が引(ひ)ける feel timorous; feel inferior; feel small; be ashamed. ◎ ～が開(ひら)く feel relieved; become merry; become cheerful. ～が広(ひろ)い be calm; be laid-back. ～が鬱(ふさ)ぐ feel depressed; be low-spirited; be low. ～が触(ふ)れる ❶ go mad; lose one's senses; Ⓢ Ⓘ lose one's marbles. ❷ be torn by conflicting emotions; be swayed. ◎ ～が減(へ)る be mentally fatigued; suffer from nervous strain; feel worn down. ◎ ～が細(ほそ)い be timid; be faint-hearted; be cautious. ～が紛(まぎ)れる be diverted (from one's worries); be (pleasantly) distracted. ～が回(まわ)る ❶ be attentive; be thoughtful; be considerate. ❷ suspect *sb* without reason; expect the worst; be prejudiced. ～が短(みじか)い have a quick

き

temper; be short-tempered. 〜が向く be inclined to do *sth*; feel like doing *sth*; be in the mood (to do *sth*). ⓞ 〜が結ぼれる become depressed; fall into a depression; become cast down. 〜が滅入る lose courage; be dispirited; be downhearted. ⓞ 〜が戻る lose interest (in doing *sth*); change one's mind; ⓒⓘ be turned off. 〜が揉める be anxious; be nervous; ⓘ wring one's hands. 〜が休まる feel relieved; feel at ease. 〜が和らぐ relent toward *sb*. ⓥⓢ 〜が行く have an orgasm. 〜が緩む slacken one's attention; ⓘ drop one's guard; let up. 〜が良い ❶ feel good; be in good spirits. ❷ be good-natured; have a friendly disposition. 〜が弱い be faint-hearted; be weak-kneed; be timid. 〜が弱る lose spirit; run out of energy; ⓔ become enervated; ⓔ lose one's zest for life. 〜が若い be young at heart.

に ⓞ 〜に合う suit one's taste; take one's fancy; like *sb*/*sth*. ⓞ 〜に当たる be offended; feel hurt. ⓞ 〜に当てる offend *sb*; hurt *sb*'s feelings. 〜に入る ❶ suit one's taste; take one's fancy; like *sb*/*sth*. ❷ humor *sb*; ingratiate oneself with *sb*; ⓘ curry favor with *sb*. 〜に掛かる ⓘ weigh on one's mind; feel uneasy about *sth*; be anxious about *sth*; be bothered by *sth*. 〜に掛ける ❶ have *sth* on one's mind; fret over *sth*; worry

about *sth*. ❷ be haunted by *sth*. 〜に適う suit one's taste. 〜に障る ❶ have *sth* on one's mind; fret over *sth*; worry about *sth*. ❷ be displeased about *sth*; be irritated by *sth*; be irked by *sth*; ⓒ ⓘ be rubbed the wrong way. Ⓐ 〜に逆う go against *sb*'s feelings; hurt *sb*'s feelings. 〜に障る be offended; feel hurt. 〜に済む ❶ feel refreshed. ❷ be satisfied; be appeased. 〜にする be bothered by *sth*; make an issue of *sth*; ⓒ let *sth* get to one. 〜に染む suit one's taste; take one's fancy; like *sb*/*sth*. Ⓐ 〜に違う be displeased; feel hurt; be put out of humor. 〜に留まる be concerned about *sth*; take notice of *sth*; draw one's attention. 〜に留める keep *sth* in mind; bear *sth* in mind. 〜になる ❶ care about; be concerned about; worry about. ❷ be in the mood (to do *sth*); feel like doing. ❸ feel as if; feel that. Ⓐ 〜に向く suit one's taste; please one's fancy. 〜に持つ ⓘ weigh on one's mind. 〜に病む worry deeply about *sth*; be worried sick; fret incessantly over *sth*.

を 〜を痛める fret over *sth*; worry about *sth*. 〜を入れる ❶ care about; make an issue of. ❷ be impatient; be eager to do *sth*. ❸ apply oneself to *sth*; do *sth* in earnest; ⓘ put one's heart into *sth*. 〜を失う ❶ lose interest; be discouraged; ⓒⓘ be turned off. ❷ lose consciousness; faint; pass out; © black out. ◎ 〜を打つ ❶ become depressed; fall into a depression. ❷ be shocked; be frightened; be startled. 〜を移す ❶ change one's mind. ❷ direct one's attention towards. 〜を奪われる be absorbed in *sth*; be engrossed in *sth*. Ⓐ 〜を得る recover one's spirit; take heart; ⓢ buck up. Ⓐ 〜を負う be eager; Ⓘ be on one's mettle (for success). ◎ 〜を置く ❶ respect *sb*'s feelings. ❷ feel relieved; be at ease. 〜を落ち着ける calm down; settle down; © regain one's composure. 〜を落とす be discouraged; be disappointed; lose heart. 〜を変える change one's mind. 〜を兼ねる ❶ feel hesitant; have scruples about (doing *sth*); hold back; shy away from. ❷ have regard for *sb*'s feelings; show constraint toward *sb*. 〜を利かす have the sense to (do *sth*); be considerate; ⓢ Ⓘ use one's loaf. 〜を腐らす be dejected; feel depressed; feel frustrated; lose courage. 〜を挫く be discouraged; lose heart. 〜を砕く fret over *sth*; worry over *sth*; © Ⓘ rack one's brains. Ⓐ 〜を下す behave oneself; act as one should. Ⓐ 〜を屈す be daunted; give in; cave in. 〜を配る pay attention; be attentive; Ⓘ be on one's guard. 〜を狂わせる drive *sb* mad. 〜を込める do *sth* with devotion. ◎ 〜を懲らす ❶ have had enough of; © be fed up with *sb*. ❷ take pains over; make strenuous

efforts. ❸ be worried by *sth*; © Ⓘ rack one's brains. 〜を静める ease one's mind; calm down; © get a hold on oneself. 〜を殺ぐ discourage *sb*; dampen *sb*'s enthusiasm. 〜をそそる arouse one's interest; be aroused by *sth*; ⓢ Ⓘ push *sb*'s buttons. ◎ 〜を背く offend *sb*'s feelings. 〜を逸らす ❶ be distracted; lose concentration. ❷ divert *sb*'s attention; distract *sb*. 〜を揃える pull together. 〜を損ずる ❶ hurt *sb*'s feelings. ❷ be disheartened. Ⓐ 〜を嗜む be determined to do; firmly resolve to do; be fully resigned (to one's fate). Ⓐ 〜を出す be full of vigor. Ⓐ 〜を扶ける put *sb* on his/her mettle. 〜を通ず have the same mind; be in agreement. 〜を遣う ❶ care about *sb*; worry about *sb*; take care of *sb*; look after *sb*. ❷ pay attention to *sth*; be mindful of *sth*. Ⓐ 〜を尽かす put one's heart and soul into *sth*; devote all one's energy to *sth*. Ⓐ 〜を尽くす ❶ exert oneself; apply oneself to *sth*. ❷ be mentally fatigued. 〜を付ける ❶ pay attention to *sth*; be mindful of *sth*. ❷ get active; be enlivened. ❸ bring *sb* round. ❹ liven *sth* up; give *sth* a boost. 〜を詰める strain one's nerves. Ⓐ 〜を通す have the sense to (do *sth*). 〜を留める pay particular attention to. 〜を取られる be diverted with *sth*; forget oneself in *sth*; lose oneself in *sth*. 〜を取り直す pluck up courage; brace oneself; Ⓢ buck up; Ⓘ pull oneself together. Ⓞ ～を取る humor *sb*; flatter *sb*; try to please *sb*; Ⓘ curry favor with *sb*. ～を直す recover one's mental strength; Ⓐ bounce back. ～を抜く ❶ relax the tension; become unconcerned about *sth*; Ⓒ let up. ❷ startle *sb*; frighten *sb*. Ⓐ ～を上す ❶ have a rush of blood to the head; feel dizzy. ❷ get excited; be worked up (over *sth*). ～を呑まれる be overwhelmed; be taken aback. ～を吐く ❶ make a good showing; do a good job; outdo oneself. ❷ brim with confidence; be in high spirits. ～を励ます rouse oneself to action. ～を晴らす cheer oneself up; take one's mind off *sth*; divert oneself (pleasantly). ～を張り詰める be on edge; be nervous; Ⓘ be on tenterhooks. ～を張る ❶ pay attention to; be watchful; be on the lookout. ❷ exert oneself; make an effort. ～を引き締める pluck up courage; brace oneself; Ⓘ pull oneself together. ～を引き立てる ❶ pluck up courage; brace oneself; Ⓘ pull oneself together. ❷ encourage *sb*; cheer *sb* up; Ⓢ buck *sb* up. ～を引く rouse *sb*'s excitement; seek *sb's* attention. Ⓐ ～を触る ❶ be offended; take offense. ❷ turn one's attention to *sth* else; be diverted by *sth*. ～を紛らす divert one's attention; take one's mind off *sth*. ～を回す be suspicious; read too much into (a situation); Ⓘ read between the lines. Ⓞ ～を迎える humor *sb*. ～を持たす ❶ encourage *sb*; embolden *sb*; ❷ raise *sb's* hopes; Ⓒ lead *sb* on. ～を揉む be anxious about *sth*; fret over *sth*; worry about *sth*; Ⓒ fidget about *sth*. ～を養う nurse one's spirit; feel refreshed. ～を休める take a rest; Ⓢ kick back. Ⓐ ～を遣る ❶ be in the mood (to do *sth*); feel like doing. Ⓥ Ⓢ ❷ have an orgasm. ～を許す ❶ relax one's attention; Ⓘ drop one's guard; Ⓘ let one's guard down. ❷ let *sb* into one's heart; open up to *sb*. ～を緩める relax one's attention; Ⓘ drop one's guard; Ⓔ unbend one's mind.

機 [E] **an opportunity; a chance**

[が] Ⓔ ～が熟す the time ripens.

[に] Ⓔ ～に応ずる act in accordance with circumstances; take the proper steps to meet the situation. Ⓔ ～に乗じる seize an opportunity. Ⓔ ～に投ずる take advantage of a situation; capitalize on an opportunity. Ⓔ ～に乗る take advantage of a situation; capitalize on a opportunity. Ⓞ Ⓔ ～に触れる be fortunate; be lucky; Ⓒ Ⓘ hit good luck.

[を] Ⓔ ～を逸する let a chance slip by; miss an opportunity. Ⓔ ～を失う lose an opportunity; let a chance slip by. Ⓔ ～を待つ wait until the time is ripe; wait for an opportunity; Ⓔ bide one's time. Ⓔ ～を見る seize an opportunity; look for an opportunity.

奇 Ⓔ strangeness; oddity
をⒺ ～を争う compete with each other in novelty; try to outdo each other in eccentricity. Ⓔ ～を好む be eccentric. Ⓔ ～を衒う affect eccentricity.

気合い a yell; a shout; spirit
が ～が入る be spirited.
に Ⓐ ～に当たる worry about. Ⓐ ～に構う ❶ be offended. ❷ fall ill.
を ～を入れる ❶ show courage; display spirit. ❷ inflict corporal punishment; punish *sb*. ❸ reprimand *sb*; Ⓒ tell *sb* off; Ⓘ haul *sb* over the coals. ～を掛ける spur *sb* on; encourage *sb*; yell at *sb*.

気炎 high spirits; big talk
が ～が上がる be in high spirits.
を ～を上げる ❶ argue heatedly in favor/against *sth*; debate *sth* hotly. ❷ brag about *sth*; boast about *sth*; Ⓘ talk big; Ⓘ blow one's own horn. ～を吐く ❶ argue heatedly in favor/against *sth*; debate *sth* hotly. ❷ brag about *sth*; boast about *sth*; Ⓘ talk big; Ⓘ blow one's own horn.

記憶 memory; recollection
が ～が良い have a good memory. ～が悪い have a poor memory.
に ～に留める register *sth* in one's memory.
を ～を失う lose one's memory. ～を辿る retrace one's memory. を取り戻す regain one's memory. ～を

呼び起こす call *sth* to mind. ～を呼び戻す recall *sth*; call *sth* to mind.

気後れ "belated spirit"
が ～がする lose one's nerve; back down; Ⓘ get cold feet.

機会 an opportunity; a chance
を ～を与える give *sb* a chance. ～を免する miss an opportunity; let a chance slip by. ～を覗う look for an occasion (to do *sth*). ～を得る find an opportunity; get a chance. ～を捕える seize an opportunity; Ⓒ grab one's chances. ～を狙う look for an opportunity. ～を逃す miss an opportunity; let a chance slip by. ～を見逃す overlook an opportunity; fail to spot an opportunity. ～を待つ wait for an opportunity. ～を持つ have an opportunity.

危害 an injury; harm; danger
を ～を受ける sustain an injury. ～を加える inflict an injury on *sb*. ～を免れる escape unhurt; Ⓒ Ⓘ save one's skin.

危機 a crisis; a critical moment
が ～が去る a crisis passes. ～が迫る a crisis approaches; danger is imminent.
に ～に襲われる be caught in a crisis; Ⓒ Ⓘ be up the creek. ～に陥る be plunged into a crisis; Ⓘ be in deep waters. ～に陥れる bring to a crisis; bring a crisis to a head. ～に

備える prepare for a crises; provide against emergencies. 〜に達する reach a crisis; come to a head. 〜に臨む face a crisis. 図 〜を切り抜ける get through a crisis; see one's way out of a crisis; ⓔ tide over a crisis; ① weather the storm. ⓔ 〜を脱する pass through a crisis. ⓔ 〜を孕む be fraught with danger.

聞き耳 attentive ears

図 〜を立てる strain one's ears; ① be all ears. ◎ 〜を潰す turn a deaf ear.

危険 danger; peril; a hazard

が 〜が迫る be in danger. 〜が伴う be fraught with danger.

に 〜に陥る fall into danger; get in harm's way; ① be in deep waters. 〜に曝す expose oneself/sb to danger; put oneself/sb in harm's way. 〜に臨む face danger. 図 〜を冒す brave danger; run a risk; take a chance. 〜を避ける avoid danger; keep out of harm's way. 〜を救う save sb from danger. 〜を免れる escape from danger; keep out of harm's way. 〜を招く court danger.

機嫌 humor; a mood

が 〜が良い be in good humor; be in a good mood. 〜が直る regain one's good humor; recover one's temper. 〜が悪い be displeased; be out of humor; be in a bad temper.

図 〜を取る flatter sb; humor sb; ① curry favor with sb; ① find sb's soft side. 〜を損ねる offend sb. 〜を直す regain one's good humor; recover one's temper.

技巧 art; craftsmanship; artifice

図 〜を懲らす employ one's skill. 〜を用いる use art. ⓔ 〜を弄する resort to artifice; use a trick.

旗幟 Ⓔ a flag; a banner

図 ⓔ 〜を鮮明する make one's position clear; take a clear stand.

記事 a (news) story; an article

図 〜を送る send in a story; submit an article. 〜を書く write an article. 〜を差し止める ban an article. 〜を取る get a story; get copy. 〜を載せる carry a story.

傷 an injury; a wound; a scar

が 〜がつく get hurt; be injured. 図 〜を受ける receive a wound; ⓔ sustain an injury. 〜を負う be wounded; ⓔ sustain an injury. 〜をつける wound sb; inflict a wound. ⓐ 〜を求む look for sb's weak points; ⓒ find sb's Achilles heel.

気勢 spirit; ardor; enthusiasm

が 〜が上がる be in high spirits; be elated.

図 〜を上げる raise sb's spirit; drum up opposition. 〜を示す display nerve; show spirit. 〜を添える inspire sb; give sb moral support. 〜

53

を殺ぐ dampen *sb's* spirit. ～を増す
be inspired; gain strength.

犠牲 self-sacrifice; sacrifice
を ～を払う make a sacrifice; pay
dearly for *sth*.

奇蹟 a miracle; a wonder
を ～を現わす achieve a miracle.
～を行う perform a miracle; work
wonders.

偽善 hypocrisy
を ～を行なう play the hypocrite.

規則 rules; a regulations; law
に ～に訴える appeal to law. ～に
拘泥する adhere to regulations. ～
に反する go against regulations. ～
による be according to regulations.
で ～で縛られる be bound by
regulations. ～で縛る tie *sb* down
by rules.
を ～を定める lay down the rules;
establish regulations; set the rules.
～を外れる deviate from the rules.
～を守る observe regulations. ～を
設ける establish regulations; lay
down rules. ～を破る flout the
rules; violate regulations; break
the law.

期待 expectation; anticipation
に ～に添う meet one's/*sb's*
expectations.
を ～を抱く harbor expectations.
～を裏切る betray one's/*sb's*
expectations.

吉兆 E an auspicious omen
を © ～を示す be auspicious; be of
good omen; augur well.

狐 a fox; a vixen
が ～が落ちる come to one's senses;
extricate oneself from a spell. ～に
つままれる be baffled; be flabbergasted; © ① be blown away.
を ～を落とす bring *sb* to their
senses; release *sb* from a spell.

規定 stipulations; provisions
に ～に従う be in conformity with
regulations; observe the rules;
comply with stipulations; ① fall
into line. ～に反する go against
regulations; be in contravention of
the rules.
を ～を設ける make provisions for;
lay down the rules. ～を作る make
provisions for; lay down the rules.
～を破る violate stipulations;
infringe the rules.

軌道 an orbit; a track; a line
に ～に乗る ❶ go into orbit; get on
track. ❷ get started; launch (a
project; © get going.

疑念 doubt; suspicion; distrust
を ～を抱く have doubts; harbor
suspicions; entertain misgivings. ～
を起こさせる raise doubts; arouse
suspicion. ～を解く dispel doubts;
clear oneself/*sb* of suspicion. ～を
晴らす clear oneself/*sb* of
suspicion; dispel doubts. ～を持つ

have doubts; harbor suspicions; entertain misgivings.

気乗り "mounted spirit"

が ～がする take interest in *sth*; be excited by *sth*; be inclined to do *sth*; ⓘ warm up to (an idea).

牙 a tusk; a fang

を Ⓐ ～を噛む ❶ grind one's teeth; gnaw one's teeth. ❷ be vexed; ⓒ be cross. ～を研ぐ ❶ sharpen one's fangs. ❷ prepare for battle; ⓘ gird up one's loins; ⓘ clear the decks. ❸ have an eye on *sb/sth*; look envious at *sb/sth*; cast covetous eyes on *sth*. ❹ watch vigilantly for (a chance); scheme against *sb*. ⓘ ～を鳴らす ❶ show one's fangs; bare one's teeth. ❷ grind one's teeth; gnaw one's teeth. ❸ snarl at *sb*; be blunt with *sb*. ～を抜く defang (an animal). ～を剥く snarl at *sb*; be blunt with *sb*.

踵 Ⓔ ⓒ the heel ▶ 踵

を ⓔ ～を返す go back; retrace one's steps. ⓔ ～を接する follow heel after heel; follow on *sb's* heels; ⓘ breathe down *sb's* neck. ⓔ ～を巡らす go back; retrace one's steps.

詭弁 sophistry; sophism

を ⓔ ～を弄する use sophistry; ⓒ ⓘ chop logic (with *sb*).

希望 hope; a wish; aspiration

に ～に生きる live on hope. ～に応

じる meet *sb's* wishes. ～に反する go against one's wishes. ～に満ちる be full of hope. ～に目覚める find renewed hope.

を ～を失う lose hope. ～を叶える fulfill one's hopes. ～を挫く stifle one's hopes; crush one's hopes. ～を捨てる give up hope; abandon one's hopes. ～を達する realize one's wishes. ～を繋ぐ hinge one's hopes (on *sth*); pin one's hopes (on *sth*). ～を取り戻す restore hope in *sth*; reassure *sb*. ～を述べる express one's hopes. ～を吹き込む infuse *sb* with hope. ～を持つ have hope; cherish an aspiration.

気前 generosity; liberality

が ～が良い be generous; ⓘ have an open hand.

を ～を見せる display one's generosity; act generously.

義務 duty; an obligation

が ～が有る have a duty; be obliged; ⓒ be bound in duty.

を ～を感じる have a sense of duty; feel an obligation. ～を尽くす do one's duty; ⓒ discharge one's duty; ⓒ honor one's obligations. ～を怠ける neglect one's duties; shirk one's responsibilities. ～を果たす do one's duty; ⓒ discharge one's duty; ⓒ honor one's obligations.

肝 the liver; courage; pluck

が ⓘ ～が煎れる feel vexed; be

き

55

き

annoyed; be irritated. ～が大きい be daring; be brave; ⓒ have pluck. ～が据る ❶ have nerves of steel; be brave; have a lot of pluck. ❷ regain one's presence of mind; ⓔ recover one's composure; ① pull oneself together; ① gather one's wits. ～が小さい be cowardly; be fainthearted; ⓢ be chicken. ～が潰れる be terrified; ① be scared out of one's wits; ⓢ be scared stiff. ◎ ～が抜ける be terrified; ① be scared out of one's wits; ⓢ be scared stiff. ～が冷える be struck with terror; ① be scared to death. ① break into a cold sweat. ～が太い have courage; be bold; be brave; ⓒ have guts; ⓒ have pluck. ◎ ～が焼ける feel vexed; be annoyed; be irritated.

に ～に堪える be shocked; be upset. ～に染みる be deeply impressed; be deeply moved. ～に染む be deeply impressed; be deeply moved. ～に銘ずる be deeply impressed; be brought home to one; ⓔ have sth impressed on one's mind; ① take sth to heart.

を ～を煎る ❶ endure great hardships; be upset; be nettled. ❷ become eager; become enthusiastic. ❸ take care of sb; help sb out; give assistance to sb. ～を落とす lose heart; be discouraged; be disheartened. ～を砕く ❶ be on edge; be nervous; ① be on tenterhooks. ❷ ponder on; ⓔ exercise one's ingenuity; work out a plan.

～を消す be terrified; ① be scared out of one's wits; ⓢ be scared stiff. ～を焦がす fret over sth; worry about sth. ～を据える resolve to do sth; make up one's mind. ～を潰す be terrified; ① be scared out of one's wits; ⓢ be scared stiff. ～を取られる be terrified; ① be scared out of one's wits; ⓢ be scared stiff. Ⓐ ～を嘗める ❶ make sacrifices for future success. ❷ have a bitter experience; suffer hardships. ～を抜かす be terrified; ① be scared out of one's wits; ⓢ be scared stiff. ～を冷やす be struck with terror; ① be scared to death. ① break into a cold sweat. Ⓐ ～を焼く fret over sth; worry about sth.

肝心 the liver and the heart

が Ⓐ ～が騒ぐ feel a presentiment; have a sense of foreboding; feel uneasy; ⓔ experience a flutter of heart.

を ～を失せる faint for fear. ～を砕く ❶ take pains over sth; make strenuous efforts. ❷ be worried by sth; ⓒ ① rack one's brains. ❸ be terrified; ① be scared out of one's wits; ⓢ be scared stiff. Ⓐ ～を惑わす be confused by; be deluded by sb/sth.

疑問 doubt; a question; a query

を ～を抱く be wary of sb/sth; have doubts; be skeptical. ～を挟む be wary of sb/sth; have doubts; be skeptical.

急 urgency; an emergency

[に] 〜に応じる meet an urgent need. 〜に赴く respond to an emergency; meet a crisis. 〜に備える provide against an emergency. 〜に止まる stop short.

[を] 〜を救う help *sb* in distress; help *sb* out of danger. 〜を告げる ❶ give a distress signal; raise the alarm. ❷ become critical; grow threatening; be urgent. 〜を要する demand immediate attention; be pressing.

牛耳 Ⓔ the ears of an ox

[を] ◎ Ⓔ 〜を取る take the lead; head a group.

急所 a vital spot; the vitals

[を] 〜を蹴る kick *sb* in the groin. 〜を逸れる miss the vital parts. 〜を掴む grasp the crux (of a matter); get it right; ① be on the mark; ◎ ① get the point. 〜を突く hit on a vital spot; ① be on the mark; ① be to the point. 〜を握る have a hold over *sb*. 〜を外れる fail to understand the crux (of a matter); get it wrong; ① be off the mark; ① miss the point. ◎ 〜を遣る hit *sb* in the vitals; ① go for the jugular.

窮地 Ⓔ a predicament

[に] Ⓔ 〜に在る be in a sad plight; be in a quandary. Ⓔ 〜に追い込む drive *sb* into a corner; corner *sb*. Ⓔ 〜に陥る be driven into a corner; ◎ ① get into a scrap; ◎ ① be up the creek.

[へ] Ⓔ 〜へに追い込む drive *sb* into a corner; corner *sb*.

[を] Ⓔ 〜を訴える complain of one's sad plight; Ⓔ lament one's predicament. Ⓔ 〜を察する empathize with *sb's* predicament. Ⓔ 〜を救う help *sb* out of a predicament. 〜を打開する resolve a predicament. Ⓔ 〜を脱する get out of a predicament; ① weather the storm.

挙 Ⓔ a plan; a project; a scheme

[に] Ⓔ 〜に出る act upon a plan; put a plan into action.

居 Ⓔ a dwelling; a house

[を] Ⓔ 〜を構える make (a place) one's home; settle somewhere. Ⓔ take up residence. Ⓔ 〜を卜する make (a place) one's home (having consulted a fortune teller); settle somewhere; Ⓔ take up residence.

虚 Ⓔ emptiness; hollowness

[に] Ⓔ 〜に乗じる take advantage of an unguarded moment; catch *sb* off guard.

[を] 〜を突かれる be caught off guard. 〜を衝く catch *sb* off guard; take (the enemy) unawares.

興 interest; fun; amusement

[が] 〜がある be interesting; ◎ be fun. 〜が乗る become interested in; be excited by *sth*.

[に] 〜に入る be absorbed in *sth*; ◎ get in the mood (for *sth*). 〜に乗ずる be driven by curiosity.

き

を④ 〜を栄(さか)す arouse *sb's* interest; ⑤ ① push *sb's* buttons. 〜を醒(さ)ます spoil the fun; dampen the mood. 〜を添(そ)える add to the merriment. 〜をそそる arouse *sb's* interest; ⑤ ① push *sb's* buttons. ⓞ 〜を尽(つ)きる enjoy oneself; ⓒ have fun.

共感(きょうかん) sympathy; empathy
を 〜を得(え)る gain *sb's* sympathy. 〜を覚(おぼ)える feel sympathy for *sb*. 〜を呼(よ)ぶ excite *sb's* sympathy.

胸襟(きょうきん) E the heart; the soul
を ⓒ 〜を開(ひら)く open oneself up to *sb*; take *sb* into one's confidence; ① pour out one's heart to *sb*; ⓒ unbosom oneself.

教訓(きょうくん) a (moral) lesson
を 〜を与(あた)える give *sb* a lesson. 〜を得(え)る learn a lesson from (an experience). 〜を織(お)り込(こ)む attach a moral to (a story). 〜を引(ひ)き出(だ)す draw a lesson from (an experience).

郷愁(きょうしゅう) homesickness; nostalgia
に 〜に駆(か)られる feel homesick; ⓒ be stricken by homesickness. 〜に耽(ふけ)る be given to nostalgia; pine for home; ⓒ give oneself over to feelings of nostalgia.
を 〜を感(かん)じる feel homesick; long for home.

教壇(きょうだん) a platform
に 〜に立(た)つ take the platform to teach; be a teacher.

を 〜を追(お)われる be removed from one's teaching post.

胸中(きょうちゅう) one's bosom; one's heart
に 〜に浮(う)かぶ enter one's mind; spring to mind; occur to one. 〜に秘(ひ)める keep *sth* to oneself.
を 〜を明(あ)かす open oneself up to *sb*; take *sb* into one's confidence; ① pour out one's heart to *sb*; ⓒ unbosom oneself. 〜を察(さっ)する sympathize with *sb*; empathize with *sb*; feel for *sb*.

恐怖(きょうふ) fear; terror; angst
で 〜で死(し)ぬ die from fear.
に 〜に襲(おそ)われる be seized with fear; be struck with terror. 〜に戦(おのの)く tremble with fear; give a shudder; be terrified.
を 〜を感(かん)じる be afraid of *sb*/*sth*; be frightened at *sth*; be scared.

興味(きょうみ) interest; zest; curiosity
を 〜を失(うしな)う lose interest in *sth*. 〜を起(お)こさせる arouse interest in *sth*. 〜を覚(おぼ)える take an interest in *sth*. 〜を添(そ)える add zest to *sth*. 〜を殺(そ)ぐ spoil *sb's* pleasure; ⓒ spoil the fun. 〜を持(も)つ take an interest in *sth*. 〜を養(やしな)う foster *sb's* interest in *sth*.

局(きょく) a bureau; a department
に 〜に当(あ)たる take charge; deal with a situation; ⓐ step in.
を ⓞ 〜を結(むす)ぶ bring *sth* to a conclusion.

局面 a situation; a phase
囲 ～が一変する　a situation changes; ⑩ the tables are turned; ⓒ be a new ball game.
囮 ～を改善する　improve the situation. ～を打開する　bring a deadlock to an end; ⑩ break the ice.

虚勢 a bluff; a bold front
囮 ～を張る　make a bluff; ⑩ put on a bold front. ～を挫く　⑩ call *sb's* bluff.

去就 one's course of action
囲 ～に迷う　be at a loss (about what to do); ⑩ be at one's wits' end; ⑩ be all at sea.
囮 ～を誤る　take the wrong course of action. ～を決する　decide on one's course of action.

距離 a distance; an interval
囲 ～がある　be distant; be different from. ～が開く　get a lead on *sb*; lag behind *sb*. ～が勝つ　get a lead on *sb*; lag behind *sb*.
囮 ～を置く　leave an interval. ～を保つ　keep a distance. ～を詰める　catch up on; reduce *sb's* lead. ～を走る　run (a certain) distance.

虚礼 Ⓔ empty formalities
囲 Ⓔ ～に陥る　slip into empty formalities; lapse into empty formalities.
囮 Ⓔ ～を廃する　do away with empty formalities; dispense with empty formalities.

義理 duty; debt; gratitude
囲 ～が有る　be bound by duty. ～が立つ　be vindicated; ⑩ save one's face.
囲 ～に欠ける　fail in one's duties; ⓒ swerve from the path of duty. ～に絡まれる　be bound by duty. ～に迫る　be dictated by one's sense of duty. ～に詰まる　stand to reason.
囮 ～を欠く　fail in one's duties. ～を立てる　do one's duty (by *sb*); be loyal (to *sb*). ～を詰める　dictate *sb* by a sense of duty; appeal to *sb's* sense of duty. ～を張る　stick to one's duties.

規律 order; discipline; rules
囲 ～に反する　violate the rules; go against the rules.
囮 ～を正す　restore discipline; put *sth* in order. ～を守る　observe discipline; act according to the rules; ⑩ toe the line. ～を乱す　loosen discipline; upset the order. ～を破る　break the rules.

記録 a record; a document
囲 ～に載る　be recorded; be on record. ～に残す　put *sth* on record.
囮 ～を更新する　better one's record; establish a new record. ～を作る　make a record. ～を取る　keep a record of *sth*; put *sth* on record. ～を破る　break a record.

議論 an argument; a discussion
囮 ～で遣り込める　corner *sb* in an argument.

国 ～に勝つ win an argument. ～に負ける lose an argument.
囮 ～を仕掛ける challenge *sb* to an argument. ～を覆す demolish an argument. ～を戦わす take issue with *sb*; ⓔ engage in a battle of words; ⓘ cross swords with *sb*. ～を始める start an argument; get into an argument (with *sb*). ～を申し進める pursue an argument. ～を持ち出す put forward an argument.

疑惑 doubt; suspicion; mistrust
囮 ～を抱く be wary of *sb*/*sth*; have misgivings about *sb*/*sth*. ～を解く clear one's doubts. ～を招く invite suspicion; arouse suspicion.

金看板 a gold-lettered signboard
囮 ～を掛ける ❶ assume an air of importance; make *sth* look more important than it is. ❷ be true to one's name; ⓘ sail under one's true colors.

均衡 equilibrium; balance
囮 ～を失う lose the balance. ～を回復する restore the balance. ～を保つ maintain the equilibrium; keep the balance. ～を取る put *sth* in balance; get the right balance. ～を求める find a balance. ～を破る upset the balance; ⓘ rock the boat.

琴線 the strings of a *koto*
国 ～に触れる be touched by *sth*; ⓘ tug at one's heartstrings; ⓘ strike a (sympathetic) chord.

巾着 Ⓐ a purse; a money pouch
囮 ～を切る pinch *sb's* wallet; pick *sb's* pocket. ⓞ ～を叩く empty one's purse.

緊張 tension; strain
囮 ～を欠く lack seriousness. ～を高める heighten tensions; raise the pressure. ～を解す wind down; ⓒ ⓘ take it easy. ～を緩める ease the tensions; ⓘ break the ice.

金的 the bull's eye
囮 ～を射止める ❶ hit the bull's eye; hit the mark. ❷ have great success; ⓒ ⓘ bring home the bacon.

ク

苦 pain; hardships; privation
国 ⓐ ～に掛ける worry about *sth*; fret over *sth*. ～にする ⓘ take *sth* to heart; be anxious about. ～になる ⓘ weigh on one's mind; cause one anxiety. ～に病む ⓘ take *sth* to heart; be anxious about.

愚 folly; stupidity; silliness
国 ⓞ ～に返る go senile; grow feeble minded; ⓔ fall into one's dotage; ⓢ go gaga. ⓞ ～にする fool *sb*; make a fool of *sb*.
囮 ⓐ ～を守る play the fool; feign ignorance.

空 space; emptiness ▶空 ▶空
国 ～に消える vanish into thin air.

～に帰^きする come to nothing; ⓘ go up in smoke.

[を] ～を打^うつ beat the air; hit empty air. ～を切^きる cut the air. ～を掴^{つか}む clutch at thin air; claw the air.

釘^{くぎ} a nail; a spike

[が] ～が利^きく be effective.

[で] ～で打^うち付^つける nail *sth* down.

[に] Ⓐ ～になる be frozen stiff; freeze with cold.

[を] ～を打^うつ drive in a nail. ～を刺^さす remind *sb* (of *sth*); tell *sb* off; ⓘ haul *sb* over the coals. ～を抜^ぬく pull out a nail; draw out a nail.

草^{くさ} grass; weeds; herbs

[を] ～を刈^かる mow the grass. ～を食^くう feed on grass. ～を取^とる weed (the garden). Ⓐ ～を結^{むす}ぶ ❶ return a favor; repay *sb* for received favors. ❷ stay at an inn; pass a night on one's journey; sleep rough. ❸ leave roadmarks; point the way.

楔^{くさび} a wedge; a chock

[と] ～となる be the tie that binds.

[を] ～を打^うち込^こむ ❶ ⓒ drive in a wedge. ❷ drive a wedge between (one's opponents); wedge (two parties) apart. ～を打^うつ drive in a wedge. ～を刺^さす remind *sb* of *sth*; call *sb's* attention to *sth*; make sure of *sth*; tell *sb* emphatically of *sth*.

苦汁^{くじゅう} Ⓔ a bitter broth

[を] ⓒ ～を嘗^なめる suffer a bitter experience; have a hard time.

癖^{くせ} a habit; a way; a kink; a friz

[が] ～が有^ある ❶ have a habit; be in the habit (of doing *sth*). ❷ have kinks; have frizzy hair. ～が付^つく fall into a habit; get into a habit; ⓔ contract a habit.

[を] ～を付^つける form a habit. ～を直^{なお}す ❶ get out of a habit; ⓔ break oneself of a habit; ⓒ ⓘ kick the habit. ❷ iron out a friz; straighten (one's hair).

管^{くだ} a pipe; a tube

[を] ～ を巻^まく blather about *sb*/*sth*; ⓒ blurt *sth* out.

口^{くち} the mouth; the lips

[が] ～ が合^あう understand each other; get on well; agree with each other. ～ が上^あがる ❶ become eloquent; become a good talker. ❷ lose one's means of living; lose one's livelihood. ～が開^あく ❶ have a vacancy; a position is open. ❷ make a beginning. ❸ find a clue; have a key to *sth*. ～が旨^{うま}い be glib-tongued; be fair-spoken; ⓒ ⓘ have the gift of the gab. ～が煩^{うるさ}い be much talked about; be notorious. ～が多^{おお}い ❶ be talkative; ⓔ be loquacious; ⓒ be a chatterbox; ⓘ talk people's head off. ❷ have many mouths to feed; have a large family to support. ～が奢^{おご}る be used to exquisite food; have an expensive taste. ～ が重^{おも}い be incommunicative; be taciturn; be slow of speech. ～ が堅^{かた}い be discreet; be tight-lipped; be able to keep a secret. 〜が掛かる be offered a position; be called in; be given a job. 〜が軽い be indiscreet; Ⓐ have a loose tongue. 〜が利く❶ have a fluent tongue; be eloquent; ⓒⓘ have the gift of the gab. ❷ be influential; have authority. 〜が利ける be able to speak. 〜が臭い have bad breath. 〜が肥える be a gourmet. 〜が過ぎる go too far in what one says; say too much. 〜が滑るⓘ make a slip of the tongue; ⓘ let sth fall/slip; ⓒ blurt sth out. 〜が早いⒶ have a loose tongue; be loose-lipped. 〜が干上がる lose one's means of living; lose one's livelihood; run out of food; fall on hard times. 〜が殖える have new mouths to feed. 〜が減る❶ have fewer mouths to feed. ❷ have no reply; be lost for words; ⓘ throw in the towel. 〜が解れる start to talk; become talkative. 〜が曲がる be extremely bitter (in taste). Ⓐ 〜が脆いⓒ have a loose tongue; be loose-lipped. 〜が悪い be foul-mouthed; Ⓐ have a venomous tongue.

に 〜に合う suit one's taste; find sth to one's taste. Ⓐ 〜に入る❶ be lionized; ⓒⓘ become the talk of the town. ❷ be edible. 〜に掛かる be the topic of conversation; be talked about. 〜に掛ける say sth; express sth; put sth into words. Ⓐ 〜に藉く give a pretext; make an excuse. 〜にする❶ put (food) into

one's mouth. ❷ speak of sb/sth; mention sb/sth; be on one's lips. 〜に出す put sth into words; give voice to sth; ⓘ let sth fall. 〜に絶つ❶ fast; abstain from food. ❷ remain silent. 〜に上せる talk about sth. 〜に上るbe the topic of conversation; be talked about. 〜に乗せる deceive sb; ⓘ take sb in; ⓒⓘ lead sb by the nose. 〜に乗る❶ be the topic of conversation; be talked about. ❷ be deceived; ⓘ be taken in. 〜に入るbe able to eat; be edible. 〜に運ぶ bring (the bowl) to one's lips. 〜に任せる say what comes into one's mind; talk without thinking.

を Ⓐ 〜を開く❶ open one's mouth. ❷ be staggered; be amazed. 〜を開ける❶ open one's mouth. ❷ say what is on one's mind; make a confession; own up to sth. 〜を合わす arrange not to contradict each other; make each other's stories match. 〜を入れる interrupt sb; ⓘ put in a word; ⓘ put a word in edgeways; ⓘ cut in; ⓢ butt in. 〜を掩う laugh up one's sleeve. ⓒ 〜を置く shut one's mouth. 〜を掛ける ❶ make pre-arrangements. ❷ get in touch; call sb in; hire sb. 〜を固める impose silence on sb; forbid sb to say anything; muzzle sb. 〜を利く❶ speak to sb; pass a remark. ❷ be influential; have authority. ❸ have a fluent tongue; be eloquent; ⓒⓘ have the gift of the gab. ❹ mediate between (two

parties); speak up for *sb*. ～を切る
❶ open the conversation; speak
out; break the silence. ❷ broach a
matter; ⓘ break the ice. ❸ open (a
bottle/a box). ～を極める be
persuasive; go out of one's way to
express (praise). ◎ ～を消す
❶ remain silent; ⓘ bite one's lip;
ⓒ ⓘ button one's lips. ❷ withdraw
one's testimony. ～を捜す look for
work; ⓔ seek employment. ～を吸
う give *sb* a kiss; kiss *sb*. ～を過ぎ
る make a living; earn one's daily
bread; support oneself. ～を過ごす
❶ make a living; earn one's daily
bread; support oneself. ❷ say too
much; go too far. ～を滑らす
ⓘ make a slip of the tongue; ⓘ let
sth fall/slip; ⓒ blurt *sth* out. ～を
窄める purse one's lips. ～を添える
❶ take a sip. ❷ speak on *sb's*
behalf; second *sb*. ～を揃える
❶ speak with one voice; sing in
chorus. ❷ make each other's stories
match. ～を出す ❶ interrupt *sb*;
ⓘ put one's oar in; ⓘ put a word in
edgeways; ⓘ cut in; ⓢ ⓘ butt in.
❷ interfere in (*sb's* affairs); meddle
with; interfere with; ⓒ ⓘ poke
one's nose into (the affairs of others). ◎ ～を叩く be garrulous;
babble. ～を立てる ❶ make an
assertion; point *sth* out. ❷ make a
living; earn one's daily bread; support oneself. ◎ ～を垂れる speak
subserviently; speak obsequiously.
～を噤む hold one's tongue; keep
silent; ⓒ ⓘ button one's lips. ～を

付ける taste *sth*; eat *sth*. ～を慎む
be careful in speech; ⓘ weigh
one's words; ⓘ guard one's words,
ⓘ curb one's tongue. ～を窄める
purse one's lips. ～を尖らす ❶ pout
one's lips. ❷ be upset; sulk over
sth. ～を閉ざす remain silent;
ⓘ bite one's lip; ⓒ ⓘ button one's
lips. ～を直す take the nasty taste
out of one's mouth; take off the
aftertaste. ～を抜く tap; broach (a
barrel). ～を拭う feign ignorance;
pretend not to know. ～を濡らす
❶ make one's living; eke out a living; ⓒ get by; make ends meet;
ⓘ keep the pot boiling. ❷ live on
rations. ～を糊するmake a meager
living. ～を挟む ❶ interrupt *sb*;
ⓘ put one's oar in; ⓘ cut in;
ⓢ ⓘ butt in. ❷ interfere in (*sb's*
affairs); meddle with; interfere
with; ⓒ ⓘ poke one's nose into (the
affairs of others). ～を開く ❶ open
one's mouth; begin to speak; start
talking. ❷ open a bottle; uncork a
bottle. ～を封じる silence *sb*; shut
sb up. ～を塞ぐ silence *sb*; shut *sb*
up. ～を見つける find work; find
employment; ⓒ get a job. Ⓐ ～を毟
る wheedle *sth* out of *sb*; milk *sb*
for (information). ⓒ ～を割る
break one's silence; speak out;
confess to *sth*; own up to *sth*.

口占 Ⓔ infer *sth* from *sb's* words
Ⓒ Ⓔ ～で察する gather *sth* from
sb's words; infer *sth* from what *sb*
says; ⓘ read between the lines.

を ～を合わせる make each other's stories match; arrange to tell the same story.

口車 "mouth cart"
に ～に乗る be taken in by *sb*; be cajoled into *sth*.

口先 a mouth; a snout; tongue
が ～が旨い have a clever tongue; © ⓘ have the gift of the gab.

で ～でごまかす talk one's way out of a situation; ⓔ rub along with honeyed words. ～で騙す talk one's way out of a situation; ⓔ rub along with honeyed words.

に ～に出掛かる ⓐ be on the tip of one's tongue.

嘴 a bill; a beak
が ～が黄色い be immature; be inexperienced; ⓘ be green.

を ～を入れる ❶ interrupt *sb*; ⓘ put one's oar in; ⓘ put a word in edgeways; ⓘ cut in; ⓢ ⓘ butt in. ❷ interfere in *sb's* affairs; meddle with; © ⓘ poke one's nose into the affairs of others. ⓐ ～を鳴らす ❶ chatter about *sth*; babble over *sth*. ❷ repent one's actions. ～を挟む ❶ interrupt *sb*; ⓘ put one's oar in; ⓘ put a word in edgeways; ⓘ cut in; ⓢ ⓘ butt in. ❷ interfere in *sb's* affairs; meddle with; © ⓘ poke one's nose into the affairs of others.

口火 a fuse; a spark plug
と ～となる trigger *sth*; touch off.

を ～を切る ❶ ignite a fuse. ❷ start on *sth*; begin *sth*; trigger off (an incident); touch *sth* off.

唇 the lips
が ～が薄い be talkative; ⓔ be loquacious; © be a chatterbox; ⓘ talk people's head off.

を ～を奪う kiss *sb* unexpectedly; ⓘ steal a kiss. ⓐ ～を返す slander *sb*; speak ill of *sb*. ～を噛む swallow one's frustration; suppress one's anger; ⓘ bite one's lip. ～を尖らす pout one's lips. ⓐ ～を翻す slander *sb*; speak ill of *sb*.

苦杯 Ⓔ a bitter cup
を ⓔ ～を嘗める drink a bitter cup; suffer a defeat.

首 the neck; the head
が ～が危ない ❶ be in grave danger; ⓔ be in peril of one's life. © ❷ be on the point of being fired. ～が落ちる be beheaded; be decapitated. ～が繋がる keep one's position; hang on to one's job. ～が飛ぶ ❶ be beheaded; be decapitated. ❷ lose one's job; be dismissed © be fired; ⓢ ⓘ get the sack. ⓐ ～が細る be in danger of one's life. ～が回らない be deeply in debt; ⓘ be in dire straits.

に ～にする ❶ break off connections with *sb*; break with *sb*. ❷ dismiss *sb*; © fire *sb*; ⓢ ⓘ give *sb* the sack. ～になる ❶ be beheaded; be decapitated. ❷ lose one's job; be dismissed Ⓒ be fired; Ⓢ ① get the sack. ～に齧り付く throw one's arms around *sb's* neck.

Ⓦ ～を集める confer with each other; Ⓔ counsel together; Ⓒ get together; ① compare notes. ～を折る ❶ Ⓒ break one's/*sb's* neck. ❷ drop one's head; hang one's head. Ⓐ ～を掻く ❶ behead *sb*; decapitate *sb*. ❷ scratch one's head (with bewilderment). ～を賭ける ❶ risk one's life; stick out one's neck. ❷ risk one's job; ① put one's head on the block. ～を傾げる incline one's head in doubt; look doubtful; be skeptical. ～を切る ❶ behead *sb*; decapitate *sb*. ❷ dismiss *sb*; Ⓒ fire *sb*; Ⓢ ① give *sb* the sack. ～を縊る hang oneself; strangle oneself; commit suicide. ～を曝す gibbet a head. ～を竦める shrug one's shoulders; duck one's head (to avoid a blow). ～を挿げ替える replace *sb*. ～を揃える confer with each other; Ⓔ counsel together; Ⓒ get together; ① compare notes. ～を出す look out of (a window); Ⓒ pop one's head out of (a doorway). ～を垂れる droop one's head; let one's head hang; bow one's head. ～を縮める duck one's head; shrug one's shoulders. ～を突っ込む ❶ delve into *sth*; Ⓒ plunge (headlong) into *sth*. ❷ interfere in (*sb's* affairs); get involved in *sth*; Ⓒ ① stick one's nose into (the affairs of others). ～を繋ぐ ❶ pardon *sb*. ❷ keep *sb* on

(in his/her job). ～を吊る hang oneself; strangle oneself; commit suicide. ～を長くする stretch one's neck; crane one's neck. Ⓞ ～を延ばす stretch one's neck; crane one's neck. ～を刎ねる behead *sb*; decapitate *sb*. ～を捻る ❶ twist one's/*sb's* neck. ❷ think hard about *sth*; Ⓒ ① rack one's brains. ～を振る shake one's head in denial; turn *sth* down; refuse to do *sth*.

踵 the heel

Ⓦ ～を返す go back; retrace one's steps. ～を接する follow heel after heel; follow on *sb's* heels; ① breathe down *sb's* neck. ～を巡らす go back; retrace one's steps.

工夫 a device; a means; a plan

Ⓝ Ⓐ ～に落つ hit on (a plan); think *sth* out; call *sth* to mind.

Ⓦ ～を凝らす work out a plan; Ⓔ tax one's ingenuity.

組み a class; a party; a group

Ⓓ ～で働く work in groups.

Ⓝ ～になる join forces; co-operate with *sb*; team up with *sb*. ～に分ける divide into groups.

Ⓦ ～を選ぶ choose sides. ～を作る create a group; make up a party.

雲 a cloud; the clouds

Ⓖ ～が切れる clouds are breaking.

Ⓝ ～に隠れる be hidden by the clouds; Ⓔ be shrouded in clouds. ～に聳える reach into the skies; rise

above the clouds; soar sky-high. Ⓐ
～に臥す live in the mountains.
を ～を凌ぐ rise above the clouds.
～を掴む be at a loss (about what
to do); Ⓓ be in the dark. ～を衝く
pierce the skies; soar into the sky;
be extremely tall. ～を吹き払う
blow away the clouds.

蔵 a storehouse; a treasury
を ～が建つ become rich; become
a millionaire.

位 grade; rank
が ～が上がる rise in rank. ～が下
がる fall in rank. ～が付く gain in
dignity.
に ～に付く ascend to the throne;
accede to the throne.
を ～を落とす lower sb in rank;
demote sb. ～を返す resign from
one's post; leave office. ～を極む
rise to the highest rank; reach high
office. ～を進める raise sb in rank;
promote sb. ～を付ける invest sb
with esteem; bestow dignity on sb.
～を取られる be overwhelmed; be
browbeaten. ～を取る ❶ show
dignity. ❷ give oneself airs; be
pompous; Ⓔ be ostentatious; Ⓘ put
on airs; Ⓢ Ⓘ be stuck-up. ～を譲る
abdicate.

暮し a living; livelihood
に ～に困る be in financial
trouble; Ⓔ be in straitened circumstances; be in dire straits.
を ～をする live. ～を立てる make

a living; earn one's daily bread;
support oneself.

車 a wheel; a car; a vehicle
に Ⓐ ～に切る cut sth in round
slices; cut clockwise. ～に乗る get
into a car; take a cab; get a taxi.
を ～を降りる get out of a car. Ⓐ
～を懸く step down from office;
Ⓔ retire from public office; leave
government service. Ⓐ ～を擢く be
abandoned; be frustrated; Ⓘ be
out on a limb. ～を捨てる get out
of a car; Ⓔ alight from a car. ～を
飛ばす hurry somewhere in a car.
～を拾う get a taxi; get a cab. ～
を呼ぶ call a taxi; call a cab.

苦労 hardships; difficulty
を ～をかける give sb trouble;
cause sb anxiety. ～を忘れる
forget one's troubles.

鍬 a hoe; a mattock; a grub hoe
が Ⓐ ～が抜ける ❶ be perplexed;
be puzzled; be baffled; be at a loss
(about what to do); Ⓒ be in a fix.
❷ relax one's attention; Ⓘ drop
one's guard; be careless. ❸ be
exhausted; become tired out; Ⓢ be
knackered.
で ～で掘る hoe the soil.
を ～を入れる break ground;
cultivate land. ～を取る hoe (in
the field); engage in farming. Ⓐ ～
を抜かす ❶ be perplexed; be
puzzled; be baffled; be at a loss
(about what to do); Ⓒ be in a fix.

❷ relax one's attention; ⓘ drop one's guard; be careless. ❸ be exhausted; become tired out; ⓢ be knackered.

群 くん a crowd; a flock; a swarm

[を] 〜を為す flock together; form a crowd. 〜を抜く outdo one's peers; outstrip *sb*; stand out; ⓔ rise above the common herd.

軍配 くんばい a *sumo* umpire's fan

[を] (人に)〜を揚げる declare *sb* the winner; decide in favor of *sb*.

訓練 くんれん training; drilling

[が] 〜が行き届く be well trained.
[を] 〜を受ける be disciplined; be trained. 〜を重ねる drill *sb* over and over again.

ケ

毛 け hair; feathers; down

[が] 〜が抜ける lose one's hair.
[を] 〜を染める dye one's hair. 〜を縮らす frizzle one's hair. 〜を抜く pull out a hair; pluck feathers.

刑 けい punishment; a penalty

[に] 〜に処する sentence *sb*. 〜に服する serve a sentence; ⓒ ⓘ do time; ⓢ ⓘ do one's bird.
[を] 〜を言い渡す pass sentence on *sb*; ⓔ pronounce a sentence on *sb*. 〜を受ける be penalized; be punished. 〜を加える inflict a penalty on *sb*. 〜を勤める serve a sentence; ⓒ ⓘ do time; ⓢ ⓘ do one's bird. 〜を逃れる escape punishment; ⓢ ⓘ beat the rap. 〜を免れる escape punishment; ⓢ ⓘ beat the rap.

芸 げい an art; an accomplishment

[が] 〜が立つ be master of an art; be proficient in an art. 〜が無い be good for nothing; have no (saving) virtues. 〜が細かい be mindful of details.
[を] 〜を教える teach (an animal) tricks. 〜を覚える learn a trick. 〜をさせる teach (an animal) tricks. 〜を仕込む train *sb* in the arts. 〜を磨く cultivate an art.

敬意 けいい respect; regard; esteem

[を] 〜を表わす show one's respect; pay homage to *sb*. 〜を払う pay *sb* respect.

警戒 けいかい caution; precaution

[を] 〜を緩める relax one's attention; ⓘ drop one's guard. 〜を要する require caution.

計画 けいかく a plan; a project

[を] 〜を起こす set a plan in action. 〜を覆えす upset a plan; ⓘ rock the boat. 〜を進める proceed with a plan; ⓘ carry a plan forward. 〜を立てる make a plan.

景気 けいき things; business

[を] 〜を上げる boost one's business;

67

liven up; be enlivened. ～を付ける boost one's business; liven up; be enlivened. ～を直す revive the economy; mend one's market.

経験 experience

が ～がある have experience; be experienced. ～が増す grow in experience.

に ～に富む have vast experience; be widely experienced.

を ～を生かす make use of one's experience; employ one's experience. ～を得る gain experience. ～を積む gather experience. ～を広げる widen one's experience.

警告 a warning; a caution

に ～に従う heed a warning; take warning from.

を ～を受ける receive a warning; be warned. ～を発する issue a warning.

掲示 a notice; a bulletin

を ～を出す put up a notice.

形式 form; formality

に ～に流れる become formal.

を ～を廃する do away with formalities. ～を踏む go through the formalities.

傾聴 E attentive listening

を ⓒ ～に値する be worth listening to; be noteworthy; be worth one's attention. ⓔ ～を怠る fail to listen carefully; ① drop one's guard.

軽蔑 contempt; disdain; scorn

を ～を表わす express one's contempt. ～を受ける be held in contempt; be despised. ～を示す show contempt.

警報 an alarm; a warning signal

を ～を伝える give an alarm. ～を解く give an all clear. ～を鳴らす sound the alarm; beat an alarm.

逆鱗 E Imperial wrath

に ⓔ ～に触れる incur the wrath of sb in power.

けじめ a line; a distinction

を Ⓐ ⓢ ～を食う be discriminated against; be looked down upon. ～を付ける ① draw a line; make a distinction. ～を守る honor a tradition; adhere to a custom; observe the difference between (good and bad); stick to the rules.

桁 a figure; a unit; a beam

が ～が違う be no match for one; ① be in a different league; ① be on different scales.

下駄 *geta*; wooden clogs

を ～を預ける pass authority to sb else; pass the ball to sb else; leave sth to sb else; ① pass the buck. ～を履かせる inflate the figures; pad the results. ～を履く ❶ put on *geta*. ❷ take graft; accept a bribe; be bribed. ～を脱ぐ take off one's *geta*; remove one's *geta*.

けち stinginess; meanness
を ～を付ける find fault with *sb*/*sth*; carp at *sb's* faults.

穴 Ⓥ Ⓢ the butt; the arse ▶穴
が Ⓥ Ⓢ ～が青い be immature; Ⓒ be green; Ⓔ be callow; Ⓒ Ⓘ be wet behind the ears. Ⓞ Ⓥ Ⓢ ～が痒い be slightly offended; feel somewhat vexed; Ⓘ go against the grain.
を Ⓥ Ⓢ ～を捲る come out fighting; take the offensive; Ⓒ stick one's chin out. Ⓥ Ⓢ ～を見せる run away; take flight. Ⓥ Ⓢ ～を向ける be against *sth*; turn *sth* down. Ⓥ Ⓢ ～を割る ❶ expose oneself; Ⓘ make a clean breast of *sth*. ❷ betray oneself; reveal one's true character; Ⓘ give oneself away; Ⓘ show one's true colors. ❸ give up halfway; Ⓘ throw in the towel. ❹ go bankrupt; go out of business; Ⓢ go bust.

結果 a result; a consequence
を ～を生む produce results. ～を得る obtain results. ～を収める secure results. ～を及ぼす have an effect. ～を齎す bring about a result.

血気 hot blood; youthful vigor
に ～に逸る be impetuous; have youthful ardor.

結婚 marriage; matrimony
を ～を取り消す annul a marriage; dissolve a marriage. ～を取り持つ be a matchmaker; arrange a marriage; act as a go-between. ～を延ばす postpone a marriage; Ⓒ put off a marriage. ～を申し込む propose marriage; ask a girl's hand in marriage; Ⓢ Ⓘ pop the question.

決心 resolve; determination
が ～が鈍る be weakened in one's resolution; lose resolve; Ⓒ Ⓘ get cold feet.
を ～を動かす shake one's resolve. ～を固める stiffen one's resolve. ～を翻す break one's resolve; change one's mind; have second thoughts.

決定 a decision; a settlement
を ～を延ばす postpone a decision; defer a settlement; put off a decision. ～を待つ await a conclusion.

欠点 a fault; a flaw; a mistake
を ～を揚げる point out *sb's* flaws. ～を補う cover up *sb's* faults. ～を捜す find fault with *sb*; carp at *sb's* faults. ～を直す correct a fault; mend a mistake.

結論 a conclusion
に ～に来る come to a conclusion. ～に達する reach a conclusion. ～になる come to a conclusion. ～に導く lead to a conclusion; bring about a conclusion.
を ～を与える give a conclusion. ～を急ぐ hasten to a conclusion. ～を下す draw a conclusion. ～を出す form a conclusion.

気配 a sign; indications
[を] 〜を感じる discern the signs of.
〜を示す show signs of.

煙 smoke; fumes
[と] 〜と消える go up in smoke; vanish into thin air.
[に] 〜になる go up in smoke. 〜に巻かれる be suffocated. 〜に巻く ❶ envelop *sth* in smoke. ❷ be evasive; be ambiguous.
[を] 〜を出す emit smoke. Ⓐ 〜を立てる make a living; earn one's daily bread; support oneself. 〜を吐く belch forth smoke; puff out smoke.

権 authority; power
[に] ◎ 〜に借る hide behind *sb's* authority; abuse (one's father's) authority; ① ride on *sb's* coat-tails. 〜に付く attach oneself to *sb* of authority. ◎ 〜に募る give oneself airs under the protection of *sb's* authority.
[を] ◎ 〜を冠る hide behind *sb's* authority; abuse (one's father's) authority; ① ride on *sb's* coat-tails. 〜を取る seize power; hold power.

剣 a sword; a blade
[を] 〜を帯びる put on a sword; wear a sword. 〜を構える hold one's sword. 〜を研ぐ sharpen a sword; burnish a sword. 〜を抜く draw a sword. 〜を振るう brandish a sword. 〜を学ぶ study the art of fencing. 〜を磨く polish a sword; burnish a sword.

言 a word; a remark; speech
[を] Ⓐ 〜を絶つ be unspeakable. Ⓐ 〜を食む ① take back one's words; ① eat one's words. Ⓐ 〜を践む act on one's word; carry out what one has said. 〜を守る keep one's word; live up to one's words. 〜を用いる follow *sb's* advice.

権威 authority; influence
[が] 〜が有る have authority.
[に] 〜に従う submit to authority.
[を] 〜を与える give *sb* influence (over *sth*). 〜を落とす debase oneself. 〜を添える lend authority to (a claim). 〜を握る seize power. 〜を奮う wield power; exercise authority. 〜を持つ have authority.

喧嘩 a fight; a quarrel; a row
[を] 〜を売る spoil for a fight; look for a fight. 〜を収める settle a dispute; ① bury the hatchet. 〜を買う take up a quarrel; ⓒ pick a fight with *sb*. 〜を仕掛ける start a fight; pick a fight with *sb*. 〜をする have a fight. 〜を始める have a quarrel; ① come to blows. 〜を吹っかける pick a fight with *sb*. 〜を止める put down a fight.

玄関 the porch; the vestibule
[を] ◎ 〜を張る make an outward show; ① keep up appearances.

嫌疑 suspicion; doubt; distrust
[が] 〜が掛かる be under suspicion; come under suspicion.

70

を ～を受ける be under suspicion. ～を掛ける cast suspicion on *sb*; suspect *sb* (of a crime). ～を晴らす dispel suspicion; clear oneself/*sb* of suspicion. ～を招く invite suspicion; arouse suspicion.

元気 vigor; vitality; energy

が ～が衰える lose vigor; be enfeebled; ⓔ fall into low spirits. ～が付く be encouraged; take heart; cheer up; ⓔ become heightened in spirits; ⓢ buck up. ～が出る be encouraged; take heart; ⓔ become heightened in spirits; ⓢ buck up.

に ～になる ❶ recover from an illness; improve in health; get better. ❷ be refreshed; take heart; cheer up; ⓢ buck up.

を ～を失う lose vigor; be enfeebled; ⓔ fall into low spirits. ～を出す brace oneself; cheer oneself up; ⓢⓘ get up steam. ～を付ける encourage *sb*; cheer *sb* up; ⓘ put *sb* on his/her mettle; ⓢⓘ buck *sb* up.

権限 authority; competence

を ～を与える authorize *sb*; empower *sb*. ～を越える exceed one's power; go beyond one's authority. ～を持つ have power; have authority.

健康 health; wholesomeness

に ～に適する be good for one's health; be wholesome. ～に響く affect one's health. ～に恵まれる be blessed with good health

を ⓔ ～を害する injure one's health; damage one's health. ～を損なう injure one's health; damage one's health. ～を保つ preserve one's health.

見当 an estimate; a guess

が ～が付く be possible to guess; have a general idea. ～が外れる guess wrong; ⓘ be off the mark.

を ～を付ける ❶ take aim at *sth*; aim at *sth*; ❷ make an estimation; have a guess.

現場 the scene (of a crime)

を ～を押えられる be caught in the act; ⓘ be caught red-handed.

権利 a right; a claim; a title

を ～を与える give *sb* rights. ～を争う contest the rights. ～を失う lose one's rights. ～を売る sell the rights. ～を犯す infringe on a right. ～を買う purchase a claim to *sth*; buy the rights. ◎ ～を踏む trample upon *sb's* rights.

権力 power; influence

に ～に屈する yield to power.

を ～を与える give *sb* power; empower *sb*; ⓔ invest *sb* with power. ～を得る gain power; ⓔ be in the ascendant. ～を掴む seize power. ～を握る seize power; hold power. ～を揮う wield power; have a hold on *sb*/*sth*.

コ

子 a child; children
[を] 〜を生む give birth to a child. 〜を下ろす have an abortion. 〜を持つ have children.

粉 powder; flour; meal; dust
[が] 〜が吹く have a bloom; be (sugar) coated.

[に] 〜にする ❶ grind *sth* to powder; pulverize *sth*. ❷ give one's all; do one's utmost; do what lies in one's power; ⓘ keep one's nose to the grindstone; ⓘ work one's fingers to the bone. 〜に碾く grind *sth* to powder; pulverize *sth*.

碁 *go* [boardgame]
[を] 〜を打つ have a game of *go*.

期 a time; an occasion
[を] Ⓐ 〜を押す call *sb's* attention to *sth*; make sure of *sth*; tell *sb* twice; Ⓒ ⓘ rub it in. Ⓐ 〜を突く call *sb's* attention to; make sure of *sth*; tell *sb* twice; Ⓒ ⓘ rub it in.

恋 love; tender passion
[に] 〜に泣く pine for love. 〜に悩む be lovesick; be lovelorn. 〜に破れる be thwarted in love.

[を] 〜を打ち明ける declare one's love. 〜を囁く whisper words of love. 〜を仕掛ける make love to *sb*; flirt with *sb*. 〜を知る know what it is to be in love. 〜をする fall in love; be in love.

功 Ⓔ merit; services; success
[を] 〜を争う claim credit for *sth*; Ⓔ contend for distinction. 〜を急ぐ be too eager for success. Ⓐ 〜を入る have a long experience (in a specific field); work for many years on *sth*. Ⓐ 〜を終える complete one's task; accomplish one's mission. Ⓔ 〜を奏する be successful; ⓘ bring home the bacon. 〜を立てる distinguish oneself in duty; Ⓔ render meritorious services. 〜を積む exert oneself in one's service. 〜を誇る boast of one's success; ⓘ blow one's own trumpet. 〜を認める give *sb* credit for *sth*; recognize *sb's* qualities.

香 incense; fragrance
[を] 〜を聞く smell incense. 〜を焚く burn incense. ◎ 〜を闘わす play a game of incense smelling. 〜を練る make incense.

劫 Ⓔ long years; long experience
[を] Ⓔ 〜を経る live to an old age; gain years of experience.

甲 a shell; armor; grade "A"
[に] Ⓐ 〜に着る hide behind *sb's* authority; do *sth* under *sb's* shelter.

[を] ◎ 〜を付ける give *sb* grade "A". ◎ 〜を取る get grade "A".

貢 Ⓐ tribute
[を] 〜を納め占める levy tribute on. 〜を納める pay tribute to.

孝 E filial piety
を © ～を尽くす be devoted to one's parents; be faithful to one's parents; be filial.

稿 E a draft; a manuscript
を © ～を改める ❶ alter a draft; rewrite a manuscript. ❷ discuss an issue with a different group of people. ～を起こす start on a draft; begin on a novel. © ～を脱す finish writing; complete a novel.

業 E karma; one's actions
が ◎ © ～が煎れる lose patience; be vexed; have one's patience tried. Ⓐ © ～が蹲う be sinful; be full of sins; © be beyond redemption. ◎ © ～が煮える lose patience; be vexed; have one's patience tried. © ～が深い be sinful; be full of sins. © be beyond redemption. © ～が滅する be absolved of one's bad karma; pass away; die in peace. ◎ © ～が湧く lose patience; be vexed; have one's patience tried.
に © ～に沈む be past saving; © be beyond redemption.
を © ～を曝す be disgraced; suffer ignominy as a result of one's past deeds. ◎ © ～を煮やす be vexed; lose patience. © ～を晴らす suffer the retributions of one's past misdeeds. © ～を沸かす lose patience; be vexed.

号 a number; a title; a pen name
を ～を追う follow each other in number. ～を付ける use a pen name; use a pseudonym.

公安 public order; public peace
を ～を保つ maintain public order. ～を破る disturb the peace.

好意 goodwill; kindness
に ～に報いる return sb's favors.
を ～を得る receive sb's favors. ～を持つ mean well; © be favorably disposed toward sb. ～を寄せる convey one's good wishes to sb.

公益 public interest
を © ～を害する harm public interest. ～を図る work for the public good.

好感 a good feeling
を ～を与える make a good impression on sb; give sb a good feeling. ～を抱く be well disposed toward sb; like sb; © be favorably disposed to sb.

後患 E future troubles
を © ～を断つ remove the source of future trouble. © ～を宿す © sow the seeds of future trouble.

好機 a good opportunity
を ～を逸する miss a golden opportunity; let slip a good chance. ～を捕える seize a good opportunity; © take the tide as it offers. ～を待つ wait for a good opportunity.

交誼 こうぎ E friendship; amity; favor
〔を〕ⓒ 〜を請う　request *sb's* (continued) favor. ⓔ 〜を結ぶ cultivate a friendship with *sb*; make friends with.

厚誼 こうぎ E kindness
〔に〕ⓔ 〜に報いる return a favor.
〔を〕ⓔ 〜を謝す thank *sb* for a favor.

肯綮 こうけい E the point; a vital point
〔に〕ⓔ 〜に中る be relevant; ⓒ ⓘ be to the point; ⓘ be on the mark; ⓘ hit the nail on the head.

攻撃 こうげき an attack; an assault
〔を〕〜を受ける be attacked. 〜を加える launch an attack. 〜を撃退する repel an attack. 〜を防ぐ defend oneself against an attack.

公言 こうげん big talk; a boast; a brag
〔を〕〜を吐く boast about *sth*; brag about *sth*; ⓒ ⓘ talk big.

巧言 こうげん E flattery; fair words
〔を〕ⓒ 〜を用いる use sweet words; flatter *sb*; say nice things to *sb*.

江湖 こうこ E the public; the world
〔に〕ⓔ 〜に訴える appeal to the public. ⓔ 〜に勧める commend (a work of art) to the public.

光彩 こうさい E luster; brilliancy
〔を〕〜を失う lose luster; go into eclipse. ⓔ 〜を添える add luster; enhance a reputation; crown an achievement. 〜を放つ cut a brilliant figure; outshine others; eclipse others.

公私 こうし public and private (affairs)
〔を〕〜を混同する mix up public and private (affairs). 〜を分ける keep public and private (affairs) separate.

好餌 こうじ E a bait; a lure
〔と〕〜となる fall prey to; be a victim of.
〔に〕ⓒ 〜にぱくつく snap at the bait (of easy money).

後事 こうじ E future affairs
〔を〕ⓔ 〜を托す entrust *sb* with future affairs.

口実 こうじつ an excuse; a pretext
〔を〕〜を作る trump up an excuse. 〜を設ける trump up an excuse.

口上 こうじょう a verbal message
〔で〕〜で伝える convey a message verbally; inform *sb* by word of mouth. 〜で述べる deliver a verbal message.
〔を〕〜を述べる deliver a verbal message.

向上心 こうじょうしん ambition; aspiration
〔を〕〜を抱く have ambitions; aspire to greatness. 〜を養う inspire aspirations in *sb*.

後塵 こうじん E a trail of dust
〔を〕ⓔ 〜を拝する play a subordinate

role; ⓒ ⓘ eat *sb's* dust; ⓘ take second billing to *sb*; ⓒ ⓘ play second fiddle to *sb*.

構想(こうそう) a conception; an idea

[を] ～を立(た)てる devise a plan; work out an idea. ～を練(ね)る think hard about *sth*; ⓒ ⓘ rack one's brains.

紅茶(こうちゃ) black tea

[を] ～を入(い)れる make tea. ～を沸(わ)かす brew tea.

高潮(こうちょう) high tide; the climax

[に] ～に達(たっ)する reach the climax; attain the zenith.

行動(こうどう) action; behavior; an act

[に] ～に表(あら)わす show *sth* in one's conduct. ～に移(うつ)す put (a plan) into action. ～に入(はい)る go into action.

[を] ～を起(お)こす set to work; make a move. ～を取(と)る take action.

後難(こうなん) [E] future trouble

[を] ～を恐(おそ)れる fear future trouble. ～を避(さ)ける avoid future trouble. ～を残(のこ)す Ⓔ sow the seeds of future trouble.

好評(こうひょう) [E] favorable criticism

[を] Ⓔ ～を博(はく)する be well received; Ⓔ be lauded; Ⓔ meet with public acclaim; ⓘ have good press.

幸福(こうふく) happiness; well-being

[に] ～に溢(あふ)れる be full of happiness. ～に暮(く)らす live a happy life; Ⓢ sit pretty. ～に死(し)ぬ pass away in peace; die happily.

[を] ～を祈(いの)る wish *sb* happiness. ～を受(う)ける enjoy happiness. ～を失(うし)う forfeit happiness. ～を羨(うらや)む envy *sb's* happiness. ～を得(え)る secure happiness (in life). ～を傷(きず)つける injure *sb's* happiness; spoil *sb's* happiness. ～を掴(つか)む gain happiness.

紅粉(こうふん) [E] rouge and powder

[を] Ⓔ ～を施(ほどこ)す powder one's face.

口吻(こうふん) [E] one's manner of speaking

[を] Ⓔ ～を真似(まね)る mimic *sb's* manner of speaking. Ⓔ ～を洩(も)らす ❶ betray one's feelings; Ⓔ give vent to one's feelings. ❷ hint at; intimate *sth*; imply *sth*.

公平(こうへい) impartiality; equity

[を] ～を欠(か)く be partial. Ⓔ ～を期(き)する attempt to be fair; seek to be impartial. ～を保(たも)つ maintain impartiality.

後報(こうほう) [E] further news

[を] ～を待(ま)つ await further details.

甲羅(こうら) a shell; a carapace

[を] ～を経(へ)る have long experience (in an office); work for many years. ～を干(ほ)す sun oneself; Ⓔ bask in the sun.

劫臈(こうろう) [E] long years of service

[を] ～を経(へ)る have long experience (in an office); work for many years.

声 a voice; a cry; notes; a song

[が] 〜が掛かる ❶ be called; be hailed. ❷ be encouraged; ⓒ be lauded; ⓒ be cheered on. ❸ be asked; be invited. 〜が嗄れる grow hoarse. 〜が詰まる speak in a choked voice. 〜が通る have a piercing voice.

[を] 〜を上げる raise one's voice; cry out; speak up. 〜を合せる talk in unison; speak with one voice. 〜を落とす lower one's voice. 〜を掛ける ❶ call out; hail *sb*. ❷ encourage *sb*; cheer *sb* on. 〜を嗄らす shout oneself hoarse. ⓒ 〜を曇らす speak in a tearful voice; falter out; murmur wistfully. 〜を殺す talk in a low voice; speak in a whisper. 〜を絞る ❶ strain one's voice. ❷ speak in a whisper; ⓒ speak with bated breath. 〜を揃える talk in unison; speak with one voice. 〜を立てる cry out; raise one's voice. 〜を尖らす speak harshly; sneer at *sb*. 〜を呑む swallow one's words; be speechless. 〜を励ます raise one's voice. 〜を弾ませる shout for joy. 〜を放つ shout out; ⓒ blare *sth* out. 〜を張り上げる yell at the top of one's voice. ⓒ 〜を潜める lower one's voice; speak in a whisper; ⓒ speak with bated breath. 〜を振り絞る cry at the top of one's voice; strain one's voice.

戸外 outdoors; the open air

[に] 〜に出る go out of doors. 〜に飛び出す dash out of the door.
[へ] 〜へ追い出す show *sb* the door; ① give *sb* the door; ⓒ throw *sb* out; ⓢ kick *sb* out.

古稀 [E] seventy years of age

[に] 〜に達する reach seventy.
[を] 〜を過ぎる pass seventy; be on the wrong side of seventy.

黒白 [E] black and white

[を] 〜を争う argue the rights and wrongs (of an issue). 〜を付ける decide on the merits and demerits (of a case). 〜を分かつ tell right from wrong; discriminate between right and wrong. ⓒ 〜を弁う be able to tell right from wrong.

虎穴 [E] a tiger's den

[に] ⓒ 〜に入る ❶ enter a tiger's den. ❷ put oneself in danger; ① put one's head in the lion's mouth.

糊口 [E] bare livelihood

[を] 〜を凌ぐ eke out a living; ⓒ get by; ① make ends meet; ⓒ ① keep the pot boiling.

故国 [E] one's homeland

[に] ⓒ 〜に帰る go back to one's homeland; return home.
[を] 〜を思う pine for home; yearn for one's homeland. 〜を去る leave one's homeland; go into exile. 〜を離れる leave one's homeland; go into exile.

小言 a scolding; a rebuke

[を] 〜を言う give *sb* a scolding; find fault with *sb*; rebuke *sb*.

心 the spirit; the heart ▶ 心

[が] 〜が洗われる feel purified; feel spiritually cleansed. 〜が動く ❶ become interested in *sb/sth*; ⓒ take a fancy to *sb/sth*. ❷ be moved; be tempted. ❸ be swayed; be unsettled; ⓔ be torn by conflicting emotions. 〜が躍る get carried away; get excited. 〜が通う understand each other. 〜が軽い be cheerful; be light-hearted. 〜が変わる fall out of love; be fickle; be unfaithful. 〜が利く be alert; keep an eye out. 〜が腐る be corrupted; have a wicked heart. 〜が挫ける be discouraged; lose heart. 〜が籠る be considerate; be thoughtful; be tactful. 〜が定まる make up one's mind. 〜が騒ぐ feel uneasy; be ill at ease. 〜が沈む be in low spirits; feel depressed. 〜が進む be in the mood for; be willing (to do *sth*). 〜が狭い be intolerant; be narrow-minded. ⓔ 〜が通ずる (be able to) convey one's feelings to *sb* else. ⓐ 〜が付く ❶ notice *sth*. ❷ come round. 〜が咎める have a guilty conscience; feel guilty; be sorry. 〜が解ける be cheered up; feel refreshed. 〜が届く ❶ be careful; be attentive (to details). ❷ be tactful; be considerate. ❸ communicate one's feelings; convey one's feelings. 〜が弾む be elated; feel excited; be proud. 〜が引かれる be attracted by; be interested in; be concerned with. 〜が引き締まる be tense; brace oneself. 〜が広い be tolerant; be broad-minded. 〜が触れ合う see things the same way; see eye to eye. 〜が乱れる be distracted; be distraught; become upset. 〜が揉める be anxious; be nervous. ⓞ 〜が悪い feel strange; feel weird; feel unwell.

[に] 〜に合う be agreeable; be pleasing. 〜に抱く cherish (a thought); harbor (a feeling); entertain (an idea). 〜に入る pierce the heart; sting to the quick. 〜に浮かぶ cross one's mind; come to mind. 〜に描く picture *sth* in one's mind; imagine *sth* vividly; come before one's eyes. 〜に思う think to oneself. 〜に懸かる ❶ be troubled by; fret over *sth*; ① weigh on one's mind. ❷ rely on *sb's* benevolence; appeal to *sb's* mercy. ⓐ 〜に掛く take *sth* into consideration; bear *sth* in mind; ① take *sth* on board. 〜に適う meet one's taste; suit one's fancy. 〜に刻む be deeply impressed by *sth*; ⓐ be engraved on one's memory; ① take *sth* to heart. ⓐ 〜に障る be annoying; be irritating. 〜に染みる penetrate one's heart; ⓔ have *sth* impressed on one's mind. 〜に留める bear *sth* in mind; keep *sth* in mind; ⓐ make a mental note of *sth*. 〜に残す leave (an impression) in *sb's* (one's) heart. 〜に残る linger in one's mind; remain in one's heart. 〜に触れる touch one's heart. 〜に任せる do as one pleases; have one's way.

[を] ～を暖(あたた)める warm one's heart; be heartwarming. ～を改(あらた)める change one's habits; ⓘ turn over a new leaf. ～を合(あ)わせる put one's hearts and minds together; be in accord; be of one mind. ◎ ～を致(いた)す devote oneself to. ～を痛(いた)める be worried by *sth*; fret over *sth*. ～を入(い)れ替(か)える change one's habits; ⓘ turn over a new leaf. ～を入(い)れる apply oneself to *sth*; do *sth* in earnest. ～を動(うご)かす unsettle one; stir one up; move one. ～を打(う)たれる be touched by *sb/sth*; be moved by *sb/sth*; be impressed by *sb/sth*. ～を打(う)つ touch *sb*; move *sb*; impress *sb*. ～を移(うつ)す change one's mind; have a change of heart. ～を奪(うば)う charm *sb*; ⓘ steal *sb's* heart; ⓘ put a spell on *sb*. ～を奪(うば)われる be fascinated by; be spellbound by; be captivated by. ◎ ～を置(お)く ❶ take *sth* into consideration; bear *sth* in mind; ⓘ take *sth* on board. ❷ be attached to; hold fast to; cling to. ❸ be modest; be shy. ❹ be cautious; ⓘ be on one's guard; be on the alert. Ⓐ ～を起(お)こす pluck up courage; brace oneself. ～を躍(おど)らせる make one's heart leap; grow excited; be worked up (about *sth*). ～を掛(か)ける ❶ pay attention to *sb/sth*; take note of *sb/sth*. ❷ give one's heart to *sb*; take a fancy to *sb*; set one's heart on *sth*. ❸ have faith in *sb*; pray for *sb/sth*. ～を傾(かたむ)ける ❶ be absorbed in *sth*; be keen on *sth*; apply oneself to *sth*. ❷ take an interest in *sb*; take to *sb*; have sympathy for *sb*. ～を固(かた)める prepare oneself for *sth*; get ready for *sth*; resolve to do *sth*; ⓘ gird up one's loins. ～を通(かよ)わせる reach an understanding. ～を交(か)わす feel a deep sympathy for each other. ～を決(き)める make up one's mind. ～を砕(くだ)く ❶ worry about *sth*; Ⓒ ⓘ rack one's brains. ❷ pay attention to; make strenuous efforts; take pains over *sth*. ～を配(くば)る ❶ be careful; be attentive. ❷ be watchful; be vigilant. (人(ひと)の)～を汲(く)む sympathize with *sb*; empathize with *sb*. ～を焦(こ)がす pine for *sb*; languish for *sb*. ～を込(こ)める apply oneself to *sth*; give one's heart to *sth*; Ⓔ devote one's mind to *sth*. ～を凝(こ)らす think hard on *sth*; Ⓔ apply one's mind to *sth*; Ⓢ ⓘ use one's loaf. ～を定(さだ)める make up one's mind; resolve to do *sth*. ～を察(さっ)する read *sb's* mind. ～を騒(さわ)がす upset one; be disturbing; be disquieting. ～を締(し)め付(つ)ける break *sb's* heart; be heartrending. ～を静(しず)める ease ones heart; compose oneself. ～を据(す)える be prepared; be resigned to (one's fate). ～を注(そそ)ぐ pour one's heart into *sth*; devote oneself to *sb/sth*. ～をそそる arouse one's interest; be aroused by *sth*; Ⓢ ⓘ push *sb's* buttons. ～を逸(そ)らす be distracted; be distraught. ～を遣(つか)う be considerate; care about. ～を掴(つか)む win *sb's* heart. ～を尽(つ)くす ❶ devote oneself to *sth*. ❷ fret over *sth*; worry about *sth*; fidget about *sth*. 〜を付ける ❶ give *sb* a tip; take *sb* into consideration (financially). ❷ revive *sb*; bring *sb* round. 〜を留める bear *sth* in mind; keep *sth* in mind; Ⓐ make a mental note of *sth*. 〜を捉える attract *sb's* attention; draw *sb's* attention. 〜を取られる be diverted with; forget oneself; lose oneself in *sth*. 〜を取り直す pluck up courage; brace oneself. 〜を慰める ease one's mind. 〜を悩ます fret over *sth*; be troubled by *sth*; worry about *sth*. 〜を煮やす lose patience; be vexed; have one's patience tried. Ⓐ 〜を延ぶ ❶ feel relieved; feel reassured. ❷ pluck up courage; brace oneself. 〜を馳す think about; long for; pine for. 〜を引く ❶ sound *sb* out; feel *sb* out; ⓒ check *sb's* mood. ❷ attract one's/*sb's* attention; be appealing. 〜を開く open one's heart; unbosom oneself; ⓓ pour out one's heart to *sb*. 〜を翻す be penitent; mend one's ways; ⓘ turn over a new leaf. Ⓐ 〜を回す ponder over *sth*; turn *sth* over in one's mind. 〜を向ける direct one's attention toward *sth*. 〜を用いる take care; give attention to *sth*. 〜を安んずる ease one's mind; set one's heart at rest. Ⓐ 〜を遣る ❶ cheer oneself up; divert oneself (pleasantly). ❷ do as one pleases; have one's own way. ❸ think about (home); long for *sb*; pine for *sb*/*sth*. 〜を和

らげる appease *sb*; disarm *sb*; calm *sb* down. Ⓐ 〜を行かす satisfy oneself; be satisfied with *sth*; be happy with *sth*. 〜を許す ❶ relax one's attention; ⓘ drop one's guard. ❷ give one's heart to *sb*; trust *sb* blindly. (人に)〜を寄せる take an interest in *sb*; warm to *sb*; take to *sb*; have sympathy for *sb*.

こころざし
志 Ⓔ **will; resolve; spirit**

Ⓦ 〜を得る attain one's aim; achieve one's goal; realize one's aspirations. 〜を立てる set an aim in life; have a purpose in life; aspire after *sth*; resolve to do *sth*. 〜を継ぐ carry out (one's father's) ambitions. Ⓐ 〜を尽くす be faithful; be trusting. 〜を遂げる attain one's aim; achieve one's goal; realize one's aspirations. 〜を果す attain one's aim; achieve one's goal; realize one's aspirations. 〜を翻す change one's mind. 〜を養う cultivate one's spirit; foster one's spirit.

こころだま
心魂 Ⓔ **the soul; the spirit**

Ⓝ Ⓐ 〜に乗る be keen to do *sth*; show interest in *sth*; display enthusiasm for *sth*.

Ⓦ Ⓐ 〜を込める be careful; take care; be prudent; be cautious. Ⓐ 〜を飛ばす be terrified; be scared out of one's wits; ⓢ be scared stiff.

こし
腰 **the waist; the loin; the hip**

Ⓦ 〜が落ち着く take root; get

settled. ～が重(おも)い be unwilling to work; be slow to act; Ⓘ drag one's heels. ～が折(お)れる be frustrated; suffer a setback; be disheartened. ～が軽(かる)い ❶ be quick to act; be willing to work. ❷ be agile; be nimble. ～が砕(くだ)ける lose one's stance; lose enthusiasm. ～が据(すわ)る be at ease. ～が高(たか)い ❶ be arrogant; be haughty; be high-handed. ❷ [*sumō*] lack stability. ～が強(つよ)い ❶ take a firm stand; be firm. ❷ be resilient; be flexible. ❸ be firm; be sticky; be chewy. [sports] ❹ have a powerful lift. ～が抜(ぬ)ける ❶ lose one's legs; Ⓒ be floored. ❷ lose heart; get scared; Ⓘ get cold feet. ～が低(ひく)い ❶ be courteous; be humble; Ⓘ keep a low profile. ❷ [*sumō*] have stability. ～が弱(よわ)い ❶ be weak-kneed; lack firmness. ❷ be limp; be thin (in texture); be soggy.

[に] ～に付(つ)ける ❶ wear (a sword). ❷ take possession of *sth*; make *sth* one's own.

[を] ～を上(あ)げる ❶ stand up; rise to one's feet. ❷ take action; come into action. ～を入(い)れる set about in earnest; commit oneself to *sth*; Ⓘ put one's shoulders to the wheel; Ⓢ go for it. ～を浮(う)かす get ready to stand up; be about to rise. ～を押(お)す ❶ push (a cart). ❷ support *sb*; back *sb*; stand behind *sb*. ❸ put *sb* up; egg *sb* on. ～を落(お)ち着(つ)ける settle down; unwind. ～を折(お)る ❶ bend over; stoop at. ❷ yield to (pressure); be subordinate to *sb*. ❸ interrupt *sb*; spoil a story. ❹ Ⓘ take the wind out of *sb's* sails. ～を下(お)ろす drop into a chair; plop oneself down. ～を屈(かが)める ❶ stoop; bend over. ❷ greet *sb*; make a bow; bow to *sb*. ～を掛(か)ける sit oneself down; seat oneself. ～を据(す)える ❶ steady oneself; sit tight. ❷ settle down (to do *sth*); Ⓒ buckle down (to do *sth*). ～を突(つ)く be discouraged; lose heart. ～を抜(ぬ)かす ❶ lose one's legs. ❷ Ⓐ grow weak at the knees; lose heart; get scared; Ⓘ get cold feet. ～を伸(の)ばす straighten up; stand up straight; stretch one's limbs. ～を引(ひ)く ❶ [*jūdō*] throw one's waist backwards (to throw one's opponent). ❷ limp along; walk with a limp. ～を振(ふ)る swing one's hips. ～を曲(ま)げる bend over; stoop at. ～を持(も)つ support *sb*; back *sb*; stand behind *sb*. Ⓐ ～を縒(よ)る fall over laughing; Ⓒ kill oneself laughing ～を割(わ)る [*sumō*] take a firm stance.

小癪(こしゃく) impudent; saucy; pert

[に] ～に障(さわ)る feel somewhat vexed; be slightly offended; Ⓘ go against the grain.

鐺(こじり) a chape; the tip of a sheath

[が] ◎ ～が詰(つ)まる be in financial trouble; Ⓘ be in dire straits.

個性(こせい) personality; individuality

[を] ～を失(うしな)う lose one's dignity. ～

を抑える suppress one's ego. 〜を欠く lack individuality. 〜を伸ばす cultivate one's personality. 〜を発揮する display individuality. 〜を持つ have personality.

戸籍 census; registration
⟨を⟩ 〜を洗う check sb's family register. 〜を調べる inquire into sb's family register; take the census.

五臓 Ⓔ the five viscera
⟨を⟩ Ⓐ 〜を絞る suffer extreme hardships. Ⓐ 〜を煮やす be irate; burn with rage/resentment. Ⓐ 〜を揉む regret sth bitterly; feel chagrined (at sth); be grieved (at sth); feel sorry for sb.

滑稽 Ⓔ comic; humor
⟨を⟩ 〜を言う make a joke; Ⓒ crack jokes; Ⓒ be witty. Ⓔ 〜を解する have a sense of humor.

骨髄 the marrow (of a bone)
⟨に⟩ Ⓐ 〜に入る sting to the quick; pierce the heart. Ⓐ 〜に撤る pierce the heart; sting to the quick.
⟨を⟩ Ⓐ 〜を砕く have a hard time; suffer great hardships.

孤独 solitude; loneliness
⟨を⟩ 〜を愛する love one's own company; Ⓒ be a loner. 〜を味わう experience loneliness. 〜を感じる feel solitude; feel lonely. 〜を楽しむ enjoy one's own company; be reclusive; Ⓒ be a loner.

言葉 words; speech; language
⟨が⟩ 〜が過ぎる say too much. 〜が通じる be understood. 〜が尖る speak stern words.

⟨に⟩ 〜に甘える take sb's word for it. 〜に余る be lost for words; be beyond description. 〜に表わす put into words. Ⓐ 〜に付く comply with sb's wishes; do as sb says. 〜に詰まる be at a loss for words. 〜に触れる let sth fall; blurt sth out. 〜に任せる comply with sb's words; do as sb says.

⟨を⟩ 〜を返す rebuke sb; talk back; Ⓒ give sb backtalk. 〜を交わす have a word with sb; talk with sb. 〜を換える change one's words. 〜を掛ける address sb; speak to sb. 〜を飾る use fancy words; use fine language. 〜を固める commit oneself; make a promise. 〜を交わす ❶ exchange words with sb; have a word with sb; talk with sb. ❷ make a verbal agreement. 〜を下げる ❶ speak in a humble way. ❷ be rude in one's speech; patronize sb; speak down to sb. 〜を添える speak up for sb; put in a good word for sb. Ⓐ 〜を番う commit oneself; make a promise. 〜を継ぐ resume one's speech; Ⓘ pick up the thread. 〜を尽くす exhaust one's words. (人の)〜を咎める censure sb's words; criticize sb; rebuke sb. 〜を直す speak formally; use polite words. 〜を濁す speak ambiguously; be vague. 〜を練る choose one's words carefully;

① weigh one's words. 〜を残す ❶ leave things unsaid. ❷ say *sth* for posterity. 〜を呑む swallow one's words. 〜を挟む interrupt *sb*; butt in. Ⓐ 〜を外す parry a remark. 〜を放つ speak unreservedly; ① shoot off one's mouth. Ⓐ 〜を食む ❶ take back what one has said; ⓒ eat one's words. ❷ break one's word; go back on one's word.

子供 a child; children

が 〜が出来る conceive a child; be with child.

を 〜を生む give birth; have a child. 〜を下ろす have an abortion; abort a pregnancy.

小鼻 the nostrils

が 〜が落ちる be emaciated; be close to dying.

を 〜を蠢かす ❶ be elated; look triumphant. ❷ be haughty; ① have airs and graces; ⓒ ① have a swelled head; ⓢ ① be stuck-up.

小腹 Ⓔ a (small) stomach

が 〜が立つ be slightly annoyed; be slightly irritated. 〜が減る feel slightly hungry.

を 〜を立てる get slightly annoyed; get slightly irritated.

媚び flattery; cajolery

を Ⓐ 〜を入る sound *sb's* feelings; ⓔ consult *sb's* pleasure. 〜を売る sell one's favors. ⓔ 〜を呈する use flattery; use blandishments.

胡麻 sesame; a sesame seed

を 〜を擦る ❶ grind sesame seeds. ❷ flatter *sb*; ① curry favor with *sb*.

小股 short steps; the groin

に 〜に歩く walk with short steps; take short steps; mince one's steps.

を 〜を掬う [*sumō*] trip *sb* up; sweep *sb's* legs from under him. 〜を取る ❶ [*sumō*] trip *sb* up; sweep *sb's* legs from under him. ❷ exploit *sb's* weak point.

小耳 a (small) ear

に 〜に挟む overhear *sth*; come to one's knowledge; ① hear *sth* on the grapevine.

声色 tone of voice

を 〜を遣う imitate *sb's* voice.

根 a root; a radical; stamina ▶根

が 〜が尽きる lose patience with *sb*/*sth*.

を 〜を詰める apply oneself to (one's studies); concentrate on *sth*; work hard on *sth*.

根源 Ⓔ the origin; the root

に ⓔ 〜に遡る trace *sth* to its origin. ⓔ 〜に触れる touch on the root of (a matter).

を ⓔ 〜を究める trace *sth* to its origin; go to the root of *sth*. 〜を絶つ root out the cause of trouble.

根底 Ⓔ the root; the bottom

を 〜を築く lay the basis for (an

idea); pave the way for (a move-ment). © ～を究める reach bedrock; get down to the root of (a matter). © ～を為す form the basis (of a theory); be the foundation of (a belief).

困難 difficulties; trouble

に ～に遭う encounter difficulties; run into trouble. ～に打ち勝つ overcome difficulties; ① weather the storm. ～に陥る fall into difficulties; get into trouble; ① be in deep waters. ～に堪える endure hardships; ① weather the storm. ～に臨む face difficulties.

を ～を感じる find *sth* difficult. ～を切り抜ける overcome problems; surmount difficulties; get out of trouble; ① weather the storm; ① get out of the woods. ～を除く relieve one's difficulties. ～を招く invite difficulties; ask for trouble.

サ

座 a seat; a position; status

が ◎ ～が醒める ❶ the mood is spoiled; spoil an occasion. ❷ inter-est wanes; lose interest. ～が白ける the mood is spoiled; spoil an occasion. ◎ ～が長い outstay one's welcome; stay too long.

に ～に着く ❶ take a seat; assume a position. ❷ occupy a position; hold a post. ～に連なる attend a meeting; join a party. ～に直る sit

down on one's own seat; sit down on one's seat; sit up straight.

を ～を構える take a seat. ～を組む sit cross-legged. ～を冷ます cast a chill over a room; spoil the mood; ① be a wet blanket. ～を占める ❶ take a seat; assume a posi-tion. ❷ occupy a position; hold a post. ～を立つ leave one's seat; slip out of the room. ～を取り持つ mediate between two parties; act as a go-between. ～を守る maintain one's position; stay in power; hold a post; © ① stay in the saddle. ～を持つ carry on a conversation; entertain a compa-ny. ～を外す leave one's seat; slip out of the room. ～を譲る offer one's seat to *sb*.

才 talent; ability; aptitude

が ～がある have talent.

に ～に溺れる rely too much on one's talent; be too confident in one's talents.

を ◎ ～を頼む rely too much on one's talent; be too confident in one's talents. ～を伸ばす develop one's talent. ～を働かす exercise one's talents.

財 money; riches; wealth

を ～を惜しむ be parsimonious; © be tight-fisted. ～を作る make a fortune. ～を積む amass a fortune; grow rich. ～を成す accumulate riches; grow rich. ～を残す leave an estate. ～を貪る covet riches.

最期 one's last moment

⎡を⎤ 〜を飾る ⓒ bring glory to one's last moments. 〜を遂げる die a pitiful death; meet with a tragic end; ⓒ come to an untimely end. 〜を見届ける be at *sb's* deathbed.

災難 a calamity; a misfortune

⎡に⎤ 〜に遭う meet with misfortune. ⎡を⎤ 〜を避ける avert a calamity. 〜を免れる escape disaster.

裁判 justice; a trial; a hearing

⎡に⎤ 〜に勝つ win a court case. ◎ 〜に付ける put (a case) on trial; bring *sb* to justice. 〜になる be brought to trial; go to court. 〜に負ける lose a court case.

⎡を⎤ 〜を仰ぐ submit (a case) to the court; bring a suit against *sb*; ⓒ sue *sb*. 〜を受ける come up for trial; be on trial. 〜を行う pass judgment on *sb*; try *sb*. 〜を開く hold a court.

財布 a purse; a wallet

⎡を⎤ 〜を落とす drop one's purse. 〜を取り出す draw out one's purse. 〜を叩く empty one's purse. 〜を満たす fill one's purse.

境 a border; a frontier

⎡に⎤ Ⓐ 〜に入る reach a high status; attain a superior position.

⎡を⎤ 〜を荒らす harass the frontier. 〜を決める set up a borderline; define the boundary. 〜を接する border on (a place). 〜を為す represent a border. 〜を広げる extend the border(s). Ⓐ 〜を隔つ leave this world (behind); pass away; draw one's last breath; ⓒ ① breathe one's last.

盃 a (sake) cup

⎡を⎤ 〜を上げる ❶ drink sake; have a drink. ❷ raise one's cup; toast to *sth*. 〜を合わせる touch (sake) cups. 〜を受ける accept a (sake) cup. 〜を返す offer a (sake) cup in return. 〜を重ねる drink one (sake) cup after another. 〜を傾ける have a drink. 〜を差す offer a (sake) cup. 〜をする drink a parting cup. 〜を伏せる reserve a (sake) cup. 〜を回す pass the (sake) cup around. 〜を貰う pledge one's loyalty (over a sake cup).

先 the head; the future ▸ 先

⎡が⎤ 〜が有る be promising; have potential. 〜が見える ❶ be able to see into the future; be clairvoyant; be far-sighted. ❷ be within reach; near completion; ① see light at the end of the tunnel.

⎡に⎤ 〜に行く go before *sb* else; go first. 〜にする give priority to *sth*. 〜に立つ ❶ be in the lead; ① be in the front van. ❷ be a priority; be placed above others. Ⓐ (人を)〜に使う involve *sb*; use *sb's* name (in one's excuse). 〜に出る come out first; top the list; be the first. 〜になる get ahead of *sb*; get the lead.

さ

回 ～を争う strive to be first. ～を急ぐ rival *sb* for priority; try to be first. ⒜ ～を追う clear the way (for a dignitary). ⒜ ～を折る spoil *sb's* enthusiasm; ⓘ be a wet blanket. ⒜ ～を駆く take the lead; be in the forefront; ⓘ set the tune. ～を担ぐ lead the way; ⒜ pave the way (for *sb*). ⒜ ～を切る ❶ cut the tip off. ❷ cut across *sb*; speak before one's turn. ⒜ ～を潜る forestall *sb*; get a start on *sb*; preempt *sb's* actions; anticipate *sb* (in doing). ～を越す forestall *sb*; get a start on *sb*; pre-empt *sb's* actions; anticipate *sb* (in doing *sth*). ⒜ ～を払う ❶ pay in advance; ⓒ pay up front. ❷ pay on delivery. ❸ clear the way (for a dignitary). ⒜ ～を回す forestall *sb*; get a start on *sb*; pre-empt *sb's* actions; anticipate *sb* (in doing). ～を見る look ahead. ～を譲る give *sb* the lead; ⓔ yield precedence to *sb*. ～を読む look into the future; plan ahead.

策 a step; a measure; a means

回 ～が尽きる be at the end of one's resources; ⓘ be driven to the wall; ⓘ be at one's wits' end; ⓒ be in a fix. ～が無い unresourceful. 回 ～に窮する be at the end of one's resources; ⓘ be driven to the wall; ⓘ be at one's wits' end; ⓒ be in a fix. ～に富む be resourceful; be a shrewd tactician. 回 ～を与える instill wisdom in *sb*; furnish *sb* with knowledge; ⓘ teach

sb the ropes. ～を誤る take the wrong step; go astray. ⓔ ～を講ずる devise a means; consider the (necessary) means. ～を立てる formulate a plan. ～を施す adopt measures; take steps. ～を廻らす devise a scheme; draw up a plan. ⓔ ～を弄する use artifice; ⓔ resort to wiles; play tricks on *sb*.

朔 H New Year's Day [lunar]

回 ⓞ ～を奉く submit to a new emperor; accept the rule of a new emperor.

さく E a ridge; a rib; a row

回 ⓞ ⓔ ～を切る till the soil.

探り a spy; a probe; a stylet

回 ～を入れる sound *sb* out; probe a wound; plunge a probe into *sth*.

酒 sake; wine; liquor

回 ⒜ ～に痛む destroy oneself with drinking; ⓢ get dead drunk; ⓢ get smashed. ～に耽る indulge in sake; give oneself up to drinking. ⓞ ～に回される be enslaved to drinking; lose oneself in liquor. 回 ～を傾ける drink from a sake cup. ～を嗜む be fond of the bottle. ～を出す serve sake; put out sake. ⒜ ～を使う do *sth* under the influence of liquor; do *sth* with Dutch courage. ～を注ぐ pour out sake. ～を慎む refrain from drinking; abstain from alcohol. ～を飲む drink sake; take wine.

匙 (さじ) a spoon

が Ⓐ 〜が回る excel in the art of medicine; be good at mixing medicine.

を 〜を投げる give *sth* up as hopeless; Ⓘ throw in the towel.

瑣事 (さじ) Ⓔ a trifle; trivialities

に 〜にこだわる bother about trifles; Ⓘ split hairs.

指図 (さしず) directions; instructions

に 〜に従う obey *sb's* directions.

を 〜を仰ぐ ask for instructions. 〜を受ける receive instructions. 〜を待つ await instructions. 〜を守る obey *sb's* directions.

鯖 (さば) a mackerel

を 〜を読む cheat in counting; give *sb* the wrong number; misrepresent one's age.

鞘 (さや) a sheath; a scabbard; a case

を 〜を取る take a commission; take a percentage. 〜を払う draw a sword; unsheathe a sword. Ⓞ 〜を寄せる narrow the spread.

左右 (さゆう) left and right

に Ⓞ 〜に托する dodge an issue; Ⓔ equivocate on an issue; Ⓘ beat about the bush; Ⓒ Ⓘ pussyfoot on an issue. Ⓞ 〜に侍る wait on *sb*; attend on *sb*. 〜に揺れる roll from side to side. 〜に分ける part left and right.

を 〜を顧みる look around. 〜を見る look left and right; look around.

産 (さん) Ⓔ childbirth; a fortune

を Ⓞ Ⓔ 〜を傾ける ❶ waste a fortune; exhaust one's fortune; Ⓔ dissipate one's possessions. ❷ invest one's family fortune; use private funds. Ⓔ (お)〜をする give birth to a child; have a baby. Ⓔ 〜を成す amass a fortune; grow rich; Ⓢ make one's pile. Ⓞ Ⓔ 〜を破る lose one's fortune; go bankrupt; Ⓢ go bust.

算 (さん) Ⓗ Chinese divining blocks

を Ⓐ 〜を置く see into the future; divine the future; prophesy the future. Ⓐ 〜を散らす upset the ranks; throw the ranks into confusion; cause mayhem. Ⓐ 〜を乱す cause mayhem; upset the ranks; throw the ranks into confusion.

賛 (さん) Ⓔ praise; eulogy; a legend

が Ⓐ 〜が付く be criticized; be reviewed.

を Ⓐ 〜を打つ criticize (a work of art); review (a book). Ⓐ 〜をする write a legend (on a picture). Ⓐ 〜を付ける criticize (a work of art); review (a book).

賛辞 (さんじ) Ⓔ a eulogy; a compliment

を Ⓔ 〜を呈する pay tribute to *sb*; speak highly of *sb*.

賛成 (さんせい) approval; agreement

を 〜を得る gain *sb's* approval. 〜を示す express one's approval. 〜を求める seek *sb's* approval.

シ

死 death; decease; demise

[に] (人を)〜に至らしめる cause *sb's* death. ⓞ 〜に着く meet death; meet one's end; ⓘ bite the dust. 〜に臨む face death; ⓔ look death in the face.

[を] ⓐ ⓔ 〜を致す pass away; ⓔ ⓘ breathe one's last. ⓔ (人の)〜を悼む mourn *sb's* death; lament over *sb's* death. 〜を祈る wish *sb* dead. 〜を恐れる fear death. 〜を期する expect to die; be ready to die. 〜を決する be resolved to die. ⓗ 〜を賜る be allowed to commit suicide. 〜を遂げる meet one's end. 〜を賭す risk one's life; hazard one's life; ⓔ put one's life at stake. 〜を早める hasten *sb's* death. 〜を免れる escape death. 〜を招く court death.

歯 ⓔ teeth; old age; frailty

[を] ⓐ ⓔ 〜を没す pass away; reach the end of one's life; ⓔ ⓘ breathe one's last.

字 a character; a letter

[を] 〜を書く write a character. 〜を崩す reduce a square Chinese character to the running style; write cursively. 〜を加える add a character. 〜を削る erase a character.

地 ground; texture; reality ▶ 地

[が] ⓞ 〜が積む be dense in texture.

〜が出る one's true nature comes through; ⓘ show the cloven hoof.

[で] 〜で行く put *sth* into practice; experience *sth* in reality; come true.

[を] 〜を均す roll the ground; level the ground. ⓞ 〜を弾く play accompaniment.

次 ⓔ order; degree; sequence

[を] 〜を追う follow a sequence; go in order; do *sth* in sequence.

思案 thought; consideration

[に] 〜に余る be at a loss (about what to do); ⓘ be at one's wits' end; ⓘ be all at sea. 〜に落ちる be satisfied; be convinced; ⓒ ⓘ get the point. 〜に暮れる be lost in meditation; ponder over *sth*; be lost in thought. 〜に沈む think *sth* over; ponder over *sth*; be lost in thought. 〜に尽きる be at the end of one's resources; ⓘ be at one's wits' end; ⓘ be all at sea. 〜に耽る be sunk in meditation; be lost in thought. ⓞ 〜に塞がる think *sth* over; ponder over *sth*; be lost in thought.

[を] 〜を凝らす bury oneself in meditation. 〜を廻らす think hard about *sth*; ⓔ cast *sth* about in one's mind; ⓒ ⓘ rack one's brains over *sth*.

辞意 one's intention to resign

[を] 〜を翻す reconsider one's resignation. 〜を洩らす hint at one's resignation; ⓔ intimate one's intention to resign.

支援 support; aid; backing

を ～を与える give *sb* support; support *sb*; Ⓒ back *sb* up. ～を求める ask for support; Ⓔ seek *sb's* support; look for support.

私怨 Ⓔ a personal grudge

を ～を抱く hold a grudge against *sb*; Ⓑ harbor a private malice; Ⓒ have it in for sb; ⓓ have a chip on one's shoulder. ～を晴らす satisfy one's grudge.

紫煙 Ⓔ tobacco smoke

を ～を燻らす send up a puff of smoke; pull away at one's cigarette; have a leisurely smoke.

塩 salt; seasoning with salt

が Ⓐ ～が浸む go through a lot of hardships; suffer all sorts of privations.

に ～に漬ける preserve *sth* in salt; salt *sth* down.

を Ⓐ ～を踏む experience lot of hardships; have a hard time.

潮 the tide; a current

が ～が上げる the tide comes in. ～が引く the tide goes out. ～が満ちる the tide is at the full.

に ～に乗る take the tide.

を Ⓐ ～を踏む go through a lot of hardships; suffer all sorts of privations. ～を待つ ❶ await a favorable tide. ❷ wait until the time is ripe; wait for a chance; Ⓒ bide one's time.

潮時 time and tide

を ～を外す ❶ miss a favorable tide. ❷ miss an opportunity; let a chance slip by. ～を待つ ❶ await a favorable tide. ❷ wait until the time is ripe; wait for a chance; Ⓒ bide one's time. ～を見る ❶ wait for a favorable tide. ❷ watch for an opportunity; look for an opportunity; Ⓒ bide one's time.

資格 qualifications; capability

が ～が有る be qualified; have the qualifications (for a post).

を ～を与える qualify *sb* (for a post). ～を失う be disqualified; lose one's qualifications. ～を奪う disqualify *sb* (for a post). ～を得る qualify (for a post); ⓘ become eligible (for a post). ～を取る obtain qualifications; get a license.

地金 ground metal; bullion

を ～を現わす betray oneself; reveal one's true character; ⓘ show one's true colors. ～を出す betray oneself; reveal one's true character; ⓘ show one's true colors.

時間 an hour; time

が ～が有る have time; be free; be vacant; have time on one's hands. ～が掛かる take time; be time-consuming. ～が迫る be under time pressure; time is closing in. ～が立つ time passes by.

に ～に遅れる be behind time; be late. ～に追われる be pressed for

time; run out of time. 〜に縛られ
る be pressed for time; run out of
time.

图 〜を得る gain time; win time.
〜を稼ぐ play for time; buy time.
〜を繰り合わせる arrange hours.
ⓢ 〜を食う be time-consuming;
take time. ⓞ 〜を消す while away
time. 〜を過ごす pass the time;
spend time (on *sth*). 〜を進める
bring time forward. 〜を費す
spend time; waste (precious) time.
〜を潰す fill the time; ⓒ kill time.
〜を取る take time. ⓞ 〜を塞ぐ fill
in the hour. 〜を守る be on time;
be punctual; ⓢ ① be on the button.
〜を持て余す have enough time;
① have time on one's hands.

時機 Ⓔ an opportunity; a chance
に ⓒ 〜に投ずる take advantage of
a situation; ⓒ capitalize on an
opportunity.
图 〜を捕える take one's chances;
grab the chance; ⓒ seize an opportunity. ⓒ 〜を逸する let a chance
slip by, miss an opportunity.

時儀 Ⓔ seasonal compliments
图 〜を交わす exchange seasonal
compliments. ⓒ 〜を述べる give
the compliments of the season.

児戯 Ⓔ child's play; puerile
に ⓒ 〜に等しい be puerile; be
childish; be mere child's play. ⓒ 〜
に類する be puerile; be childish;
be mere child's play.

敷居 a threshold; a doorsill
图 〜が高い feel awkward to visit
sb; have leaden feet.
图 〜を跨ぐ cross a threshold;
enter/leave a house.

色彩 a color; a hue; a tint
に 〜に富む be colorful; be rich in
color.
图 〜を与える give color to *sth*. 〜
を帯びる take on color.

色情 desire; sexual appetite
图 〜が起こる be seized with desire.
图 〜をそそる arouse one's desire;
excite one's sexual appetite.

事業 an enterprise; a project
图 〜を営む run a business. 〜を起
こす start an enterprise. 〜を引き
受ける undertake a business. 〜を
目論む have a project in view.

資金 funds; capital
图 〜が切れる run out of funds.
图 〜を集める raise funds. 〜を出
す provide funds; put up funds.

死刑 capital punishment
に 〜に処する put *sb* to death.
图 〜を下す condemn *sb* to death;
pass a death sentence on *sb*. 〜を
免れる escape capital punishment.

刺激 a stimulus; an impetus
图 〜を与える give impetus to *sth*;
give a stimulus to *sb*. 〜を受ける
receive a stimulus; be stimulated.

し

試験 an examination; a test

[に] ～に受かる pass an exam. ～に落ちる fail an examination; Ⓢ flunk a test.

[を] ～を受ける take a test; sit for an examination. ～を行う organize an examination; hold a test.

事件 an event; an incident

[を] ～を起こす cause an incident; start trouble; stir up trouble; Ⓘ raise Cain. ～を引き受ける take up a matter. ～を揉み消す hush up a scandal; cover up an affair; Ⓘ sweep *sth* under the carpet.

嗜好 [E] a taste; a fancy; a liking

[に] Ⓔ ～に適う suit one's taste. Ⓔ ～に投じる catch the (public) taste; capture *sb's* fancy.

仕事 work; labor; a job

[に] ～に在り付く find work; Ⓒ Ⓘ land a job. ～に追われる be pressed with business. ～に掛かる set to work; get down to business. ～に疲れる be tired with work; be workworn.

[を] ～を宛がう assign work to *sb*. ～を終える finish work; Ⓒ round off a job. ～を捜す look for work; hunt for a job. ～を始める start work; get on with the job. ～を任せる entrust *sb* with work. ～を見付ける find work; Ⓒ Ⓘ land a job. ～を求める seek employment. ～を休む absent oneself from work; take time off from work. ～を辞める quit work; Ⓒ Ⓘ throw up one's job.

指示 instructions; directions

[に] ～に従う comply with *sb's* directions; follow *sb's* instructions.

[を] ～を与える give instructions. ～を受ける receive directions.

市場 a market; a mart

[に] ～に出す put (a product) on the market. ～に出る come on the market; Ⓒ hit the market.

[を] ～を操る manipulate the market. ～を荒らす spoil the market; upset the market. ～を築く build up a market. ～を狂わせる upset the market; spoil the market. ～を見付ける find a market.

私情 personal feeling

[に] ～に駆られる be swayed by personal feelings.

[を] ～を差し挟む take personal feelings into consideration. ～を捨てる set aside one's personal feelings. ～を挟む bring one's personal feelings into play.

私心 self-interest; selfishness

[を] ～を捨てる discard selfish feelings. ～を差し挟む act out of self-interest; Ⓘ have an axe to grind; Ⓘ have a hidden agenda.

自信 self-confidence

[が] ～が有る have self-confidence; be confident; Ⓒ be cocky. ～が付く acquire confidence in oneself.

[を] ～を失う lose confidence; become insecure; Ⓢ lose one's

cool. ～を得る gain confidence; become sure of oneself; Ⓒ get cocky. ～を欠く lack confidence; be insecure. ～を覆す undermine *sb's* self-confidence. ～を付ける acquire confidence in oneself. ～を持たせる give *sb* self-confidence. ～を持つ have self-confidence; be confident; Ⓒ be cocky.

自説 one's own view
[を] ～を改める revise one's views. ～を捨てる give up one's own view. ～を曲げる change one's position.

視線 one's gaze; a glance
[を] ～を集める attract the public gaze. ～を浴びる attract *sb's* attention. ～を避ける avoid *sb's* gaze. ～を逸らす avert one's eyes; look away. ～を向ける turn one's gaze upon *sb/sth*.

慈善 charity; benevolence
[を] ～を行う do good; perform an act of charity. ～を施す render aid (to the poor); do good.

自尊心 self-esteem; pride
[を] ～を失う lose one's self-esteem. ～を押える swallow one's pride. ～を傷つける hurt *sb's* pride. ～を保つ maintain one's self-esteem.

舌 the tongue; a clapper ➧ 舌
[が] ～が肥える develop a taste for *sth*; be a gourmet. ～が滑る Ⓘ make a slip of the tongue; Ⓘ let *sth* fall/slip; Ⓒ blurt *sth* out. ～が長い be talkative; Ⓔ be loquacious; Ⓒ be a chatterbox; Ⓘ talk people's head off. ◎ ～が伸びる exaggerate *sth*; overstate *sth*; Ⓘ stretch the facts; Ⓢ Ⓘ pile it on. ～が回る have a glib tongue; be a good talker; Ⓒ Ⓘ have the gift of the gab.
[を] ～を打つ click one's tongue (with displeasure). ◎ ～を返す come back on what one has said; Ⓘ change one's tune. ～を噛む bite one's tongue. Ⓢ ～を食う bite off one's tongue and die. ～を滑らす blurt *sth* out; come out with *sth* inadvertently; let (a secret) slip out of one's mouth. ～を出す ❶ make a fool of *sb* (behind their back); talk behind *sb's* back; Ⓒ poke fun at *sb* (behind their back); Ⓒ Ⓘ thumb one's nose at *sb*. ❷ be embarrassed; be ashamed. ～を鳴らす ❶ click one's tongue with (dis)pleasure. ❷ marvel at *sth*; be struck with wonder. Ⓐ ～を吐く be appalled by *sth*; be disgusted with *sth*; Ⓘ be fed up with *sth*. Ⓐ ～を引く hold one's tongue; fall silent; Ⓢ shut up. Ⓐ ～を翻す be struck dumb; be astonished; be flabbergasted; Ⓢ Ⓘ be blown away. Ⓐ ～を振る be terrified; Ⓘ be scared out of one's wits. ～を振う ❶ speak fluently; make an eloquent speech. ❷ be talkative; Ⓔ be loquacious; Ⓒ be a chatterbox; Ⓘ talk people's head off. ❸ be terrified; Ⓘ be scared out of one's

し

wits. ～を巻く ❶ be silenced; fall silent. ❷ be dumfounded; marvel at *sth*; Ⓢ Ⓘ be blown away. ～を見るexamine *sb's* tongue.

事端（じたん） [E] **the origin of an affair**

[を] Ⓔ ～を構えるfind a pretext for a deed. ◎ Ⓔ ～を繁くするgive rise to complications; stir up troubles.

質（しち） **quality; nature; matter** ▶質（しつ）

[が] ～が良いbe of good quality. ～が流れるforfeit a pawn. ～が悪いbe of bad quality.

[を] ～を落とすreduce the quality of *sth*; Ⓔ debase the quality of *sth*. ～を下げるdebase the quality of *sth*.

死地（しち） [E] **the jaws of death**

[を] ～に追い込む drive *sb* into a corner; corner *sb*. ～に陥る be driven into a corner; Ⓒ Ⓘ get into a scrap; Ⓒ Ⓘ be up the creek. Ⓔ ～に赴く face certain destruction; Ⓘ throw oneself into the jaws of death; Ⓘ burn one's boats/bridges (behind one).

[を] ～を求める face death; Ⓔ look death in the face; court destruction.

質（しつ） **a pawn; a pledge** ▶質（しち）

[が] ～が流れるforfeit a pawn.

[に] ～に入れる give *sth* in pledge; give *sth* as collateral; pawn *sth*; Ⓒ give *sth* in hock. ～に置く ❶ offer *sb* as a hostage; leave *sb* as a hostage. ❷ give *sth* as collateral; give *sth* in pledge; pawn *sth*; Ⓒ give *sth* in hock. ～に取る ❶ accept *sth* in pledge; take *sth* in pawn. ❷ take a hostage; hold *sb* hostage.

[を] Ⓐ ～を受ける pay off one's pledge. ～を置く give *sth* as collateral; give *sth* in pledge; pawn *sth*; Ⓒ give *sth* in hock. ～を埋める give *sth* as collateral; give *sth* in pledge; pawn *sth*; Ⓒ give *sth* in hock. ～を流すforfeit a pawn.

実（じつ） **the truth; the fruit** ▶実（み）

[を] ～を明かす reveal the truth; expose the truth. ～を挙げるbring *sth* to fruition; realize a goal; achieve an aim; live up to one's principles. ～を言う speak the truth. ◎ ～を立てる keep faith with *sb*. ◎ ～を尽くすbe truthful; act sincerely toward *sb*; show fidelity toward *sb*. ◎ ～を告げる tell *sb* how things stand; undeceive *sb*. ◎ ～を吐く confess the truth; Ⓒ own up to the truth.

失言（しつげん） **a slip of the tongue**

[を] ～をする Ⓘ make a slip of the tongue; Ⓘ let *sth* fall/slip; Ⓒ blurt *sth* out. ～を取り消す take back what one has said; Ⓒ eat one's words. ～を詰る reproach *sb* (for their indiscretions); scold *sb*; Ⓒ tell *sb* off ～を詫びる apologize for one's indiscretions.

失策（しっさく） **a blunder; a mistake**

[を] ～を演じる commit a blunder; make a mistake; Ⓒ Ⓘ drop the ball.

尻尾 a tail; the end; the tip

〔が〕Ⓐ ～が裂ける be bewitched by *sb/sth*; be under *sb's* spell. ～が出る betray oneself; reveal one's true character; Ⓘ reveal one's true colors; Ⓘ show the cloven hoof.

〔に〕～に着く queue up; join a queue.

〔を〕Ⓐ ～を嗅がれる be caught out; be exposed; be found out. ～を切る take a percentage; Ⓒ take a rake-off. ～を出す betray oneself; reveal one's true character; Ⓘ reveal one's true colors; Ⓘ show the cloven hoof. ～を掴む ❶ obtain evidence; uncover a scandal. ❷ find fault with *sb*; catch *sb* out. ～を振る ❶ wag its tail. ❷ ingratiate oneself with *sb*; Ⓘ curry favor with *sb*. ～を巻く acknowledge one's inferiority; beat a retreat; Ⓢ Ⓘ hightail it. ～を見せる betray oneself; reveal one's true character; Ⓘ reveal one's true colors; Ⓘ show the cloven hoof.

質問 a question; a query

〔に〕～に応ずる respond to a question. ～に答える answer a question; reply to a question.

〔を〕～を受ける be questioned; answer a question; Ⓒ take a question. ～を受け流す turn a question aside; Ⓒ parry a question. ～を打ち切る bring an interview to a close; put an end to the questioning. ～を逸らす turn a question aside; Ⓒ parry a question. ～を放つ fire questions at *sb*; Ⓒ hurl questions at *sb*. ～を向ける address a question to *sb*; put a question to *sb*.

指導 guidance; leadership

〔を〕～を与える give *sb* guidance. ～を誤る lead *sb* amiss. (人の)～を受ける receive guidance. (人の)～を求める turn to *sb* for guidance.

品 a thing; quality; coquetry♪ 品

〔が〕Ⓞ ～が落ちる be inferior in quality; be cheap; Ⓘ be below par. ～が劣る be inferior in quality; be cheap. ～が切れる run out of stock. Ⓒ ～がだぶつく there is glut in the market; be overabundant. ～が違う be different in quality.

〔を〕～を落とす reduce the quality of *sth*; Ⓔ debase the quality of *sth*. ～を作る behave coquettishly; play the coquette; give oneself airs; Ⓘ put on airs; Ⓢ Ⓘ be stuck-up. ～を付ける ❶ find a pretext; Ⓔ assign a reason for *sth*; make an excuse. ❷ behave coquettishly; give oneself airs; play the coquette; Ⓘ put on airs; Ⓢ Ⓘ be stuck-up. Ⓐ ～を踏む gather experience; make headway. Ⓐ ～を遣る behave coquettishly; play the coquette; Ⓘ put on airs.

鎬 Ⓗ ridges on a sword blade

〔を〕Ⓒ ～を削る fight desperately; engage in a fierce competition; fight to the death.

芝居 a play; a drama; a fake

〔を〕～を演じる perform a play;

し

enact a scene. ～を打つ ❶ stage a play; play a piece. ❷ play a trick on *sb*; Ⓢ put *sb* on; Ⓘ put up a false show. ～を見る see a play.

自腹(じばら) [S] **"one's own stomach"**
[を] Ⓢ ～を切る pay out of one's own pocket; Ⓐ untie one's purse strings; Ⓘ foot the bill.

支払い(しはらい) **payment; disbursement**
[を] ～を受ける receive payment. ～を断る refuse payment. ～を迫る press *sb* for payment. ～を停止する suspend payment; stop a check. ～を延ばす postpone payment.

地盤(じばん) **the ground; the base**
[を] ～を得る gain a foothold. ～を固める solidify the foundation. (市場に)～を築き上げる get a footing (in a market). ～を築く lay the foundation; establish a constituency. ～を造る prepare the ground. ～を作る establish a foothold. ～を取り戻す recover one's footing; regain one's foothold. (地方に)～を持つ have a foothold in (a district). ～を養う nurse one's constituency.

慈悲(じひ) **mercy; charity; pity**
[を] ～を掛ける do an act of charity; show mercy (to *sb*). ～を請う beg for mercy; plea for mercy. Ⓐ ～を垂れる have mercy on *sb*.

痺れ(しびれ) **a cramp; numbness**
[を] ～を切らす ❶ have a cramp. ❷ lose one's patience; grow impatient; Ⓒ get tired of waiting.

時分(じぶん) **time; hour; season**
[を] ～を窺う watch for a (good) moment; look for an opportunity; Ⓔ bide one's time.

辞柄(じへい) [E] **a pretext; an excuse**
[を] Ⓔ ～を設ける find an excuse; give a pretext; make excuses.

資本(しほん) **a capital; a fund**
[を] Ⓞ ～を下ろす lay out capital (in a venture); put in capital. ～を出す provide capital; finance (an enterprise). ～を投じる invest capital (in). ～を寝かせる let capital lie idle.

始末(しまつ) **circumstances; settlement**
[に] ～に困る be hard to deal with.
[を] ～を付ける settle one's accounts; do away with *sth*.

死命(しめい) [E] **life and death; fate**
[を] Ⓔ (人の)～を制する have a hold upon *sb*; have *sb* in one's power.

締め括り(しめくくり) **control; conclusion**
[を] ～を付ける round (a matter) off; settle (an affair); put an end to *sth*; bring *sth* to a close. Ⓞ ～を遣る control (a department); supervise (an activity).

奢侈(しゃし) [E] **luxury; extravagance**
[に] ～に流れる fall into luxurious

habits. 〜に耽る indulge in luxury.
［を］〜を戒める admonish against luxurious living.

視野 one's field of vision
［に］〜に入る come into view; come in sight.
［を］〜を去る go out of sight. 〜を広げる broaden one's outlook; widen one's mental/intellectual horizon.

邪気 malarial air; malice
［を］〜を払う purge noxious vapors.

癪 spasms; convulsions
［が］Ⓐ 〜が上る have a spasm; suffer a fit; have convulsions.
［に］〜に障る be offended; feel vexed; take offense; Ⓘ go against the grain.
［を］Ⓐ 〜を言う say offensive things; hurt *sb's* feelings; upset *sb*.

尺 a *shaku* (0.9 ft.); a measure
［を］Ⓞ 〜を打つ measure the length of *sth*; take *sb's* measurements. 〜を取る measure the length of *sth*; take *sb's* measurements.

酌 serving sake at a table
［を］〜をする pour sake into *sb's* cup; help *sb* to sake; serve sake. Ⓞ 〜を取る pour sake into *sb's* cup; help *sb* to sake; serve sake.

錫 Ⓗ a priest's staff
［を］Ⓐ Ⓔ 〜を飛ばす travel on foot; go on a pilgrimage; Ⓒ hit the road.

弱点 a weak point; a defect
［に］(人の)〜に触れる touch *sb* on a sore spot; Ⓒ hit *sb's* Achilles heel; Ⓘ touch *sb* on the raw. Ⓔ (人の)〜に乗ずる take advantage of *sb's* weak point.
［を］〜を暴く expose a defect. 〜を突く strike (the enemy) at a weak point; Ⓒ hit where it hurts; Ⓔ hit *sb's* Achilles heel. 〜を握られる Ⓘ give a handle (to the enemy). 〜を見抜く see *sb's* weak points; Ⓔ find *sb's* Achilles heel; Ⓘ get the length of *sb's* foot. 〜を持つ have a weak point; have a flaw; Ⓔ have an Achilles heel.

邪慳 cruelty; hardheartedness
［に］〜にする be hard on *sb*; be cruel to *sb*; treat *sb* with cruelty.

邪魔 a hindrance; cumbersome
［に］〜になる be in *sb's* way; be a hindrance; stand in the way.
［を］〜をする disturb *sb*; interrupt *sb*; thwart *sb's* plans.

邪念 an evil thought; malice
［が］〜が有る have wicked thoughts.
［に］〜に耽る indulge in wicked thoughts.
［を］〜を払う free oneself of evil thoughts.

朱 Ⓔ cinnabar; vermilion ◆朱
［に］Ⓔ 〜に交わる associate with the wrong people; keep bad company.
［を］Ⓔ 〜を入れる red-pencil *sth*;

し

95

correct *sth*. ⓐ ⓔ 〜を雪ぐ go purple
with rage; be flushed with rage.

綬 ⊞ a ribbon (of office)
を ⓜ ⓔ 〜を釈く step down from
office; ⓔ retire from public office;
leave government service. ⓜ ⓔ 〜
を結ぶ take up public office.

銃 a rifle; a gun; arms
を 〜を担ぎ変える change arms.
〜を構える hold a rifle at the
ready. 〜を組む stack arms. 〜を捧
げる present arms. 〜を解く
unstack arms. 〜を担う shoulder a
rifle. 〜を向ける point a gun at *sb*.

自由 liberty; freedom
に 〔人を〕〜にする ❶ set *sb* free;
liberate *sb*. ❷ have one's will with
sb; ⓘ wrap *sb* round one's little finger. ❸ deceive *sb*; ⓘ take *sb* in;
ⓒ ⓘ lead *sb* by the nose. 〔人の〕〜
になる be at *sb's* beck and call; be
at *sb's* disposal; be at *sb's* mercy;
be at *sb's* will.
を 〜を与える set *sb* free; give *sb*
liberty. 〜を失う lose one's
freedom; ⓔ be robbed of one's liberty. 〜を得る gain one's liberty.
〜を尊ぶ value liberty; ⓔ hold
freedom dear; prize freedom.

銃火 rifle fire; musket fire
を 〜を冒す brave enemy fire. 〜
を浴びる come under fire. 〜を交
える exchange fire; fight a battle;
ⓔ engage an enemy.

習慣 a custom; usage; habit
が 〜が有る have a habit/custom.
〜が付く pick up a habit; take to a
habit; ⓔ acquire a custom.
に 〜に従う stick to one's habit.
を 〜を捨てる abandon a usage; do
away with custom; break off a
habit; discard a custom. 〜を付け
る form a habit; ⓔ cultivate a custom. 〜を取り入れる adopt a
custom; take over a habit. 〜を直
す mend a habit; change a custom.
〜を発する abolish a custom;
ⓔ abrogate a custom. 〜を守る
observe an old custom; adhere to
old customs; ⓒ stick to old habits.

銃口 the muzzle of a rifle
を 〜を向ける level a gun at *sb*;
point a rifle at *sb*; hold a gun on *sb*.

十字 a cross
を 〜を切る cross oneself; cross
one's heart. ⓜ 〜を引く cross out
(a word).

十字架 a crucifix; a cross
に 〜に懸ける crucify *sb*.
を 〜を背負う bear one's cross;
carry a cross.

十字路 a crossroads
に 〜に立つ stand at a crossroads;
be at a crossroads.

主義 a principle; a cause
に 〜にこだわる stick to one's principles; ⓘ stick to one's guns. 〜に

殉じる　die for one's principles; sacrifice oneself for a cause.

を ～を捨てる　give up a cause; abandon one's principles. ～を曲げる　compromise one's principles. ～を守る　defend a cause; live up to one's principles; ① stick to one's guns.

授業 teaching; class; a session

に ～に出る　attend lessons; go to school.

を ～を受ける　take lessons; be taught; receive instruction. ◎ ～をサボる　dodge a lesson; play truant. ～を休む　miss a lesson; stay away from a lesson.

手段 a means; a measure; a way

が ～が尽きる　be at the end of one's resources; ① be at the end of one's tether; ① be at one's wits' end.

を ～を誤る　Ⓐ take a wrong step; use the wrong methods; go astray. ～を選ばず　try all possible means; stop at nothing. ～を講じる　devise a means; work out a way. ～を尽くす　leave no means untried; try every means; ① leave no stone unturned. ～を取る　take measures; resort to (certain) means.

術計 Ⓐ a ploy; a ruse; a scheme

が ◎ ～が尽きる　pass away; reach the end of one's life; Ⓔ ① breathe one's last.

に ◎ ～に陥る　become the victim of a plot; Ⓐ fall into a trap.

寿命 one's span of life

を ～を縮める　shorten one's span of life. ～を延ばす　lengthen one's span of life.

順 order; a turn

が ～が来る　be next in line; one's turn comes round. ～が狂う　be out of order.

に ～に送る　pass sth on. ～に並ぶ　stand in order. ～に並べる　put sth in order. ～に回す　pass sth around. ◎ ～に遣る　take one's turn.

を ～を追う　go in order; do sth in sequence. ～を変える　change the order. ～を繰り上げる　move up in order. ～を狂わす　put sth out of order. ～を待つ　await one's turn.

順序 order; sequence

が ～が違う　be out of order; be inappropriate.

に ～に従う　go in order; do sth in sequence.

を ～を誤る　follow the wrong order. ～を狂わす　upset the order; disturb the order; put sth out of order. ～を立てる　put sth in order. ～を整える　adjust the order. ～を踏む　follow procedures; Ⓒ go through due formalities. ～を乱す　disturb the order; put sth out of order.

順番 order; turn; rotation

に ～に働く　work in shifts; take turns.

を ～を狂わす　upset the order; put sth out of order. ～を待つ　await

one's turn. ～を守る keep one's turn; observe the order.

賞（しょう） a prize; a reward

[を] ～を与える bestow a reward on *sb*; award a prize to *sb*; give *sb* a reward. ～を争う compete for a prize (with *sb*). ～を受ける receive a prize. ～を懸ける offer a prize (for *sth*); (人の首に) put a price on (*sb's* head). ～を攫う carry off an award. ～を取る win an award.

性（しょう） nature; disposition

[が] ～が合う ❶ have the same temperament. ❷ have the same social standing. ◎ ～が付く be steady; be resolved; be firm. ～が抜ける become feeble-minded; lose vigor.

[に] ～に合う agree with one; come natural to one; Ⓔ be congenial to one.

掌（しょう） [E] the palm of the hand ➧ 掌（てのひら）

[を] ～を返す ❶ be easy (to do); be simple (to understand). ❷ be fickle; be inconstant; be changeable. ～を指す be clear; be apparent.

情（じょう） feelings; sentiments

[が] ～が有る have a kind heart. ～が薄い be unfeeling; be heartless; hardhearted; be coldhearted. ～が移る become attached to *sb*; begin to love *sb*. ～が強い be headstrong; be obstinate; be stiff-necked. Ⓐ ～が張る refuse to give in; be obstinate; be stubborn. ～が深い ❶ be warmhearted; be kindhearted. ❷ have a passionate disposition; © be a great lover.

[に] Ⓐ ～に入れる apply oneself to; do *sth* in earnest. ～に脆い have a tender heart; be sentimental; © have a soft spot.

[を] ◎ ～を明かす confide in *sb*; tell things as they are. ～を売る prostitute oneself; Ⓔ sell one's favors. ◎ (人の)～を起こす affect *sb's* emotions; touch *sb's* heart. ～を覚える be swayed by emotions; feel (a surge of) passion. ～を交わす have sexual intercourse; sleep with each other. ～を込める sympathize with *sb*; empathize with *sb*; feel for *sb*. ～を立てる be faithful to *sb*. ◎ ～を矯める repress one's desires; restrain one's passions. (人と)～を通じる ❶ have an affair (with *sb*); Ⓢ carry on with *sb*. ❷ make secret overtures (to the enemy). ～を張る refuse to give in; be obstinate; be stubborn. ～を燃やす burn with love (for *sb*); lust after *sb*. (人の)～を催す affect *sb's* emotions; touch *sb's* heart. ～を寄せる make overtures to *sb*.

錠（じょう） a padlock; a snaplock

[が] ～が下りる ❶ (the door) locks. ❷ be settled; be brought to an end. ～が掛かる (the door) locks.

[を] ～を開ける remove a lock; unlock (a door). ～を下ろす ❶ fasten a lock; lock (a door). ❷ grow stubborn; become set in one's ways. ～を掛ける fasten a lock; lock (a door). ◎ ～を狂わす hamper a lock; meddle with a lock. ～を抉じ開ける prize open a lock; force a lock. ～を付ける put a lock on (a door). ～を捩じ切る prize open a lock; force a lock. ～を外す remove a lock; unlock (a door).

障害（しょうがい） **an obstacle; a barrier**
[と] ～と成る become an obstacle.
[に] ～に遭う meet with difficulties; run into difficulties; [C] [I] hit a snag. ～に打ち勝つ overcome an obstacle. ～に成る be an obstacle. ～にぶつかる encounter an obstacle; [C] [I] hit a snag.
[を] ～を築く build a barrier; erect a barrier. ～を飛び越える [sports] clear a hurdle. ～を乗り越える overcome an obstacle; surmount difficulties.

正気（しょうき） **consciousness; sanity**
[に] ～に返る recover one's sanity; come to oneself; come to one's senses.
[を] ～を失う ❶ lose consciousness; pass out; [C] black out. ❷ lose one's senses; go mad; [S] [I] lose one's marbles; [S] go crazy.

衝撃（しょうげき） **a shock; an impact**
[を] ～を与える give *sb*/*sth* a shock. ～を受ける receive a shock.

情交（じょうこう） **friendship; liaison**
[を] ～を迫る force attentions upon *sb*. ～を結ぶ keep company with *sb*; become intimate with *sb*; have a relationship with *sb*.

情実（じょうじつ） **personal considerations**
[を] ～を排する set aside personal considerations.

消息（しょうそく） **news; word; a letter**
[を] ～を聞く hear of *sb*; get news of *sb*. ～を伝える bear news of *sb*.

承諾（しょうだく） **consent; acceptance**
[を] ～を与える give one's consent. ～を得る obtain *sb's* consent.

常道（じょうどう） [E] **the beaten track**
[を] ◎ [E] ～を辿る follow the beaten track. ～を踏み外す stray from the beaten track; get out of compass.

性根（しょうね） **nature; disposition**
[が] ～が腐る be corrupted; be depraved. ～が付く ❶ come to one's senses; come to oneself; be oneself again. ❷ be penitent; mend one's ways; [I] return to the straight and narrow; [I] turn over a new leaf. ～が曲がる have a warped mind; be corrupted; be depraved.
[に] ◎ ～に返る recover one's sanity; come to oneself; come to one's senses.
[を] ～を入れ換える mend one's ways; [I] turn over a new leaf. ◎ ～を失う ❶ lose consciousness; pass out; [C] black out. ❷ lose one's senses; go mad; [S] go crazy; [S] [I] lose

one's marbles. ⑩ 〜を奪う drive *sb* mad; ⓔ rob *sb* of his/her senses; corrupt *sb's* mind. 〜を定める make up one's mind; decide to do *sth*; resolve to do *sth*. 〜を叩き直す straighten *sb* out; set *sb* right. Ⓐ 〜を付ける ❶ pluck up courage; brace oneself; become emboldened. ❷ bring *sb* round to his/her senses.

錠前 a lock

を 〜を開ける remove a lock; unlock (a door). 〜を下ろす fasten a lock; lock (a door). 〜を掛ける fasten a lock; lock (a door). 〜を狂わす hamper a lock; meddle with a lock. 〜を抉じ開ける prize open a lock; force a lock. 〜を付ける put a lock on *sth*. 〜を捩じ切る prize open a lock; force a lock. 〜を外す remove a lock; unlock (a door).

将来 the future (prospects)

に 〜に備える prepare for the future.

を 〜を戒める warn for the future. 〜を考える have the future in mind; think of the future. ⓔ 〜を卜する predict the future; see into the future; tell *sb's* fortune.

勝利 victory; triumph

を 〜を得る gain a victory. 〜を収める gain victory; ① gain the upper hand. 〜を占める gain a victory; be victorious. 〜を誇る boast of victory; revel in one's success; ⓔ glory in victory; ⓒ ① blow one's own horn (trumpet).

条例 a usage; a custom

に 〜に従う follow precedent; do *sth* in the conventional way. 〜に背く be contrary to custom; ① go against the grain.

私欲 selfish desires

に 〜に走る pursue one's selfish desires.

を 〜を離れる rise above one's selfish desires. 〜を満たす gratify one's selfish desires.

職 work; a post; a calling

に 〜に就く take employment; get a job. 〜に留まる remain in office; stay in a job.

を 〜を与える employ *sb*; give *sb* employment; hire *sb*. 〜を失う be dismissed; lose one's job; ⓢ ① get the sack. 〜を得る obtain a position; secure employment; get a job. ⑩ 〜を覚える learn a trade. 〜を代える change one's job; switch jobs. 〜を探す seek employment; look for a job. ⑩ 〜を仕込む teach *sb* a trade. ⓔ 〜を辞する resign one's office; tender one's resignation; leave one's job. 〜を解かれる be dismissed from one's post. 〜を投げ打つ resign from office; leave one's post. 〜を奉ずる hold office. 〜を辞める resign one's office; leave one's job. ⑩ 〜を汚す abuse one's position.

食 <small>しょく</small> a meal; food; appetite

[が] ～が進<small>すす</small>む have a good appetite.

食欲 <small>しょくよく</small> appetite

[を] ～を失<small>うしな</small>う lose one's appetite. ～をそそる excite one's appetite. ～を殺<small>そ</small>ぐ dull one's appetite.

助言 <small>じょげん</small> advice; counsel

[を] ～を得<small>え</small>る get counsel from *sb*. ～を求<small>もと</small>める seek *sb's* counsel; ask for *sb's* advice.

女色 <small>じょしょく</small> Ⓔ feminine charms

[に] Ⓔ～に耽<small>ふけ</small>る indulge in lewdness; Ⓔ be given up to amours. Ⓔ～に迷<small>まよ</small>う be infatuated with a woman; Ⓔ be enamored of a woman.

[を] Ⓔ～を好<small>この</small>む be lascivious; be licentious. Ⓞ Ⓔ～を近付<small>ちかづ</small>ける keep company with woman; Ⓔ have commerce with women.

処置 <small>しょち</small> a measure; disposition

[に] ～に窮<small>きゅう</small>する be at a loss; Ⓘ be at one's wits' end; Ⓘ be all at sea.

[を] ～を誤<small>あやま</small>る take the wrong measures; make an error. ～を得<small>え</small>る reach a solution; solve (a matter). ～を取<small>と</small>る take measures; deal with *sth*; Ⓔ use one's discretion.

助力 <small>じょりょく</small> help; aid; assistance

[を] ～を仰<small>あお</small>ぐ ask for help; seek aid; Ⓔ turn to *sb* for assistance. ～を得<small>え</small>る receive assistance; get help. ～を求<small>もと</small>める seek *sb's* assistance; ask for *sb's* help.

白 <small>しら</small> white; blank

[を] ～を切<small>き</small>る pretend not to know; feign ignorance; Ⓘ play the innocent.

尻 <small>しり</small> the rear; the buttocks; the hips

[が] Ⓐ ～が有<small>あ</small>る have long-term consequences. Ⓒ～が暖<small>あたた</small>まる stay on; linger behind (at a place). Ⓒ～が重<small>おも</small>い be lazy; Ⓔ be indolent; be slow; Ⓘ drag one's heels. Ⓒ～が軽<small>かる</small>い ❶ be quick; be nimble. ❷ act light-heartedly; Ⓒ be flighty. Ⓥ Ⓢ❸ be promiscuous; have loose morals; Ⓔ be wanton; Ⓒ sleep around; Ⓒ Ⓘ put oneself about. ～が切<small>き</small>れる stop *sth* midway; leave *sth* unfinished. Ⓐ ～が来<small>く</small>る be complained about; Ⓔ have a complaint lodged against one. Ⓐ Ⓒ～が肥<small>こ</small>える shirk one's duties; be lazy; be impudent. Ⓐ Ⓒ～がこそばゆい be ill at ease; have a guilty conscience; feel awkward. Ⓒ～が据<small>す</small>わる Ⓐ be glued to a spot; Ⓒ stay put; Ⓘ stick it out. Ⓐ ～が出<small>で</small>る be complained about; Ⓔ have a complaint lodged against one. Ⓒ～が長<small>なが</small>い outstay one's welcome; stay too long. Ⓒ～が抜<small>ぬ</small>ける be slothful; be forgetful; Ⓒ be sloppy. Ⓐ ～が剥<small>は</small>げる be exposed; be found out. Ⓐ ～が早<small>はや</small>い ❶ be quick to boil. Ⓥ Ⓢ❷ be promiscuous; have loose morals; Ⓔ be wanton; Ⓒ sleep around. Ⓒ Ⓘ put oneself about. Ⓐ Ⓒ～が破<small>やぶ</small>れる be exposed; be found out. Ⓐ Ⓒ～が揉<small>も</small>める have

し

troubles; be troubled (by *sth*); have a dispute. ⓞ ⓢ ～が割れる be exposed; be found out.

に ⓞ (妻の)～に敷かれる be dominated by one's wife; ① be tied to one's wife's apron strings; ⓒ ① be henpecked. ⓐ ⓒ ～に聞かす listen without interest; pay little attention; pass over *sth*. ⓐ ～に立つ ❶ follow *sb* closely; ① breathe down *sb's* neck. ❷ accompany *sb* through life. ⓒ ～に付く ❶ follow on *sb's* heels; ① breathe down *sb's* neck. ⓒ ❷ imitate *sb*; copycat *sb*. ⓥ ⓢ ～に挟む ignore *sb*; make light of *sth*; ① close one's eyes to *sth*.

を ⓒ ～を上げる ❶ get up; stand up; rise up. ❷ speak with a rising intonation. ⓒ ～を暖める ❶ warm one's buttocks. ❷ remain in the same position (for a long time); hold a post (for many years). ⓒ (女の)～を追い回す dangle after a girl; chase a girl. ⓒ (人の)～を押す ❶ give *sb* assistance. ❷ encourage *sb*; egg *sb* on; ⓒ ① fire *sb* up. ❸ abet *sb* in a crime. ⓒ ～を落ち着ける make oneself at home; linger behind (at a place). ⓒ ～を掛ける ❶ sit oneself down; take a seat. ❷ cause *sb* trouble; leave a problem for *sb* else (to settle). ～を絡げる tuck one's *kimono* (into one's *obi*). ⓐ ～を切る stop mid-sentence; check oneself; break off short. ⓐ ⓢ ～を食う set matters right; wind *sth* up; deal with the aftermath (of an affair). ⓐ ⓢ ～を

括る do *sth* with great care; stay concentrated (to the end). ⓒ ～を下げる ❶ sit down. ❷ speak with a falling intonation. ⓐ ⓒ ～を捌く set matters right; wind *sth* up; deal with the aftermath (of an affair). ⓒ ～を据える ❶ squat on one's haunches. ❷ settle down; resolve to do *sth*; ⓒ buckle down. ⓒ (人の)～を叩く encourage *sb*; egg *sb* on; ⓒ ① fire *sb* up. ⓐ ⓒ ～を溜める make oneself at home. ⓐ ⓒ ～を突く press *sb* to settle an affair; demand that *sb* clear their debts. ⓞ ⓢ (人の)～を拭う bear *sb's* burden; bear the consequences of *sb's* error; pay off *sb's* debt; ⓐ clean up *sb's* mess. ⓞ ⓢ (人の)～を剥ぐ bring *sth* to light; expose *sb*. ～を端折る ❶ tuck one's *kimono* (into one's *obi*). ❷ cut short (one's stay); abridge (a story). ⓒ ～を引く remain unsettled; remain unresolved. ⓒ ～を振る swing one's hips; wag one's behind. ⓒ ～を捲る assume a defiant attitude. ⓒ ～を向ける turn one's back on *sb*; ① give *sb* the cold shoulder. ⓐ ～を結ぶ finish *sth* off; put an end to *sth*; bring a matter to a (satisfactory) close. ⓒ ～を持ち込む complain about *sb*; ⓔ lodge a complaint; seek a settlement. ⓐ ⓢ (人の)～を割る bring *sth* to light; expose *sb*.

私利 ⒠ self-interest

を ～を計る look to one's own interests; be self-seeking; ⓒ ① look after number one; ⓘ feather one's own nest.

自利 Ⓔ one's own interest
名 ⓔ ～を図る be self-seeking; ⓒ consult one's own interests; ⓘ look after number one.

事理 Ⓔ reason; facts; propriety
名 ⓔ ～を弁える be sensible; have good sense; listen to reason.

尻馬 a byrider on a horse
に ～に乗る go along with *sb's* ideas; ⓘ climb onto the bandwagon; ⓘ ride on *sb's* coattails.

時流 Ⓔ the current of the times
に ⓔ ～に阿る ⓘ curry favor with (the public). ⓔ ～に逆らう be out of tune with the times; go against the stream. ⓔ ～に従う go along with the current; follow the fashion of the day; ⓘ climb onto the bandwagon. ⓔ ～に投じる catch the public fancy. ⓔ ～に乗る go with the times; be trendy.
名 ⓔ ～を追う pursue the fashion of the day; follow the latest fad.

信 faith; fidelity; trust; truth
名 ⓞ ⓔ ～を致す have a deep faith; deeply believe. ～を失う lose *sb's* confidence; lose credit. ～を得る gain *sb's* confidence; get credit; enjoy *sb's* trust. ～を置く rely upon *sb*; put confidence in *sb/sth*; give credence to *sb/sth*; ⓔ repose trust

in *sb/sth*. Ⓐ ～を取る ❶ take *sth* to be true; accept *sth* as true. ❷ gain *sb's* trust; win *sb's* confidence; uphold *sb's* trust. Ⓐ ～を為す ❶ take *sth* to be true; trust in *sth*; put one's faith in *sb/sth*; place reliance on *sb/sth*. ❷ deepen one's faith; strengthen one's belief.

心 heart; mind, soul; core ▸ 心
が ～が腐る ❶ ⓒ have a rotten core. ❷ Ⓐ be rotten at the core; be corrupted; have a warped nature. ～が疲れる suffer from nervous stress; be mentally fatigued; be sapped of vitality.
名 ～を入れる line a coat; pad a sash. ～を切る snuff a candle; trim a wick. ～を出す turn up the wick; screw up a lamp. ⓒ ～を止める top a tree; make a pollard. ～を取る core (an apple).

真 Ⓔ truth; genuineness ▸ 真
に ⓔ ～に迫る be lifelike; be true to nature.
名 ⓒ ～を保つ stay lifelike; remain true to nature.

神 god; spirit; divinity ▸ 神
に ～に入る reach a superior level of attainment (in an art); have divine skills.

寝 a bed; a bedstead; a birth
に ～に着く go to bed; turn in for the night; ⓔ retire to rest; ⓒ ⓘ hit the hay.

紳 ⊞ a wide sash (of office)
　⃝ に ◎ ⓔ 〜に書す keep *sth* in mind; ⓔ commit *sth* to memory; make a mental note of *sth*.

陣 a camp; quarters
　⃝ を 〜を固める close the ranks. 〜を構える pitch a camp; take up a position; encamp (for battle). 〜を敷く pitch a camp; take up a position; encamp (for battle). 〜を撤去する break camp. 〜を取る pitch a camp; take up a position; occupy a place; seize a position. 〜を張る pitch a camp; take up a position.

塵界 ⓔ the dusty world
　⃝ を ⓔ 〜を脱する ❶ escape from the madding crowd; get away from the hustle and bustle of the world. ❷ go into seclusion; become a hermit; renounce the world; ⓒ retire from the world. ❸ become a Buddhist priest; take the tonsure; ⓒ retire into religion.

仁義 humanity and justice
　⃝ を 〜を切る greet a fellow *yakuza*. 〜を通す do what is right; ① stick to the straight and narrow. 〜を守る do what is right; ① stick to the straight and narrow.

神経 a nerve; nerves
　⃝ が 〜が高ぶる become nervous; become excited; be on edge.
　⃝ に 〜に堪える be a strain on one's nerves. 〜に触る grate on one's nerves; wear one down.
　⃝ を 〜を苛立たせる set one's nerves on edge; get on one's nerves; jar *sb's* nerves. ◎ 〜を起こす get excited; become nervous. 〜を静める soothe one's nerves. 〜を摩り減らす grate on one's nerves; wear one down. 〜を疲らせる exhaust one's nerves. 〜を尖らす set one's nerves on edge. ◎ 〜を悩ます worry about *sth*; fret over *sth*. 〜を抜く ① extract a nerve.

信仰 (religious) faith; belief
　⃝ に 〜に殉じる be a martyr for one's faith. 〜に入る find faith.
　⃝ を 〜を固める strengthen one's faith. 〜を実践する practice one's faith. 〜を捨てる forsake one's faith; renounce one's beliefs. 〜を深める deepen one's faith.

親交 friendship; intimacy
　⃝ を 〜を得る win *sb's* friendship. 〜を図る promote friendly relations. 〜を断つ break off one's friendship with *sb*; ⓒ sever connections with *sb*. 〜を結ぶ cultivate a friendship with *sb*; make friends with *sb*.

辛酸 ⓔ hardships; privations
　⃝ が ◎ ⓔ 〜が滲む experience the hardships of life; ⓒ suffer life's vicissitudes.
　⃝ を 〜を嘗める go through a lot of hardships; suffer all sorts of privations; ⓒ suffer life's vicissitudes.

人心 じんしん E people's hearts
を © ～を収める win the hears of the people. © ～を静める appease the people. © ～を惑わす mislead the public.

身代 しんだい one's property
を ～を継ぐ inherit *sb's* property; come into a fortune. ～を潰す lose one's property; © dissipate one's fortune; go bankrupt; © go bust. ～を減らす damage one's fortune.

診断 しんだん a diagnosis; diagnostication
を ～を誤る make a wrong diagnosis. ～を受ける have one's case diagnosed. ～を下す give a diagnosis.

陣頭 じんとう the head of an army
に ～に立つ be at the head of an army; lead the vanguard; © be in the front van.

人道 じんどう E humanity
に © ～に背く be inhumane; go against humanity; be cruel. © ～に悖る go against humanity; be inhumane; be cruel.

心配 しんぱい anxiety; worry
を ～を掛ける cause *sb* to worry. © ～を去る relieve *sb's* anxiety.

進歩 しんぽ progress; improvement
を ～を妨げる hinder progress. ～を遂げる make progress. ～を見せる show progress.

陣容 じんよう battle array; a lineup
を ～を立て直す ❶ close ranks. ❷ reshuffle (a cabinet) ～を整える marshal an army; array the formation of troops; get ready for battle; © clear the decks.

人倫 じんりん E humanity; morality
に © ～に背く go against humanity; transgress morality; be inhumane.

信頼 しんらい trust; reliance; faith
に ～に値する deserve *sb's* trust; © be worthy of *sb's* trust. ～に答える be reliable; be trustworthy; © prove oneself worthy of *sb's* trust. ～に背く betray *sb's* trust; © let *sb* down.
を ～を失う lose *sb's* trust. ～を裏切る betray *sb's* trust. ～を得る win *sb's* trust; gain *sb's* confidence. ～を置く put one's trust (in *sb*).

針路 しんろ a course; a flight path
を ～を誤る take the wrong course. ～を定める set one's course. ～を取る take (a certain) course.

ス

図 ず a drawing; a picture; a map
が ⓐ ～が外れる go wrong; guess wrong; © get it wrong.
に ～に当たる go according to plan; prove a success; work out well. ～に乗る ❶ go according to plan;

prove a success; work out well.
❷ get carried away; be elated; get excited. ❸ be haughty; be puffed up; show off; ⓘ have airs and graces; ⓢ ⓘ be stuck-up.

[を] ⓐ 〜を失う be stupefied; be dumfounded; be struck dumb; ⓢ ⓘ be blown away. ⓐ 〜を抜かす ❶ miss an opportunity; let a chance slip by. ❷ relax the tension; ⓘ break the ice. ⓐ 〜を外す let a chance slip by; miss an opportunity. 〜を引く draw (up) a plan.

頭 Ⓔ the head; the brain ▸ 頭 ▸ 頭

[が] ⓔ 〜が高い be arrogant; be haughty; have an overbearing attitude; be proud.

衰運 declining fortune

[に] 〜に向かう begin to decline; go downhill; be on the wane.
[を] 〜を挽回する retrieve one's fortunes.

姿 a figure; a form; an aspect

[を] 〜を現わす show oneself; come into sight; make one's appearance. 〜を隠す hide oneself; cover one's traces. 〜を消す drop from view; fade away; ⓘ keep a low profile. 〜を窶す disguise oneself (as *sb*).

隙 an opening; a gap; a space

[に] 〜に乗じる take advantage of an unguarded moment; catch *sb* off guard.
[を] 〜を伺う seek an opening;

watch for an unguarded moment; try to catch *sb* off guard. 〜を狙う watch for an opportunity; ⓒ bide one's time. 〜を見せる lay oneself open to attack; ⓘ drop one's guard. 〜を見付ける find an opportunity (to attack).

救い rescue; relief; salvation

[が] 〜が無い be past saving; ⓔ be beyond redemption.
[を] ⓞ 〜に与る ❶ find relief; be saved. ❷ find salvation; ⓔ partake of salvation. 〜に行く go to *sb's* rescue; help *sb* in distress.
[を] 〜を見出す find salvation; be converted. 〜を求める ❶ ask for help; seek relief. ❷ seek salvation.

筋 a muscle; a fiber; logic

[が] ⓞ 〜が切れる make progress; get better. 〜が立つ be reasonable; be logical; stand to reason; be right. 〜が違う be unreasonable; do not stand to reason; be in the wrong. 〜が通る be reasonable; stand to reason; be right. 〜が良い have talent; have an aptitude; have a head for (figures). 〜が悪い ❶ have a bad nature; have a bad temperament. ❷ have little talent; lack artistic skill.
[を] ⓞ 〜を言う be argumentative; make a complaint; object to *sth*; find fault with *sb*; ⓘ split hairs. 〜を書く form a plan; have *sth* in mind. ⓐ 〜を出す lose one's temper; ⓒ ⓘ fly off the handle;

Ⓢ Ⓘ blow a fuse. ～を通（とお）す ❶ be steadfast; stick to one's principles; Ⓘ stick to one's guns. ❷ follow the correct procedures; go through the proper channels.

素性（すじょう） birth; lineage; origin

[が] ～が怪（あや）しい have no clear family background; have a shady lineage; have doubtful antecedents. ～が良（い）い be of good birth; come from a good family; Ⓔ be of gentle birth. ～が卑（いや）しい be lowborn; Ⓔ be of humble birth.

[を] ～を暴（あば）く disclose *sb's* identity; Ⓒ Ⓘ blow *sb's* cover. ～を隠（かく）す conceal one's identity; hide one's history. ～を調（しら）べる inquire into *sb's* background; Ⓒ check *sb* out; Ⓘ give *sb* the once over.

煤（すす） soot

[を] ～を払（はら）う sweep away soot; clean the house.

鈴（すず） a bell

[を] ～を鳴（な）らす ring a bell.

裾（すそ） the skirt; the cuffs; the base

[を] ◎ ～を掻（か）く ❶ trip *sb* up; sweep *sb's* legs from under him/her. ❷ outwit *sb*; cheat on *sb*. ～を絡（から）げる tuck in a skirt. ◎ ～をする clean the hoofs of a horse. ◎ ～を揃（そろ）える tidy one's hair. ◎ ～を遣（つか）う clean the hoofs of a horse. ～を曳（ひ）く trail the skirt (of a wedding dress). ～を捲（まく）る roll up the cuffs (of one's trousers). ～を持（も）つ hold up the train (of a wedding dress).

脛（すね） the leg; the shin; the shank

[が] ◎ ～が流（なが）れる lose out against *sb*; lose ground; give way; give in.

[に] ～に疵（きず）持（も）つ have a guilty conscience; Ⓔ feel the pangs of conscience.

[を] ◎ ～を掛（か）ける stay at (a place); make a stay (at a place). ～を齧（かじ）る live on *sb's* expenses; be dependent on *sb*; Ⓒ sponge on *sb*. ◎ ～を払（はら）う trip *sb* up; sweep *sb's* legs from under him/her. ◎ ～を拾（ひろ）う refrain from going somewhere.

住居（すまい） a dwelling; an abode

[を] ～を定（さだ）める take up one's abode; make (a place) one's home. ～を尋（たず）ねる ask for *sb's* address.

寸法（すんぽう） measurements; a plan

[に] ～に入（い）れる take *sth* into consideration; Ⓘ take *sth* on board. ～を取（と）る take a measurement.

図星（ずぼし） [S] the bull's-eye; the mark

[を] Ⓢ ～を指（さ）される have one's plans seen through; be exposed. Ⓢ ～を指（さ）す guess right; Ⓘ be on the mark; Ⓘ hit the nail on the head.

セ

背（せ） the back; the spine ➧ 背（せい）

[が] ～が高（たか）い be tall; be of great

stature. 〜が低い be short; be of small stature.

に 〜に負う carry *sth* on one's back; shoulder (a load). 〜にする ❶ carry *sth*; shoulder (a load); ❷ leave *sb/sth* behind. ❸ turn one's back toward *sth*; put one's back against *sth*.

を 〜を伸ばす straighten one's back. 〜を曲げる bend one's back. 〜を見せる turn one's back on *sb*. 〜を向ける reject *sb/sth*; ⓘ give *sb* the cold shoulder; ⓘ turn one's back on *sb/sth*. ⓐ 〜を縒る writhe in agony; be in agony.

瀬 a torrent; a rapid; a current
に 〜に乗り上げる run ashore; be grounded; ⓔ take the ground.
を 〜を下る descend a rapid. 〜を乗り切る pass a rapid. 〜を渡る ford a rapid.

精 spirit; vigor; vitality
に ⓞ 〜に入る pay attention to detail. 〜に入れる ❶ do *sth* with heart and soul; ⓘ put one's heart into *sth*. ❷ take pains over *sth*; fret over *sth*; ⓒ ⓘ rack one's brains.

を ⓞ 〜を入れる do *sth* with heart and soul; ⓘ put one's heart into *sth*; throw oneself into *sth* heart and soul. ⓞ 〜を落とす lose courage; be discouraged; be dejected; be disappointed; be frustrated. ⓞ 〜を切る breathe hard; gasp for breath. 〜を出す exert oneself; apply oneself (to one's work). ⓞ 〜を尽かす be

discouraged; be dejected; lose courage; be disappointed; be frustrated. 〜を付ける invigorate *sb*; tone *sb* up; cheer *sb* on. ⓞ 〜を励ます be devoted to *sth*; be enthusiastic about *sth*; do *sth* with zeal.

背 stature; height; tallness ▸ 背
が 〜が高い be tall; be of great stature. 〜が立つ be able to stand with one's head above water. 〜が伸びる grow in stature; grow taller. 〜が低い be short; be of small stature.
を 〜を測る measure *sb's* height.

生 Ⓔ life; living
を ⓒ 〜を営む lead a life; ⓔ spend one's days. ⓔ 〜を享ける come into the world; be born. ⓐ ⓔ 〜を偸む outlive one's span of life; live to no purpose; live a useless life.

姓 a surname; a family name
を ⓐ 〜を冒す use the name of *sb* else; misappropriate *sb's* name. 〜を変える change one's name; assume a new name.

贅 Ⓔ luxury; extravagance
を ⓐ 〜を言う boast about *sth*; brag about *sth*; ⓘ blow one's own horn; ⓘ talk big. 〜を尽くす indulge in luxury; behave extravagantly. ⓐ 〜を張る show off; be vain. ⓐ 〜を遣る ❶ show off; be vain. ❷ boast about *sth*; brag about *sth*; ⓘ talk big.

税 <ruby>税<rt>ぜい</rt></ruby> **a tax; a duty**
> 〔を〕 ～を<ruby>納<rt>おさ</rt></ruby>める pay a tax. ～を<ruby>課<rt>か</rt></ruby>する levy a tax; impose a tax. ～を<ruby>取<rt>と</rt></ruby>り<ruby>立<rt>た</rt></ruby>てる collect taxes; draw a tax.

誠意 <ruby>誠意<rt>せい い</rt></ruby> **sincerity; good faith**
> 〔を〕 ～を<ruby>疑<rt>うたが</rt></ruby>う question *sb's* sincerity. ～を<ruby>欠<rt>か</rt></ruby>く lack sincerity. ～を<ruby>示<rt>しめ</rt></ruby>す show one's good faith.

生気 <ruby>生気<rt>せい き</rt></ruby> **vitality; vigor; life; verve**
> 〔に〕 ～に<ruby>満<rt>み</rt></ruby>ちる brim with vitality.
> 〔を〕 ～を<ruby>与<rt>あた</rt></ruby>える give animation to *sth*; put life into *sth*. ～を<ruby>奪<rt>うば</rt></ruby>う sap the vitality of *sb/sth*.

制限 <ruby>制限<rt>せいげん</rt></ruby> **a restriction; a limit**
> 〔を〕 ～を<ruby>受<rt>う</rt></ruby>ける be subject to restriction. ～を<ruby>越<rt>こ</rt></ruby>える exceed restriction levels. Ⓔ ～を<ruby>付<rt>ふ</rt></ruby>する place restrictions on *sth*.

成功 <ruby>成功<rt>せいこう</rt></ruby> **success; a coup; a hit**
> 〔を〕 ～を<ruby>焦<rt>あせ</rt></ruby>る be (too) eager for success; hunger for success. ～を<ruby>祈<rt>いの</rt></ruby>る pray for success; wish *sb* success. ～を<ruby>祝<rt>いわ</rt></ruby>う celebrate one's success; congratulate *sb* on his/her success. ～を<ruby>収<rt>おさ</rt></ruby>める achieve success; be successful; Ⓒ make a hit ～を<ruby>期<rt>き</rt></ruby>する expect success; be sure of success; anticipate success.

正鵠 <ruby>正鵠<rt>せいこう</rt></ruby> Ⓔ **the bull's eye; the point**
> 〔を〕 ～を<ruby>射<rt>い</rt></ruby>る be relevant; Ⓘ be to the point; Ⓘ hit the nail on the head. Ⓔ ～を<ruby>失<rt>しっ</rt></ruby>する be irrelevant; Ⓘ be off the mark; Ⓘ miss the point.

贅沢 <ruby>贅沢<rt>ぜいたく</rt></ruby> **luxury; extravagance**
> 〔に〕 ～に<ruby>暮<rt>く</rt></ruby>らす live in luxury; lead a life of luxury. ～に<ruby>育<rt>そだ</rt></ruby>つ be brought up in luxury; be raised in the lap of luxury.
> 〔を〕 ～を<ruby>言<rt>い</rt></ruby>う ask for too much; expect too much. ～をする indulge in luxury; Ⓘ have one's bread buttered on both sides. ～を<ruby>尽<rt>つく</rt></ruby>す make *sth* exquisite; explore the boundaries of luxury. ～を<ruby>慎<rt>つつし</rt></ruby>む abstain from luxuries. ～を<ruby>始<rt>はじ</rt></ruby>める take to extravagance.

掣肘 <ruby>掣肘<rt>せいちゅう</rt></ruby> Ⓔ **restraint; restriction**
> 〔を〕 Ⓔ ～を<ruby>受<rt>う</rt></ruby>ける be retrained; be restricted. Ⓔ ～を<ruby>加<rt>くわ</rt></ruby>える put *sb* under restraint.

正道 <ruby>正道<rt>せいどう</rt></ruby> Ⓔ **the right path**
> 〔に〕 ～に<ruby>就<rt>つ</rt></ruby>く be on the right track. ～に<ruby>立<rt>た</rt></ruby>ち<ruby>返<rt>かえ</rt></ruby>らせる lead *sb* back to the right way. ～に<ruby>外<rt>はず</rt></ruby>れる be astray from the right path. ～に<ruby>導<rt>みちび</rt></ruby>く guide *sb* to the right path. ～に<ruby>戻<rt>もど</rt></ruby>る get back on the right path; mend one's ways; Ⓘ return to the straight and narrow.
> 〔を〕 ～を<ruby>逸<rt>そ</rt></ruby>れる deviate from the right path. ～を<ruby>外<rt>はず</rt></ruby>す stray from the right path. ～を<ruby>踏<rt>ふ</rt></ruby>む keep to the right path; pursue an honest career; Ⓘ stick to the straight and narrow; Ⓒ do the right thing.

生命 <ruby>生命<rt>せいめい</rt></ruby> **life; existence; the soul**
> 〔を〕 ～を<ruby>預<rt>あず</rt></ruby>ける put one's life in *sb's* hands; Ⓔ entrust one's life to *sb*. ～

せ

を失う lose one's life. ～を奪う take *sb's* life. ～を賭ける risk one's life. ⓔ ～を捧げる devote one's life (to a cause). ～を救う save *sb's* life. ⓔ ～を托す place one's life in *sb's* hands; ⓔ entrust one's life to *sb* ⓒ ～を賭する risk one's life. ～を尊ぶ value life; ⓔ hold life dear. ～を投げ打つ throw one's life away. ～を狙う seek *sb's* life; ⓔ have a design on *sb's* life.

誓約 せいやく a vow; an oath; a pledge
を ～を果たす fulfill one's vow; live up to one's word. ～を守る keep one's vow; be true to one's word. ～を破る break one's word; ⓔ violate one's pledge.

勢力 せいりょく influence; power; weight
が ～がある have influence; exercise power; wield power. ～が増す gain in influence; win gravity.
を ～を得る acquire influence. ～を挫く undermine *sb's* influence. ～を張る establish one's influence. ～を挽回する regain power. ～を揮う wield power; ⓔ hold sway. ～を増す increase one's influence.

席 せき a seat; a gallery
に ～に着く take one's seat; seat oneself. ～に戻る return to one's seat.
を ～を改める ❶ change seats. ❷ find another occasion (to do *sth*). ～を移す change venues; ⓔ adjourn to another room. ～を替える

change one's seat; change seats. ～を蹴る leave (a meeting) in a row; ⓒ storm out of the room. ～を進める come closer to; draw near to; be drawn into. ～を取る take *sb's* seat. ～を外す leave one's seat; make a seat free; leave the room. ～を離れる leave one's seat; quit one's seat. ～を譲る ❶ offer one's seat to *sb*. ❷ hand over one's position to *sb*; make place for *sb* else.

責任 せきにん responsibility; duty
を ～を失う lose responsibility. ～を移す turn over a duty to *sb* else; shift the responsibility (for one's actions) to *sb* else; ⓒ ⓘ pass the buck to *sb* else. ～を負う bear the responsibility for (one's actions); be responsible. ～を感じる feel responsible; have a sense of responsibility. ～を避ける avoid responsibility; ⓒ shirk one's duty. ～を棄てる desert one's duty; abandon one's responsibilities. ～を問う call *sb* to account. ～を解く relieve *sb* from his/her duty. ～を取る assume responsibility; take responsibility. ～を果たす fulfill one's duty; carry out one's responsibility; do one's duty. ～を放棄する relinquish one's responsibilities. ⓔ abdicate responsibility. ～を持つ be responsible; hold responsibility.

世間 せけん the world; the public
が ～が狭い have a small circle of acquaintances. ⓐ ～が立つ do one's

worldly duties. Ⓐ ～が詰まる be unable to manage (financially); Ⓒ hit hard times. Ⓐ ～が張る make a great outlay (to impress people); Ⓔ be ostentatious. ～が広い have a wide circle of acquaintances.
[に] ～に知れる become public; come to light; Ⓘ spread abroad; Ⓘ take wind. ～に出る go out into the world; enter the real world. Ⓞ ～に成る return to secular life; renounce the cloth. ～に広まる gain publicity; become widely known; gain repute. Ⓐ ～に凭れる follow the world; do as others do; Ⓒ go with the flow.
[へ] ～へ出る go out into the world; enter the real world.
[を] ～を恐れる be afraid of people's opinions; fear what people will say. Ⓐ ～を兼ねる take account of the public eye; Ⓘ keep up appearances. ～を騒がす be much talked about; create a sensation; Ⓘ make a stir. Ⓐ ～を済ます fool the world; Ⓘ lead the public by the nose. Ⓐ ～を包む hide *sth* from the outside world; keep *sth* secret. ～を憚る be wary of people's opinions; heed public opinion. Ⓐ ～を張る play the *bon vivant*; show off; Ⓔ be ostentatious. Ⓐ ～を塞げる lose contact with the world; be shut off from the outside world. ～を見る see the world; gain in worldly experience. Ⓐ ～を辞める ❶ go into seclusion; become a hermit; Ⓔ retire from the world; renounce the world. ❷ become a Buddhist priest; take the tonsure; Ⓔ retire into religion. ～を渡る go through the world.

世間体（せけんてい） **appearances**
[を] ～を構う take account of the public eye; heed public opinion. ～を繕う save appearances; Ⓘ keep up appearances.

節（せつ） **a season; constancy** ▶ 節（ふし）
[を] Ⓞ ～を売る prostitute oneself; Ⓔ sell one's honor. ～を折る yield to *sb*; give in to *sb*. ～を屈する yield to *sb*; give in to *sb*. Ⓞ ～を捨てる abandon one's principles; Ⓘ desert one's colors. ～を遂ぐ achieve one's aim; win through. ～を曲げる betray one's principles; Ⓢ sell out. ～を守る be faithful; remain constant; stick to one's principles; stand firm; Ⓘ hold to one's colors; Ⓘ stick to one's guns. Ⓞ ～を破る stain one's virtue; be unchaste.

拙（せつ） [I] **poor; unskillful; clumsy**
[を] Ⓐ Ⓔ ～を蔵す hide one's flaws. Ⓐ Ⓔ ～を守る be content with one's mediocrity; accept one's flaws.

舌（ぜつ） **the tongue** ▶ 舌（した）
[に] ～に掛ける win *sb* over; get round *sb*; seduce *sb*.

是非（ぜひ） **right and wrong**
[を] ～を極める distinguish right from wrong. ～を問う call *sth* into

せ

question. 〜を弁じる distinguish between right and wrong. 〜を論じる discuss the pros and cons (of an issue).

世話 care; assistance; help

[が] 〜が焼ける give *sb* trouble; require care.

[に] ⓞ 〜に砕ける speak in a plain and friendly manner. 〜になる be under *sb's* care; receive assistance.

[を] 〜をする look after *sb*. 〜を掛ける trouble *sb*. Ⓐ 〜を拾う carry the burden. 〜を焼かす give *sb* trouble; require care. Ⓐ 〜を病む take utmost care; look after *sb* at one's own cost.

先 the future; priority ▶ 先

[を] 〜を越す anticipate *sb*/*sth*; take the initiative; get a start on *sb*; be the first to act. 〜を取る get a lead on *sb*; preempt *sb's* actions; get ahead of *sb*.

選 selection; choice

[に] 〜に入る be selected; be chosen. 〜に漏れる be rejected; be left out of the selection.

線 a line; a wire; a route; a track

[を] 〜を引く ❶ draw a line. ❷ make a distinction between two things; ① draw the line.

膳 a (small) table; a tray

[に] 〜に出す serve a meal; put a meal on the table. 〜に就く sit down to table. 〜に向かう sit down to table.

[を] 〜を片付ける clear the table; remove the tablecloth. 〜を据える put a tray in front of *sb*; lay the table; set a table. Ⓐ 〜を引く clear the table; remove the tablecloth.

善 good; goodness; virtue

[を] 〜を成す do good; practice virtue.

前後 before and behind; order

[を] 〜を見回す look around one. 〜を忘れる forget oneself; be at a loss; be distraught.

善根 Ⓔ a good deed; charity

[を] Ⓔ 〜を積む lead a good life; accumulate good deeds. Ⓔ 〜を施す do good; practice charity.

全盛 the height of prosperity

[を] 〜を極める attain the highest stage of prosperity. 〜を誇る be in all its glory.

戦争 war; a battle; warfare

[に] 〜に訴える resort to arms. 〜に勝つ win a battle; win the day. 〜に出る go to war; go into battle. 〜に備える prepare for war; Ⓔ make ready for battle; ① clear the decks. 〜に負ける be defeated in battle; lose a battle.

[を] 〜を逃れる escape from war; Ⓔ be spared from (the ravages) of war. 〜を始める open hostilities.

そ

先手 the first move
を ～を打つ forestall *sb*; get a start on *sb*; anticipate *sb* (in doing). ～を取る get a lead on *sb*; preempt *sb's* actions; get ahead of *sb*.

先頭 the forefront; the lead
に ～に立つ lead the vanguard; take the lead; spearhead (a campaign); ⓘ be in the front van. を ～を切る take the lead; ⓘ be in the front van (of a campaign).

善美 ⒠ the good and beautiful
を ～を極める make *sth* exquisite; explore the boundaries of luxury. ～を尽す make *sth* gorgeous; furnish *sth* lavishly.

前非 ⒠ one's past folly
を ⒠ ～を悔いる repent of one's past sins. ⒠ ～を悟る see the error of one's own ways.

先鞭 ⒠ the initiative; the lead
を ～を付ける take the initiative.

全貌 ⒠ the whole picture/story
を ～を現わす come into full view; ⒸⒸ emerge into view. ～を示す give *sb* the full details; Ⓒ put *sb* in the picture. ～を掴む grasp the full story; Ⓒ get the whole picture. ⒸⒸ ～を尽す give an exhaustive account; describe *sth* in all its details.

全力 all one's power
を ～を上げる muster all one's strength; exert all one's power; Ⓒ go all out. ～を注ぐ pour all one's energy into *sth*. ～を尽す do one's utmost; do everything in one's power; give one's all.

先例 a precedent; an example
と ～とする take *sth* as a precedent. ～となる become a precedent (for). に ～に背く contravene precedent; depart from precedent. ～による be according to precedent; comply with precedent. を ～を作る set a precedent. ～を破る violate a precedent.

洗礼 baptism
を ～を受ける be baptized. ～を施す baptize *sb*.

ソ

爪牙 ⒠ nails and fangs; clutches
に ⒠ ～に掛かる fall victim to (*sb's* evil intent); fall into *sb's* clutches. を ⒠ ～を脱する free oneself from *sb's* hold; get out of *sb's* clutches. ⒠ ～を研ぐ ❶ sharpen its clutches. ❷ keep a vigilant eye on *sb*/*sth*; have an eye on *sb*/*sth*.

想像 imagination; fancy
が ～がつく be imaginable; be understandable; have a notion; Ⓒ get the idea. に ～に描く make a mental picture

of *sth*; picture *sth* to oneself; see *sth* in one's imagination. 〜に絶する defy all imagination. 〜に基づく be a figment of one's imagination. 〔を〕〜を廻らす be imaginative; use one's imagination; ponder over *sth*.

俗 ぞく 〔E〕 customs; manners
〔を〕 ◎ 〔E〕 〜を追う pursue worldly things. 〔E〕 〜を脱する rise above the world.

俗塵 ぞくじん 〔E〕 the world; earthly affairs
〔を〕 〜を洗う disengage one's mind from worldly cares. 〜を避ける live secluded from the world; keep aloof from everyday life.

束縛 そくばく a restraint; a restriction
〔を〕 〜を受ける be placed under restraint. 〜を加える impose restraints upon *sb*; put restrictions on *sb*. 〔E〕 〜を脱する free oneself from restraint; 〔E〕 throw off a yoke.

底 そこ the bottom; the bed
〔が〕 〜が浅い ❶ ◎ be shallow; have little depth. ❷ Ⓐ be shallow; Ⓐ have no depth; be superficial. 〜が知れない be unfathomable; be a mystery. 〜が深い ❶ ◎ be deep; have depth. ❷ be profound; Ⓐ have depth; ◎ be deep. 〜が見える be seen through. 〜が割れる be exposed; be seen through; ◎ be shown up (for what one is). 〔に〕 〜に着く find bottom; touch bottom; reach the bottom.

〔を〕 Ⓐ 〜を入れる ❶ have a starter; have an appetizer. ❷ make sure of *sth*; tell *sb* twice; bring *sth* home to *sb*; ◎ Ⓘ rub it in. ❸ reach the rock-bottom price; ◎ bottom out. Ⓐ 〜を押す remind *sb* (of *sth*); call *sb's* attention to *sth*; make sure of *sth*; tell *sb* emphatically of *sth*. 〜を極める master the essence of *sth*. Ⓐ 〜を叩く ❶ empty (a vessel) totally. ❷ reach the rock-bottom price. 〜を突く ❶ touch bottom; reach the bottom. ❷ exhaust (one's savings); run out of (petrol). ⊕ 〜を付ける fail in dying fabric. 〜を抜く knock out the bottom (of a box). Ⓐ 〜を叩く empty (a vessel) totally. Ⓐ 〜を払う empty (a vessel) totally. ◎ 〜を割る ❶ open one's heart to *sb*; unbosom oneself; speak one's mind; Ⓘ pour out one's heart to *sb*. ❷ (prices) fall through the bottom. ◎ 〜を破る expose (a secret); reveal the truth.

訴訟 そしょう a lawsuit; an action
〔に〕 〜に勝つ win a lawsuit. 〜に負ける lose a lawsuit.
〔を〕 〜を起こす raise a suit; go to court. 〜を取り下げる drop a suit.

俎上 そじょう 〔E〕 a chopping block
〔に〕 〜に載せる ❶ put (meat) on the chopping block. ❷ put *sth* under review; take *sth* up for discussion.

袖 そで a sleeve; an arm; a wing
〔に〕 Ⓐ Ⓢ 〜に食らう hide *sth* in one's

114

sleeve; ⓒ pinch *sth*; ⓢ nick *sth*. Ⓐ
〜に時雨る cry in one's sleeve;
shed tears. 〜に縋る ❶ hang on to
sb's sleeve; cling to *sb's* sleeve.
❷ entreat *sb* for mercy; appeal to
sb's compassion. Ⓐ 〜に墨付く be
the object of *sb's* desires; be
loved. 〜にする jilt one's lover;
rebuff *sb*; ① leave *sb* in the lurch;
① give *sb* the cold shoulder.

を Ⓗ 〜を返す turn one's sleeve
inside out (in the hope of dreaming
of one's lover). Ⓐ 〜を片敷く have
a rest; have a (cat)nap; have a
snooze. 〜を絞る cry in one's
sleeve; be moved to tears. ⓞ 〜を
連ねる go along with *sb*; go in the
company of *sb*. 〜を通す put on a
garment (for the first time). 〜を
捕える hold *sb* by the sleeve;
ⓒ ① buttonhole *sb*. 〜を濡らす cry
in one's sleeve; shed tears. 〜を払
う brush (an obstacle) aside. 〜を
引く ❶ pull *sb* by the sleeve; pluck
sb's sleeve. ❷ woo a woman; try to
win a girl. ❸ warn *sb*; call *sth* to
sb's attention. ⓞ 〜を拡ぐ beg for
alms. 〜を分かつ part from *sb*;
part company with *sb*; break off
relations with *sb*.

外 the outside; outdoors

で 〜で遊ぶ play outdoors; play in
the open.

に 〜にいる be outside; be out. 〜
に立つ stand outside (the door). 〜
に漏れる come to light; leak out;
① spread abroad; ① take wind.

へ 〜へ出る go outside; go out of
doors. 〜へ向ける turn outward.

を 〜を見る look outside; look out
of (the window).

傍 a side; vicinity; proximity

に 〜にいる be at *sb's* side. 〜に置
く keep *sth*/*sb* near at hand. 〜に
座る sit down next to *sb*. 〜に寄る
draw near to *sb*.

を 〜を通る pass *sb* by. 〜を離れる
leave *sb's* side.

空 the sky; the air ▸空 ▸空

で 〜で覚える learn *sth* by heart;
know *sth* by heart. 〜で読む recite
sth from memory; read *sth* by rote.

に 〜に舞い上がる pierce the
skies; soar into the sky.

を (旅の)〜を仰ぐ be in a strange
land; be away from home. Ⓐ 〜を歩
む be on edge; be nervous; ① be on
tenterhooks. ⓞ 〜を使う pretend
not to know; feign ignorance. 〜を
飛ぶ fly in the air. 〜を眺める look
at the sky. 〜を見上げる look up at
the sky. 〜を渡る cross the skies;
sail across the sky.

空鼾 feigned snoring

を 〜を掻く pretend to be asleep;
feign sleep (by snoring).

反り a warp; a curve; an arch

が (人と)〜が合う be like-minded;
get along with *sb*; ① see eye to eye;
ⓒ ① hit it off. 〜が有る be curved.
ⓞ 〜が来る become warped.

を (人と)〜を合わせる try to get along (with *sb*). Ⓐ 〜を打つ ❶ be ready to draw one's sword; have one's sword at the ready. ❷ have a recurved shape; be bent backwards. Ⓐ 〜を返す turn one's sword (so that the curve faces downward); be ready to draw one's sword; have one's sword at the ready.

損 a loss; damage; a drawback
が Ⓐ 〜が立つ result in a loss.
に 〜になる result in a loss.
を 〜を埋める recoup a loss; make good a loss. 〜を掛ける cause a loss; inflict a loss upon *sb*. 〜を被る sustain a loss; suffer damage. 〜をする suffer a loss. 〜を償う recoup a loss; make good a loss.

尊敬 respect; esteem; regard
を 〜を受ける receive respect; be esteemed; get respect. 〜を得る earn *sb's* respect; gain *sb's* esteem. 〜を払う pay one's respect to *sb*; show respect.

存在 existence; being
を 〜を疑う doubt the existence of. 〜を認める recognize *sb's* existence.

タ

田 a rice field; a paddy field
を 〜を植える plant rice seedlings. 〜を打つ plow a rice field; till a rice field. 〜を耕す plow a rice field; till a rice field. 〜を作る crop a rice field; cultivate a rice field; grow rice; till a rice field.

体 the body; an object ▶ 体
を 〜を預ける [*sumō*] throw one's full weight against one's opponent. 〜を躱す dodge (a blow); get out of the way. 〜を成す take form; get into shape; be organized. Ⓞ 〜を引く draw back; withdraw (one's body).

太鼓 a drum; a tomtom
を 〜を打つ beat a drum. 〜を叩く ❶ pound on drums. ❷ flatter *sb*; ① chime in with *sb*; ① curry favor with *sb*. 〜を鳴らす beat a drum. (人の)〜を持つ flatter *sb*; ① chime in with *sb*; ① curry favor with *sb*.

太鼓判 Ⓔ a large seal
を Ⓔ 〜を押す give one's seal of approval; sponsor *sb/sth*; give *sb* a clean bill of health.

体重 body weight
が 〜が減る lose weight. 〜が増す gain weight; put on weight.
を 〜を計る weigh oneself. 〜を減らす reduce one's weight.

態度 an attitude; a manner
を 〜を改める revise one's attitude. 〜を変える change one's attitude. 〜を決める determine one's attitude. 〜を持する retain

one's attitude. ～を取る take a stand; adopt an attitude.

大砲 a canon; an artillery gun
図 ～を据える mount a gun. ～を造る build a gun. ～を放つ fire a gun. ～を向ける train a gun.

体面 appearances; face; honor
図 ～を重んじる respect *sb's* honor; ⓔ ⓘ keep *sb* in countenance. ～を汚す be disgraced; ⓔ bring disgrace upon oneself; ⓘ lose face. ～を保つ ⓘ save one's face; ⓘ keep up appearances. ～を繕う ⓘ keep up appearances.

高 a quantity; an amount; a sum
図 ～が知れる be not worth considering; be of little account. 図 ～を括る make light of *sth*; take *sth* lightly; think little of *sth*.

箍 a (metal/bamboo) hoop
図 ～が外れる feel relieved; feel relaxed. ～が緩む ❶ the hoop comes off. ❷ feel relieved; feel relaxed. ❸ lose one's vigor; ⓘ go out of gear. 図 ～を掛け代える put on new hoops; rehoop a barrel. ～を掛ける put on a hoop; bind a barrel. ～を外す ❶ take the hoops off; unhoop a barrel. ❷ free oneself from restrictions; ⓔ throw off the yoke; ⓔ cast off the fetters. ❸ have fun; make merry; ⓘ paint the town red; ⓒ ⓘ let one's hair down.

戦い war; a battle; a struggle
図 ～に倦み疲れる be tired of fighting; ⓔ be battle weary. ～に赴く go to war; go to the front; head for the battlefield. ～に勝つ gain victory; win a game; win a battle; ⓘ win the day. ～に備える prepare for battle; make oneself ready for combat; ⓘ clear the decks. ～に出る go to the front; go off to war; ⓔ take the field. ～に負ける be defeated; lose a game; ⓘ lose the day.
図 ～を挑む offer battle; challenge *sb* to a game; ⓘ throw down the gauntlet to *sb*. ⓔ ～を宣する declare war (against a country). ～を交える join battle (with *sb*); ⓔ do battle; engage the enemy. ～を求める seek battle; challenge *sb* to battle.

立場 a standpoint; a position
図 (人の)～に在る be in *sb's* position; ⓘ be in *sb's* shoes. (人の)～に成る put oneself in *sb's* place; ⓘ put oneself in *sb's* shoes.
図 ～を失う lose one's footing. ～を奪う cut the ground from under *sb's* feet. ～を得る gain one's footing. ～を換える change one's ground; take a different standpoint. ～を尊ぶ respect *sb's* position. ～を取る take a (certain) position; take a stand. ～を守る hold one's ground.

手綱 a bridle; the reins
図 ～を取る hold the reins; be in

control; Ⓢ Ⓘ call the shots. Ⓞ ～を控える draw in the reins; rein in (a horse); call *sb* to order. ～を引き締める tighten the reins; rein in (a horse); call *sb* to order; Ⓘ keep a tight rein. ～を引く pull the reins; draw in the reins. ～を緩める slacken the reins; give the reins (to a horse); give *sb* free rein; Ⓘ allow a free rein. ～を渡す pass the reins to *sb* else; make place for *sb* else; transfer control.

盾 (たて) **a shield; a buckler**

[に] ～に突く use *sth*/*sb* as a shield. ～に取る ❶ use *sth*/sb as a shield; Ⓛ hide oneself behind *sth*. ❷ use *sth* as an excuse; Ⓐ hide behind *sth*; Ⓐ shield oneself behind *sth*.

[を] Ⓐ ～を突く set oneself against *sb*; rebel against *sb*; defy *sb*.

棚 (たな) **a shelf; a rack; a trellis**

[に] ～に上げる ❶ (物を) put *sth* on a shelf. ❷ (事を) be blind to one's own faults; shut one's eyes to one's own faults; Ⓘ fail to see the beam in one's own eye.

[を] ～をつる put up a shelf.

掌 (たなごころ) **the palm of the hand ▶ 掌** (てのひら)

[に] ～にする ❶ make *sth* one's own. take possession of *sth*. ❷ do as one pleases; have one's own way.

[を] ～を返す ❶ be easy (to do); be simple (to understand). ❷ be fick-le; be inconstant; be changeable. Ⓐ ～を指す be clear; be apparent.

種 (たね) **a seed; a stone; a kernel**

[を] ～を明かす reveal a secret; explain a trick. ～を蒔く Ⓛ sow seeds; Ⓐ sow seeds (of discontent). ～を宿す become pregnant; have *sb's* child. Ⓐ ～を割る expose *sb*; reveal a secret.

魂 (たましい) **the soul; the spirit**

[を] ～が据わる recover one's presence of mind; come to oneself.

[を] ～を入れる breathe (new) life into *sth*. ～を入れ替える have a change of heart; mend one's ways; Ⓘ turn over a new leaf. ～を打ち込む throw oneself into *sth* heart and soul; Ⓘ put one's heart into *sth*. ～を奪う charm *sb*; Ⓘ steal *sb's* heart; Ⓘ put a spell on *sb*. ～を抜く charm *sb*; Ⓘ steal *sb's* heart; Ⓘ put a spell on *sb*. ～を冷やす be struck with terror; Ⓘ be scared to death. Ⓘ break into a cold sweat. ～を吹き込む breathe (new) life into *sth*.

駄目 (だめ) **no good; useless; futile**

[に] ～にする spoil *sth*; ruin *sth*. ～になる be spoiled; be ruined; go wrong; go bad.

[を] ～を押す make doubly sure; tell *sb* twice; Ⓒ Ⓘ rub it in. ～を出す reject *sth*; turn *sth* down. Ⓞ ～を踏む do *sth* in vain; do *sth* that is to no avail; waste one's time.

袂 (たもと) **a sleeve; a sleeve pocket**

[に] ～に入れる put *sth* in one's (*kimono*) sleeve; pocket *sth*. ～に

縋る ❶ hang on to *sb's* sleeve; cling to *sb's* sleeve. ❷ appeal to *sb*; ⓔ beseech *sb* (to grant a favor).
⓪ 〜を絞る shed a flood of tears; ⓔ weep bitterly. ◎ 〜を連ねる (do *sth*) in a body; all together. 〜を分かつ part from *sb*; break off relations with *sb*; part company with *sb*.

胆 the liver; spirit; guts; pluck
ⓖ 〜が据る ❶ have nerves of steel; be brave; have a lot of pluck. ❷ regain one's presence of mind; ⓔ recover one's composure; ① pull oneself together; ① gather one's wits.
⓪ ◎ 〜を奪う strike terror into *sb's* heart; ① scare the living daylights out of *sb*. ◎ 〜を練る muster courage; gather one's nerves; ① gird up one's loins.

短 ⓔ shortness; brevity; a fault
⓪ ⓔ 〜を補う make up for one's defects. ⓔ 〜を捨てる do away with what is bad.

痰 sputum; phlegm; spittle
⓪ (人に)〜を掛ける spit on *sb*. 〜を吐く cough up phlegm; spit out.

端 ⓔ origin; beginning
⓪ ⓔ (事に)〜を発する originate in *sth*; have its origin in *sth*; arise from *sth*; stem from *sth*.

端緒 ⓔ the beginning; a start
ⓣ 〜と成る lead to (a success); become the first step (to a success); pave the way to success.
⓪ 〜を失う lose the clue; lose the plot. 〜を得る find a clue; have a key (to a mystery). 〜を捜す look for a clue; search for a key (to a problem). 〜を掴む find a clue; have a key to. (事に)〜を発する originate in *sth*; have its origin in *sth*; arise from *sth*. 〜を開く make a beginning; pave the way.

丹精 ⓔ "one's true heart"
⓪ ⓐ 〜を致す do one's utmost. 〜を尽くす exert oneself. 〜を凝らす spare no pains; make every effort.

嘆声 ⓔ a sigh of grief/wonder
⓪ ⓔ 〜を発する gasp with wonder; sigh with despair. 〜を漏らす gasp with wonder; sigh with despair.

チ

血 blood
ⓖ 〜が通う be made of flesh and blood; be kindhearted; be humane. 〜が騒ぐ tingle with excitement; become worked up; get excited. 〜が繋がる be related by blood; be a blood relative. 〜が出る blood oozes out; lose blood. 〜が付く be tainted with blood. 〜が止まる stop bleeding; the bleeding stops. 〜が上る ❶ feel dizzy; be giddy. ❷ lose one's temper; fly into a rage; ◎ ① fly off the handle;

③ ① blow a fuse. 〜が引く ❶ turn pale (with fright); go white (in the face). ❷ shudder with fear; shiver with horror. 〜が沸く be exiting; be stirring.

Ⓒ 〜に飢える thirst for blood; be bloodthirsty. 〜に狂う go mad at the sight of blood. 〜に染まる be tainted with blood. Ⓗ 〜に啼く utter a sorrowful cry; sing sorrowfully. 〜に塗れる be smeared with blood. 〜に迷う lose control; behave irrationally; forget oneself; ① lose one's head.

Ⓦ 〜を上げる have a rush of blood to the head; feel dizzy; feel giddy. 〜を受ける descend from; inherit one's parents' traits. 〜を通わす liven up (an occasion). 〜を清める purify the blood. Ⓐ 〜を啜る vow solemnly; make a solemn oath. 〜を出す draw blood. 〜を止める staunch blood; arrest the bleeding. 〜を流す cause blood to flow; shed blood; inflict casualties. 〜を吐く cough up blood. 〜を引く carry the same blood; descend from; inherit one's parents' traits. 〜を見る cause casualties; lead to bloodshed. 〜を沸かす cause the blood to tingle; Ⓒ inflame the blood; be thrilling; be stirring. 〜を分ける be related by blood; be blood relatives. 〜を汚す spoil the blood.

地 the earth; soil; a place ♦ 地

Ⓒ 〜に墜ちる lose vigor/power; be in decline; be cast down. 〜に 墜つ be at a low ebb. 〜に塗れる suffer a crushing defeat; be defeated; lose a contest; ① bite the dust.

Ⓦ 〜を固める strengthen one's foothold; secure a foothold. Ⓐ 〜を払う disappear from the face of the earth; go up in smoke. 〜を掘る dig the ground.

智 Ⓔ intellect; intelligence

Ⓦ 〜を磨く improve one's mind; sharpen one's mind; polish one's intellect. Ⓒ 〜を巡らす devise a stratagem; work out a plan.

治安 public peace; public order

Ⓦ 〜を保つ maintain public order. 〜を破る disturb the peace.

地位 a position; a rank; a post

Ⓖ 〜が上がる climb in rank; rise in social standing. 〜が高い have a high rank; be of high social standing. 〜が違う differ in social standing. 〜が低い have a low rank; be of low social standing.

Ⓒ 〜に就く take a position.

Ⓦ 〜を争う contest a position. 〜を維持する maintain a position. 〜を得る acquire a position. 〜を向上する improve one's position. 〜を占める occupy a position; hold a post. 〜を捨てる abandon one's position; give up a position. 〜を高める elevate one's position; raise one's status. 〜を求める seek a position; apply for a post. 〜を譲る

yield one's position to; make room for *sb*; step down for *sb*. 〜を乱用する abuse one's position. 〜を弁える be aware of one's position.

知恵 wisdom; intelligence

[が] 〜がある be wise; be intelligent; be full of ideas. 〜が尽きる be at the end of one's tether; ⓘ be at one's wits' end; ⓘ be all at sea. 〜が付く grow wise; ⓒ get smart. 〜が増す gain in wisdom; grow wiser. 〜が回る be resourceful; be inventive.

[を] 〜を貸す give *sb* advice; offer counsel to. 〜を借りる ask for *sb's* advice. 〜を絞る think hard about *sth*; ⓒ ⓘ rack one's brains. 〜を出す show wisdom. 〜を付ける give *sb* a hint; plant an idea in *sb's* head; incite *sb* to *sth*. 〜を磨く cultivate wisdom; sharpen one's intellect; polish one's intellect.

地下 underground; in the grave

[に] 〜に埋める bury *sth* in the earth. 〜に潜る go into hiding; ⓘ go to earth; ⓘ go to ground. 〜に眠る sleep in the grave; rest in peace.

誓い a vow; an oath; a pledge

[を] 〜を交す exchange vows. 〜を立てる make a vow. 〜を守る honor one's vow; stand by one's oath; be true to one's word. 〜を破る break one's word; ⓒ violate one's pledge.

力 strength; force; power

[が] 〜がある be strong; have strength. 〜が尽きる be spent; ⓒ ⓐ be wrung out; ⓢ be knackered. 〜が付く gain strength; gather strength. 〜が抜ける be enervated; lose strength.

[と] 〜と頼む rely on *sb*.

[に] 〜に余る be beyond one's powers; lie outside one's ability. 〜に屈する yield to (brute) force. 〜にする ❶ be reinvigorated; be strengthened by. ❷ rely on *sb*; get (moral) support from *sb*. 〜になる be a help; be a source of strength.

[を] 〜を合わせる work together; join forces. 〜を入れる put one's back into *sth*. 〜を失う lose strength. 〜を得る gain strength from *sth*; be encouraged by *sth*. 〜を落す be weakened; lose courage; be discouraged. 〜を貸す give assistance to *sb*; stand by *sb*. 〜を借りる ask for *sb's* help; enlist *sb's* help. 〜を比べる measure one's strength with *sb*. 〜を込める put one's back into *sth*. ⓐ 〜を立つ put one's back into *sth*. 〜を尽くす exert oneself; make efforts. 〜を付ける encourage oneself/*sb*; cheer oneself/*sb* up; put *sb* on his/her mettle; brace oneself. 〜を取り戻す regain one's strength. 〜を揮う exert force; be influential.

契り a pledge; a vow

[を] ⓐ 〜を籠む make a solemn vow. 〜を結ぶ make a pledge.

知識 knowledge; learning

[が] 〜が進む advance in knowledge. 〜が増す grow in knowledge.

[を] 〜を与える impart knowledge to *sb*. 〜を得る obtain knowledge. 〜を積む accumulate knowledge; gather knowledge. 〜を広める broaden one's knowledge. 〜を増す increase one's knowledge. 〜を磨く improve one's knowledge.

恥辱 disgrace; shame; a stigma

[を] 〜を与える humiliate *sb*; put *sb* to shame; Ⓘ take *sb* down a peg. 〜を受ける be humiliated; be insulted; Ⓘ be taken down a peg. ◎〜を来たす bring shame upon *sb*. 〜を被る suffer disgrace. 〜を忍ぶ suffer an insult; Ⓘ eat humble pie. 〜を濯ぐ wipe away a stigma; clear one's name. 〜を招く invite the taunt of slander; disgrace oneself; bring shame upon one's head.

乳 milk; the breast; a breast

[を] 〜を絞る milk (a cow). 〜を飲ませる suckle a baby; breastfeed a baby. 〜を飲む take the breast; suck milk. 〜を離す wean a child.

地歩 a foothold; a stand

[を] 〜を失う lose ground; lose one's foothold. 〜を得る gain a foothold; establish a foothold. 〜を固める strengthen one's foothold; secure a foothold. 〜を築く establish a foothold 〜を占める gain a footing; secure a niche; take one's stand. 〜を保つ maintain one's foothold; keep one's footing. 〜を取り戻す regain one's foothold; recover lost ground.

茶 green tea; nonsense

[に] 〜にする ❶ make fun of *sb*; slight *sb*; insult *sb*. ❷ have a short rest; Ⓒ have a nap; Ⓒ have a breather. (お)〜に呼ぶ invite *sb* to a tea party.

[を] Ⓐ 〜を言う talk nonsense; Ⓘ talk through one's hat; Ⓢ talk rubbish. 〜を入れ替える make fresh tea. 〜を入れる make (a pot of) tea. 〜を煎じる make tea; brew tea. 〜を出す serve tea. 〜を点てる ❶ make tea (the formal way); hold a tea ceremony. ◎ ❷ hold a Buddhist mass. 〜を注ぐ pour out tea. 〜を摘む pick tea. (お)〜を濁す ❶ do *sth* in a halfhearted way; muddle on. ❷ give an evasive reply; Ⓘ beat about the bush; Ⓒ Ⓘ pussyfoot on (an issue). 〜を飲む drink tea. 〜を挽く grind tea. (お)〜を引く have no engagement; be without engagement. 〜を焙じる roast tea. 〜を沸かす ❶ make tea; brew tea. ❷ be greatly tickled at *sth*; Ⓘ split one's sides with laughter.

茶代 [E] a tip; a gratuity

[を] 〜を受け取る receive a tip. 〜を置く leave a tip (on the plate). 〜を弾む tip *sb* generously; give *sb* a big tip. 〜を遣る give *sb* a tip.

茶柱 an erectly floating tea stalk
が ～が立つ be auspicious; be lucky; ⓒ Ⓐ hit good luck.

宙 space; the air; midair
で ⓞ ～で言う ① say *sth* off the top of one's head. ⓞ ～で読む recite *sth* from memory; read *sth* by rote.
に ⓞ ～に行く be unresolved; ① be up in the air; ① be in limbo. ～に浮く ❶ float in midair. ❷ be unfinished; be unresolved; ⓒ be in limbo. ～に舞う drift in midair; flutter in the air. ⓞ ～に迷う be unfinished; be unresolved; be in limbo.
を ～を掛ける ① have wings on one's heels. ～を飛ぶ ❶ fly in the air. ❷ ① have wings on one's heels.

注意 attention; notice; heed
が ～が行き届く be very careful; take great care.
を ～を与える give *sb* advice. ～を促す call *sb*'s attention to *sth*. ～を怠る be careless; be negligent. ～を逸らす divert one's attention. ～を捕える capture *sb*'s attention. ～を払う pay attention to *sth*. ～を引く draw *sb*'s attention. ～を向ける turn one's attention to *sth*.

忠告 advice; counsel
に ～に従う follow *sb*'s advice. ～に背く go against *sb*'s advice.
を ～を与える give *sb* (a piece of) advice; ⓔ counsel *sb*. ～を容れる accept *sb*'s advice. ～を聞く ask *sb*'s advice; listen to *sb*'s advice. ～を守る act upon *sb*'s advice; heed *sb*'s advice; ⓒ stick to *sb*'s advice. ～を求める seek *sb*'s advice.

注文 an order; a request
に ～に応じる accept an order.
を ～を集める collect orders. ～を受ける accept an order. ～を促す invite orders. ～を付ける make conditions; make special requests. ⓞ ～を取り極める close an order. ～を取り消す cancel an order; call off an order. ～を取る take orders; secure an order. ～を流す fail to secure an order.

中立 neutrality; independence
を ～を侵す violate (a country's) neutrality. ～を守る maintain neutrality.

聴覚 hearing; auditory sense
が ～が鋭い have good hearing; have a sharp ear.
に ～に訴える appeal to the ear.
を ～を失う lose one's hearing. ～を働かす use one's ears.

調査 an investigation; an inquiry
を ～を打ち切る discontinue an investigation. ～を行う conduct an investigation. ～を進める pursue an investigation; ⓒ look into *sth*. ～を始める start an investigation.

調子 a tune; a pitch; a manner
が ～が合う be in tune. ～が良い feel good; be in good condition. ～

が高い be in a high key; have a high pitch. ～が出る warm up (to work); ⓔ get into one's stride. ～が低い be in a low key; have a low pitch. ～が悪い feel unwell; ① be out of sorts; be out of order; be not well tuned; be awry.

に ～に乗る ❶ get into one's stride; get on the ball; get into the swing of things. ❷ get carried away; be elated; ⓒ ① let oneself loose. ❸ be haughty; be puffed up; show off; ① have airs and graces; ⓢ ① be stuck-up.

を ～を上げる raise the pitch. ～を合わせる keep in tune (with *sb*); keep in step (with *sb*); play along with *sb*. ～を落とす slow down; be in recession. ～を変える modulate one's tone; ⓒ change one's tune. ～を崩す lose condition. ～を下げる lower the pitch. ～を示す show a trend; display a tendency. ～を揃える be in tune; be in harmony. ～を高める raise one's pitch. ～を付ける intone (a poem). ～を整える work on one's shape; tone up one's condition; fine tune (a machine). ～を取り戻す regain one's form. ～を取る beat time; mark time. ～を飲み込む learn how to do *sth*; ⓒ get the knack of *sth*. ～を外す strike a false note; be out of tune. ～を乱す put *sth* out of tune.

ちょうしょう 嘲笑 ridicule; derision; scorn
を ～を招く invite ridicule. ～を浴びせる cast ridicule upon *sb*.

ちょうちん 提灯 a (paper) lantern
を ～を持つ ❶ carry a lantern. ❷ flatter *sb*; ① curry favor with *sb*.

ちょうへい 徴兵 conscription
に ～に出る serve in the army. ～に取られる be enlisted; ① join up.

ちょうわ 調和 harmony
を ～を欠く lack harmony. ～を損なう disturb the harmony.

ちり 塵 dust; dirt; the madding crowd
に Ⓐ ～に立つ a rumor spreads. Ⓐ ～に継ぐ inherit *sb's* legacy; take over *sb's* unfinished work. Ⓗ ～に同ず submerge oneself in the (workaday) world; go up in the madding crowd; keep company with the vulgar; hide one's virtues. Ⓐ ～に交わる ❶ submerge oneself in the (workaday) world; go up in the madding crowd; ① keep one's head down; ① keep a low profile. ❷ hide one's talents; ① hide one's light under a bushel. ～に塗れる be defeated; lose in a contest.

を Ⓐ ～を出づ ❶ escape from the madding crowd; get away from the hustle and bustle of the world. ❷ go into seclusion; become a hermit; ⓔ retire from the world; renounce the world. ❸ become a Buddhist priest; take the tonsure; ⓔ retire into religion. ～を切る [*sumō*] rub the salt off one's hands (by way of purification). Ⓐ ～を据える mar one's good name; put a

blot on one's reputation. ⓐ 〜を絶
つ ❶ go into seclusion; ⓔ retire
from the world; renounce the
world. ❷ be peerless; outstrip one's
peers. ⓐ 〜を逃れる escape from
the madding crowd; get away from
the hustle and bustle of the world.
〜を払う dust *sth* off. ⓐ 〜を捻る
squirm (in one's seat); fidget with
embarrassment. ⓐ 〜を攪てる
upset a settled matter; ① stir up
dust; ① raise a dust. ⓐ 〜を結ぶ
❶ send a gift out of mere courtesy.
❷ [*sumō*] rub the salt off one's
hands (by way of purification).

治療 medical treatment

[を] 〜を受ける receive medical
treatment. 〜を施す subject *sb* to
medical treatment.

沈黙 silence; reticence; quiet

[を] 〜を守る remain silent; ① bite
one's lip; ⓒ ① button one's lips. 〜を
破る break one's silence; break the
silence; speak out.

ツ

唾 spit; spittle; saliva

[を] ⓐ ⓒ 〜を返す rebuke *sb*; talk
back; ⓒ give *sb* backtalk. 〜を呑む
hold one's breath; catch one's
breath; be intensely anxious. ⓐ 〜
を引く ❶ hold one's breath; catch
one's breath; be intensely anxious.
❷ drool with envy; lust for *sth*.

柄 a hilt, a haft; a handle

[を] ⓐ 〜を取る be at home in (a
subject); get used to *sth*; ⓔ be well
versed in (a subject). ⓐ 〜を握る be
at home in (a subject); get used to
sth; ⓔ be well versed in (a subject).

疲れ fatigue; exhaustion

[が] 〜が出る begin to suffer from
fatigue; look run down. 〜が取れる
recover from one's fatigue; feel
refreshed. 〜が抜ける recover
from one's fatigue; feel refreshed.
[を] 〜を癒す relieve one's fatigue;
freshen up. 〜を覚える feel tired;
be done in; ⓢ be knackered. 〜を
取る relieve one's fatigue; freshen
up. 〜を抜く relieve one's fatigue;
freshen up. 〜を休める rest
oneself; take a rest.

土 earth; soil; mud; the ground

[が] 〜が付く [*sumō*] be defeated;
lose a fight; ① bite the dust.
[に] 〜に埋める bury in the ground.
〜に帰る pass away; return to dust.
〜に親しむ live close to the soil;
feel kinship with the earth. ⓐ 〜に
成る be buried; ⓔ be laid to rest.
[を] 〜を懸ける heap up earth;
cover *sth* with earth. 〜を掘る dig
in the ground. 〜を踏む set foot on
(foreign) soil.

綱 a rope; a cord; a string

[を] 〜を打つ make rope. 〜を繰り
出す pay out a rope; let out a
rope. 〜を手繰る haul in a rope. 〜

を張る ❶ stretch a rope; rope off (an area). ❷ [*sumō*] become a grand champion. 〜を放す let go the rope. 〜を引く pull a rope; haul in a rope.

角 a horn, an antler ▶ 角

国 〜が生う ❶ sprout horns. ❷ get mad; lose one's temper; be vexed by *sth*; ⓢ ⓘ blow a fuse. ❸ exhibit jealousy; become jealous; be envious. 〜が折れる ❶ lose its horns. ❷ become obedient; become tractable. ❸ be nonplussed; be embarrassed; ⓒ be stumped. 〜が生える ❶ sprout horns. ❷ get mad; lose one's temper; be vexed by *sth*; ⓢ ⓘ blow a fuse. ❸ exhibit jealousy; become jealous; be envious.

で 〜で突く gore *sth* with its horns; horn *sth*.

を 〜を落とす dehorn (an animal). 〜を折る give in to *sb's* demand; drop one's stubborn attitude. 〜を出す display jealous anger; ⓢ ⓘ get one's back up. (人と)〜を突き合わせる be at odds with *sb*; ⓘ be at daggers drawn with *sb*; ⓘ be at loggerheads with *sb*. 〜を付ける attach horns to *sth*. 〜を生やす be jealous of *sb*; envy *sb*; ⓔ have a fit of jealousy; ⓘ wear horns. ⓒ 〜を引っ込ます draw in its feelers. 〜を振り上げる lift up its horns.

鍔 a handguard; the guard

を ⓒ 〜を割る fight desperately; have fierce competition.

粒 a grain; a kernel; a drop

国 〜が揃う be of even quality; be the same size; be well matched.

潰し crushing; smashing

国 〜が効く ❶ be good for some other work; be widely skilled; ⓔ have marketable skills. ⓒ ❷ sell *sth* for the price of the material; have scrap value.

に 〜にする demolish *sth*; melt *sth* down; pulp (books).

壷 a pot; a jar; a vessel

に 〜に嵌まる ❶ go according to plan; prove a success; work out well. ❷ grasp the crux (of a matter); get it right; ⓘ be on the mark; ⓒ ⓘ get the point.

褄 H a skirt

を Ⓐ ⓔ 〜を重ねる make love; have sexual intercourse; have sex. 〜を取る ❶ hold up a skirt; tuck in a skirt. ⓔ ❷ become a *geisha*.

罪 a crime; an offense; a sin

国 〜が無い be harmless; be innocent; be innocuous. 〜が深い be sinful; be full of sin.

に 〜に陥れる incriminate *sb* in a crime. 〜に問う accuse *sb* of a crime; bring a charge against *sb*; charge *sb* with an offense. 〜に服する admit an offense; submit to a sentence; plead guilty.

を 〜を購う atone for one's sins; do penance. 〜を暴く disclose a

crime; Ⓔ bring a misdemeanor to light. ～を負う take (the guilt for) an offense; hold oneself accountable for an offense. ～を犯す commit a crime; commit a sin; Ⓔ perpetrate a misdemeanor. ～を行なう do wrong. ～を隠す hide an offense; Ⓔ cloak a sin. ～を重ねる commit one crime after another. ～を着せる put the guilt on *sb*; pin the blame on *sb*; Ⓘ lay the blame at *sb's* door. ～を着る take the blame for an offense; Ⓒ Ⓘ take the fall. ～を定める sentence *sb* for an offense. ～を正す inquire into an offense. ～を作る act criminally; do *sth* outrageous. ～を鳴らす accuse *sb* of an offense. ～を免れる evade punishment. ～を認める plead guilty to an offense. ～を許す condone an offense.

旋毛(つむじ) **a whorl of hair**

[を] ～を曲げる become mean; be cantankerous; Ⓒ get cross (at *sth*).

爪(つめ) **a nail; a claw; a talon**

[を] ～を隠す ❶ draw in one's claws. ❷ hide one's talents. ～を切る cut one's nails; trim one's nails. ～を銜える ❶ bite on one's nails. ❷ covet *sth*; look enviously at *sb*/*sth*; watch *sb* with envy. ❸ remain an onlooker; stand by idly; Ⓘ sit on the fence. ～を染める paint one's nails. ～を研ぐ ❶ sharpen its claws. ❷ prepare oneself for a fight; resolve to do *sth*; Ⓘ gird up one's loins. ～を延ばす ❶ let one's nails grow long. ❷ lust after *sth*. ～を弾く ❶ snap one's nails. ❷ shun *sb*.

艶(つや) **gloss; luster; glaze**

[が] ～が消える lose its luster. ～が出る a gloss appears.

[を] ～を消す take off the gloss; subdue the luster. ～を出す make *sth* glossy; give luster to *sth*; polish *sth* up. (話に)～を付ける give color to a story; make a story colorful. ～を取る take away the luster.

露(つゆ) **dew; dewdrops; tears**

[が] ～が降りる dew falls.

[と] ～と消える end one's days; fade away; sink into oblivion.

[に] ～に濡れる be moist with dew. Ⓞ ～に結ぶ be frosted with dew. (目に)～を宿す be reduced to tears; Ⓔ melt into tears.

[を] ～を帯びる be covered with dew. ～を払う brush off the dew.

面(つら) [S] **a face; the surface** ▶ 面(おもて) ▶ 面(めん)

[が] Ⓢ ～が良い be cheeky; be impudent. Ⓢ ～が大きい be proud; be haughty; be arrogant. Ⓢ ～が憎い hate the sight of *sb*; detest *sb*.

[を] Ⓢ ～を売る make oneself known; gain influence. Ⓐ Ⓢ ～を食わす hit *sb* in the face; strike *sb* in the face. Ⓢ ～を下げる act with good grace; be unashamed; be unabashed. Ⓢ ～を顰める make a grimace; scowl. Ⓢ ～を出す make an appearance; show one's face;

visit *sb*; call on *sb*. Ⓐ Ⓢ ～を拭う pocket one's pride; swallow one's pride. Ⓢ ～を膨らす show one's displeasure. Ⓢ ～を踏む injure *sb's* dignity; cause *sb* to lose face; Ⓔ blight *sb's* honor. Ⓞ Ⓢ ～を見返す ❶ look back at *sb*; glare back at *sb*. ❷ put a former enemy to shame; Ⓘ get one's own back.

テ

手 the hand; the arm

[が] ～が上がる ❶ show greater skill; get better at *sth*; improve one's hand(writing); (be able to) drink more. ❷ be at a loss (about what to do); Ⓘ be at one's wits' end; Ⓘ be all at sea. ～が空く have time (for *sb*); be free; be vacant; Ⓘ have time on one's hands. ～が有る ❶ have means at one's disposal; have options open to one. ❷ have assistance; be in no short supply of hands. ❸ be skilled with one's hands; Ⓔ be dexterous. ～が掛かる require a great deal of trouble; be troublesome; Ⓒ be a handful. ～が利く be skilled; be good with one's hands; Ⓒ Ⓘ be a dab hand at *sth*. ～が切れる break off (relations) with *sb*; fall out with *sb*. ～が込む be elaborate; be intricate. ～が冴える be skilled; be good with one's hands; Ⓒ Ⓘ be a dab hand at *sth*. ～が下がる lose one's skill; get out of practice. ～が空く have time (for *sb*); be free; be vacant; Ⓘ have time on one's hands. ～が尽きる be at a loss (about what to do); Ⓘ be at one's wits' end; Ⓘ play one's last card; Ⓘ be all at sea. ～が付く ❶ set about (doing *sth*); start out on *sth*. ❷ become intimate with (a servant); enter into a sexual relation with (a maid). ～が付かない be unable to settle down; be restless. ～が付けられない ❶ be out of control; be unmanageable. ❷ be incorrigible; be beyond help. ～が詰まる be busy; be occupied; Ⓘ have one's hands full. ～が出ない ❶ be beyond one's means; be too expensive. ❷ be too difficult for one; lie outside one's ability. ～が届く ❶ be thorough; offer good service; Ⓘ go the whole hog. ❷ lie within one's ability; be within one's sphere of influence. ❸ be within reach of (a goal); get close to (an objective); be getting on for (a certain age). Ⓞ ～が長い be a kleptomaniac; be light-fingered; Ⓔ be given to pilfering. ～が入る ❶ correct *sth*; process *sth*; refine *sth*; ❷ take charge; take control; Ⓘ take *sth* in hand; Ⓐ step in. ～が離れる become independent; be no longer connected with; Ⓘ cut the cord. ～が省ける save one trouble. ～が早い ❶ be quick; be nimble. ❷ be a lady's man; Ⓢ be a quick mover. ❸ be quick to fight; be quick-tempered. ～が塞がる Ⓘ have one's hands full; be fully occupied. ～が回る ❶ attend to everything; leave nothing undone; be attentive to *sb*. ❷ be on *sb's* track. ～が見える be exposed; see through *sb*; ⓘ see in *sb's* cards. ～が焼ける be troublesome; be a bother. ～が良い write in a good hand; be good at *sth*; have nimble hands. ～が笑う lose control over one's hands; have shaky hands. ～が悪い write in a bad hand; be a poor hand at *sth*; ⓘ have two left hands.

[に] ～に余る be beyond one's control; lie outside one's powers; be too much for *sb* (to handle). ～に入れる ❶ gain possession of *sth*; get one's hands on *sth*; come by. ❷ do *sth* with complete control; do *sth* with perfect freedom. ～に落ちる come under *sb's* control; ⓘ fall into *sb's* hands. ～に掛かる ❶ be looked after; be taken care of; be dealt with. ❷ ⓘ fall into *sb's* hands; ⓘ die by *sb's* hand; ⓘ bite the dust. ～に掛ける ❶ take care of *sth/sb*; look after *sb*. ❷ kill *sb* with one's own hands. ～に帰す fall into *sb's* hands; come under *sb's* control. ～にする take *sth* into one's hands; come into the possession of *sth*; make *sth* one's own. ◎ ～に立つ be worthy of *sb's* attention; have effect on *sb*. ～に足る be worthy of *sb's* attention; have effect on *sb*. ～に付かない be unable to settle down; be restless. ～に唾する ❶ ⓘ spit in one's hands.

❷ get ready; ⓘ roll up one's sleeves. ～に取る take *sth* into one's hands. (人の)～に成る be by *sb's* hand; be the work of *sb*. ～に握る be in one's hands; be under one's control; ⓢ ⓘ call the shots. ～に乗る fall into a trap; be taken in; ⓘ play into (the enemy's) hands. ～に入る take possession of *sth*; make *sth* one's own. ～に渡す hand *sth* to *sb*; place *sth* in *sb's* hands. ～に渡る pass into *sb's* possession; fall into *sb's* hands.

[を] ～を上げる ❶ raise one's hands; throw up one's hands. ❷ improve one's skill; get better at *sth*; improve one's hand(writing); (be able to) drink more. ❸ throw one's fists around; attack *sb*; be violent; ◎ throw a punch. ❹ give up; give in; yield to; ⓘ throw in the towel. ～を洗う wash one's hands. ～を合わす ❶ fold one's hands (in prayer). ❷ have a game with *sb*; have a bout with *sb*. ～を入れる ❶ put one's hand into *sth*; reach into *sth*. ❷ touch *sth* up; smarten (a place) up. ❸ meddle with *sth*; ⓘ cook the books. ❹ sound *sb* out; ⓘ put up a trial balloon. ❺ devise a means to *sth*; find a means to *sth*. ❻ make a raid on; conduct a raid (into). ～を失う be deprived of a means. ～を打つ ❶ clap one's hands. ❷ adopt a measure; take action; make a move. ❸ come to an understanding; strike a bargain; close a deal; ⓘ shake hands on *sth*. ～を負う be

129

wounded; be hurt. Ⓐ 〜を置く ❶ be at a loss (about what to do); ① be at one's wits' end; ① be all at sea. ❷ be reserved; hold back. ❸ stand back; acknowledge *sb's* superiority; yield to *sb*. (人の)〜を押える seize *sb* by the hand. Ⓐ 〜を斂む ❶ restrain one's hands. ❷ salute *sb*; give a salute. 〜を返す ❶ be easy (to do); be simple. ❷ be volatile; be changeable; be fickle. 〜を変える change one's approach; resort to other means. Ⓐ 〜を掻く signal with one's hands. ◎ 〜を書く have a taste for calligraphy; be fond of writing. 〜を掛ける ❶ take charge; get a hold on *sth*; ① take *sth* in hand; Ⓐ step in. ❷ lay one's hands on *sth*; take *sth*; ⓒ pinch *sth*; ⓢ nick *sth*. ❸ take trouble over *sth*; elaborate on *sth*; concern oneself with *sth*. 〜を翳す shield one's eyes with one's hand. 〜を貸す assist *sb*; give *sb* help; help *sb*; ① lend *sb* a helping hand. 〜を借りる receive help; ask for help; call in *sb's* aid. 〜を切る ❶ cut one's hand. ❷ (人と) break off (relations) with *sb*. ⓢ 〜を食う be deceived; ① be taken in; ⓒ ① be led by the nose. ◎ 〜を砕く exert oneself; ⓔ give *sth* one's all. 〜を下す ❶ do *sth* in person. ❷ set out to do *sth*; undertake *sth*. 〜を配る make arrangements; take (the necessary) steps. 〜を組む ❶ fold one's arms; link arms with *sb*. ❷ cooperate with each other; work together; join forces; ① join hands. 〜を加える correct *sth*; process *sth*; refine *sth*. 〜を拱く ❶ fold one's hands in prayer. ❷ fold one's arms. ❸ stand by idly; remain an onlooker; ① sit on the fence. 〜を込める give full play to one's skill; exercise one's utmost skill. Ⓐ 〜を下げる beg *sb's* pardon; express one's regret. 〜を差し出す hold out one's hands; offer one's hand. 〜を縛られる have one's hands tied. 〜を締める ❶ squeeze *sb's* hand; give *sb's* hand a squeeze. ❷ close a deal; strike a bargain. ❸ tighten (the rules); draw in the reins; ① keep a tight rein. 〜を擦る rub one's hands; wring one's hands. 〜を添える ① lend *sb* a helping hand. 〜を染める ❶ set out to do *sth*; make a start; Ⓐ get one's hands dirty. ❷ be involved in; ① have a hand in (a plot); ⓢ ① be in cahoots. 〜を揃える gather to do *sth*; work together. 〜を出す ❶ throw one's fists around; attack *sb*; be violent; ⓒ throw a punch. ❷ meddle with *sth*; dabble in (stocks); get involved in *sth*; ① turn one's hand to *sth*. ❸ take *sth*; ⓒ pinch *sth*; ⓢ nick *sth*. ❹ make advances to *sb*; make a move; get involved with a woman. 〜を携える take *sb's* hand; hold *sb's* hand. 〜を叩く ❶ clap one's hands. ❷ strike a deal. 〜を使う ❶ use one's hands. ❷ resort to (every possible) means. 〜を束ねる ❶ fold one's arms. ❷ stand by idly;

て

remain an onlooker; ⓘ sit on the fence. 〜を突く put both hands on the floor (when greeting). 〜を尽くす do one's utmost; do all one can; leave no stone unturned. ⒶÓ 〜を造る put one's hands together (in worship). 〜を付ける ❶ lay one's hand on *sth*; touch *sth*. ❷ set out to do *sth*; take *sth* on; ⓘ take *sth* in hand. ❸ become intimate with (a maid); enter into a sexual relation with *sb* (below one's standing). ❹ embezzle money; pocket (other people's) money. 〜を繋ぐ fold one's hands; join hands. 〜を通す put on a garment (for the first time). 〜を取る ❶ take *sb* by the hand; grab *sb's* hand. ❷ introduce *sb* into an art; teach *sb* kindly. ❸ be flurried; be baffled; be at a loss (about what to do); ⓘ be at one's wits' end; ⓘ be all at sea. ❹ be deceived; ⓘ be taken in; © ⓘ be led by the nose. ❺ [*sumō*] use a technique; resort to a trick. 〜を握る ❶ clench one's fists; wring one's hands. ❷ shake *sb's* hand; grasp *sb's* hand. ❸ form an alliance; cooperate with *sb* on *sth*. ❹ make peace with *sb*; ⓔ be reconciled; © make up (with *sb*). 〜を抜く skimp one's work; ⓘ cut corners; ⑤ ⓘ skate on the job. ⑩ 〜を舐る ❶ © spit in one's hands. ❷ get ready; ⓘ roll up one's sleeves. 〜を延ばす ❶ stretch one's arms. ❷ try one's hand at (*sth* new); venture into (a new area);

ⓘ turn one's hand to *sth*. 〜を放す let off *sth*; loose one's hold on *sth*. 〜を離れる ❶ be out of one's hands; be off one's hands. ❷ become independent; stand on one's own feet; ⓘ cut the cord. 〜を省く skimp one's work; ⓘ cut corners; ⑤ ⓘ skate on the job. 〜を引く ❶ lead *sb* by the hand. ❷ draw one's hands away. ❸ withdraw oneself from *sth*; retreat from a controversy; ⓘ wash one's hands of *sth*; opt out © back out. 〜を広げる ❶ spread one's arms. ❷ be finished; be done for. ❸ extend one's activities; expand a business. ❹ go on a spending spree; © live it up. 〜を振る wave one's hand. 〜を触れる touch *sth*. (人の)〜を経る pass through *sb's* hands. 〜を真似る imitate *sb's* hand(writing). 〜を回す ❶ make full arrangements; take measures; work out a plan. ❷ resort to spying; employ an agent; ⓘ send out tracers. 〜を結ぶ join forces with *sb*; cooperate with *sb*; form an alliance with *sb*. 〜を揉む ❶ rub one's hands together; wring one's hands. ❷ fret over *sth*. 〜を焼く ❶ burn one's hands. ❷ be at a loss (about what to do); ⓘ be put out by *sb*; ⓘ have one's hands full (with a child). ❸ have a bitter experience; be unsuccessful (in dealing with *sth*); ⓘ burn one's fingers. 〜を休める have a rest; take a break; stop doing *sth*. 〜を緩める loose one's grip on *sth*; relax one's hold; make allowances; slacken in vigilance. 〜を汚す ❶ dirty one's hands. ❷ set out to do *sth*; make a start; ⓘ get one's hands dirty; ⓢ get cracking. 〜を分つ ❶ divide work; mete out work. ❷ break off relations; ⓔ sever one's connections with *sb*. ❸ divorce *sb*; get divorced; get separated; ⓒ secure a divorce; ⓒ split up. 〜を煩わす trouble *sb* with *sth*; bother *sb*; rely on *sb's* help; be a burden to *sb*.

手足 arms and legs
🈁 〜を伸ばす stretch one's arms and legs; relax; unwind.

貞操 chastity; constance; virtue
🈁 〜を売る sell one's chastity; prostitute oneself. 〜を捧げる surrender one's chastity. 〜を守る remain faithful; ⓔ defend one's virtue; be chaste. 〜を弄ぶ trifle with (a girl's) chastity. 〜を破る lose one's chastity. 〜を汚す defile (a girl's) chastity; deflower a girl.

敵 an enemy; a foe; a rival
🈁 〜に襲われる be attacked by the enemy. 〜に勝つ conquer the enemy. 〜に付く go over to the enemy; desert to the enemy. 〜に投じる go over to the enemy; desert to the enemy. 〜に成る become enemies; turn against each other. 〜に臨む face the enemy; confront the enemy. 〜に回す

antagonize *sb*; make an enemy of *sb*; have *sb* for an enemy.
🈁 〜とする antagonize *sb*; make an enemy of *sb*; have *sb* for an enemy. 〜と戦う fight with the enemy. 〜と渡り合う engage an enemy; close with the enemy.
🈁 〜を愛する love the enemy. ⓞ 〜を受ける be under attack from the enemy; be attacked by the enemy. 〜を押える check the enemy; keep the enemy in check; pin down the enemy. 〜を襲う make a raid on the enemy; attack the enemy. 〜を作る make enemies.

手心 Ⓔ consideration; allowance
🈁 〜を加える use one's discretion; make allowances (for *sb*); ⓒ go easy on *sb*; ⓢ ⓘ pull one's punches.

手先 the fingers; a tool; a pawn
🈁 〜が痺れる get numb fingers.
🈁 〜で稼ぐ live by one's finger's end.
🈁 〜に使う involve *sb* in (one's excuses); use *sb* as a tool; ⓘ make a cat's paw of *sb*. 〜に成る be an agent in *sth*; act as an instrument.

手塩 Ⓔ table salt
🈁 〜に掛ける raise (a child) with tender loving care.

手玉 a hand ball; a small ball
🈁 〜に取る trifle with a person; ⓘ take *sb* in; ⓒ ⓘ lead *sb* by the nose; ⓒ ⓘ twist *sb* round one's little finger.

轍 E a wheel track; a rut

を ～を踏む repeat *sb's* mistake; share *sb's* fate; C follow in the wake of *sth*; I fall into the same rut.

鉄槌 E an iron hammer

を ～を下す deal a crushing blow (to *sb/sth*); crack down on *sb/sth*. ～を加える deal a crushing blow (to *sb/sth*); crack down on *sb/sth*.

掌 the palm of the hand ▶ 掌

に ～に隠す palm (a card/coin).
を ～を返す be inconstant; be changeable; be fickle.

出端 E the outset; the start

を (人の)～を折る snub *sb*; spoil *sb's* headstart; dampen *sb's* initial enthusiasm. (人の)～を挫く snub *sb*; spoil *sb's* headstart; dampen *sb's* initial enthusiasm.

天 the heavens; the sky

に ～に謝す heaven be thanked!; thank heaven! ◎ E ～に冲する soar into the sky; shoot up skyward. ～に衝く soar into the sky; shoot up skyward. ◎ ～に則る submit to the will of heaven; follow the way of heaven. ～に任せる put one's faith in heaven; trust to providence; rely on fate.
を ～を仰ぐ look up to heaven; raise one's gaze skyward. ～を恐れる fear the gods. (火が)～を焦がす (flames) scorch the heavens. Ⓐ E ～を摩する touch the heavens.

点 a spot; a point; a mark

が ～が甘い be (too) liberal in marking; be (too) lenient in marking. ～が辛い be strict in marking; be severe in marking. ～が良い have good marks. ～が悪い have bad marks.
を ～を与える award marks. ～を得る gain a point. ～を打つ ❶ mark *sth* with a dot; punctuate a sentence. ❷ criticize *sb*; point out *sb's* shortcomings. ～を稼ぐ gain (good) marks; get a good score. ◎ ～を記す keep the score. ～を付ける give marks; mark *sb's* work. ～を取る get a rating; score a point.

天下 the whole country

を ～を治める pacify the whole country; rule over the whole country. ～を取る conquer the whole country; take the reigns of government; gain absolute control.

天秤 a pair of scales

に ～に掛ける weigh the pros and cons (of a matter).

ト

戸 a door; a sliding door

を ～を開ける open a door. Ⓐ ～を下ろす ❶ close a door; bolt the door. ❷ go out of business; go bankrupt; S go bust. Ⓐ ～を鎖す ❶ close a door; bolt the door. ❷ go out of business; go bankrupt; S go

133

bust. 〜をしめ直す reclose a door.
〜を閉める close a door. 〜を叩く
knock on a door.

堵 E a fence; an enclosure

が A E 〜に安んず ❶ live in peace;
enjoy the safety of peace. ❷ be
relieved; be at ease; feel at ease.

度 a degree; an extent

が 〜が過ぎる be excessive; go too
far; © Ⓘ be over the top. A 〜が抜
ける ❶ have bad timing. ❷ relieve
the tension; Ⓘ break the ice.
に A 〜に当たる be moderate; be
in the right degree.
を 〜を失う be rattled; lose one's
presence of mind; be flustered; be
flurried; Ⓘ lose one's head. 〜を過
ごす go too far in *sth*; Ⓘ take *sth*
too far; Ⓘ carry things too far.

当 E right; justice; fairness

を 〜を得る be right; be in order;
be proper; Ⓘ be to the point. E 〜
を失する be wrong; be improper;
E be ill conceived; Ⓘ be off the
mark; Ⓘ be beside the point.

薹 E a flower stalk; a peduncle

が E 〜が立つ ❶ go to seed; run to
seed. ❷ go hard; become fibrous.
❸ pass one's prime; E lose the
bloom of youth; A get old and
rusty; Ⓘ be over the hill.

胴 the trunk; the body

が A 〜が据わる be resolute; pluck

up courage; brace oneself; gather
one's strength. 〜が長い have a
long trunk. 〜が短い have a short
trunk; have a short waist.
に ⓪ 〜に上げる toss *sb* into the
air. A 〜に突く toss *sb* into the air.
を A 〜を据える pluck up courage;
become emboldened.

堂 a hall; a temple; a shrine

に 〜に入る become an expert;
master a craft; be at home in (a
certain field of expertise).

頭角 E the top of the head

を 〜を現わす distinguish oneself;
stand out (among one's peers);
Ⓘ cut a dashing figure.

峠 a (mountain) pass; a crisis

を 〜を越す ❶ cross over a ridge;
traverse a (mountain) pass. ❷ pass
the critical point; Ⓘ turn the corner; © Ⓘ be over the hump.

答弁 E a reply; an answer

に E 〜に窮する be at a loss for an
answer; be speechless.
を E 〜を差し控える reserve one's
answer. E 〜を求める call *sb* to
account; require an explanation.

時 time; an occasion; a chance

が 〜がある have time. 〜が掛かる
take time. 〜が立つ time passes;
time goes by; time elapses.
に A 〜に遇う have luck; have
one's day. 〜に当たる be at the

right time. 〜に従う go with the times; go with the flow. Ⓐ 〜につく bend to the powers that be. 〜に臨む meet the occasion; Ⓒ face the music; Ⓒ bite the bullet. 〜に因る go with the times. Ⓐ 〜に寄る bend to the powers that be.

を 〜を与える give *sb* time; allow *sb* time (to do *sth*). 〜を争う fight for time; try to buy time. 〜を窺う watch for an opportunity; Ⓔ bide one's time. 〜を失う ❶ miss an opportunity; lose a chance; be untimely. ❷ be out of touch with the times; go into eclipse; go down in the world. 〜を打つ chime the hour; strike the hour. 〜を得る ride the wave of opportunity; Ⓔ have one's day. 〜を置く (do *sth*) at regular intervals; (do *sth*) periodically. 〜を惜しむ spare time; be sparing of one's time. 〜を貸す give *sb* time. 〜を稼ぐ play for time; buy time. 〜を切る (do *sth*) at regular intervals; (do *sth*) periodically. 〜を裂く find the time. 〜を過ごす pass time; spend one's time. 〜を費やす spend time; waste time. 〜を撞く toll the time; chime the hour; strike the hour. Ⓐ 〜を作る announce the dawn; crow (at dawn). 〜を告げる announce the hour; toll the time. 〜を潰す idle one's time away; waste one's time; Ⓒ kill time. 〜を待つ wait until the time is ripe; wait for an opportunity; Ⓔ bide one's tim. 〜を忘れる forget the time; lose the time.

度胆 Ⓒ "the very liver"

を Ⓒ 〜を抜かす ❶ be appalled; be dumfounded; be taken aback. ❷ be terrified; Ⓒ be scared out of one's wits.

度胸 courage; pluck; grit

が 〜が据る have great courage; have nerves of steel.

を 〜を据える pluck up courage; gather one's strength.

毒 poison; venom; malice; spite

に 〜に中る be poisoned; get poisoned. 〜に成る be venomous; be noxious; be harmful.

を Ⓐ 〜を言う say malicious things; Ⓔ speak venomous words; Ⓐ spit venom. 〜を消す counteract the effects of poison; neutralize poison. 〜を盛る administer poison to *sb*; poison *sb*.

蟠 a coil

を 〜を巻く ❶ coil oneself up. ❷ hang around; loaf about; loiter around.

床 a bed; a sickbed; a kip

に 〜に就く ❶ go to bed; retire to bed; turn in. ❷ take to a sickbed; be taken ill; be ill in bed; be laid up (with illness). 〜に入る go to bed; get into bed.

を 〜を上げる ❶ put away the bedding. ❷ get better; leave one's sickbed; Ⓒ be up and about. 〜を敷く prepare a bed; lay out the

と

bedding; make a bed. 〜を取る
prepare a bed; lay out the bedding; make a bed. 〜を離れる
❶ get out of bed. ❷ leave one's
sickbed; get better; ⓒ be up and
about. 〜を払う ❶ put away the
bedding. ❷ get better; leave one's
sickbed; ⓒ be up and about.

所 (ところ) a place; a spot; a scene
に Ⓐ 〜に置く ❶ stand back; give
way to *sb*; yield ground to *sb*. ❷ be
reserved; hold back. Ⓐ 〜に付く
fall into place; find a niche; find
one's feet; feel at home.
を 〜を得る ❶ be in (one's) place;
be in one's element. ❷ fall into
place; ⓒ attain a position; find a
niche; ⓓ 〜を教える tell *sb* one's
address; give *sb* one's address. 〜
を変える change one's position;
change place.

年 (とし) a year; years; age ⬧ 年 (ねん)
が 〜が明ける the year opens; the
year begins. 〜が改まる ❶ the new
year comes round. ❷ the era name
changes; enter a new era. 〜が行
く ❶ grow old; reach old age. ❷ a
year passes by; the year draws to a
close. 〜が替る ❶ the new year
comes round. ❷ the era name
changes; enter a new era. 〜が長
ける put on years; grow older. 〜
が立つ years pass. 〜が寄る grow
old; reach old age.
を 〜を惜しむ fear old age; regret
the passing of the years. 〜を隠す

conceal one's age. (人の)〜を聞く
ask *sb* his/her age. ⓢ 〜を食う put
on years; grow older. 〜を越す
❶ send off the old year and greet
the new. ❷ keep *sth* over the win-
ter. 〜を取る ❶ put on years; grow
older; gain in years. ❷ welcome
the new year. ⓓ 〜を拾う take a
new lease of life. 〜を跨ぐ extend
from one year to the next; bridge
the new year. 〜を迎える welcome
the new year.

土地 (とち) soil; land; a lot; a locality
を 〜を買う buy a lot. 〜を借りる
lease land. 〜を切り開く clear the
land. 〜を肥やす enrich the soil.
〜を耕す till the soil.

止め (とど) Ⓔ a finishing blow
を ⓔ 〜を刺す ❶ kill *sb* by a stab in
the neck. ❷ deal *sb* a decisive
blow; clinch an argument; ⓘ put
the lid on *sth*.

帳 (とばり) Ⓔ a curtain; hangings
が ⓔ 〜が降りる darkness falls;
night falls.
に ⓔ 〜に包まれる be shrouded in
mystery.

途方 (とほう) an aim; reason; logic
に 〜に暮れる be bewildered; ⓘ be
at one's wits' end; ⓘ be all at sea.

富 (とみ) riches; a fortune; wealth
が ⓓ 〜が落ちる win a prize (in a
lottery).

[を] ～を作る create wealth; make a fortune. ～を積む amass a fortune; accumulate wealth; build up a fortune. ～を成す accumulate riches; create wealth; grow rich. ～を残す leave an estate (to *sb*). ～を誇る grow arrogant through one's wealth; be purse-proud.

虎 a tiger; a tigress

[に] ～になる get roaring drunk; get riotously drunk; be high on drink.

鳥肌 goose bumps; gooseflesh

[が] ～が立つ give *sb* goose bumps; get goose pimples.

泥 mud; dirt; mire

[を] ～を被る assume *sb* else's responsibility; take the blame for *sb*; Ⓒ Ⓘ take the fall. ～を塗る sling mud at *sb*; stain *sb's* good name; ; Ⓘ take *sb* down a peg. Ⓢ ～を吐く confess the truth; admit one's guilt; Ⓒ own up (to a crime). Ⓐ ～を踏む have an unsteady gait; be unsteady on one's feet.

ナ

名 a name; a title; esteem ➧ 名

[が] ～が売れる be widely known; be popular; be esteemed. Ⓐ ～が朽ちる disgrace one's good name; lose one's reputation. ～が廃れる lose one's reputation; lose ground. ～が立つ have a reputation; Ⓒ Ⓘ be the talk of the town. ～が通る be well known; be renowned. Ⓐ ～が流れる win fame; become widely known. ～が泣く reflect badly on one's name; fall short of one's reputation. ◎ ～が触れる be well known; be famous; be celebrated.

[に] ～に負う ❶ (do *sth*) in one's own name; (do *sth*) in the name of (honor). ❷ be true to one's name. ❸ be famous; have a great reputation. ～に係わる compromise one's reputation; reflect on one's good name. ～に聞く hear of *sth*; listen to *sth*; Ⓘ give rumor the ear. ～に背く belie one's name; be untrue to one's name; do not live up to one's name. Ⓐ ～に立つ be well known; be famous; be celebrated. Ⓐ ～に流る win fame; become widely known; rise in the world. Ⓐ ～に旧る have an illustrious name. ◎ ～に触れる be well known; be famous; be celebrated.

[を] ～を明かす disclose one's/*sb's* name. ～を揚げる ❶ win fame; gain reputation; become celebrated. ❷ advertise oneself; make oneself well known; distinguish oneself. ～を挙げる mention *sb's* name; name *sb*. ～を現わす reveal one's/*sb's* name. ～を言う say one's name; mention *sb's* name. ～を偽る assume a false name; give a wrong name. Ⓐ ～を埋む fade into obscurity; bury one's name. ～を売る achieve fame; acquire a reputation. Ⓐ ～を得る become famous;

gain reputation; win popularity. ～
を惜しむ hold one's name high;
honor one's name; be jealous of
one's reputation. ～を落とす
damage one's (good) name; lose
one's reputation. Ⓐ ～を折る injure
one's/*sb's* reputation; mar one's/*sb's*
reputation. ～を変える change
one's name. Ⓐ ～を掛く ❶ enter
one's name; allow one's name to be
added (to a list). ❷ gain fame; grow
in reputation. ❸ call *sb's* name. ～
を貸す lend one's name (to a
cause). ～を騙る assume *sb's* name;
impersonate *sb*. ～を借りる ❶ do
sth in *sb's* name; use *sb's* name.
❷ do *sth* under a pretext. Ⓐ ～を腐
す wreck one's/*sb's* name; ruin
one's/*sb's* reputation. ～を汚す
damage one's/*sb's* name; disgrace
one's/*sb's* name. ～を指す mention
sb by name; point out *sb's* name. ～
を示す name oneself; publish one's
name. ～を濯ぐ clear one's/*sb's*
name; restore one's/*sb's* reputation.
～を雪ぐ clear one's/*sb's* name;
restore one's/*sb's* reputation. ～を
出す put forth one's name; give
one's name. Ⓐ ～を正す tell right
from wrong; define one's moral
obligations. ～を立てる ❶ win
fame; gain a reputation; become
celebrated. ❷ start a rumor; set
afloat a rumor. ～を保つ defend
one's/*sb's* honor. Ⓐ ～を散らす
achieve fame; acquire a good reputation; ⓒ ① be the talk of the town.
～を付ける give *sb* a name; christen

a child. ～を連ねる enter one's
name (on a list); have oneself
enlisted. Ⓐ ～を釣る seek fame;
make oneself well known; distinguish oneself. Ⓐ ～を遂げる attain
a (certain) reputation; distinguish
oneself. ～を留む leave one's name
behind; become immortal; ⓔ leave
one's mark. Ⓗ ～を唱える state
one's name (to the enemy). ～を取
る win fame; become famous. ～を
流す cause a scandal; be talked
about; ⓒ ① be the talk of the town.
～を成す acquire a name for
oneself; win fame; become well
known. ⑩ ～を偸む gain an
unjustified reputation. ～を残す
leave one's name behind; become
immortal; ⓒ leave one's mark. ～を
辱める insult *sb's* reputation;
disgrace oneself; ⓔ bring disgrace
upon one's/*sb's* name. ～を馳せる
win fame; become widely known.
Ⓐ ～を揮う do one credit; reflect
well on one's name. Ⓐ ～を許す
recognize *sb's* reputation. ～を汚す
soil one's name; mar one's reputation. ～を呼ぶ call *sb* by name.

中 the inside; the interior

で ～で待つ wait inside (a place).
に (危険の)～に居る be in danger;
be in the midst of danger. ～に埋
める bury *sth* in (the sand/soil). ～
に数える number *sb* among (the
great). ～に佇む stand amid (a
crowd). ～に立つ ❶ stand inside (a
place). ❷ mediate between (two

parties); come between (two parties). 〜に入_いる ❶ go into a place; enter (a building); go inside. ❷ mediate between (two parties); come between (two parties).

凵 〜へ入_いれる put *sth* into (a box). 〜へ立_たつ mediate between (two parties); come between (two parties). 〜へ入_{はい}る ❶ go into a place; enter (a building); go inside. ❷ mediate between (two parties); come between (two parties).

囪 〜を取_とる ❶ take the middle course; Ⓒ go middle. ❷ mediate between (two parties); come between (two parties). 〜を直_{なお}す reconcile (two parties); make peace. 〜を行_ゆく take the middle course; go middle.

仲_{なか} relations; relationship

囵 〜が良_いい be good friends; be on good terms; get on well. Ⓞ 〜が旨_{うま}い be good friends; be on good terms; get on well. 〜が悪_{わる}い be enemies; be on bad terms; ① be at daggers drawn; Ⓒ ① be on the out with *sb*.

囶 〜に立_たつ mediate between (two parties); come between (two parties). 〜になる fall in love with each other; come to love each other. 〜に入_{はい}る mediate between (two parties); come between (two parties). 〜に挟_{はさ}まる be caught between (the conflicting interests of) two parties.

凵 〜へ立_たつ mediate between (two

parties); come between (two parties). 〜へ入_{はい}る mediate between (two parties); come between (two parties).

囫 〜を裂_さく divide (two parties); drive a wedge between (two parties); estrange two people. 〜を塞_せく divide (two parties); drive a wedge between (two parties); estrange two people. 〜を取_とり持_もつ act as a go-between; be a match-maker. 〜を取_とる mediate between (two parties); come between (two parties). 〜を直_{なお}す reconcile (two parties); make peace.

流れ_{なが} a flow; a stream; a school

囶 〜に逆_{さか}らう go against the flow; swim against the current. 〜に従_{したが}う go with the flow; swim with the current.

囫 〜を下_{くだ}る go downstream. 〜を汲_くむ ❶ drink from a stream. ❷ follow in a tradition; belong to a school (of thought); belong to the same bloodline. Ⓐ 〜を立_たてる become a prostitute. 〜を上_{のぼ}る go upstream. 〜を乱_{みだ}す wade through a stream; cross a stream.

泣き_な crying; weeping; lament

囵 Ⓞ (芸_{げい}に)〜が入_{はい}る become highly accomplished at an art; master a skill.

囫 〜を入_いれる plead for mercy; beg for mercy; Ⓒ implore *sb*. 〜を見_みる be in trouble; ① come to grief; Ⓒ get oneself into a fix.

慰め comfort; consolation

[を] 〜を得る take comfort in *sth*; draw comfort from *sth*. 〜を求める seek for solace; take comfort in *sth*; find solace in (prayer).

情け sympathy; pity; charity

[を] 〜を売る ❶ sell one's favors; prostitute oneself. ❷ be kind to *sb*; show *sb* sympathy. 〜を掛ける be kind to *sb*; show kindness; treat *sb* with sympathy; take pity on *sb*. 〜を交わす love one another; treat each other with affection. 〜を乞う ask *sb* for mercy; beg for mercy; plead for mercy. 〜を知る know pity; have pity. 〜を尽す do good; practice charity.

鍋釜 pots and pans

[が] ⒶⒶ 〜が賑わう live in luxury; live the good life; be well off. Ⓐ 〜が割れる have a domestic quarrel.

波 a wave; a billow; a sea

[が] 〜が高い the waves are high; have high seas; Ⓒ be choppy. 〜が立つ be wavy; have high seas; Ⓒ be choppy.

[に] 〜に攫われる be carried away by the waves; be swept away by the waves. 〜に漂う drift on the waves. 〜に呑まれる be swallowed up by the waves. 〜に乗る ❶ ride a wave; surf on a wave. ❷ ride on the waves (of opportunity); ride the crest (of a movement).

[を] 〜を打つ be wavy; have high seas; Ⓒ be choppy. 〜を被る ship water; be washed by the waves. 〜を切る plow the waves; cleave the waves; cut through the waves.

涙 tears; crying; sympathy

[に] 〜に暮れる ❶ weep one's eyes out; cry one's eyes out. ❷ live in misery; live a life of misery. 〜に沈む weep one's eyes out; cry one's eyes out; drown in sorrow; Ⓒ be dissolved in tears. Ⓐ 〜に迷う be distraught with grief; be lost in grief. 〜に咽ぶ be choked with tears.

[を] 〜を浮かべる tears stand in one's eyes. 〜を打ち払う dash one's tears away. 〜を押える fight back one's tears; repress one's tears. 〜を誘う move *sb* to tears; be a tear-jerker. 〜を流す shed tears. 〜を拭う wipe one's tears away; wipe one's eyes. 〜を呑む ❶ swallow one's tears; gulp down one's tears. ❷ pocket an insult; brook an insult; Ⓘ keep a stiff upper lip. 〜を払う dash one's tears away. 〜を拭く dry one's tears. 〜を催す melt into tears; be moved to tears.

縄 a rope; a cord; bonds

[に] 〜に掛かる be bound with a rope; be put in bonds; be arrested.

[を] 〜を入る measure the acreage (of a plot of land); take the measurements of a plot. 〜を打つ ❶ bind *sb* with a rope; arrest *sb*;

seize *sb*. ❷ measure the acreage (of a plot of land); take the measurements of a plot. ❸ stretch a rope; rope off (a place); draw a cordon. 〜を掛ける ❶ bind *sb*/*sth* with a rope; tie *sb* up; put *sb* in bonds. ❷ arrest *sb*; put *sb* under arrest. 〜を解く ❶ unbind *sb*/*sth*; untie *sb*/*sth*; untie *sb's* bonds. ❷ release *sb*; set *sb* free; ⓒ let *sb* go. 〜を綯う twist a rope; strand a rope. 〜を張る rope off (a place); draw a cordon; demarcate an area; mark one's territory. 〜を引く pull a rope. ⓗ 〜を結ぶ knot a rope (to convey a message).

縄張り roping off; territory

|を| 〜を荒らす intrude into *sb's* domain; trespass on *sb's* territory. 〜を争う contest a sphere of influence; quarrel over (one's) territory. 〜をする rope off (a place); draw a cordon; demarcate an area; mark (one's) territory. 〜を広げる extend one's territory; widen one's beat. 〜を守る defend one's territory; protect an area.

縄目 Ⓔ bonds; fetters; chains

|に| ⓔ 〜に遭う ❶ be bound with a rope; be put in bonds. ⓔ ❷ be arrested; be put under arrest.

|を| ⓔ 〜を切る untie one's bonds. ⓔ 〜を擦り抜ける free oneself from one's bonds; slip one's bonds. ⓔ 〜を解く ❶ unbind *sb*/*sth*; untie *sb*/*sth*; untie *sb's* bonds. ❷ release

sb; set *sb* free; ⓒ let *sb* go. ⓔ 〜を免れる escape arrest.

難 trouble; difficulty; hardship

|に| 〜に遭う meet with disaster. 〜に当たる face (up to) difficulty; tackle a difficult situation.

|を| 〜を言う point out *sb's* flaws. Ⓐ 〜を構える take issue with *sb*; ⓔ engage in a battle of words; ⓘ cross swords with *sb*. 〜を避ける take refuge in (a place). 〜を免れる escape danger; escape censure.

荷 a load; a cargo; a burden

|が| 〜が重い be a heavy load; be a taxing burden. 〜が下りる be relieved from one's duty; be acquitted of one's responsibilities. 〜が勝つ be too heavy a load for one; be unequal to the task.

|に| 〜になる be a burden to one.

|を| 〜を送る send freight; consign goods. 〜を下ろす ❶ unload (a ship); unpack (a horse). ❷ fulfill one's duty; relieve oneself of one's responsibilities. ⓓ 〜を付ける load (a cart); pack (a horse). 〜を積む load (a cart); pack (a horse); take on cargo. 〜を解く unpack a box. 〜を担う carry a load on one's shoulders. 〜を刎ねる throw cargo overboard; jettison (part of) the cargo. 〜を引き取る receive goods; take delivery of goods.

に

匂 a smell; a scent; an odor

[を] 〜を嗅ぐ smell *sth*. 〜を付ける perfume *sth*. 〜を取る take the smell off *sth*. 〜を抜く remove an odor. 〜を放つ give out a scent.

肉 flesh; meat; the flesh

[が] 〜が落ちる lose weight. 〜が付く put on weight.

[に] 〜に飢える thirst for the flesh.

[を] 〜を切る carve meat. 〜を付ける fatten up; flesh out.

肉欲 lust; passion; carnal desire

[に] 〜に耽る indulge in sensual pleasures.

[を] 〜を制する suppress one's carnal desires; restrain one's passions; be continent. 〜を満たす gratify one's lusts; satisfy one's carnal desires.

逃げ flight; escape

[を] 〜を打つ ❶ attempt to escape; try to get away; plan one's escape. ❷ excuse oneself; dodge (a question); ⓒ back out (of a promise). 〜を張る ❶ attempt to escape; try to get away; plan one's escape. ❷ excuse oneself; dodge (a question); ⓒ back out (of a promise).

逃げ場 a refuge; a shelter

[を] 〜を失う have one's escape cut off; be cut off from escape; be trapped. 〜を作る provide for one's retreat; find a pretext; set up one's escape.

錦 Japanese brocade

[を] 〜を飾る return home in glory; ⓔ have a glorious homecoming; ⓒ ⓘ bring home the bacon.

にち Ⓐ wheedling; extortion

[を] Ⓐ 〜を入れる wheedle *sb* into *sth* by false arguments; talk *sb* into *sth*; ⓒ importune *sb* by illicit means.

日限 a date; a term

[が] 〜が切れる the term expires. 〜が来る fall due.

[を] 〜を定める fix a term; set a date. 〜を早める advance the date.

荷物 a load; a burden; luggage

[を] 〜を預ける have one's baggage checked. 〜を下ろす unload (a cart). 〜を抱え込む bear a responsibility; carry a (heavy) burden. 〜を運ぶ carry a load. 〜を纏める pack up.

任 a duty; a responsibility

[に] 〜に当たる take charge of a duty; ⓒ undertake a responsibility; ⓒ take on a job. 〜に在る be in office; hold a post. 〜に赴く leave for one's post. 〜に帰る return to one's post. 〜に堪える be equal to the task; be up to the job. 〜に就く take up one's duties; take office. 〜に適す be fit for a post.

[を] 〜を辞す resign from one's post; ⓔ tender one's resignation; step

down from office; leave office. 〜
を果たす fulfill one's duties.

認可 approval; permission

を 〜を得る obtain authorization;
be authorized.

人気 popularity; public interest

が 〜がある be popular; be in
favor; be in vogue. 〜が落ちる fall
in popularity; lose favor; go out of
fashion; ⑩ fall from grace. 〜が増す
win popularity; gain in popularity.

を 〜を失う lose popularity; go
out of fashion. 〜を得る gain
favor; become fashionable. 〜を落
とす lose popularity; become
unpopular. 〜を高める increase
one's popularity; heighten one's
popularity. 〜を取る become
popular; win favor; ⓒ catch on. 〜
を呼ぶ be much talked about;
create a sensation; ⑩ make a stir.

人数 the number of persons

を 〜を限る limit the number of
people. 〜を数える count heads;
ⓒ ⓐ tell noses. 〜を揃える
assemble the required number of
people. 〜を増やす increase the
number of persons. 〜を減らす
reduce the number of persons.

人相 looks; appearance

を 〜を教える describe sb's looks.
〜を変える disguise oneself. 〜を
見る tell sb's destiny by their face;
read sb's face.

ヌ

縫い揚げ a tuck (of a garment)

を 〜を下ろす let out a tuck. 〜を
する tuck (a garment).

縫い目 a seam; a stitch

が 〜が綻びる a seam opens. 〜が
解ける a seam starts.
を 〜を解く undo a seam.

盗み stealing; theft; larceny

に 〜に入る break into a house;
burglarize an estate.
を 〜を働く steal *sth*; ⓒ commit
larceny.

濡れ衣 a false charge

を 〜を着せる accuse *sb* unjustly;
bring a false charge against *sb*. 〜
を着る be falsely charged; be
wrongly accused (of a crime).

ネ

根 a root; the source; nature ▶ 根

が 〜が付く ❶ ⓛ take root. ❷ catch
on; ⓐ take root. 〜が生える
❶ ⓛ take root. ❷ ⓐ take root; settle down.

に 〜に持つ ❶ bare *sb* ill will;
harbor a grudge against *sb*; have
an underlying motive; ⑩ have an
axe to grind. ❷ entertain (an idea);
hold *sth*; harbor *sth*; hide *sth*.

を ⓐ 〜を押す pay attention to
sth; elaborate on *sth*. 〜を下ろす

ぬ

take root; settle down. Ⓐ 〜を切る ❶ cure *sb* radically; Ⓔ effect a radical cure. ❷ root out a longstanding abuse; eradicate an old evil. 〜を差す ❶ Ⓒ take root. ❷ arise from *sth*; originate in *sth*; Ⓐ take root in *sth*. 〜を絶つ root out (a problem); eradicate the roots (of evil). 〜を摘む ❶ nip a root. ❷ grasp *sb's* purpose; understand *sb's* motives. 〜を抜く root up; pluck up by the roots. 〜を生やす ❶ Ⓒ take root. ❷ Ⓐ take root; settle down. 〜を張る ❶ Ⓒ take root. ❷ catch on; Ⓐ take root. Ⓐ 〜を引く sow the seeds (of discord). Ⓒ 〜を回す dig round the roots (of a tree).

音 Ⓔ a sound; a tone; a tune

が Ⓔ 〜が良い sound sweet. Ⓔ 〜が悪い sound harsh.

に Ⓔ 〜に聞く listen to rumors; lend rumor the ear; Ⓘ hear *sth* on the grapevine. Ⓐ Ⓔ 〜に立つ raise one's voice; call out. Ⓔ 〜に泣く burst out crying; wail.

を Ⓔ 〜を上げる ❶ complain about *sth*; make complaints; Ⓒ Ⓘ sing small. ❷ give in; admit one's defeat; Ⓒ Ⓘ cry uncle. Ⓐ Ⓔ 〜を立つ raise one's voice; call out. Ⓔ 〜を泣く burst out crying; wail.

値 a price; a cost; a value

が 〜が上がる rise in price; go up in price. 〜が決まる fix a price; set a price. 〜が下がる fall in price; go down in price. 〜が出る fetch a

good price; improve in price. Ⓐ 〜が成る ❶ fix a price. ❷ come to an understanding; arrive at an agreement; come to terms. 〜が張る be expensive; be dear.

を 〜を上げる raise the price. 〜を押える peg the price. 〜を聞く ask the price; inquire after the price. 〜を決める fix a price; set a price. 〜を下げる lower the price. 〜を競り上げる bid up the price. 〜を付ける ❶ put a price on *sth*; set a price on *sth*; price (an article). ❷ name a price; make an offer; estimate a price. 〜を踏む ❶ put a price on *sth*; set a price on *sth*; price (an article). ❷ name a price; make an offer; estimate a price.

値打ち value; worth; merit

が 〜が上がる ❶ rise in value; gain value. ❷ go up in public estimation; gain prestige. 〜が有る have value; be worthy (of *sth*). 〜が落ちる ❶ fall in value; lose value. ❷ go down in public estimation; lose prestige. 〜が下がる lose value; drop in value; go down in public estimation. 〜が出る become of value. 〜が増す ❶ gain in value; increase in value. ❷ go up in public estimation; gain prestige; be widely recognized.

を 〜を付ける put a value on *sth*. 〜を増す increase the value of *sth*; make *sth* more valuable. 〜を認める appreciate the value of *sth*; recognize the merit of *sth*.

寝返り tossing about in bed

[を] 〜を打つ ❶ toss about in bed; turn over in one's sleep. ❷ betray an ally; play *sb* false; double-cross *sb*; go over to the enemy; defect to the other side; ① be a turncoat.

猫 a cat

[を] 〜を飼う keep a cat. 〜を被る conceal one's real personality; feign ignorance; play the hypocrite; simulate modesty.

螺子 a screw; a spring

[が] 〜が緩む ❶ a screw loosens. ❷ loosen up; relax in tension.

[で] 〜で締める screw *sth* down. 〜で停める screw *sth* up; fix *sth* with a screw; fasten *sth* with a screw.

[を] 〜を締める drive home a screw. 〜を抜く remove a screw. 〜を巻く ❶ wind up (a watch). ❷ rouse *sb* to action; spur *sb* into action; call *sb* to order. 〜を回す turn a screw. 〜を戻す unscrew a screw. 〜を緩める loosen a screw.

熱 heat; temperature; fever

[が] 〜が上がる one's temperature rises; increase one's fever. 〜がある have a temperature; be feverish; run a fever. 〜が籠る be filled with enthusiasm. 〜が下がる one's temperature falls; ⓔ one's fever subsided. 〜が冷める lose one's enthusiasm. 〜が高い have a high fever; have a temperature. 〜が出る run a temperature; become feverish. 〜が入る get carried away by *sth*; get into *sth*; put one's mind to *sth*; ① warm up to *sth*. 〜が引く one's temperature falls; ⓔ one's fever subsided.

[に] 〜に浮かされる ❶ be delirious with fever; fall into delirium. ❷ be obsessed with *sth*.

[を] 〜を上げる ❶ push up the temperature; raise the heat. ❷ be enthusiastic about *sb/sth*; enthuse over *sb/sth*; be enthralled by *sth*; ① be mad about *sb*; have a crush on *sb*. 〜を加える apply heat to *sth*. 〜を冷ます ❶ cool down; chill down. ❷ dampen one's enthusiasm; ① be a wet blanket. 〜を計る take one's temperature. Ⓐ 〜を吐く ❶ argue heatedly in favor/against *sth*; debate *sth* hotly. ❷ brag about *sth*; boast about *sth*; ① talk big; ① blow one's own horn.

眠気 sleepiness; drowsiness

[が] 〜がさす become sleepy; feel drowsy; be overcome with drowsiness.

[に] 〜に襲われる be overcome with drowsiness.

[を] 〜を覚ます keep oneself awake; shake off sleepiness; get over a sleepy spell. 〜を払う shake off sleepiness; get over a sleepy spell. 〜を催す become sleepy; feel drowsy.

眠り a sleep; a slumber; a nap

[が] 〜が浅い have a poor sleep;

145

sleep lightly; be a light sleeper. 〜
が深い have a sound sleep; sleep
deeply; be a good sleeper.

［に］ 〜に落ちる fall asleep; drop off
to sleep. 〜につく go to sleep; go
to bed; ⓔ retire to bed.

［を］ 〜を覚ます arouse *sb* from
sleep. 〜を催させる make *sb* feel
drowsy; induce sleep.

念 ⓔ a sense; an idea; a wish

［が］ ⓔ 〜が入る be attentive to
detail; be prudent; be careful. ⓔ
〜が届く ❶ have one's wish come
true; see one's dream fulfilled.
❷ be tactful; be considerate; be
attentive. ⓔ 〜が残る be unable to
give *sth* up. ⓔ 〜が晴れる clear
one's mind.

［と］ ⓞ ⓔ 〜とする be of concern.

［に］ ⓔ 〜に掛ける be troubled by *sth*;
fret over *sth*; ⓘ weigh on one's mind.

［を］ ⓔ 〜を入れる ❶ pay attention to
detail; take care with *sth*; do *sth*
with care. ❷ put *sb* to trouble; give
trouble to *sb*; make trouble. ⓔ 〜
を押す remind *sb* (of *sth*); call *sb's*
attention to *sth*; make sure of *sth*;
tell *sb* emphatically of *sth*. ⓔ 〜を
凝らす meditate on *sth*; ponder
over *sth*. ⓞ ⓔ 〜を突く make sure
of *sth*; call *sb's* attention to *sth*;
remind *sb* of *sth*. ⓔ 〜を残す pass
away with regrets. ⓔ 〜を晴らす
clear one's mind.

年 a year; a grade; a term ▶ 年

［が］ 〜が明ける ❶ end one's term of

service; end one's apprenticeship.
❷ end one's role; ⓔ bring one's mission to an end. ❸ go out of use;
lose its effectiveness.

［に］ ⓞ 〜に行く be apprenticed to
sb; apprentice oneself to *sb*.

［を］ ⓞ 〜を入れる go through a long
period of training; put in a great
deal of time; apply oneself to *sth*
over many years. ⓞ 〜を沈める be
apprenticed to *sb*; apprentice oneself to *sb*.

年功 ⓔ long years of service

［を］ ⓔ 〜を積む have long
experience (in an office); apply
oneself to *sth* over many years;
work for many years; serve long.

ノ

軒 the eaves

［を］ 〜を争う stand close together.
〜を借りる take shelter under the
eaves (of *sb's* house). 〜を連ねる
stand side by side; stand in a row.
〜を並べる stand side by side;
stand in a row.

望み hope a wish; aspirations

［が］ 〜が有る there is hope.

［に］ 〜に叶う meet one's hopes;
answer one's prayers.

［を］ 〜を抱く have an ambition;
harbor a wish; ⓔ cherish a desire.
〜を失う lose hope; despair of
achieving one's ambition. (人に)〜

を掛ける expect much of *sb*; set one's hopes on *sb*. 〜を叶える fulfill *sb's* wishes. 〜を捨てる abandon one's dreams; give up hope. (人に)〜を託す pin one's hopes on *sb*. 〜を繋ぐ cling to one's (last) hopes. 〜を遂げる realize one's dream; attain one's object; effect one's purpose. ⓒ 〜を懐く entertain hopes (of success); aspire to *sth*.

喉 the throat; a voice

が 〜が渇く ❶ be thirsty. ❷ be envious; be greedy; covet *sth*. 〜が詰まる be choked. 〜が鳴る smack one's lips; ⓢ ⓘ lick one's chops.

に 〜に支える have *sth* stuck in one's throat; get *sth* stuck in one's throat. 〜に引っ掛かる have *sth* stuck in one's throat; get *sth* stuck in one's throat.

を 〜を潤す quench one's thirst. 〜を押える hold one's/*sb's* throat; seize *sb* by the throat. 〜を聞かす sing to others. 〜を締める grip *sb's* throat; strangle *sb*. 〜を絞る shout at the top of one's voice. 〜を突く stab oneself/*sb* in the throat. 〜を鳴らす purr. ⓒ 〜を干す feel hungry; go hungry; starve from hunger.

暖簾 a shop curtain; reputation

に 〜に関わる affect the name of a shop; reflect on the reputation of an enterprise.

を 〜を売る sell out one's business.

〜を下ろす ❶ close down (a shop); go out of business; ⓑ retire from business. ❷ close shop; put up the shutters; ⓒ wind up business. Ⓐ 〜を掛ける go out of business; go bankrupt; ⓢ go bust. 〜を傷つける harm the name of a shop; damage the reputation of an establishment. 〜を潜る frequent an establishment; visit a shop. 〜を汚す harm the reputation of a shop. 〜を分ける start up in the same business; open up a branch store.

ハ

歯 a tooth; grinders; a cog

が 〜が痛む have a toothache. 〜が浮く be grating; be nauseating; be disgusting; ⓘ set one's teeth on edge. Ⓐ 〜が利く ❶ be effective; be of use. ❷ have influence; ⓘ carry weight. 〜が立つ ❶ be edible. ❷ be within one's reach; be able to handle *sth*; be able to resist *sb*.

に Ⓐ 〜に合う meet one's taste; be suitable.

を Ⓐ 〜を噛む grind one's teeth; gnash one's teeth. 〜を食い縛る clench one's teeth; grit one's teeth. Ⓐ 〜を切る clench one's teeth; grit one's teeth. Ⓐ ⓔ 〜を切す clench one's teeth; grit one's teeth. ⓗ 〜を染める blacken one's teeth. ⓒ 〜を出す ❶ show one's teeth; bare one's teeth. ❷ get

は

angry; be irate. ～を立てる sink one's teeth into *sth*. ～を抜く pull out a tooth; extract a tooth. ～を穿る pick one's teeth. ～を磨く brush one's teeth; polish one's teeth. ～を見せる show one's teeth; grin. ～を剥く ❶ show one's teeth; bare one's teeth. ❷ get angry; be irate; ⓒ ⓘ blow a fuse.

覇 Ⓔ supremacy; leadership
ⓦ ～を争う contend for mastery; ⓔ vie for supremacy. ⓔ ～を唱える hold sway; assume the leadership; reign supreme.

刃 a blade; an edge ♦ 刃
ⓦ ⓞ ～を付ける sharpen a sword; give an edge to a blade; sharpen a knife; set a razor. ⓞ ～を拾う polish a sword; finish a sword blade.

羽 feathers ♦ 羽
ⓖ ⓐ ～が利く have influence; ⓘ carry weight (with *sb*).
ⓦ ⓐ ～を伸す exert one's influence.

場 a place; a spot; a site
ⓖ ～が開く the market opens. ～が立つ a session is held.
ⓦ ～を取る occupy space. ～を外す quit a place; ⓒ ⓘ slip away.

場当たり grandstand play
ⓦ ～を言う tune one's talk to the company; ⓘ pay lipservice. ～を取る ⓘ win the gallery. ⓞ ～を遣る play to the gallery.

肺肝 Ⓔ lungs and liver
ⓦ ⓐ ⓔ ～を明かす unbosom oneself; ⓔ admit *sb* into one's confidence ⓘ pour out one's heart to *sb*. ⓐ ⓔ ～を出だす unbosom oneself; ⓔ admit *sb* into one's confidence ⓘ pour out one's heart to *sb*. ⓐ ⓔ ～を穿つ see through *sb's* heart; penetrate *sb's* mind. ⓐ ⓔ ～を砕く think hard about *sth*; ⓔ tax one's ingenuity; ⓒ ⓘ rack one's brains. ⓐ ⓔ ～を苦しむ think hard about *sth*; ⓔ tax one's ingenuity; ⓒ ⓘ rack one's brains. ⓐ ⓔ ～を出す unbosom oneself; ⓔ admit *sb* into one's confidence ⓘ pour out one's heart to *sb*. ⓐ ⓔ ～を尽くす think hard about *sth*; ⓔ tax one's ingenuity; ⓒ ⓘ rack one's brains. ⓐ ⓔ ～を披く unbosom oneself; ⓔ admit *sb* into one's confidence ⓘ pour out one's heart to *sb*.

敗北 defeat; a reverse; a rout
ⓦ ～を喫する meet with defeat; taste defeat. ～を招く court defeat. ～を認める admit defeat; acknowledge one's defeat.

墓 a grave; a tomb; a sepulcher
ⓝ ～に葬る consign (sb) to the grave. ～に参る visit *sb's* grave.
ⓦ ～を暴く dig open a grave. ～を建てる raise a tomb; erect a tombstone. ～を掘る dig a grave.

捗 Ⓔ progress; advance
ⓖ ～が行く make good progress.

は

馬鹿 a fool; a simpleton
に ～にする make a fool of *sb*; make fun of *sb*; slight *sb*; insult *sb*. ～になる become benumbed; grow dull; go blunt; go flat.
を ～を言う talk nonsense; ⓘ talk through one's hat; © talk rubbish. ～を見る make a fool of oneself; feel like a loser; be disappointed. ～を遣る make a mistake; commit a stupidity; make a blunder.

場数 experience
を ～を踏む gain experience; add to one's experience.

馬脚 a horse's legs
を ～を現わす betray oneself; reveal one's true character; ⓘ show the cloven hoof.

箔 (metal) foil; gold/silver leaf
が ～が落ちる ❶ the gilt comes off. ❷ lower one's dignity; lose prestige; lose one's reputation; reflect badly on one. ～が付く gather prestige; gain in reputation. ～が剥げる ❶ the gilt comes off. ❷ lower one's dignity; lose prestige; lose one's reputation; reflect badly on one.
を ～を置く gild (an object); cover *sth* with gold/silver leaf. ～を付ける make one/*sth* look more important; add to *sth*'s value; add to one's reputation; reflect well on one. ～を塗る gild (an object); cover *sth* with gold/silver leaf).

馬具 horse gear; harness
を ～を付ける harness a horse. ～を外す unharness a horse.

白紙 blank paper; white paper
に ～に戻す return to the drawing board; start all over again.

拍車 a spur
に (馬)に～を入れる spur on (one's horse). ～を掛ける spur *sth* on; give impetus to *sth*.

博打 gambling; speculation
を ～を打つ gamble; play for money; take a gamble. ～を止める give up gambling.

薄氷 thin ice
を ～を踏む tread on thin ice; be on thin ice.

箸 chopsticks
が ～が進む eat a lot; eat one's fill.
を ～を置く put one's chopsticks down. ◎ ～を下ろす start eating; begin to eat. Ⓐ ～を試みる ❶ taste *sth*; sample food; try the taste of *sth*. ⓥ ⓢ ❷ sleep with a woman; ⓔ have intercourse with a woman; ⓢ lay a woman. ～を使う use chopsticks. ～を付ける start eating; begin to eat. ～を取る ❶ hold chopsticks; take up one's chopsticks. ❷ start eating; begin to eat. ～を休める ❶ put one's chopsticks down. ❷ finish eating.

149

恥 shame; ignominy; disgrace

を ～を掻く be put to shame; be embarrassed; be humiliated; ⓘ be taken down a peg. Ⓐ ～を雪む exorcize one's feelings of shame. ～を堪える bear the shame; endure the ignominy. ～を曝す disgrace oneself; bring shame upon oneself. ～を忍ぶ swallow one's pride; suppress one's feelings of shame. ～を知る have a sense of shame/honor; be sensible to shame. ～を雪ぐ vindicate one's honor; clear one's name. Ⓐ ～を捨つ be unashamed. Ⓐ ～を見す put *sb* to shame; humiliate *sb*; ⓘ take *sb* down a peg.

旗 a flag; a banner; a standard

を ～を揚げる ❶ raise a flag; hoist a flag. ❷ rise in arms; raise an army. ❸ set out (to do *sth*); set up in business. ～を押し立てる unfurl a flag. ～を下ろす take down a flag; strike a flag; lower the flag. ～を掲げる hoist a flag; put up a flag. ～を出す hang out a flag. ～を立てる hoist a flag; put up a flag. ～を振る ❶ wave a flag. ❷ lead a group. ⓞ ～を開く unfurl a flag; put up a flag. ～を広げる unfurl a flag. ⓞ ～を巻く ❶ furl a flag. ❷ withdraw from the battlefield; ⓒ back out (of a situation). ❸ close down (a shop).

旗色 flag color; the situation

を ～を見る remain an onlooker; ⓘ see how the wind blows; ⓘ sit on the fence; ⓒⓘ watch which way the cat jumps.

肌 the skin; the grain

が ～が合う be like-minded; get along well; ⓔ be congenial to one; ⓘ see eye to eye; ⓒⓘ hit it off.

で ～で感じる have first-hand experience; know *sth* from experience.

に ～に合う suit one; be right for one. (女の)～に触れる know a woman; sleep with a woman; ⓔ have carnal knowledge of a woman; ⓢ lay a woman.

を ～を合わせる ❶ be close to *sb*; ⓢⓘ be in cahoots with *sb*. ❷ have sexual intercourse; sleep with each other. ～を脱ぐ ❶ strip oneself to the waist; bare one's shoulders. ❷ exert oneself; do one's utmost. (男に)～を許す give oneself to a man; sleep with a man; ⓒⓘ go all the way. ～を汚す stain one's/sb's virtue; be unchaste; rape a woman.

裸 a naked body; a nude

に ～にする undress *sb*; strip *sb* naked; strip (a tree) of leaves. ～になる ❶ strip oneself naked; get undressed; take off one's clothes. ❷ lose all one's money; become penniless; ⓒ go broke; ⓢ go bust.

畑 a field; a farm; a plantation

が ～が違う lie outside one's field of expertise.

罰 Ⓒ divine punishment ▶ 罰

が Ⓒ ～が当たる be punished by the gods; be served right; Ⓔ feel the wrath of Heaven; Ⓔ incur divine punishment.

ばつ Ⓢ an occasion; a situation

が Ⓢ ～が悪い be embarrassed; feel awkward; be ashamed; be abashed.

を Ⓞ Ⓢ ～を合わせる make one's story sound plausible; arrange to tell the same story; say *sth* to suit the occasion; ① chime in with *sb*.

罰 punishment; penalty ▶ 罰

を ～を受ける be punished. ～を加える inflict punishment on *sb*; impose a penalty on *sb*; mete out punishment.

発破 a blast

を ～を掛ける ❶ blast *sth* with explosives. ❷ urge *sb* to do *sth*; spur *sb* on (to do *sth*); egg *sb* on.

花 a flower; a blossom; youth

が ～が咲く ❶ Ⓒ be in bloom; be in blossom. ❷ be prosperous; do well. ❸ grow lively; liven up.

と ～と散る be killed in action; fall in battle; die on the battlefield.

を ～を活ける arrange flowers; put flowers in (a vase). Ⓐ ～を折る have good looks; have a graceful figure. ～を飾る decorate *sth* with flowers; dress *sth* up. ～を切る cut flowers. ～を咲かせる ❶ make

something prosperous; make *sth* flourish; invigorate *sth*. ❷ win fame; be successful; ① bring home the bacon. ～を添える add luster to *sth*. Ⓐ ～を散らす pass away before one's time; die young. ～を作る grow flowers. ～を摘む pick flowers; gather flowers. ～を引く play cards. ～を持たせる let *sb* have the credit for (a success); give *sb* credit; Ⓔ bestow favors on *sb*. Ⓐ ～を遣る make *sth* exquisite; explore the boundaries of luxury.

鼻 a nose; a muzzle; a trunk

が Ⓐ ～が明く be disappointed; be frustrated. ～が利く ❶ have a good nose; have a good scent. ❷ be good at making money; ① have a nose for *sth*. ～が高い be proud; be vain; be haughty; Ⓔ have a high opinion of oneself; Ⓢ be stuck up. ～が詰まる have a stopped up nose. Ⓐ ～が拉げる be discouraged; be squashed; be crushed; give way. ～が凹む be talked down; be cornered; ① be brought to bay. ～が曲がる smell offensive.

で ～であしらう treat *sb* with contempt; snub *sb*; ① thumb one's nose at *sb*. ～で笑う laugh sardonically at *sb*; Ⓒ snicker at *sb*.

に ～に当てる boast about *sth*; be proud of *sth*; take pride in *sth*. ～に掛ける boast about *sth*; be proud of *sth*; take pride in *sth*. ～に付く ❶ smell offensive; be disgusting. ❷ get sick and tired of *sth*; Ⓒ be

は

fed up with *sth*. 〜にぶら下げる boast about *sth*; be proud of *sth*; take pride in *sth*.

|を| (人の)〜を明かす ❶ forestall *sb*; get a start on *sb*; preempt *sb's* actions; anticipate *sb* in doing *sth*. ❷ outwit *sb*; surprise *sb*. 〜を蠢かす be elated; be puffed up with pride. 〜を折る humble *sb's* pride; ① put *sb's* nose out of joint; ① take *sb* down a peg. Ⓐ 〜を欠く suffer a loss; incur a setback. (人の)〜を出し抜く ❶ forestall *sb*; get a start on *sb*; preempt *sb's* actions; anticipate *sb* in doing *sth*. ❷ outwit *sb*; surprise *sb*. 〜を突き合わせる be face to face. 〜を衝く ❶ assail the nostrils; smell offensive. ❷ be disinherited; be cut off. ❸ have a clash of personalities; have a conflict; fall out with *sb*. 〜を撮まれる be disliked; put people off. 〜を撮む hold one's nose. 〜を鳴らす ❶ sniff one's nose. ❷ coo at *sth*; sulk over *sth*; behave like a spoilt child. 〜を並べる line up (horses). Ⓐ 〜を舐る loaf around; idle away one's time. ◎ 〜を放る sneeze. 〜を弾く ❶ assail the nostrils; smell offensive. ❷ humble *sb's* pride; ① put *sb's* nose out of joint. 〜を穿る pick one's nose.

鼻息 nasal breath
|が| 〜が荒い ❶ breathe hard through the nose. ❷ be arrogant; be haughty; be proud; have an overbearing attitude.

|を| ◎ 〜を仰ぐ sound out *sb's* feelings; Ⓒ consult *sb's* pleasure. 〜を窺う sound out *sb's* feelings; Ⓒ consult *sb's* pleasure.

鼻毛 nasal hair
|が| 〜が長い be infatuated with a woman; be keen on a girl; Ⓒ be besotted with a woman.

|を| Ⓐ 〜を数える make fun of *sb* who is infatuated with one; ① wrap *sb* round one's little finger; Ⓒ poke fun at one's suitor. 〜を抜く ❶ pull out one's nasal hair. ❷ outwit *sb*; deceive *sb*; ① take *sb* in; Ⓒ ① lead *sb* by the nose; ⒮ dupe *sb*. 〜を延ばす be infatuated with a woman; be keen on a girl; Ⓒ be mad about a woman; Ⓒ be besotted with a woman. ◎ 〜を読む make fun of *sb* who is infatuated with one; ① wrap *sb* round one's little finger; Ⓒ poke fun at one's suitor.

鼻薬 "nose medicine"; a bribe
|を| 〜を嗅がせる offer *sb* a bribe; bribe *sb*; Ⓒ ① grease *sb's* palm. 〜を効かせる offer *sb* a bribe; bribe *sb*; Ⓒ ① grease *sb's* palm.

話 a talk; a chat; a rumor
|が| 〜が合う understand each other; get on well; agree with each other. ◎ 〜が落ちる talk wildly; talk indecently; talk lewdly. 〜が違う be a different matter; be a different story. 〜が付く reach an agreement; come to an under-

standing; strike a bargain; close a deal; ① shake hands on *sth*. 〜が弾む have a lively conversation. 〜が纏まる come to an agreement; reach a settlement; ⓒ wrap *sth* up. 〜が分かる ❶ understand *sb*; empathize with *sb*. ❷ be sensible; know what is what.

に 〜に乗る give *sb* counsel; counsel *sb*. 〜にならない be not worth mentioning; be not worth one's while; be too ridiculous for words. 〜に触れる touch upon a subject; broach a subject.

を 〜を変える change the subject (of conversation). 〜をし掛ける speak to *sb*; accost *sb*. 〜を切り出す broach a subject; raise an issue. 〜を逸らす turn the conversation to a different subject; steer the conversation in a different direction. 〜を付ける settle a matter; make arrangements with *sb*; negotiate with *sb*. 〜を続ける continue to talk; keep up the conversation. 〜を始める start a conversation; begin a story. 〜を端折る make a long story short; cut the matter short; ⓒ ① get to the point; ① cut to the chase. 〜を纏める come to an agreement with *sb*; reach a settlement; ⓢ wrap *sth* up. 〜を持ち掛ける approach *sb* with a matter; make *sb* a proposal. 〜を持ち込む propose a matter; make *sb* a proposal. 〜を持ち出す bring up a subject; put forward a matter; broach a subject.

鼻柱 the bridge of a nose; pride

を 〜を折る snub *sb*; ⓔ humble *sb's* pride; ① take *sb* down a peg.

羽 a feather; a wing ▶ 羽

が ⓞ 〜が付く be settled; be brought to an end. 〜が抜ける shed feathers. 〜が生える fledge.

を Ⓐ 〜を交す act like two turtle doves; have a loving marriage. ⓞ 〜を付ける settle *sth*; bring *sth* to an end. 〜を畳む fold the wings. Ⓗ 〜を垂る ❶ go down on one's knees; grovel in the dirt. ❷ surrender oneself; capitulate (to the enemy); submit to one's rival; ① hoist a white flag. ⓞ 〜を取る ❶ take a percentage; take a rake-off. ❷ be a great success; be a big hit; ① pull off a great coup; ⓢ ① hit the jackpot. Ⓐ 〜を並べる ❶ act like two turtle doves; be a loving man and wife; have a loving marriage. Ⓐ ❷ give collective counsel to (one's lord). 〜を伸ばす have a good time; Ⓐ spread one's wings; ⓢ ① kick up one's heels. 〜を広げる spread the wings.

幅 width; breadth; influence

が 〜が利く have influence with *sb*; be influential.

に Ⓐ 〜に成る gain prestige; win fame; be widely recognized.

を 〜を利かす make one's influence felt; lord it over *sb*; assert one's power. ⓞ 〜をする be vain; show off; ⓔ be ostentatious;

は

be haughty. 〜を取る ❶ occupy a wide space. ❷ make one's influence felt; assert one's power. ㋑ 〜を成す ❶ make one's influence felt; lord it over *sb*; assert one's power. ❷ make oneself at home; put oneself at ease. ㋺ 〜を遣る make one's influence felt; lord it over *sb*; assert one's power.

羽目 a panel; a situation; a pass

㋺ 〜に陥る be in a quandary; be in a sad plight; ⓒ be in a fix; ⓢ ① be up the creek. 〜になる be in a quandary; be in a sad plight; ⓒ be in a fix.

㋲ 〜を外す make merry; make a racket; ⓒ ① let one's hair down.

波紋 a water ring; a ripple

㋓ 〜が広がる ❶ create a ripple (on a pond); ripple out. ❷ have repercussions; the rumor spreads; ① make a stir.

㋲ 〜を描く ❶ create a water ring; ripple out. ❷ have repercussions; ① make a stir. 〜を投じる have major repercussions; ① make a stir. 〜を投げ掛ける have major repercussions; cause a sensation; ① make a stir.

腹 the stomach; the abdomen

㋓ ⓐ 〜が合う be like-minded; get along well; ⓔ have the same disposition; ⓔ be congenial to one; ① see eye to eye; ⓒ ① hit it off. 〜が有る harbor a secret; have a hidden

agenda; have an ulterior motive; ① have an axe to grind. ⓐ 〜が癒える ❶ settle old scores; ① get one's own back; revenge oneself on *sb*; wreak one's wrath. ❷ cool one's anger; calm down; ⓐ cool down; work off one's grudge. ❸ vent one's spleen; give vent to one's feelings. 〜が痛む have a stomachache; have the gripes. ⓐ 〜が居る cool one's anger; vent one's spleen; give vent to one's feelings. 〜が大きい be magnanimous; be big-hearted 〜が収まる calm down; ⓐ cool down. 〜が決まる have one's mind made up; be resolved; be determined. 〜が腐る be corrupted; be despicable. 〜が下る have loose bowels; suffer from diarrhea. 〜が黒い be treacherous; be perverted; be blackhearted. 〜が据る have the stomach to do *sth*; ⓒ have guts; have pluck; be bold. 〜が立つ get angry; lose one's temper; ⓢ ① blow a fuse. ⓢ 〜が突く have an empty stomach; be hungry. 〜が出来る ❶ be full; have eaten one's fill. ❷ have one's mind made up; be resolved; be determined. 〜が出る have a potbelly; ⓢ ① have a spare tire. ⓢ 〜が無い ❶ be ungenerous; be mean. ❷ lack courage; be timid; be cowardly. 〜が煮え繰り返る be infuriated; be irate; be furious; ⓔ be beside oneself with rage. 〜が煮える become irritated; be upset over *sth*; be cross with *sb*. 〜が張る be fully

は

fed; feel bloated. 〜が減る have an empty stomach; be hungry. 〜が膨れる ❶ be full; have eaten one's fill. Ⓥ Ⓢ ❷ become pregnant. ❸ hold a grudge against *sb*; Ⓔ harbor a private malice; Ⓘ have an axe to grind; Ⓘ have a chip on one's shoulder. ❹ be frustrated; feel thwarted. 〜が太い ❶ be brazen; be cheeky. ❷ be magnanimous; be generous; be big-hearted. 〜が見え透く be seen through; be exposed.

[に] Ⓐ 〜に合う understand *sb*; get on well with *sb*; agree with *sb*; Ⓘ see eye to eye with *sb*; Ⓒ Ⓘ hit it off. Ⓞ 〜に入る grasp the meaning of *sth*; learn how to do *sth*; master the art of *sth*. 〜に落ちる be convinced; be persuaded; come round to *sb's* point of view; give one's consent. 〜に据え兼ねる be intolerable; be unbearable; Ⓔ be insufferable.

[へ] Ⓐ 〜へ落ちる be convinced; be persuaded; come round to *sb's* point of view; give one's consent.

[を] Ⓞ 〜を合わす collaborate with *sb*; conspire with *sb*; Ⓢ Ⓘ be in cahoots with *sb*. 〜を痛める ❶ give birth. ❷ suffer financial losses. 〜を癒す ❶ settle old scores; Ⓘ get one's own back; revenge oneself on *sb*; wreak one's wrath. ❷ cool one's anger; calm down; Ⓐ cool down; work off one's grudge. ❸ vent one's spleen; give vent to one's feelings. Ⓐ 〜を入れる apply oneself to *sth*; do *sth* wholeheartedly. 〜を抉る wring one's heart; Ⓘ turn one's stomach upside down; Ⓒ feel gutted. 〜を抱える Ⓘ hold one's sides with laughter; Ⓘ laugh one's head off; Ⓒ Ⓘ kill oneself laughing. 〜を固める make up one's mind; resolve to do *sth*; Ⓘ gird up one's loins. 〜を決める make up one's mind; resolve to do *sth*; Ⓘ gird up one's loins. 〜を切る ❶ disembowel oneself; commit suicide. ❷ resign from office; leave office; step down from office. ❸ take responsibility; Ⓒ Ⓘ face the music; Ⓒ Ⓘ bite the bullet. ❹ Ⓘ hold one's sides with laughter; Ⓒ Ⓘ kill oneself laughing. 〜を括る brace oneself; resolve to do *sth*; Ⓘ gird up one's loins. Ⓞ 〜を拵える have a meal to fortify oneself; satisfy one's appetite; eat one's fill. 〜を肥やす enrich oneself; Ⓘ line one's pocket; Ⓘ feather one's nest. 〜を壊す have stomach trouble; upset one's stomach. 〜を探る sound *sb* out; feel *sb* out; Ⓒ check *sb's* mood. 〜を摩る rub one's stomach. Ⓐ 〜を締める brace oneself; resolve to do *sth*; Ⓘ gird up one's loins. 〜を据える ❶ make up one's mind; prepare oneself for *sth*; Ⓘ gird up one's loins. ❷ calm oneself; collect one's senses. ❸ cool one's anger; vent one's spleen; give vent to one's feelings. 〜を空かす work up an appetite. 〜を立てる get angry; take offense at *sth*; get worked up over *sth*; lose one's temper; Ⓢ Ⓘ blow a fuse. ～を見抜く see through *sb*; read *sb's* mind. Ⓐ ～を召す disembowel oneself; commit suicide. ～を捩じる Ⓘ hold one's sides with laughter; Ⓘ laugh one's head off; Ⓒ Ⓘ kill oneself laughing. ～を読む fathom *sb's* thoughts; read *sb's* mind. ◎ ～を縒る Ⓘ split one's sides with laughter; Ⓘ hold one's sides with laughter. ～を割る speak one's mind; be outspoken; be candid; be frank.

腸（はらわた） the intestines; the bowels

[が] ～が腐る become depraved; be perverted; be corrupted. ～が千切れる wring one's heart; be heart-broken; Ⓒ feel gutted. ～が煮え返る be infuriated; be irate; be furious. ～が見え透く be exposed; be seen through.

[に] ～に沁みる ❶ have a pleasant sensation (when drinking alcohol). ❷ sink deeply into one's mind; be deeply impressed.

[を] ～を抉る wring one's heart; Ⓘ turn one's stomach upside down; Ⓒ feel gutted. ～を掻き毟る wring one's heart; Ⓘ turn one's stomach upside down; Ⓔ rend one's heart; break one's heart. ◎ ～を切る roll over laughing; Ⓘ laugh one's head off; Ⓒ Ⓘ kill oneself laughing. ～を探る sound *sb* out; feel *sb* out; Ⓒ check *sb's* mood. ～を絞る wring one's heart; Ⓔ rend one's heart; Ⓘ turn one's stomach upside down; break one's heart. ～を断つ ❶ wring one's heart; Ⓔ rend one's heart; Ⓘ turn one's stomach upside down; break one's heart. ❷ roll over laughing; Ⓘ laugh one's head off; Ⓒ Ⓘ kill oneself laughing. ～を抜く remove the guts; gut (a fish).

針（はり） a needle; a pin; a pointer

[を] ◎ ～を含む have a sting.

馬力（ばりき） horse power

[が] ～が有る have stamina.

[を] ～を掛ける exert oneself; Ⓘ work one's fingers to the bone.

春（はる） spring; springtime

[を] ～を売る sell one's chastity; prostitute oneself. ～を鬻ぐ sell one's chastity; prostitute oneself.

判（はん） a (hand) stamp; a seal

[を] ～を押す seal (a bond); affix a seal. ◎ ～を貸す stand surety for *sb*; go bail for *sb*.

範（はん） [E] an example; a model

[を] ～を示す set an example. ～を垂れる set an example. ◎ ～を採る follow *sb's* example. ◎ ～を似倣う copy *sb's* example.

番（ばん） watch; guard; one's turn

[が] ◎ ～が明ける be off watch.

[に] ～に当たる be on duty. ～に立つ be on guard; stand guard.

[を] ～を狂わせる disturb the order. ～をする watch over (a house);

は

stand guard; look after *sth*. 〜を待つ wait for one's turn.

範囲 an extent; a scope; a sphere

を 〜を限る set limits; limit (the scope of) *sth*; fix the limits of *sth*. 〜を越える exceed a limit; transcend the boundaries.

反感 animosity; antipathy

を 〜を抱く hold a grudge against *sb*; harbor ill feelings toward *sb*. 〜を買う arouse *sb's* antipathy; incur *sb's* ill feeling. 〜を示す show one's antipathy. 〜をそそる provoke antipathy.

反旗 E a banner of revolt

を E 〜を翻す rise in revolt; take up arms (against *sb*); E raise the standard of revolt.

反響 an echo; reverberation

を 〜を起こす cause repercussions; be much talked about; ① make a stir. 〜を呼び起こす evoke a response; ① make a stir.

半畳 half a *tatami*

を Ⓐ 〜を入れる jeer at *sb*; hoot at *sb*; heckle *sb*; Ⓒ ① give *sb* the bird. Ⓐ 〜を打つ jeer at *sb*; hoot at *sb*; heckle *sb*; Ⓒ ① give *sb* the bird.

判断 judgment; decision

を 〜を誤る err in one's judgment; judge wrongly. 〜を下す take a decision; make a judgment.

万難 E innumerable difficulties

を E 〜を排する do *sth* at all costs; overcome all kinds of difficulties.

反乱 a rebellion; a revolt

を 〜を起こす rise in revolt; rebel against. 〜を静める put down a revolt; pacify a rebellion.

ヒ

日 the sun; a day; a date

が 〜が上がる the sun rises; the sun goes up. 〜が浅い be not long since; be only recent. 〜が当たる ❶ be in the sun; bask in the sun. ❷ be favored by circumstances; ① have one's day in the sun. 〜が落ちる the sun goes down; the sun sets. 〜が傾く the sun is getting low; the sun declines. 〜が陰る the sun goes behind the clouds; the sun is eclipsed. 〜が暮れる it grows dark; night falls; the day declines. ◎ 〜が込む take time; be time-consuming. 〜が差す the sunlight stings. 〜が沈む the sun sets; the sun goes down. 〜が高い the sun is high; the day is (still) high; be still early days. 〜が詰る the days grow shorter. 〜が出る the sun rises; the sun goes up. 〜が長い the days are long. 〜が昇る the sun rises. 〜が入る the sun sets; the sun goes down. 〜が短い the days are short. 〜が悪い have a bad day.

に ～に当てる bask in the sun; sun oneself; expose *sth* to the sun. ～に干す dry *sth* in the sun. ～に焼ける get sunburned.

を ◎ ～を入れる let in the sunlight. ～を選ぶ choose a date; name the day. ～を重ねる gather time. ～を数える count the days. ◎ ～を切る give a time limit; set a deadline. ～を暮らす pass one's days; spend one's time. Ⓐ ～を消す pass one's days; spend one's time. ～を定める fix a date; set a date. ～を延ばす put *sth* off; postpone *sth*. ◎ ～を旧る gather years; grow old. ～を経る pass the days; go through the days. ～を見る cast a horoscope for the day. ～を避ける avoid the sun; keep off the sun; shield oneself from the sun.

火 a fire; a flame; a blaze

が ～が移る the fire spreads; catch on fire. ～が付く ❶ catch fire. ❷ a (crisis) breaks out; erupt into a crisis); (war) breaks out. ～が出る see stars; see red. Ⓐ ～が降る be badly off; ① be in dire straits. ～が燃える a fire is burning.

に ～に当たる warm oneself at a fire. ～に掛ける put *sth* over a fire. ～に焼べる put *sth* into the fire; throw (logs) on the fire.

を ～を扇ぐ fan a fire. Ⓐ ～を挙ぐ ❶ make a fire; light a fire. ❷ make a living. ◎ ～を活ける bank up a fire; damp down a fire. ～を打つ strike a spark; make a fire. ～を起こ

す build a fire. ～を落とす rake out a fire. Ⓗ ～を易う purify a ritual fire. ～を掻き立てる stir a fire. ～を掛ける ❶ set fire to *sth*; set *sth* alight. ❷ open fire (on the enemy); take (the enemy) under fire. Ⓓ ～を被る be overcome with grief; grief over *sth*; Ⓐ cover oneself in ashes. ～を切る strike a spark; make fire. ～を消す ❶ put out a fire; extinguish a fire. ❷ turn off the light; switch off the light. ～を失す cause a fire by accident. Ⓐ ～を摩る ❶ make fire by friction. ❷ burn with resentment; boil with dissension. ～を焚き付ける kindle a fire; make a fire. ～を出す have a fire started. ～を立てる signal by way of making a fire. ～を散らす fight vehemently; debate an issue hotly; Ⓔ engage in a fierce contest. ～を使う use fire. ～を注ぐ replenish a fire. ～を付ける ❶ set fire to *sth*; set *sth* alight. ❷ turn on the light; switch on the light. ❸ trigger an event; start a conflict. Ⓔ instigate a row. ～を通す heat *sth* up; warm *sth* up. ～を灯す light a lamp. ～を吐く spit fire; emit fire; erupt into flames. ～を放つ set fire to *sth*. ～を噴く ❶ blow life into a fire. ❷ erupt into flames; emit fire; breathe fire. Ⓐ ～を振る ❶ stir a fire; rake up a fire. ❷ start a quarrel with *sb*; pick a fight with *sb*. ～を弄ぶ play with fire. ～を燃やす make a fire; light a fire; start a fire.

非 a fault; an injustice; a wrong

を ～を暴く discover one's faults. ◎ ～を打つ point out an injustice; criticize *sb*. ～を飾る hide one's faults. ～を悟る realize one's error. ～を鳴らす denounce (a traitor). ～を認める admit one's error; acknowledge one's faults.

眉宇 E the brow

を E ～を輝かす beam (with joy).

美観 a nice view; a fine spectacle

を ～を傷つける mar the beauty of *sth*; spoil the view. ～を添える add to the beauty of *sth*; lend beauty to *sth*. E ～を呈する present a fine spectacle.

髭 a beard; a mustache

を ～を剃る shave oneself; have a shave. ◎ ～を取る shave off one's beard/mustache. ～を撫でる stroke one's beard/mustache. ～を生やす grow a beard/mustache; have a beard/mustache. ～を捻る twirl one's mustache.

鼻孔 the nostril

を ～を膨らませる flare one's nostrils.

膝 the knee; one's lap

が ～が流れる have weak knees. ～が抜ける one's knees give way. ～が笑う be unsteady on one's legs.

を Ⓐ ～を容れる ❶ set foot in (a place. ❷ join the party; join the conversation; © join in. ～を打つ ❶ agree with *sb*. ❷ be impressed by *sth*. ❸ call *sth* to mind. ～を折る ❶ sit on one's knees; bend one's knees. ❷ bow to *sb*; yield to *sb*; submit to *sb*. ～を屈める ❶ bend one's knees. ❷ bow to *sb*; yield to *sb*; submit to *sb*. ～を崩す ❶ relax one's knees; sit at ease. ❷ yield to *sb*; give in (to a demand). ～を組む cross one's legs; sit cross-legged. ～を進める come closer to; draw near to *sb*; be drawn into *sth*. ～を抱く ❶ be lonely; © be forlorn. ❷ entreat *sb* (for mercy); implore *sb*. ～を叩く ❶ agree with *sb*. ❷ be impressed by *sth*. ❸ call *sth* to mind. ～を正す sit upright. ～を立てる draw up one's knees. ～を突き合わせる have a serious talk. ～を突く go down on one's knees. Ⓐ ～を直す relax one's knees; sit at ease. ～を曲げる bend one's knees. ～を交える have an informal chat; have a heart-to-heart; © have a chinwag.

肘 an elbow; an arm

を ～を当てる restrain *sb*; hold *sb* down. ～を押し退ける elbow *sb* aside. © ～を食う be rebuffed; be rejected; get snubbed. Ⓐ ～を極める ignore *sb*; make light of *sth*. ～を突く elbow *sb*; poke one's elbow (into *sb's* side); rest one's elbow. ～を張る ❶ square one's elbow; spread out one's elbows. ❷ refuse to give in; © ① dig in one's heels;

hold on. ～を引(ひ)く pull *sb's* arm. Ⓘ ～を曲(ま)げる ❶ make one's arms into a pillow; rest on one's arms. ❷ enjoy a life of honest poverty.

肘鉄砲(ひじでっぽう) [S] a rebuff; a snub

[を] Ⓢ ～を食(く)う be rejected; get snubbed; Ⓔ suffer a rebuff; Ⓢ be kicked Ⓘ get the mitten.

顰(ひそ)み frowning; a frown

[に] ～に倣(なら)う follow *sb's* example; imitate *sb* slavishly.

額(ひたい) the forehead; the brow

[に] ～に汗(あせ)する do *sth* with all one's might; try as hard as one can; work flat-out.

[を] ～を集(あつ)める confer with each other; Ⓔ counsel together; Ⓒ get together; Ⓘ compare notes. ～を合(あ)わせる sit close together; be close to each other.

ひ

媚態(びたい) [E] coquetry

[を] ～を示(しめ)す play the coquet. ～を作(つく)る behave coquettishly.

跛(びっこ) [S] lameness; a cripple

[に] Ⓢ ～に成(な)る become lame; become crippled.

[を] Ⓢ ～を引(ひ)く have a limp.

人(ひと) a human being

[と] ～と成(な)る ❶ grow up; become an adult; reach adulthood. ❷ come to oneself; Ⓔ recover one's sanity; come to one's senses.

[を] Ⓢ ～を食(く)う make a fool of *sb*; Ⓒ poke fun at *sb*; Ⓢ Ⓘ take the mickey (out of *sb*); Ⓢ Ⓘ take the piss (out of *sb*). ～を立(た)てる send a messenger; dispatch an intermediary; mediate between two parties.

美徳(びとく) virtues; good deeds

[を] ～を積(つ)む accumulate virtues. ～を養(やしな)う cultivate virtuous habits.

人手(ひとで) *sb*'s hand; a worker; help

[に] ～に掛(かか)かる die by *sb's* hands; be murdered. ～に渡(わた)る pass into *sb's* hands; change hands.

[を] ～を借(か)りる get *sb's* assistance; ask *sb* for assistance. ～を加(くわ)える be man-made; be artificial; Ⓔ be by the hand of man.

瞳(ひとみ) the pupil

[を] ～を凝(こ)らす strain one's eyes; Ⓔ rivet one's eyes on *sb/sth*; look hard at *sb/sth*.

人目(ひとめ) the public eye

[に] ～に余(あま)る be overconspicuous; be excessive. ～に晒(さら)す bring *sth* to light. ～に立(た)つ be conspicuous; draw people's attention; stand out. ～に付(つ)く be conspicuous; attract attention; draw people's attention.

[を] ～を奪(うば)う steal *sb's* attention; captivate the public. ～を避(さ)ける avoid public notice; shun public notice. ～を忍(しの)ぶ avoid public notice; do *sth* in secret. Ⓐ ～を包(つつ)む shun the company of others;

avoid others. 〜を盗む do *sth* in secret; ⓔ steal one's way (into a place). 〜を憚る fear to be seen by others; ⓒ be shady. 〜を引く attract attention; draw people's attention.

非難 criticism; blame; reproach

を 〜を浴びる be the focus of criticism; come in for criticism. 〜を招く incur *sb's* criticism; lay oneself open to censure.

火蓋 the apron of a gun

を 〜を切る ❶ open fire; fire the first gun; take (the enemy) under fire. ❷ launch (a campaign).

美貌 ⓔ good looks; beauty

に 〜に迷う be captivated by *sb's* beauty; be enchanted by *sb*; ⓔ be smitten with *sb's* charms.

暇 time; spare time; leisure ▶ 暇

が ⓐ 〜が明く have time off; be free; be vacant; ⓘ have time on one's hands. ⓐ 〜が入る take up time; be time-consuming. ⓒ 〜がかる take up time; be time-con-suming.

に 〜に飽かす make full use of one's free time. 〜になる be free; be vacant; ⓘ have time on one's hands.

を ⓐ 〜を明ける ❶ take time off; make oneself free; make time (to do *sth*). ❷ divorce from (one's wife); get separated. ⓐ 〜を入れる

while away one's time; ⓒ kill time. ⓐ 〜を欠く while away one's time; waste one's time; ⓒ kill time. 〜を拵える make time (to do *sth*). 〜を割く find time (to do *sth*). 〜を出す ❶ dismiss *sb*; discharge *sb*; ⓒ fire *sb*; ⓢⓘ give *sb* the sack; ⓒⓘ send *sb* packing. ❷ give *sb* time off. ❸ get divorced (from one's wife); get separated. 〜を潰す while away one's time; ⓒ kill time. 〜を取る ❶ resign from one's post; ⓔ tender one's resignation. ❷ take time off; have a vacation. ❸ get divorced (from one's husband); get separated. 〜を盗む steal time (to do *sth*); make time (to do *sth*). 〜を弄ぶ do not know what to do with oneself; be bored. 〜を貰う ask for leave; get time off; leave *sb's* service. 〜を遣る ❶ dismiss *sb*; discharge *sb*; ⓒ fire *sb*; ⓢⓘ give *sb* the sack; ⓒⓘ send *sb* packing. ❷ give *sb* time off. ❸ get divorced (from one's wife); get separated.

秘密 a secret; a mystery

を 〜を明かす confide a secret to *sb*; share a secret with *sb*. 〜を暴く reveal a secret; disclose a secret; uncover a mystery. 〜を侵す spill a secret; intrude on *sb's* privacy; ⓘ spill the beans. 〜を教える initiate *sb* into the mysteries of (an art). 〜を探る pry into a secret; probe a secret. 〜を解く unravel a mystery. 〜を守る keep a secret; observe secrecy; ⓘ keep

ひ

sth under one's hat. ～を漏らす leak out a secret; betray a secret.

悲鳴 a shriek; a scream
🈁 ～を上げる utter a shriek; raise a howl; cry out (in anguish).

紐 a string; a cord; a braid
🈡 ～で括る tie *sth* up.
🈁 ⓞ ～を絞る fasten a string. ～を解く untie a string. ～を結ぶ tie a string. ～を緩める loosen a string.

百計 🇪 all means
🈓 ⓔ ～が尽きる be at the end of one's resources; ⓘ be at the end of one's tether; ⓘ come to the end of one's rope.
🈁 ⓔ ～を廻らす leave no means untried; try every means; ⓘ leave no stone unturned.

病気 sickness; illness
🈓 ～が治る recover from one's disease; get over one's illness; get well. ～が振り返す relapse into illness; suffer a relapse.
🈡 ～で倒れる come down with an illness; ⓔ succumb to a disease.
🈂 ～と闘う combat a disease.
🈔 ～に打ち勝つ survive an illness. ～に掛かる fall ill; take a disease; lose one's health. ～に効く be effective in curing a disease; be wholesome. ～に堪える bear one's illness. ～に成る fall ill; contract a disease; lose one's health. ～に負ける give way to one's disease.

🈡 ～を移す transmit a disease. ～を拗らす complicate a disease; develop a complication. ～を背負う carry a disease; be ill. ～を治す cure a disease. ～を防ぐ prevent a disease. ～を見舞う ask after *sb's* health; inquire after *sb's* health. ～を装う feign illness.

病根 🇪 the cause of a disease
🈡 ⓔ ～を断つ root out an illness; strike at the root of an illness.

拍子 rhythm; measure; time
🈔 Ⓐ ～に掛かる ❶ keep good time with (the music). ❷ get (too) excited; be elated; ⓘ get carried away.
🈡 ～を合わす keep good time with (the music). ～を取る keep time; beat time. ～を踏む keep time; beat time.

病床 🇪 a sickbed
🈔 ⓔ ～に就く take to a sickbed; go to bed ill; be taken ill; be ill in bed; be laid up (with illness). ⓔ ～に侍る be by *sb's* bedside; sit watch by *sb's* bedside. ⓔ ～に伏す lie in one's sickbed; lie on a bed of illness; keep one's bed; be laid up with illness; be bedridden.

病勢 🇪 the state of a disease
🈓 ⓔ ～が改まる grow worse; take a turn for the worse. ⓔ ～が衰える grow less serious; get better. ⓔ ～が募る grow worse; take a turn for the worse.

162

評判 reputation; fame; credit
ひょうばん

[が] ～が良い be popular; have a good reputation; ⓔ be well spoken of. ～が悪い be unpopular; have a bad reputation; ⓔ be ill spoken of.

[を] ～を落とす lose one's (good) reputation; fall into discredit. ～を立てる start a rumor; ① make a stir. ～を取り返す regain one's character; restore one's reputation. ～を取る win reputation; become popular; win credit.

日和 weather; fair weather
ひより

[を] ～を見る wait and see; ① see how the wind blows; ① sit on the fence; ©① watch which way the cat jumps.

品 grace; refinement ▶品
ひん   しな

[が] ～が有る be refined; have grace. ～が無い be unrefined; lack grace; be vulgar.

品位 dignity; grace; nobility
ひんい

[を] ～を落とす lose one's dignity; degrade oneself. ～を高める give sb dignity; ennoble sb. ～を保つ maintain one's dignity; keep up one's state; ⓢ keep one's cool.

貧困 poverty; destitution
ひんこん

[に] ～に喘ぐ suffer extreme poverty; ① be in dire straits. ～に陥る be impoverished; be reduced to poverty; become destitute.

[を] ⓔ ～を脱する rise from poverty; ⓔ emerge from poverty.

顰蹙 frowning
ひんしゅく

[を] ⓔ ～を買う be frowned on; disgust sb; ⓔ incur sb's displeasure.

びんた a slap on the cheek
[を] ⓢ ～を食う be slapped in the face. ⓢ ～を張る slap sb in the face; give sb a slap in the face.

敏腕 ability; capability
びんわん

[を] ⓔ ～を揮う show one's ability; ⓔ give full play to one's talents.

フ

腑 the viscera; the bowels
ふ

[が] Ⓐ ～が抜ける ❶ lose one's senses; lose one's wits; ⓢ① lose one's marbles. ❷ lose courage; have no stomach for sth. ❸ fall into one's dotage; go senile; get weak with age; ⓢ go gaga.

[に] Ⓐ ～に入る ❶ make sense of sth; grasp the meaning; catch the idea. ❷ be convinced; be won over; be persuaded. ～に落ちる ❶ make sense of sth; grasp the meaning; catch the idea. ❷ be convinced; be won over; be persuaded.

分 a percentage; a rate ▶分
ぶ   ぶん

[が] ～が有る stand a chance; have a chance (of success). ～が良い ❶ the percentage is good. ❷ have the edge; be favorable. ～が悪い ❶ the percentage is bad. ❷ have no edge; be unfavorable.

歩 an advantage; ▶ 歩
に Ⓐ 〜に合う be profitable; pay for itself. Ⓐ 〜に掛かる be profitable; pay for itself. Ⓐ 〜に回る ❶ be very profitable. ❷ draw profit from *sth*; exploit *sth*.

武 Ⓔ military/martial affairs
を Ⓔ 〜を争う struggle for military supremacy. Ⓔ 〜を講ずる practice military tactics. Ⓔ 〜を尊ぶ pursue a policy of militarism. Ⓔ 〜を練る train oneself in the arts of war. Ⓔ 〜を学ぶ study martial arts.

不安 uneasiness; anxiety
に 〜に思う be uncertain about *sth*; feel uneasy about *sth*; be anxious about *sth*. 〜になる lose one's peace of mind; grow restless; Ⓘ get cold feet.
を 〜を抱く be anxious; have misgivings; Ⓔ entertain apprehensions. 〜を感じる feel uneasy; be uncertain; be anxious; be ill at ease.

不意 sudden; unexpected
を 〜を打つ take *sb* by surprise; catch *sb* unawares. Ⓐ Ⓢ 〜を食う be taken by surprise; be caught unawares. 〜を突く take *sb* by surprise; catch *sb* unawares.

風 Ⓔ an air; a look; a trend
を Ⓔ 〜を守る stick to one's habits; adhere to a custom; keep to the (good) old ways.

封 seal; closing
を 〜を開ける open a letter. 〜を切る break open a seal; cut (a letter) open. 〜をする seal a letter; put (a letter) in an envelope.

封鎖 a blockade; blocking
を 〜を潜る run a blockade. 〜を解く lift a blockade; raise a blockade. 〜を破る break a blockade.

風説 Ⓔ a rumor; hearsay
を Ⓔ 〜を生む give rise to rumors. Ⓔ 〜を立てる set a rumor afloat.

風船 a balloon
を 〜を上げる let up a balloon; send up a balloon. 〜を飛ばす let up a balloon; send up a balloon. 〜を膨らます inflate a balloon. 〜を割る burst a balloon.

風致 Ⓔ elegance; scenic beauty
を Ⓔ 〜を害する spoil the view; disfigure the landscape. Ⓔ 〜を増す add charms to a view.

風潮 the tide; the current
に 〜に逆らう be out of tune with the times; go against the tide. 〜に従う go with the tide. 〜に乗る ride the tide.

不運 misfortune; bad luck
に 〜に遭う fall on evil days; meet with a reverse.
を 〜を忍ぶ bear misfortune.

164

不覚 ⒠ imprudence; negligence

⓪ ⒠ 〜を取る suffer a setback; be beaten; ⓘ come to grief.

武器 a weapon; arms

⓪ 〜を納める lay down arms. 〜を取る take up arms; rise in arms.

復讐 revenge; vengeance

⓪ 〜を企てる seek revenge on *sb*. 〜を誓う swear revenge on *sb*. 〜を計る plan to revenge *sb*.

武功 ⒠ military exploits

⓪ ⒠ 〜 を 立 て る distinguish oneself in war; ⒠ render distinguished military service.

節 a joint; a knuckle; a knot ▶ 節

⓰ 〜が痛む one's joints ache; feel pain in one's joints; Ⓒ have sore joints. Ⓐ 〜が立つ cause offense; arouse bitterness; aggravate *sb*; have a rough going.

⓪ 〜を合わせる play the same air. 〜を付ける ❶ set a verse to music. ❷ find fault with *sb*; pick a quarrel with *sb*.

侮辱 insult; indignity

⓪ 〜を受ける suffer an insult; be insulted. 〜を加える insult *sb*; level an insult at *sb*. 〜を忍ぶ bear an affront; brook an insult; ⓘ keep a stiff upper lip.

不審 doubt; suspicion

ⓝ 〜に思う consider *sth* to be suspicious; have doubts about *sth*; Ⓒ think *sth* odd.

⓪ ⓪ 〜を上ぐ raise suspicions; ⒠ cast doubts on *sth*. 〜を抱く have a suspicion; entertain doubts about *sth*. 〜を解く dispel *sb*'s doubts.

不信 distrust; bad faith

⓪ 〜を抱く have a suspicion; be suspicious of *sb*. 〜を買う incur suspicion; be called into question. 〜を来す cause distrust. 〜を招く incur *sb*'s mistrust.

不正 injustice; iniquity

⓪ 〜を正す redress injustice. 〜を働く do a dishonest thing; do *sb* an injustice; do wrong.

不足 shortage; want

⓪ 〜を言う vent one's discontent; express dissatisfaction. 〜を補う make good a deficiency; meet a shortage. 〜を告げる run short of *sth*; prove deficient.

蓋 a lid; a cover; a flap; a cap

⓪ 〜を開ける ❶ open a play; begin a performance. ❷ begin (work); start things up. 〜を取る take the lid of (a barrel); uncover *sth*.

札 a card; a label; a tag; a charm

⓰ ⓪ 〜が落ちる have one's tender accepted. 〜が付く get a bad reputation; ⒠ gain notoriety.

⓪ 〜を頂く receive a charm (from a shrine). 〜を切る cut the cards;

shuffle the cards. 〜を配る deal
the cards. 〜を捨てる throw up
one's cards. 〜を立てる put up a
notice board. 〜を付ける paste a
card; label *sth*; put a tag on *sth*.
〜を取る pick a card; take a card.
〜を張る paste a card; label *sth*;
put a tag on *sth*. 〜を見せる show
one's cards. 〜を捲る turn over a
card; turn down a card.

舞台 the stage
に 〜に立つ appear on the stage;
go on the stage; ⓔ come before
the footlights. 〜に載せる stage a
play; put a play on stage.
を 〜を退く leave the stage; end
one's acting career; ⓔ retire from
the stage. 〜を踏む go on the
stage; make one's debut; ⓔ come
before the footlights.

二股 Ⓔa fork; a branch
に ⓒ 〜になる fork off in two; fork
into two branches; divide into two.
を ⓒ 〜を掛ける have it both ways;
play a double game; try to have
the best of both worlds.

縁 an edge; a verge; a side ▸ 縁
に 〜に立つ stand on the edge; be
on the verge of *sth*.
を 〜を付ける frame (an area);
delimit (an area). 〜を通る hug the
side (of the road); stick to the
roadside. 〜を取る hem (an area);
border (an area). 〜を縫う border
(cloth); hemstitch (cloth).

淵 an abyss; a pit; the depths
に 〜に落ち込む sink into the
limbo of oblivion. 〜に沈む sink
into the depth (of misery); fall into
a slough (of despond).

打ち壊し ⓢ demolition
を ⓢ 〜を言う talk mischief; make
destructive criticism; ⓘ be a wet
blanket. ⓢ 〜を遣る make a mess
of things; ⓘ throw a spanner in the
works; ⓒ bungle *sth*; ⓒ botch *sth*.

不忠 Ⓔdisloyal; unfaithful
を ⓒ 〜を働く be disloyal (to one's
master/country).

物価 prices (of commodities)
を 〜を上げる raise prices. 〜を下
げる lower prices; reduce prices.
〜を調節する regulate prices.

物議 Ⓔpublic censure; unrest
を ⓒ 〜を醸す give rise to a public
discussion; cause dissent; arouse
criticism; raise a scandal.

仏事 a Buddhist mass
を 〜を営む hold a Buddhist mass.

筆 a (writing) brush; a pen
が 〜が滑る a slip of the pen;
touch the paper by accident (when
writing). 〜が立つ be facile with
one's pen; write in a good style; be
a good writer. 〜が回る be facile
with one's pen; be a good writer.
で ⓢ 〜で食う live by one's pen.

ふ

に ～に任せる let one's pen wander.

を ～を入れる make corrections; touch up (a document); add touches to (calligraphy). ～を擱く lay down one's pen; complete a draft; stop writing. ～を折る give up writing; end one's literary career. ～を下ろす ❶ use a new brush. ❷ pick up the pen; ⓒ put pen to paper; start on a (new) work. Ⓐ ～を呵す force oneself to write; make an effort to write. ～を加える fill in; make corrections; add some touches. Ⓐ ～を下す pick up the pen; put pen to paper. ～を染める ❶ pick up the pen; ⓒ put pen to paper. ❷ try one's hand at writing. ～を絶つ give up writing; end one's literary career. ～を試す try one's pen. ～を執る pick up the pen; ⓒ put pen to paper. ～を投げる stop writing in mid-sentence. ～を拭う ❶ clean one's brush; wipe one's brush. ❷ lay down one's pen; stop writing. ～を運ぶ write a draft; ⓒ move one's pen across the paper. Ⓐ ～を馳す write off; scribble away. ～を揮う wield a brush; write calligraphy; paint a picture. ⓞ ⓔ ～を弄す write in jest; doodle.

懐 the bosom; a purse

が ～が暖かい have a well-filled purse; ⓘ be well-heeled. ～が痛む be a financial burden; pay out of one's own pocket. ～が寂しい have an little money; ⓞ be hard up;

ⓘ be in dire straits. ～が寒い have little money; ⓘ have a cold purse; ⓘ feel the draught. ～が広い be generous; be hospitable.

に ～に入れる put *sth* in one's pocket; pocket *sth*; make *sth* one's own. ～にする pocket *sth*; make *sth* one's own.

を ～を暖める enrich oneself by way of graft; ⓘ line one's pocket; ⓘ feather one's own nest. ～を痛める bear a financial burden; pay out of one's own pocket. ～を肥やす enrich oneself by way of graft; ⓘ line one's pocket; ⓘ feather one's own nest. ～を見透かす see through *sb's* designs.

布団 a futon

を ～を上げる roll up one's futon. ～を被る pull one's futon over one's head. ～を敷く spread one's futon; make a bed. ～を畳む fold up one's futon; clear away one's futon.

舟/船 a boat; a ship; vessel

が Ⓐ ～が座る stay put; stay on (in power); remain in office.

に ～に乗る get on board a ship. ～に酔う get seasick.

を ～を漕ぐ ❶ row a boat. ❷ nod off; fall asleep (on the job). ～を出す put to sea; set sail; put out. ～を造る build a ship. ～を止める bring a ship to. ～を回す bring up a ship; sail a ship. ～を乗り捨てる abandon ship. ～を雇う charter a ship; hire a boat.

不評 ふひょう ill repute; a bad reputation

をする ～を買う lose one's popularity; become unpopular. ～を招く lose one's popularity; become unpopular.

不憫 ふびん pity; compassion

に ～に思う feel pity; take pity on *sb*; Ⓔ be moved to pity.

不平 ふへい discontent; dissatisfaction

を ～を言う speak one's mind; grumble over *sth*; complain of *sth*; Ⓔ voice one's discontent. ～を抱く be discontented; hold a grudge against *sb*; Ⓘ have an axe to grind; Ⓔ nurse a grievance. ～を訴える complain about *sth*; Ⓔ lodge a complaint. ～を押える restrain oneself; Ⓔ repress one's dissatisfaction. ～を鳴らす complain about *sth*; Ⓔ air one's grievances. ～を並べる grumble over; Ⓒ whine over *sth*. ～を洩す vent one's discontent; Ⓔ air one's grievances. ～をやめる stop complaining; leave off complaining; Ⓒ let it go.

不便 ふべん inconvenience

を ～を掛ける inconvenience *sb*; cause inconvenience. ～を感じる be inconvenienced. ～を忍ぶ put up with an inconvenience; endure discomfort. ～を生ずる be a source of discomfort; cause inconvenience. ～を除く remove inconveniences.

部門 ぶもん a class; a group

に ～に入れる bring *sth* under the division of *sth*; place *sth* in a (certain) category; categorize *sth*. ～に入る fall under the head of *sth*; fall into a category; belong to a category. ～に分ける classify (into orders); divide into sections.

無聊 ぶりょう Ⓔ ennui; tedium

を Ⓔ ～を慰める while away one's time; fill the time; Ⓒ kill time.

触れ ふれ an official notice

を ～を出す issue an official notice. ～を回す send round an official notice.

風呂 ふろ a (hot) bath; a public bath

に ～に行く go to a bathhouse. ～に入れる give *sb* a bath. ～に浸かる soak in a bathtub; sink into a hot bath. ～に入る take a bath.

を ～を落とす empty a bathtub; let the water out of the bath. ～を焚く heat a bath; prepare a bath. ～を立てる prepare a bath. ～を使う take a bath; use a bath. ～を沸かす heat the bath.

文 ぶん composition; writing

を ～を売る make a living by the pen; write to make a living; support oneself by writing. ～を書く write prose. Ⓔ ～を飾る embellish a composition. Ⓐ Ⓔ ～を属す make a composition; write an article. ～を作る make a composition; write a composition. ～を綴る compose an essay; frame a sentence. ～を練

る improve on one's writing; polish one's writing style. 〜を奮う write high prose; compose literature.

分 a part; one's place ▶ 分

を 〜を尽くす do one's duty; ⓒ do one's bit. 〜を守る keep to one's sphere in life; ⓘ keep within one's own province; ⓘ cut one's coat according to one's cloth. 〜を弁える know one's place; ⓘ keep within one's own province.

紛議 dissension; controversy

を 〜を醸す cause dissension.

紛擾 Ⓔ confusion; disorder

を ⓔ 〜を起こす stir up trouble; cause a disturbance; ⓔ give rise to confusion; ⓢ ⓘ raise a dust.

文壇 the literary world

に 〜に乗り出す enter upon a literary career; take up writing.

文通 correspondence

を 〜を禁じられる be held incommunicado. 〜を絶つ break off correspondence with sb. 〜を続ける maintain correspondence with sb. 〜を始める enter into correspondence with sb.

褌 Ⓒ a loincloth

を ⓒ 〜を締める brace oneself; get ready to do sth; ⓘ gird up one's loins; ⓘ put one's best foot forward; ⓢ ⓘ get up steam.

文名 Ⓔ literary fame

を 〜を馳せる win literary fame.

へ

兵 a soldier; troops; warfare

を 〜を挙げる take up arms; rise in arms; raise an army. 〜を送る send troops. 〜を募る raise an army; collect an army. 〜を解く disband an army. 〜を率いる lead an army. 〜を伏せる lay an ambush. 〜を向ける direct an army against sb.

塀 a wall; a fence

で 〜で囲む fence in (an area); put a fence around (a place).

を 〜を立てる build a wall. 〜を乗り越える climb over a wall. 〜を巡らす surround (a house) with a wall; wall in (an area).

平気 calmness; serenity

を 〜を装う affect composure; be self-composed; ⓘ keep one's head.

平衡 equilibrium; balance

を 〜を失う lose one's balance. 〜を保つ keep one's balance.

平癒 Ⓔ recovery from illness

を ⓔ 〜を祈る pray for sb's recovery.

平和 peace; harmony

を ⓔ 〜を講ずる make peace with sb. 〜を乱す disturb the harmony. 〜を破る break the peace.

臍 the navel, the belly button

が Ⓐ ～がくねる be too ridiculous for words; be preposterous; be outrageous; Ⓘ be beyond the pale.

で Ⓐ ～で笑う be too ridiculous for words; be preposterous; be outrageous; Ⓘ be beyond the pale.

を Ⓐ ～を動かす give sb fits of laughter; convulse sb with laughter. Ⓐ ～を固める be determined; make up one's mind. Ⓐ ～を噛む have regrets; be sorry for. ～を曲げる become perverse; get awkward; sulk over sth; Ⓒ get cross. ～を撚る be amused; take delight in sth; find pleasure in sth.

篦 a spatula

を Ⓐ ～を使う be ambiguous; be evasive; Ⓘ beat about the bush.

弁 speech; eloquence; a dialect

が ～が立つ have a fluent tongue; be fluent in speech; Ⓒ Ⓘ have the gift of the gab.

を ～を練る cultivate eloquence; improve one's oratory skills. Ⓔ ～を弄する ❶ use one's eloquence; Ⓔ resort to sophistry. ❷ quibble over sth; put forward a far-fetched argument; Ⓘ split hairs.

偏見 prejudice; a biased view

を ～を抱く be prejudiced; hold a biased view. ～を捨てる discard one's bias; get over one's prejudices. ～を持つ be prejudiced; hold a biased view.

辺幅 Ⓔ outward appearance

を Ⓐ Ⓔ ～を飾る be particular about one's appearance; Ⓘ keep up appearances.

片鱗 a glimpse; a part

を ～を示す get a glimpse of sb's erudition/talent.

木

歩 a step; a pace ▶歩

を Ⓐ ～を失う be at a loss (about what to do); lose one's direction. Ⓒ ～を移す step ahead. ～を進める advance; go ahead. ～を運ぶ proceed; go ahead. ～を廻らす turn back; retrace one's steps.

帆 a sail; a canvas

を ～を揚げる hoist a sail. ～を下ろす lower a sail. ～を掛ける set a sail. ～を絞る brail a sail. ～を畳む furl a sail. ～を詰める take in sail. ～を張る unfurl a sail. ～を増す make sail.

穂 an ear; a head; a spike

が ～が出る ears form (on the barley); come into ears; Ⓒ ear up.

に Ⓐ ～に出る come out into the open; become noticed; be revealed. ～になる ears form (on the barley); come into ears; Ⓒ ear up.

を ～を出す ears form (on the barley); come into ears; Ⓒ ear up. (話の)～を継ぐ take up the thread

ほ

(of a story); take up (one's story); resume (one's story).

秀 excellence
に ◎ 〜に出づ become noticed; become apparent; come out into the open; be revealed.

棒 a rod; a stick; a club
に 〜に振る make a mess of *sth*; waste *sth*; bring ruin on *sth*.
を ◎ 〜を折る be a failure; give up halfway; ① bite the dust. 〜を引く draw a line; cross *sth* out; strike *sth* off. 〜を揮う conduct music.

砲火 gunfire; artillery fire
を 〜を開ける open fire; fire the first gun; take (the enemy) under fire; ⓒ open hostilities. 〜を浴びる be under fire. 〜を蒙る be subjected to fire; be brought under fire. 〜を交える exchange fire; fight a battle; ⓒ engage an enemy.

方角 a direction; a bearing
に 〜に迷う lose one's bearings; lose direction; lose one's way.
を 〜を失う lose one's bearings; lose one's way. 〜を見る find one's bearings; take a bearing.

暴虐 ⓔ an outrage; an atrocity
を ⓒ 〜を行う commit atrocities.

謀計 ⓔ a plot; a scheme
に ⓒ 〜に陥る become the victim of a plot; ⓐ fall into a trap.

を ⓒ 〜を巡らす conspire against *sb*; devise a stratagem.

妄言 ⓔ a reckless remark
を ⓒ 〜を吐く make a reckless remark; utter *sth* thoughtless; talk without thinking.

暴言 ⓔ violent language
を 〜を吐く use violent language; utter wild words; ① lash out at *sb*.

暴行 violence; an outrage
を 〜を加える assault *sb*; molest *sb*; employ violence against *sb*. 〜を働く resort to violence; ⓒ have recourse to violence.

帽子 a hat; a cap; headgear
を 〜を押える hold one's hat/cap. 〜を被る put on a hat/cap. 〜を取る take off one's hat/cap. 〜を脱ぐ take off one's hat/cap. 〜を振るう wave one's hat/cap.

房事 ⓔ sexual intercourse
に ⓒ 〜に耽る indulge in sexual pleasure.
を ⓒ 〜を慎む abstain from sexual intercourse.

法事 a Buddhist mass
を 〜を営む hold a Buddhist mass.

方針 a course; a line; an aim
を 〜を誤る take a wrong course. 〜を立てる frame a plan; map out one's course; decide one's policy.

ほ

171

〜を採る adopt a course; aim for *sth*; take a (certain) line.

坊主 ⓒ a Buddhist priest

に ⓒ 〜に刈る have one's hair closely cropped; trim (one's hair) closely. ⓒ 〜になる ❶ become Buddhist a priest. ❷ have one's head shaved.

法廷 a law court; a court of law

で 〜で争う go to law; take *sth* to court; ⓔ bring a suit against *sb*.

に 〜に立つ stand at the bar. 〜に引き出す take *sb* up to court; sue *sb*; ⓒ drag *sb* into court. 〜に持ち出す bring a matter before the court; take *sth* to court.

暴動 a riot; a disturbance

を 〜を起こす raise a riot; create a disturbance. 〜を静める suppress a riot; put down a riot.

法網 ⓔ the meshes of the law

を ⓔ 〜を潜る slip through the meshes (of the law.

砲門 the muzzle of a gun

を 〜を開く open fire; fire the first gun; take (the enemy) under fire.

暴利 excessive profits

を 〜を貪る make undue profits.

暴力 violence; brute force

に 〜に訴える resort to violence; ⓔ have recourse to violence.

を 〜を加える assault *sb*; molest *sb*. ⓒ employ violence against *sb*. 〜を振るう use violence on *sb*.

頬 the cheek

が 〜が弛む smile; look glad.

を 〜を染める get red in the face; blush. 〜を抓る ① pinch oneself. 〜を尖らす put on a sulky face. 〜を膨らます put on a sulky face.

墓穴 ⓔ a grave

を 〜を掘る ❶ dig a grave. ⓒ ❷ go to ruin; ① dig one's own grave; ⓢ ① go to the dogs.

保険 insurance

を 〜を掛ける take out insurance.

鉾 a halberd; arms

を 〜を収める lay down arms; stop fighting. 〜を取る take up arms; rise in arms. 〜を交える open hostilities; cross swords with *sb*; fight each other. 〜を向ける attack *sb* (in an argument); ⓒ lay into someone; ① turn one's guns on *sb*.

保護 protection; shelter

を 〜を与える give protection to *sb*. 〜を受ける be protected by *sb*. 〜を求める seek protection.

埃 dust

を 〜が溜まる become dusty; gather dust; collect dust. 〜を静める let *sth* rest; lay the dust. 〜を立てる ❶ raise dust; stir

ほ

up dust; kick up dust. ❷ cause a disturbance; ⓘ raise a dust; ⓘ stir up dust. 〜を払う brush away the dust; wipe off the dust.

誇り pride; a boast

と 〜とする take pride in *sth*; be proud of *sth*.

を 〜を傷つける hurt *sb's* pride. 〜を持つ have pride; be proud.

星 Ⓒ a star; a spot; a culprit

が ⓢ 〜が割れる find out who the culprit is.

を ⓢ 〜を挙げる ❶ arrest a culprit; seize a criminal. ❷ [*sumō*] win a match. Ⓒ 〜を戴く labor hard; work hard; Ⓔ work from dawn till dusk. Ⓒ 〜を失う be beaten; Ⓔ suffer a defeat; ⓘ bite the dust. Ⓒ 〜を落す [*sumō*] lose a match. Ⓒ 〜を稼ぐ ❶ obtain good results; get a good score; gain a point. ❷ ingratiate oneself with *sb*; ⓘ curry favor with *sb*. Ⓐ ⓢ 〜を食わす guess right; get it right; ⓘ be on the mark; Ⓒ ⓘ get the point; ⓘ hit the nail on the head. Ⓐ Ⓒ 〜を指す ❶ guess right; ⓘ be on the mark; Ⓒ ⓘ hit the mark. ❷ see through (a plot); penetrate (*sb's* heart). Ⓒ 〜を付ける take aim at; have an eye on; mark *sb* out. Ⓒ 〜を潰す [*sumō*] lose a match. Ⓗ Ⓒ 〜を唱える proclaim the year's star sign. Ⓒ 〜を拾う [*sumō*] rescue a victory; win in spite of the odds. Ⓒ 〜を見る tell *sb's* fortune.

臍 Ⓔ the navel; a tenon; a pivot

を Ⓔ 〜を固める make up one's mind; resolve to do *sth*. Ⓔ 〜を決める make up one's mind; be prepared for *sth*; be determined; be resolved (to do *sth*); ⓘ gird up one's loins. Ⓔ 〜を噛む repent *sth*; have regrets; regret *sth*. Ⓐ Ⓔ 〜を付ける have dinner; have *sth* to eat.

菩提 Buddhahood; enlightenment

を Ⓔ 〜を弔う pray for the repose of *sb's* soul; hold a memorial service; hold a mass for *sb*.

釦 a button

を 〜を押す ⓘ push a button. 〜を掛ける fasten one's buttons; button up (a coat). 〜を付ける put on a button; sew a button on (a coat). 〜を毟り取る tear off a button.

歩調 a pace; a step

が 〜が合う ❶ keep the same pace. ❷ be like-minded; get along well; ⓘ see eye to eye; Ⓔ be congenial to one; Ⓒ ⓘ hit it off.

を 〜を合わす ❶ fall into step; keep pace with *sb*. ❷ work together; act in concert. 〜を定める set the pace. 〜を揃える ❶ fall into step; keep pace with *sb*. ❷ work together; act in concert. 〜を整える set the pace. 〜を取る keep step; keep pace with *sb*. 〜を早める quicken one's pace. 〜を乱す break step; walk out of step. 〜を緩める slacken one's pace.

ほ

173

程 ほど a limit; an extent; one's place

が ～が有る have one's limits. Ⓐ ～が良い ❶ be refined; be stylish; be smart. ❷ have a clever tongue; Ⓒ ① have the gift of the gab.

を ～を越す break bounds; go too far. ～を知る know one's place; know one's limitations. ～を守る observe moderation; keep within bounds; stay within good limits.

仏 ほとけ Buddha; the departed soul

に ～になる ❶ become a Buddha. ❷ pass away; draw one's last breath; Ⓔ ① breathe one's last.

骨 ほね a bone; a frame; a skeleton

が ～が有る have fortitude; have strong convictions. ～が折れる be laborious; be a hard job; find sth hard to do. ～が太い be firm; be reliable; be sturdy; Ⓔ be steadfast.

に ～に刻む engrave sth on one's memory. ～に沁みる sink deep into one's mind; feel sth deeply. Ⓐ ～に徹る go straight to the heart; feel sth deeply; ① cut to the quick. ～になる pass away; draw one's last breath; Ⓔ ① breathe one's last.

を ～を埋める ❶ bury sb's remains; inter sb. ❷ die in (this country). ❸ make (a place) one's final home. ❹ devote one's life to (a cause); dedicate oneself to (a cause). ～を惜しむ ❶ spare oneself (the trouble); be sparing of oneself. ❷ be idle; be lazy; neglect one's duty. ～を折る ❶ break a bone;

suffer a fracture. ❷ take pains to do sth; make serious efforts; exert oneself. ❸ have a hard time of it; go through a lot of trouble. ～を刺す be frozen to the bones; have one's bones ache with cold. ～を曝す be reduced to a skeleton. ～を違える dislocate a limb. ～を接ぐ set a broken bone. ～を抜く ❶ bone a fish. ❷ emasculate sth; take the backbone out of sth; ① water sth down. Ⓐ ～を盗む ❶ cause sb a lot of work; be a burden to sb. ❷ be idle; be lazy; neglect one's duty. ～を拾う ❶ gather a deceased's ashes. ❷ look after a deceased's affairs; take the place (of a fallen comrade). ～を休める take a rest; Ⓒ have a breather.

骨身 ほねみ flesh and bones

に ～に応える be chilled to the bone. ～に沁みる sink deep into one's mind; feel sth deeply. ～に徹する feel sth deeply; ① come home to one; ① cut to the quick.

を ～を削る ❶ work hard; do one's best; ① work one's fingers to the bone. ❷ suffer great hardships.

法螺 ほら a boast; a brag; big talk

を ～を吹く boast about sth; brag about sth; ① tell a tall tale; ① talk big; Ⓒ ① talk through one's hat; ① blow one's own horn (trumpet).

襤褸 ぼろ a rag; a shred; a fault

が ～が出る have one's faults

ほ

174

exposed; be found out; ⓘ show the cloven hoof; ⓒ ⓘ show oneself up.

を ～を隠す hide one's faults; cover up one's mistakes. ～を出す expose one's faults; betray one's ignorance; ⓒ ⓘ show oneself up.

本音 the truth; real intentions

を ～を吐く reveal one's true intentions; speak out; ⓘ give oneself away.

マ

間 space; room; an interval ▶ 間

が ～が有る have the time (to do *sth*); have time (for *sth*). ～が欠ける be short of time; be too late. ～が抜ける ❶ be out of tune; be off-key; be off-bear. ❷ look stupid; be out of place; be absent-minded. ～が延びる be slovenly; be dull; be careless; be untidy. ～が持てない be unable to fill the time. ～が悪い ❶ feel awkward; be embarrassed; be ashamed. ❷ be unfortunate; be unlucky; be inauspicious.

に ～に合う ❶ be on time; be in time; meet a deadline. ❷ be of use; ⓔ be opportune; ⓒ come in handy. ❸ be enough; be sufficient; meet requirements.

を ～を開ける leave a space; space out. ～を合わす ❶ keep good time with (the music). ❷ act appropriately; do *sth* timely; ⓒ patch *sth* up for the time being. ～を窺う

watch for a good moment; ⓔ bide one's time. ～を措く leave a space; leave an interval; put a pause (between). ～を欠く be of no use; be incompetent; be to no avail. ～を貸す let a room; rent a room. ～を借りる take a room; hire a room. ～を配る leave (enough) space; arrange things spaciously. ～を詰める fill a gap; close a gap. ～を取る leave (enough) space; arrange things spaciously. ～を塞ぐ fill a space. ～を見る watch for a good moment; ⓔ bide one's time. ～を持たす fill in the time; use one's spare time (well). ⓐ ～を渡す do *sth* timely; act appropriately; act in time; meet the occasion.

魔 a demon; a devil

が ～が刺す be tempted by a devil; be possessed by an evil spirit; fall victim to temptation.

を ～を祓う exorcise an evil spirit. ～を避ける avert evil influences; keep evil spirits away.

真 truth; reality; seriousness ▶ 真

に ～に受ける take *sth* as the truth; accept *sth* as true; believe *sth* to be true; accept *sth* as true. ⓐ ～に成る get serious; straighten one's face; put on a serious look.

幕 a curtain; a hanging screen

が ～が上がる the curtain rises; the play begins; *sth* starts. ～が開く the curtain rises; the play

ま

begins; *sth* starts. ～が下りる the curtain falls; the play comes to an end; come to an end. ～が切れる an episode comes to an end. Ⓐ ～が支える be short of funds; be poorly funded. Ⓐ ～が通る ❶ make *sb* understand; get one's ideas across. ❷ become widely know; win fame.

[に] Ⓐ ～にする bring *sth* to an end; Ⓘ bring down the curtain. ～になる come to an end.

[を] Ⓐ ～を打つ close the curtain; bring *sth* to an end; Ⓘ bring down the curtain. ～を下ろす drop the curtain; bring *sth* to an end. Ⓐ ～を切る ❶ start on *sth*; set about doing *sth*. ❷ bring *sth* to an end; end *sth*; Ⓘ bring down the curtain. Ⓐ ～を通す ❶ carry the stage; command a house. ❷ make oneself understood; get one's ideas across. ～を閉じる ❶ close the curtain; drop the curtain. ❷ bring *sth* to an end; end *sth*; Ⓘ bring down the curtain on *sth*. Ⓗ ～を張る stretch a curtain. ～を引く ❶ close the curtain; drop the curtain. ❷ bring *sth* to an end; end *sth*; Ⓘ bring down the curtain.

枕（まくら） a pillow; a headrest

[と] Ⓐ ～と枕く go to sleep; curl up.
[を] ～を重ねる sleep together regularly; share the same bed regularly. ～を交わす sleep together; share the same bed. Ⓐ ～を砕く fret over *sth*; be troubled by *sth*; worry about *sth*. Ⓐ ～を付ける sleep together; share the same bed. ～を並べる ❶ sleep together; share the same bed. ❷ fall in great numbers; commit mass suicide. ～を濡らす cry in one's pillow; shed tears in bed. ～を結ぶ stay at an inn; sleep away from home; pass a night on one's journey; sleep rough. Ⓐ ～を割る be troubled by *sth*; worry about *sth*; fret over *sth*.

呪い（まじない） a spell; a charm

[を] ～を掛ける put a spell on *sb*. ～を消す break a spell. ～をする put a spell on *sb*.

待ち伏せ（まちぶせ） an ambush

[を] Ⓢ ～を食う fall into an ambush; be waylaid. ～をやめる break an ambush.

睫（まつげ） eyelashes; lashes

[を] ～を濡らす be on the alert; watch out; Ⓘ be on one's guard. Ⓐ ～を読まれる ❶ be taken in by *sb*; be cheated on. ❷ be looked down on; be slighted; be made light of; Ⓔ be held in contempt.

的（まと） a mark; a target; an object

[が] Ⓐ ～が立つ be punished by the gods; incur divine punishment; be served right.
[に] ～に当たる ❶ hit the target; hit the mark; strike home. ❷ grasp the crux (of a matter); get it right; Ⓘ hit the mark; Ⓒ Ⓘ get the point.

[を] 〜を射る ❶ hit the target; hit the mark; strike home. ❷ be relevant; ⓘ be on the mark; ⓘ hit the nail on the head; ⓘ be to the point. 〜を越す overshoot the mark. 〜を絞る focus on *sth*; set one's sights on *sth*; aim at (a target). 〜を外す ❶ fail to hit the mark; miss the mark; miss in one's aim. ❷ be irrelevant; ⓘ be off the mark; ⓘ be beside the point.

俎板 a cutting board
[に] 〜に載せる ❶ put (food) on the chopping block. ❷ put *sth* under review; take *sth* up for discussion.

瞼 an eyelid; the lid of an eye
[に] 〜に浮かぶ come before one's eyes; come to mind; occur to one; ⓔ rise in one's thoughts. 〜に残る linger before one's eyes; ⓘ be engraved on one's memory.
[を] 〜を閉じる close one's eyes; shut one's eyes.

魔法 magic; sorcery; witchcraft
[を] 〜を掛ける cast a spell on *sb*; put *sb* under a spell. 〜を使う use magic; practice witchcraft.

幻 a phantom; an apparition
[に] 〜に見る see *sth* in a vision.
[を] 〜を追う pursue phantoms.

眉 an eyebrow; one's brow
[に] 〜に迫る draw close; come into view; enter one's field of vision.

[を] 〜を上げる ❶ raise one's eyebrows. ❷ look angered. Ⓐ 〜を集める knit one's brows; ⓔ bend one's brows. Ⓐ 〜を落とす ❶ shave off one's eyebrows. ❷ get married; become *sb's* wife; ⓒ ⓘ tie the knot. 〜を描く correct one's eyebrows; pencil one's eyebrows. 〜を曇らす look troubled. 〜を顰める contract one's eyebrows; knit one's brows; ⓔ bend one's brows. 〜を皺める contract one's eyebrows; knit one's brows; ⓔ bend one's brows. 〜を引く correct one's eyebrows; pencil one's eyebrows. 〜を顰める frown on *sth*; knit one's brows; ⓔ bend one's brows. 〜を開く feel relieved; feel assured. Ⓐ 〜を広ぐ feel relieved; feel assured. 〜を寄せる frown on *sth*; knit one's brows; ⓔ bend one's brows. Ⓐ 〜を読む read *sb's* thoughts.

満 fullness; ripeness
[を] ⓔ 〜を持す ❶ draw a bow fully. ❷ wait until the time is ripe; watch for an opportunity; ⓔ bide one's time. 〜を搾る ❶ draw a bow fully. ❷ wait until the time is ripe; watch for an opportunity; ⓔ bide one's time. 〜を引く ❶ draw a bow fully. ⓒ ❷ drink to one's heart's content; have one's fill; ⓘ lift one's elbow.

万一 a contingency
[に] 〜に備える provide against contingencies.
[を] 〜を頼む trust to chance.

ま

身〔み〕 the body; the flesh; oneself

〔が〕 ～が入る become interested in *sth*; be absorbed in *sth*; ⓔ be engrossed in *sth*; ⓒ warm up to *sth*. ～が固まる settle down; get a job; get married.～が軽い ❶ be nimble; be agile. ❷ travel light; be lightly dressed. ⓓ ～が極まる settle down; get a job; get married. ～が定まる settle down; get a job; get married. ～が竦む shrink with fear; draw back from *sth*; ⓔ recoil from *sth*. ⓐ ～が詰まる be cornered; be in trouble; ⓘ be in dire straits; ⓘ be brought to bay. ⓐ ～が燃える burn with (anger). ⓐ be on fire; ⓔ be consumed (with passion). ～が入る become interested in *sth*; be absorbed in *sth*; ⓔ be engrossed in *sth*; ⓒ warm up to *sth*.

〔に〕 ～に余る be more than one deserves; be too great an honor. ⓐ ～に入れる put oneself into *sth*; take an interest in *sth*; devote oneself to *sth*. ～に代える value *sth* as much as one's own life; do *sth* in the face of death. ⓐ ～に掛かる affect one; befall one. ～に沁みる ❶ be chilled to the bone. ❷ sink deep into one's mind; ⓘ come home to one. ～に付く ❶ be nourishing; be good for one. ❷ make *sth* one's own; master (a craft). ❸ be eager to do; take an interest in *sth*; devote oneself to *sth*; ❹ be equipped with *sth*; fit one's body.

～に付ける ❶ put on (a piece of clothing/jewelry); bear a weapon; carry *sth* on one's body. ❷ acquire *sth*; be equipped with *sth*. ❸ learn (a skill); master (a skill). ～に詰まされる sympathize deeply with; feel deeply for; ⓔ empathize with *sb*. ～になる ❶ be nourishing; do one good. ❷ put oneself in *sb's* place. ～に纏う put *sth* on; be wrapped in (a garment).

〔を〕 ～を誤る go astray; ⓔ stray from virtue; ⓘ go to the bad. ～を合わす become one; ⓔ act in unison. ～を入れる put oneself into *sth*; take an interest in; devote oneself to *sth*. ⓐ ～を失う ❶ lose one's life; pass away. ❷ commit suicide; kill oneself. ❸ lay down one's life; throw away one's life. ⓐ ～を打つ indulge in *sth*; give oneself up to *sth*; abandon oneself to *sth*. ～を売る prostitute oneself; sell oneself (into slavery). ～を起こす ❶ rise up; set to work. ⓢ get cracking. ❷ rise in the world; establish oneself; make one's way up. ⓐ ～を修む get a grip on oneself; straighten oneself out. ～を落とす degrade oneself; come down in the world; be down and out. ～を踊らす ❶ jump in the air; leap (for joy). ❷ plunge into action. ⓐ ～を変える be reborn. ～を隠す hide oneself; hide one's background. ～を固める ❶ settle down; get a steady job; get married. ❷ dress up (warm); ⓒ bundle up. ❸ stand ready; take a

stance; stand on guard. ～を躱す
avoid danger; dodge an attack;
shirk one's duty; avoid responsibility; ⓘ dodge the column. ～を浄め
る purify oneself. ～を切る ❶ feel
the cold. ❷ experience great hardships. ❸ pay *sth* out of one's own
pocket. ～を砕く work oneself to
the bone; do one's utmost. ～を汚
す defile oneself; lose one's chastity. ～を削る suffer great hardships;
be in anguish. ～を焦がす burn
with (unrequited) love; ⓔ be consumed with love. ⓐ ～を懲らす do
penance; mortify one's flesh. ～を
曝す expose oneself; lay oneself
open to (an attack). ～を沈める
❶ drown oneself; throw oneself
into the water. ❷ sell one's body;
prostitute oneself. ❸ be down and
out; go to ruin; go down in the
world. ～を忍ぶ go into hiding;
hide oneself; ⓘ go to ground. ～を
捨てる ❶ lay down one's life; throw
away one's life; sacrifice one's life;
dedicate one's life (to a cause).
❷ go into seclusion; become a hermit; ⓔ retire from the world;
renounce the world. ❸ become a
Buddhist priest; take the tonsure;
ⓔ retire into religion. ❹ leave one's
body; ⓔ throw off one's mortal coil.
～を立てる rise in the world;
establish oneself (as an artist); set
oneself up (in a trade). ⓐ ～を辿る
reflect on one's life; relive one's
past life. ～を尽くす do *sth* with
one's whole heart. ～を慎む behave

prudently. ⓐ ～を抓む sympathize
deeply with; feel deeply for *sb*. ⓐ
～を詰める live frugally; lead a
frugal life. ～を挺する risk one's
life; offer one's life; throw oneself
(into the breach). ～を投じる
❶ throw oneself (into a river).
❷ plunge (headlong) into *sth*; go
into (politics); ⓘ burn one's
boats/bridges (behind one). ～を投
げる ❶ throw oneself (off a building); hurl oneself (into the water);
❷ throw oneself into *sth* heart and
soul; put one's heart and soul into
sth. ⓐ ～を逃れる avoid danger;
dodge an attack; shirk one's duty;
avoid responsibility; ⓘ dodge the
column. ⓐ ～を果たす ❶ put one's
life on the line; ⓘ throw oneself
into the jaws of death. ❷ come to
an untimely end; sacrifice one's
life. ❸ ruin oneself; go bankrupt;
ⓢ ⓘ go the the dogs. ⓐ ～を填む
throw oneself into *sth* wholeheartedly. ～を退く resign from one's
post; leave an occupation; step
down; ⓒ back out. ～を滅ぼす ruin
oneself; destroy oneself; ⓢ ⓘ go to
the dogs. (男に)～を任せる give
oneself to a man; sleep with a
man. ～を任せる ❶ throw oneself
on the mercy of *sb*. ❷ give oneself
up to (an addiction/vice). ❸ give
oneself to (a man); sleep with a
man. ～を毟る pick the flesh (from
the bones). ～を結ぶ bear fruit. ～
を持ち崩す destroy oneself; go to
the bad; ⓢ ⓘ go to the dogs. ⓐ ～を

み

持つ ❶ be independent; stand on one's own feet; Ⓒ ① cut the cord. ❷ get married; get settled; settle down. 〜を揉む writhe in agony; fret greatly over *sth*; worry about *sth*; fidget about *sth*. Ⓐ 〜を焼く ❶ suffer great agonies; be convulsed with anguish. ❷ burn with (unrequited) love; Ⓔ be consumed with love. 〜を窶す disguise oneself; dress oneself (as). 〜を寄せる live with *sb*; stay with *sb*.

実 a fruit; a nut; a berry ▸ 実

Ⓖ 〜がなる bear fruit.
Ⓦ 〜を結ばせる carry *sth* to fruition. 〜を結ぶ bear fruit; pay off.

見栄 show; display; ostentation

Ⓦ 〜を切る assume a posture; make a defiant gesture; strike an attitude. 〜を張る show off; be vain; Ⓔ be ostentatious.

磨き a polish; burnishing

Ⓦ 〜をかける ❶ give *sth* a polish; polish *sth* up. ❷ improve one's skills; work on one's technique.

見切り forsaking; abandonment

Ⓒ 〜で買う buy *sth* at a reduced price.
Ⓦ 〜を付ける give *sth* up; be through with *sb*/*sth*; be done with *sb*/*sth*.

神輿 a portable shrine

Ⓦ 〜を上げる ❶ rise from one's

seat; get up. ❷ set to work; take action; Ⓒ get on with *sth*. 〜を下ろす sit down; take a seat. 〜を担ぐ ❶ carry a portable shrine. ❷ cajole *sb* into *sth*; talk *sb* into *sth*. 〜を据える ❶ settle oneself down; plant oneself (on a chair). ❷ outstay one's welcome.

操 chastity; faithfulness

Ⓦ 〜を立てる remain faithful to *sb*; be chaste; Ⓔ defend one's virtue. 〜を破る renounce one's faith; lose one's chastity.

水 water; a flood

Ⓖ 〜が開く be in the lead. Ⓞ 〜が回る become widely known.
Ⓣ 〜で割る water *sth* down; ① put water in the wine/whiskey.
Ⓝ 〜に逆らう be out of tune with the times; go against the stream. Ⓐ 〜にする put *sth* to waste; waste *sth*; spoil *sth*; throw *sth* away. 〜に流す let *sth* pass; forgive and forget; Ⓔ let bygones be bygones; Ⓒ let *sth* go. Ⓐ 〜になる go up in smoke; come to nothing; be wasted. 〜に馴れる ❶ get accustomed to the drinking water. ❷ get used to one's new environment; settle in. 〜に浸す soak *sth* in water.
Ⓦ 〜を開ける open up a lead (between oneself and the competition). 〜を打つ water (the lawn). 〜を切る drain the water; plow the water. 〜を好む take to water; be water-loving. 〜を注す ❶ pour

water into (a kettle). ❷ estrange people from each other; cause ill feelings between people; breed bad blood. ❸ discourage *sb*; put a damper on (*sb's* enthusiasm); ⓘ be a wet blanket; ⓘ pour cold water on (*sb's* enthusiasm). ～を出(だ)す turn on the water. ～を止(と)める turn off the water. ～を抜(ぬ)く drain off (a tub). ～を弾(はじ)く repel water; be water-repellent. ～を向(む)ける distract *sb's* attention; proposition *sb* to do *sth*; win *sb* over; draw *sth* out of *sb*. ～を割(わ)る add water; dilute *sth* with water.

店(みせ) a store; a shop; a stall

[を] ～を開(あ)ける open the store. ～を買(か)う buy out a business. ～を閉(し)める ❶ close down (a shop); go out of business; ⓔ retire from business. ❷ close shop; put up the shutters; ⓒ wind up business. ～を出(だ)す open a store. ～を畳(たた)む close down (a shop); go out of business; ⓔ retire from business. ～を張(は)る open up shop. ◎ ～を引(ひ)く close shop; put up the shutters; ⓒ wind up business. ～を広(ひろ)げる extend one's business; spread (one's things) all over the place. ～を持(も)たせる set *sb* up in business. ～を譲(ゆず)る hand over one's business.

味噌(みそ) *miso* [bean paste]

[が] Ⓐ ～が腐(くさ)る ❶ the *miso* goes bad. ❷ have a bad voice (for singing).

[を] Ⓐ ～を上(あ)げる be boastful; take pride in oneself; ⓘ blow one's own horn; ⓘ talk big. ◎ ～を擂(す)る flatter *sb*; play up to *sb*; ⓘ curry favor with *sb*. ～を付(つ)ける ❶ apply *miso* to *sth*. ❷ be a failure; ⓒ make a mess of things; ⓒ bungle *sth*.

道(みち) a way; a road; the Way

[が] ～が開(あ)く have renewed hope; the prospects brighten; ⓘ see light at the end of the tunnel. ～がくねる the road twists and turns; the road meanders. ～が捗(はかど)る make good headway; the going is good; ⓔ be expeditious. ～が開(ひら)ける have renewed hope; ⓘ see light at the end of the tunnel. Ⓐ ～が行(ゆ)く make good headway; the going is good; ⓔ be expeditious.

[に] ◎ ～に欠(か)ける fail in one's duties; ⓔ swerve from the Way. ～に適(かな)う comply with the Way; be reasonable; be rational. ～に背(そむ)く stray from the Way; err from the Way. ～につく follow a road; take to the road; Ⓢ ⓘ hit the road. ～に出(で)る come out into the road; lead onto a road. ～に外(はず)れる stray from the Way; ⓘ leave the straight and narrow. ～に迷(まよ)う lose one's way; get lost.

[へ] ～へ出(で)る go out into the road.

[を] ～を開(あ)ける make way for *sb*; give way to *sb*; clear the way. ～を誤(あやま)る take the wrong turn; go astray. ～を歩(ある)く walk (up/down/along) a road; follow a road. ～を行(い)く take a road; go

み

one's way. 〜を急ぐ hurry along. 〜を失う lose one's way; be at a loss (about what to do). 〜を教える tell *sb* the way; direct *sb* to a place. (人に)〜を聞く ask *sb* the way; ask *sb* for directions. Ⓐ 〜を切る ❶ obstruct the road; cut off a path. ❷ cut off all relations with *sb*; Ⓔ sever one's connections with *sb*. 〜を立てる do one's duty; do what is right. 〜を辿る follow a road; retrace a path; follow in *sb's* path. 〜を付ける ❶ make a road; cut a path. ❷ lead the way; pave the way (for *sb*). 〜を通す drive a road through (a forest). 〜を説く expound the Way; moralize a story. Ⓐ 〜を払う make way for *sb*; give way to; clear the way. 〜を開く open up a road; break trail. 〜を拾う find one's way; pick one's way. 〜を塞ぐ stand in *sb's* way; block *sb's* passage; bar the way. 〜を踏み外す stray from the Way; Ⓘ leave the straight and narrow. 〜を守る uphold the Way; maintain one's integrity. 〜を間違える take the wrong way. 〜を求める look for a way; seek the Way; pursue the truth. 〜を譲る make way for *sb*; yield the right of way.

密計 Ⓔ a secret plan
Ⓦ Ⓔ 〜を巡らす weave a plot; devise a secret plan.

身分 status; rank; identity
Ⓖ 〜が違う have a different social

standing; differ in social standing.
Ⓦ 〜を明かす reveal one's identity; disclose one's identity. 〜を隠す hide one's identity.

耳 an ear; hearing; an edge
Ⓖ 〜が痛い ❶ have a pain in the ear. ❷ find *sth* hard to hear; be unpleasant to the ears; be embarrassed to hear *sth*. 〜が肥える have an ear for *sth*. 〜が鋭い have a keen ear; be sharp-eared. Ⓞ 〜が近い have good hearing; have a sharp ear. 〜が遠い have poor hearing; have a bad ear. 〜が鳴る have a ringing in the ears; suffer from tinnitus. 〜が早い have a quick ear; be quick of hearing. 〜が良い have a good ear. 〜が汚れる hear obscenities. 〜が悪い have poor hearing; have a bad ear.
Ⓝ Ⓞ 〜に当る be upset by what one hears; Ⓔ offend the ears. 〜に入れる ❶ tell *sb*; bring *sth* to *sb's* attention. ❷ listen to *sb*; take notice of *sth*; Ⓔ Ⓘ lend *sb* an ear. Ⓐ 〜に掛かる ❶ listen attentively; prick up one's ears. ❷ linger in one's ears; strike one's ear. Ⓐ 〜に応える be brought home to one; have effect on one. 〜に逆らう sound harsh to the ear; jar upon one's ear; Ⓔ offend the ear. 〜に障る sound harsh to the ear; jar upon one's ear; Ⓔ offend the ear. 〜にする happen to hear *sth*; find out about *sth*; Ⓒ pick up a rumor; Ⓘ get wind of *sth*. Ⓐ 〜に立つ

❶ listen attentively; prick up one's ears. ❷ linger in one's ears; strike one's ear. 〜に付く ❶ strike one's ear; linger in one's ear. ❷ be tired of hearing; be wary of hearing *sth*. 〜に留める keep *sth* in mind; linger in one's ears. Ⓐ 〜に成る have people's ears; give cause for rumor. 〜に残す linger in one's ears. 〜に入る come to one's knowledge; learn *sth* by chance; find *sth* out; Ⓘ get wind of *sth*. 〜に挟む ❶ put (a pencil/cigarette) behind one's ear. ❷ come to one's knowledge; learn *sth* by chance; find *sth* out; Ⓘ get wind of *sth*.
圏 〜を洗う ❶ clean one's ears. ❷ cleanse oneself of the impurities one has heard. 〜を疑う doubt one's own ears; cannot believe one's ears. 〜を打つ whisper *sth* into *sb's* ear; Ⓘ put a word into *sb's* ear; Ⓘ bend *sb's* ear. 〜を覆う cover one's ears (with one's hands). 〜を押える stop the ears; hold one's ears. (人に)〜を貸す listen to *sb*; Ⓘ lend *sb* an ear; Ⓘ give one's ear to *sb*. 〜を傾ける listen to *sb* attentively; pay attention to (what *sb* says); Ⓘ bend one's ear to *sb*. Ⓒ 〜を借りる whisper *sth* into *sb's* ear; Ⓘ put a word into *sb's* ear; Ⓘ have *sb's* ear; Ⓘ bend *sb's* ear. Ⓐ 〜を聞く reach one's ear; come to one's knowledge. Ⓐ 〜を擦る make an insinuating remark; Ⓘ give an indirect cut; Ⓘ talk at *sb*. 〜を肥やす develop an ear for (music). 〜を

濯ぐ cleanse oneself of the impurities one has heard. 〜を澄ます listen intently; strain one's ears; Ⓘ be all ears. 〜をそ欹てる strain one's ears; prick up one's ears. 〜を揃える make a lump-sum payment; pay in full. 〜を立てる listen intently; strain one's ears; prick up one's ears. Ⓐ 〜を潰す pretend not to listen. Ⓐ 〜を舐る ❶ whisper *sth* into *sb's* ear; Ⓘ put a word into *sb's* ear. ❷ inform on *sb*; tell on *sb*; Ⓒ let on about *sb*; Ⓘ stab *sb* in the back. ❸ cast aspersions on *sb*; slander *sb*; speak ill of *sb*; Ⓔ cast a slur on *sb's* name. Ⓐ 〜を引く share *sb's* good luck. Ⓓ 〜を吹く whisper *sth* into *sb's* ear; Ⓘ put a word into *sb's* ear. 〜を塞ぐ Ⓘ listen with half an ear; Ⓘ turn a deaf ear. 〜を穿る pick one's ear(s). Ⓐ 〜を読む count one's money.

脈 a vein; a pulse; deposits
⾃ Ⓐ 〜が上がる ❶ pass away; draw one's last breath; Ⓔ Ⓘ breathe one's last. ❷ lose hope; despair of *sth*. 〜が有る ❶ have a pulse; have life in one yet. ❷ have room for hope. Ⓒ 〜が切れる ❶ pass away; draw one's last breath; Ⓔ Ⓘ breathe one's last. ❷ lose hope; despair of *sth*.
圏 〜を打つ pulsate; throb. 〜を数える count *sb's* pulse. 〜を繋ぐ eke out a living; stay alive; keep on living. 〜を取る take *sb's* pulse; feel *sb's* pulse. Ⓐ 〜を引く sound *sb*

み

out; feel *sb* out; ⓘ feel *sb's* pulse.
〜を見る ❶ take *sb's* pulse; feel
sb's pulse. ❷ test the prospects of
sth; try the viability of *sth*.

魅力 charm; appeal; lure
が 〜が有る have an appeal; be
charming.
を 〜を失う lose one's appeal; lose
its glamour; lose one's charm. 〜を
感じる be fascinated by *sb/sth*. 〜
を添える lend charm to; give *sth*
additional charm.

ム

無 nothing; naught; nil
に 〜に帰す come to nothing; be
wasted; be a waste of time. 〜にす
る waste *sth*; put *sth* to waste. 〜
になる come to nothing; be wasted; be a waste of time.

昔 antiquity; ancient; old days
を 〜を偲ぶ look back on one's
past; think of one's younger days.

向こう the opposite side
に (人を)〜に回す rival with *sb*;
compete with *sb*.
を (人の)〜を張る oppose *sb*; set
oneself up against *sb*.

虫 an insect; a bug; a worm
が Ⓐ 〜が合う be like-minded; get
along well; Ⓔ be congenial to one;
ⓘ see eye to eye; Ⓒ ⓘ hit it off. Ⓐ

〜がある feel confident; have confidence. 〜が良い be selfish; take
things for granted; do things one's
own way. Ⓐ 〜が痛い have a
stomach ache; one's stomach
aches. Ⓐ 〜が入る ❶ be damaged;
be spoiled; be marred. ❷ keep bad
company; have a ne'er-do-well as a
lover; have a good-for-nothing
boyfriend. 〜が起こる ❶ become
fretful; get peevish. ❷ be (sexual-
ly) roused; be tempted. 〜が納ま
る regain one's temper; settle
down; Ⓔ be mollified; Ⓐ cool
down. Ⓞ 〜が落ち着く regain one's
temper; settle down; Ⓔ be mollified; Ⓐ cool down. Ⓐ 〜が降りる
feel refreshed; feel relieved. Ⓐ 〜
が齧る ❶ have a stomach ache;
one's stomach aches. ❷ feel hungry; have an appetite. ❸ go into
convulsions; have a convulsive fit;
be seized with cramps. ❹ be seized
with labor pains; go into labor. Ⓐ
〜が聞く agree fully; be in full
agreement. 〜が嫌う dislike *sb*;
have an aversion to *sb*; feel
uncomfortable with *sb*. 〜が食う
be eaten by worms. 〜が刺す ❶ be
damaged; be spoiled. ❷ keep bad
company; have a ne'er-do-well as a
lover; have a good-for-nothing
boyfriend. 〜が鎮まる calm down;
Ⓔ regain one's composure; Ⓐ cool
down. 〜が知らす have a gut
feeling; have a premonition;
Ⓔ have a sense of foreboding;
Ⓒ have a hunch. Ⓐ 〜が据る be

ready; be resigned (to one's fate); be resolved. Ⓐ 〜が堰く have a stomach ache; one's stomach aches 〜が集る ❶ get worms. ❷ become infested with worms; Ⓔ become verminous. 〜が付く ❶ be infested with insects; be insect-ridden. ❷ keep bad company; have a ne'er-do-well as a lover; have a good-for-nothing boyfriend. 〜が出る ❶ fall ill. ❷ get worms. Ⓐ 〜が動じる be surprised; be startled. Ⓐ 〜が取り上す lose one's temper; fly into a rage; Ⓢ lose one's cool. 〜が這う crawl with insects; teem with insects. Ⓐ 〜が早い ❶ be hasty; be rash. ❷ have a quick temper; be short-tempered. Ⓞ 〜が焼ける feel vexed; be annoyed; Ⓔ be chagrined. 〜が湧く get worms; become infested with worms; Ⓔ become verminous. Ⓐ 〜が悪い be hypersensitive; Ⓔ have delicate nerves; have a short temper.

に Ⓐ 〜に当たる get angry; lose one's temper; take offense; Ⓒ Ⓘ fly off the handle; Ⓢ Ⓘ blow a fuse. Ⓐ 〜に入る calm down; Ⓔ regain one's composure; Ⓐ cool down. Ⓐ 〜に障る ❶ feel unwell; have an upset stomach. ❷ feel vexed; be offended; Ⓔ be chagrined; grate on one's nerves.

を Ⓞ 〜を起こす ❶ have a stomach ache. ❷ go into convulsions; have a convulsive fit; be seized with cramps. ❸ be seized with labor pains; go into labor. Ⓞ 〜を押さえる ❶ control one's temper; contain one's anger; suppress one's feelings. ❷ have a snack. 〜を下す drive out worms; expel worms. Ⓞ 〜を殺す control one's temper; contain one's anger; suppress one's feelings. Ⓞ 〜を堪える control one's temper; contain one's anger; suppress one's feelings. Ⓐ 〜を摩る control one's temper; contain one's anger; suppress one's feelings. Ⓞ 〜を死なす control one's temper; contain one's anger; suppress one's feelings. Ⓞ 〜を持つ have a temper; be irritable. Ⓞ 〜を患う have a stomach ache; suffer from a stomach complaint.

無駄 futility; idleness; useless

に 〜にする render *sth* futile; bring *sth* to naught. 〜になる be futile; come to nothing; be wasted; Ⓘ go up in smoke.
を 〜を省く avoid waste; be efficient.

無駄足 a wasted trip

を 〜を運ぶ make a wasted a trip; Ⓘ go on a bootless errand. 〜を踏む make a wasted a trip; Ⓘ go on a bootless errand.

無駄口 idle talk; wasted talk

を 〜を叩く indulge in idle talk.

無駄玉 a wasted bullet

に Ⓞ 〜になる be to no avail; be useless; be futile; come to nothing.

む

無駄話(むだばなし) idle talk; tittle-tattle

[を] ～をする talk idly; engage in idle talk; title-tatle.

無駄骨(むだぼね) [S] wasted efforts

[に] Ⓢ ～に終(お)わる prove fruitless.
[を] Ⓢ ～を折(お)る make vain efforts; waste one's time; make useless efforts; Ⓘ catch at shadows.

無駄飯(むだめし) [S] an idle life

[を] Ⓢ ～を食(く)う lead an idle life; waste one's life.

鞭(むち) a whip; a rod; a cane

[で] ～で打(う)つ lash *sb*; give *sb* a hiding.
[を] Ⓞ ～を揚(あ)ぐ whip (a horse); lash (a horse). ～を加(くわ)える give *sb* the rod; give *sb* a thrashing. ～を鳴(な)らす crack a whip; swish a whip. ～を振(ふ)る wield a whip.

胸(むね) the breast; the chest

[が] Ⓐ ～が合(あ)う be like-minded; get along well; Ⓔ be congenial to one; Ⓘ see eye to eye; Ⓒ Ⓘ hit it off. Ⓐ ～が開(あ)ける feel relieved; Ⓘ feel a weight taken off one's chest. ～が痛(いた)む ❶ have a chest ache; one's chest aches. ❷ be in agony; be in anguish; be worried about *sb/sth*. ～が収(おさ)まる calm down; Ⓔ regain one's composure; Ⓐ cool down. ～が躍(おど)る be excited; be lifted in spirit; Ⓘ have butterflies in one's stomach. ～が決(き)まる make up one's mind; decide to do. Ⓞ ～が焦(こ)がる ❶ pine for *sb*; burn with passion for *sb*. ❷ be anxious; worry about *sb/sth*; be impatient. ～が裂(さ)ける be heartbroken; be torn apart with grief. ～が騒(さわ)ぐ have a sense of foreboding; feel a presentiment; feel uneasy; Ⓔ experience a flutter of heart. ～が空(す)く feel refreshed; feel relieved. Ⓐ ～が堰(せ)く be filled with sadness; feel wretched. Ⓞ ～が狭(せま)い be narrow-minded; be small-minded. Ⓐ ～が迫(せま)る be filled with emotions; Ⓔ feel a stirring in one's breast; be excited by *sth*; become aroused by *sth*. ～が支(つか)える lie heavy on one's stomach; feel a pressure on one's chest; Ⓘ feel a weight on one's chest. ～が潰(つぶ)れる ❶ be surprised; be startled; be taken aback; be flabbergasted. ❷ feel crushed; be heartbroken; Ⓒ feel gutted. ～が詰(つ)まる be filled with (gratitude); be overcome by (grief); Ⓘ feel a weight on one's chest; Ⓘ have a lump in one's throat; be choked up. ～が轟(とどろ)く suffer heartthrobs; feel one's heart pounding. Ⓞ ～が煮(に)える burn with (desire/rage); Ⓔ be consumed with (passion/hatred). ～が弾(はず)む be excited; be lifted in spirit. ～が張(は)り裂(さ)ける be utterly heartbroken; be torn apart by grief. Ⓐ ～が張(は)る be filled with (gratitude); be overcome by (grief); Ⓘ feel a weight on one's chest; Ⓘ have a lump in one's throat; be choked up. ～が晴(は)れる feel refreshed; feel relieved. Ⓐ ～

が開く feel relieved; ⓘ feel a weight taken off one's chest. 〜が塞がる ⓘ feel a weight on one's chest; ⓘ have a lump in one's throat; be choked up. Ⓐ 〜が燃える burn with (desire/rage); Ⓔ be consumed with (passion/hatred). 〜が焼ける have heartburn. 〜が悪い be sick to the stomach; ⓘ turn one's stomach upside down; be disgusted.

☐に 〜に当る be struck by; ⓘ come home to one; occur to one. 〜に余る feel distressed. 〜に抱く hug (an idea) to one's heart; cherish a thought. 〜に浮かぶ occur to one; ⓘ cross one's mind; ⓘ dawn on one; ⓘ strike one. 〜に描く picture sth to oneself; picture sth in one's mind. 〜に納める keep sth to oneself; ⓘ hold sth in one's heart. 〜に落ちる come to terms with sth; consent to sth; be satisfied with sth. 〜に聞く ⓘ search one's heart; ponder sth deeply; ⓘ turn sth over in one's mind; ⓒ do some soul-searching. 〜に刻む ⓘ take sth to heart; bear sth in mind. Ⓐ 〜に釘打つ feel guilty; Ⓔ weigh upon one's conscience; ⓘ feel the pricks of conscience. 〜に応える go to one's heart; ⓘ tug at one's heartstrings; ⓘ come home to one; ⓘ cut to the quick. 〜に据え兼ねる be intolerable; be unbearable; Ⓔ be insufferable. 〜に迫る be filled with emotions; Ⓔ feel a stirring in one's breast; be excited by

sth; become aroused by sth. 〜に抱きしめる press sb to one's heart. 〜に畳む keep sth to oneself; ⓘ hold sth in one's heart. 〜に支える lie heavy on one's stomach; feel a pressure on one's chest; ⓘ feel a weight on one's chest. ⓞ 〜に包む ⓘ keep sth to oneself; hold sth in one's heart. ⓞ 〜に詰まる be filled with (gratitude); be overcome by (grief); ⓘ feel a weight on one's chest; ⓘ have a lump in one's throat; be choked up. 〜に響く ⓘ take sth to heart; ⓘ come home to one. 〜に秘める ⓘ keep sth to oneself; ⓘ hold sth in one's heart.

☐を 〜を明かす unbosom oneself; speak one's mind; ⓘ get sth off one's chest; ⓘ unburden one's heart. 〜を痛める ❶ have a chest ache. ❷ be worried about sth; fret over sth. 〜を打つ be moved by sth; be impressed by sth; ⓘ tug at one's heartstrings; ⓘ strike a chord. 〜を躍らせる be excited; be lifted in spirit. 〜を貸す ❶ express one's thoughts; give sb advice. ❷ [sumō] give sb a workout. 〜を借りる ❶ ask sb's advice. ❷ [sumō] be given a workout. 〜を焦がす ❶ pine for sb; burn with passion for sb. ❷ be anxious; worry about sb/sth; be impatient. 〜を定める prepare to do sth; ⓘ make up one's mind; ⓘ gird up one's loins. Ⓐ 〜を摩る keep sth to oneself; suppress one's anger/feelings. 〜を締め付ける break one's/sb's heart;

む

be heartrending. Ⓐ 〜を据える prepare to do *sth*; ① make up one's mind; ① gird up one's loins. Ⓐ 〜を壊く be nauseated by; feel sick; be vexed at *sth*. 〜を反らす ❶ straighten oneself up. ❷ take pride in *sth*; feel bolstered by *sth*. 〜を叩く agree readily. 〜を突く ❶ be surprised; be taken aback; be flabbergasted. ❷ worry about *sb/sth*; feel anxious about *sb/sth*; ① go to the heart; ① cut one to the quick. ❸ be steep; ⓔ be precipitous. 〜を潰す ❶ upset one; be disturbing; be disquieting. ❷ be shocked; be amazed; get a start; be astonished. 〜をときめかす suffer heartthrobs; be agitated; get excited (at the thought of *sth*); ⓒ go pit-a-tat. 〜を轟かす suffer heartthrobs; feel one's heart pounding (against one's chest); ⓒ go pit-a-tat. 〜を撫で下ろす ❶ give a sigh of relief; be able to breathe again. ❷ feel relieved; be reassured; be put at ease. 〜を弾ませる ⓔ one's heart leaps with anticipation. 〜を開ける expose one's chest; bare one's breasts. 〜を晴らす get rid of an unpleasant feeling; dispel a sense of gloom; ① take a load off one's mind. 〜を張る ❶ stretch one's chest. ❷ boast about *sth*; be proud of *sth*; pride oneself on *sth*; ① puff up one's chest. 〜を冷やす be terrified; tremble with fear; give a shudder. 〜を膨らます ❶ heave one's chest.

❷ have high hopes; be full of *sth*; ⓒ be upbeat. 〜を病む suffer from a chest disease. 〜を割る speak frankly; be outspoken; be candid.

謀叛 a rebellion; a revolt

を 〜を起こす raise a rebellion; rise in revolt. 〜を企てる plot a rebellion. 〜を静める suppress a rebellion.

無理 unreasonableness

を 〜を言う be unreasonable; be cross-grained; say unreasonable things. 〜をする strain oneself; overtax oneself; go against nature.

メ

目 an eye; sight; eyesight

が 〜が合う ❶ the eyes meet. ❷ be asleep. ⓒ 〜が明く ❶ be able to see (again). ❷ Ⓐ one's eyes are opened; come to see; come to understand. ❸ [*sumō*] win a bout after a succession of defeats. 〜が粗い have a loose weave; be loosely woven. 〜が有る ❶ have a critical eye (for quality); be a connoisseur (of art). ❷ be heavy; weigh heavy. 〜が良い ❶ have good eyesight. ❷ have a critical eye (for quality); be a connoisseur. 〜が痛い have sore eyes. 〜が落ち込む have sunken eyes; have deepset eyes. 〜が霞む ❶ have a blurred vision; have one's eyes grow misty with tears; one's eye-sight grows dim (with age). ❷ lose one's powers of judgment; be uncertain of oneself. ⓒ 〜が堅い be unable to sleep; ⓔ suffer from insomnia; be wide awake; be wide awake. 〜が利く have a critical eye for *sth*; have a keen eye. 〜が眩む ❶ feel dizzy; get giddy. ❷ be blinded (by greed); be dazzled. 〜が肥える have a critical eye (for quality); be a connoisseur (of art). 〜が冴える be unable to sleep; ⓔ suffer from insomnia; be wide awake; become wide awake. 〜が覚める ❶ wake up; open one's eyes. ❷ come to one's senses; ⓔ be disillusioned; see reason. ❸ be startled; be dazzled; be amazed. 〜が鋭い be sharp-sighted; have eagle eyes. 〜が据る the eyes are set/fixed. 〜が高い have a critical eye for *sth*; have a keen eye. Ⓐ 〜が立つ be fortunate; be lucky; ⓒ ⓘ hit good luck. 〜が付く take notice of *sb*/*sth*; pay attention to *sb*/*sth*; notice *sth*. 〜が散る be distracted; be diverted; be distraught. 〜が潰れる lose one's sight; go blind. 〜が詰む have a close weave; be closely woven. 〜が出る ❶ the die is cast. ❷ (良い目) have luck on one's side; have a stroke of good luck; be lucky. 〜が届く keep an eye on *sb*/*sth*; pay careful attention; be attentive. ⓒ 〜が飛び出る ❶ be stunned (by the cost); be flabbergasted. ❷ be

severely scolded; be given a dressing-down. 〜が無い ❶ be blinded (by love); ⓔ be imprudent; ⓒ be mad about *sb*/*sth*. ❷ lack a critical eye; have no insight. 〜が早い be quick to see *sth*; be sharp-sighted. 〜が光る keep a close eye on *sb*/*sth*; keep a watch on *sb*/*sth*. 〜が回る ❶ feel dizzy; get giddy; be stunned. ❷ be extremely busy. 〜が行く ❶ notice *sth*; take to *sb*; catch one's fancy. ❷ feel dizzy; get giddy. 〜が良い have good sight. 〜が弱い have weak eyes; have poor eyes. 〜が悪い have bad sight; have poor eyesight.

Ⓒ (酷い)〜に遭う be in trouble; have a hard time. 〜に余る ❶ be too much to take in. ❷ be too much to bear; be intolerable. 〜に浮かぶ come before one's eyes; come to mind; occur to one; ⓔ rise in one's thoughts. ⓒ ⓔ 〜に映じる greet the eyes; be seen by one. 〜に懸かる ❶ come in sight; be noticed. ❷ (お目に) see *sb*; meet with *sb*. 〜に懸ける ❶ notice *sth*; ⓘ catch one's eye. ❷ take care of *sb*/*sth*; look after *sb*/*sth*. ❸ (お目に) display *sth*; put *sth* on show. Ⓐ 〜に遮る block off one's sight. 〜に曝す expose *sth* to the eye. 〜に障る ❶ be hurtful to the eye. ❷ be offensive to the eye; be an eyesore; spoil the view. 〜に染みる ❶ smart the eyes; cause the eyes to water. ❷ be vivid (in color); be dazzling; be startling. ❸ grow tired

189

of seeing *sth*; Ⓒ get an eyeful of *sth*. ～にする notice *sth*; take note of *sth*; happen to see *sth*. ～に立つ stand out; draw one's attention. ～に付く ❶ attract one's attention; be noticeable. ❷ haunt one; Ⓘ stay with one. ～に留まる ❶ attract attention; be noticed. ❷ take to *sb*; catch one's fancy; Ⓒ Ⓘ give *sb* the (glad) eye. Ⓐ ～に留める notice *sth*; Ⓘ catch one's eye. ～になる keep an eye on *sb/sth*; watch out for *sb/sth*; look out for *sb/sth* ～に残る linger before one's eyes; Ⓘ be engraved on one's memory. ～に入る catch sight of *sb/sth*; come in sight; come into view. ～に触れる attract one's attention; come into view; Ⓘ catch one's eye. ～に見える be obvious; be clear (for all to see); stand to reason. ◎ ～に見る see *sth* clearly; have *sth* before one's eyes.

[を] Ⓐ ～を明く come to one's senses; see reason; Ⓔ be disillusioned. ～を開ける bring *sb* to his/her senses; Ⓔ disillusion *sb*; Ⓐ open *sb's* eyes. ～を上げる look up; Ⓐ raise one's eyes; Ⓔ lift one's gaze. ～を遊ばす give one's eye free reign. ～を合わす ❶ close one's eyes. ❷ meet each other's gaze; run across *sb*. ～を痛める impair one's vision. ～を射る be blinding; be startling. ～を入れる cast a favorable eye on *sb*; favor *sb*. ～を疑う doubt one's eyes; question what one sees. ～を移す shift one's gaze. ～を奪う be fascinating; be an eye-catcher. ～を奪われる be fascinated by *sth*; be spellbound by *sth*; be dazzled by *sth*. ◎ ～を起こす ❶ throw the dice; Ⓔ cast the die. ❷ be fortunate; be lucky; Ⓒ Ⓘ hit good luck. ～を押える cover one's eyes. ～を落とす ❶ look down; cast a downward look. ❷ drop a stitch; let down a stitch. ◎ ❸ lose one's life; lay down one's life. ～を驚かす be astonished; be startled; be flabbergasted. ～を掛ける ❶ take care of *sb/sth*; look after *sb/sth*. ❷ watch out for *sb/sth*. ❸ be partial to *sb*; be biased toward *sb*. (人の)～を掠める do *sth* by stealth; Ⓢ do *sth* on the sly. ～を切る make a notch in *sth*; score (meat). ◎ ～を極む strain one's eyes; peer (into the distance). (人の)～を潜る elude *sb's* view. Ⓐ ～を下す take care of *sb/sth*; look after *sb/sth*; watch out for *sb/sth*. ～を配る keep a watchful eye on *sb/sth*; remain vigilant; watch *sb/sth* carefully. (涙で)～を曇らす blur the eyes (with tears). ～を晦ます deceive *sb*; Ⓘ throw dust in *sb's* eyes. Ⓒ ～を呉れる glance at *sb/sth*. Ⓐ Ⓢ ～を食わす wink at *sb*; exchange glances with *sb*. ～を肥やす ❶ feast one's eyes on *sth*. ❷ develop an eye for *sth*; nourish the eye. ～を凝らす ❶ gaze at *sb/sth*; stare a at *sb/sth*. ❷ strain one's eyes. ～を遮る bar *sth* from

め

sight; obstruct one's/*sb's* view. 〜を覚ます ❶ wake up. ❷ be startled; be surprised. ❸ become conscious of *sth*; Ⓐ have one's eyes opened; realize *sth*; awake to (the truth). ❹ come to one's senses; see reason; Ⓔ be disillusioned. ◎ 〜を曝す draw one's eyes wide open; look straight ahead; look all over *sth*. (人の)〜を忍ぶ elude *sb's* eyes. 〜を据える fix one's eyes on *sb*/*sth*; gaze at *sb*/*sth*. Ⓐ 〜を擦る rub one's eyes; wipe one's eyes. Ⓐ 〜を澄ます gaze at *sb*/*sth*; stare at *sb*/*sth*; look hard at *sb*/*sth*. 〜を注ぐ turn one's gaze toward *sb*/*sth*; keep one's eyes on *sb*/*sth*; pay attention to *sb*/*sth*. Ⓐ 〜を側める avert the eyes (in disgust); look away; look the other way. 〜を背ける avert the eyes (in disgust); look away from; look the other way. 〜を逸らす take one's eyes off *sb*/*sth*; turn the eyes away from *sb*/*sth*. Ⓐ 〜を立てる take notice of *sb*/*sth*; pay attention to *sb*/*sth*. ◎ 〜を使う use one's eyes; Ⓐ keep one's eyes open. 〜を付ける keep one's eyes on *sb*/*sth*; pay attention to; be interested in *sth*. 〜を潰す put *sb's* eye out. 〜を瞑る ❶ close one's eyes; go to sleep. ❷ pass away; draw one's last breath; Ⓔ ⓘ breathe one's last. ❸ overlook *sth*; put up with *sth*; ⓘ turn a blind eye; ⓘ wink at *sth*. 〜を通す run one's eyes over *sb*/*sth*; look *sth* over. 〜を閉じる

❶ shut one's eyes; close one's eyes. ❷ pass away; draw one's last breath; Ⓔ ⓘ breathe one's last. Ⓐ 〜を留める take notice of *sb*/*sth*; pay attention to *sb*/*sth*. 〜を慰む soothe the eyes. Ⓐ (人の)〜を抜く play a trick on *sb's* eyes; ⓘ pull the wool over *sb's* eyes. 〜を拭う wipe one's eyes. 〜を盗む do *sth* in secret. 〜を外す take one's eyes off *sb*/*sth*; turn the eyes away from *sb*/*sth*. 〜を離す let *sb*/*sth* out of one's sight; ⓘ be off one's guard. 〜を憚る shy away from the public gaze; Ⓔ shrink from people's gaze; shun publicity. 〜を光らす keep a watchful eye on *sb*/*sth*; be watchful; be vigilant. 〜を引く ❶ draw one's/*sb's* attention; attract one's/*sb's* notice. ❷ wink at *sb*; ⓘ give *sb* the eye; ⓘ make eyes at *sb*. 〜を開く ❶ open one's eyes. ❷ understand *sth*; become aware of *sth*; ⓘ dawn on one. ❸ be spiritually awakened; reach enlightenment; ⓘ see the light. ❹ become able to read; become literate. 〜を塞ぐ ❶ shut one' eyes. ❷ pass away; draw one's last breath; Ⓔ ⓘ breathe one's last. ❸ ⓘ turn a blind eye; ⓘ wink at *sth*. 〜を伏せる lower one's eyes; Ⓔ cast down one's eyes. 〜を細める close one's eyes partly; look lovingly at (a child); look through one's eyelashes; beam (with delight). 〜を回す ❶ lose consciousness; pass out; ◎ black out. ❷ be bewildered; be surprised. ❸ be extremely busy. 〜を見合わせる lock eyes with each other. 〜を見出す gaze at *sb/sth*; glare a at *sb/sth* (with jealousy). Ⓐ 〜を見す ❶ wink at *sb*; Ⓘ give *sb* the eye; Ⓘ make eyes at *sb*. ❷ cause *sb* trouble; give *sb* a hard time. ❸ show one's feelings in one's eyes. 〜を見張る ❶ open one's eyes wide. ❷ be struck with wonder; be stunned; be awestruck; be flabbergasted; Ⓢ Ⓘ be blown away. 〜を見る ❶ look *sb* in the eyes; look into *sb's* eyes. ❷ be in a (difficult) situation; Ⓒ be in a fix. ❸ discriminate between two things; recognize *sb/sth*. 〜を剥く glare at *sb/sth*; stare one's eyes out; Ⓘ look daggers at *sb*. 〜を向ける turn one's eyes to *sb/sth*; become interested in *sb/sth*; turn one's attention to *sb/sth*. 〜を遣る look at *sb/sth*; look toward *sb/sth*; Ⓒ cast one's eyes on *sb/sth*. 〜を喜ばす please the eyes; be a feast for the eyes.

芽 a bud; a sprout; a spear

Ⓖ 〜が出る ❶ sprout up; burst into leaf. ❷ begin to prosper; start to thrive. ❸ come into luck; Ⓒ get a lucky break.

Ⓦ 〜を出す ❶ put out buds; burst into leaf. ❷ begin to prosper; start to thrive. 〜を摘む ❶ nip a bud. ❷ nip (a plot) in the bud; foil *sb's* evil designs. 〜を吹く ❶ put out buds; burst into leaf. ❷ begin to prosper; start to thrive.

銘 Ⓔ an inscription; an epitaph

Ⓦ Ⓔ 〜を打つ ❶ stamp one's name (into a blade); impress a signature (onto a blade). ❷ name *sth*; style *sth*; brand *sth*. Ⓔ 〜を刻む carve an epitaph (into a stone); engrave an inscription (into stone).

名 Ⓔ distinction; greatness ▶ 名

Ⓦ Ⓔ 〜を謳う extol *sb's* name; praise *sb's* accomplishments.

命数 Ⓔ one's given span of life

Ⓖ 〜が尽きる ❶ reach the end of one's days. ❷ run out of luck.

Ⓦ 〜を知る know one's time has come.

名声 fame; renown; celebrity

Ⓖ 〜が上げる rise in fame. 〜が有る be celebrated; be popular. 〜が落ちる lose one's reputation.

Ⓦ 〜を揚げる make one's name renowned; enhance one's reputation. 〜を失う lose prestige; lose one's reputation. 〜を落す ruin one's reputation; Ⓒ lower one's reputation. 〜を傷つける damage one's name; injure one's reputation. 〜を汚す mar one's name; Ⓔ tarnish one's reputation; Ⓔ cast a slur on one's reputation. 〜を高める bring fame to one/*sb*; add to one's reputation; Ⓔ enhance one's reputation. Ⓔ 〜を博する win fame; make a name for oneself; gain a reputation. 〜を求める seek a name for oneself; desire fame.

瞑想 ⓔ meditation
⬜に ⓔ 〜に耽る be lost in meditation.

名分 ⓔ one's moral duty
⬜を ⓔ 〜を立てる justify oneself; explain one's conduct.

名望 ⓔ repute; renown; fame
⬜を ⓔ 〜を失う lose one's reputation; ⓔ fall in public estimation. 〜を得る gain reputation.

命脈 ⓔ life; the thread of life
⬜が ⓔ 〜が尽きる die out; come to an end.
⬜を ⓔ 〜を保つ remain alive; maintain life; preserve life. ⓔ 〜を繋ぐ stay alive; hang on to life; eke out a living; cling on to life.

迷夢 ⓔ an illusion; a delusion
⬜が ⓒ ⓔ 〜が覚める come to one's senses; come to oneself; be disillusioned; see reason.
⬜を ⓒ ⓔ 〜を覚ます bring sb to his/her senses; ⓔ disillusion sb; ⓐ open sb's eyes; make sb see reason.

迷惑 trouble; annoyance
⬜を 〜を掛ける ❶ cause sb trouble; get sb into trouble. ❷ annoy sb; make oneself a nuisance.

目頭 the inner corner of the eye
⬜を 〜を押える fight back one's tears. 〜を拭う wipe away one's tears.

目角 the corner of the eye
⬜に ⓐ 〜に取る see sth clearly; recognize sth clearly; ⓒ take sth in.
⬜を ⓐ 〜を利かす be sensible; be quick-witted. ⓐ 〜を立てる look fiercely at sb; ⓘ look daggers at sb.

眼鏡 a pair of spectacles
⬜が 〜が狂う misjudge a situation.
⬜に 〜に適う win sb's confidence; meet sb's approval; pass a test.
⬜を 〜を掛ける put on one's glasses. 〜を外す take off one's glasses.

目釘 Ⓗ a rivet of a sword hilt
⬜を 〜を湿す ❶ moisten the rivet of a sword hilt. ⓐ ❷ prepare for battle; make oneself ready for combat; brace oneself; ⓘ gird up one's loins.

目くじら the corner of the eye
⬜を 〜を立てる ❶ raise one's eyebrows. ❷ call sth into question; look disapprovingly at sb/sth; make a fuss over sth; ⓘ split hairs.

目先 at hand; immediate
⬜が 〜が利く be farsighted; have foresight.
⬜に 〜にちらつく see (recollect) sth vividly.
⬜を 〜を変える do something new.

目尻 the corner of the eye
⬜を 〜を下げる ❶ be all smiles; be pleased with sth. ❷ make eyes at sb; ⓔ cast amorous glances at sb; ⓘ make sheep's eyes at sb.

め

193

鍍金 plating; gilding; gilt
[が] 〜が剥げる ❶ the gilt comes off. ❷ betray oneself; reveal one's true character; ⓘ show one's true colors; ⓘ show the cloven hoof.
[を] Ⓐ 〜をさす gild *sth*; plate *sth* (with gold/silver). 〜を施す gild *sth*; plate *sth* (with gold/silver).

目褄 Ⓐ public notice; publicity
[を] Ⓐ 〜を忍ぶ avoid public notice; do *sth* in secret; meet in secret.

目処 an aim; a goal; a prospect
[が] 〜が有る have hope of doing; lie within the realm of possibilities. 〜が立つ have renewed hope; the prospects brighten; ⓘ see light at the end of the tunnel. 〜が付く have renewed hope; the prospects brighten; ⓘ see light at the end of the tunnel.

目端 ready wits
[が] 〜が利く be quick witted; be tactful; have tact; be sensible.

目鼻 the eyes and nose
[が] 〜が付く reach completion; near completion; materialize; take shape; ⓒ get somewhere.
[を] 〜を付ける give shape to *sth*; get *sth* into shape.

目星 an aim; an objective
[を] 〜を付ける ❶ keep an aye on *sb/sth*; Ⓐ fasten one's eyes on *sb/sth*. ❷ make an educated guess.

目安 a standard; a yardstick
[が] 〜が付く have a rough idea; get a general idea.
[を] 〜を置く set a standard. 〜を立てる set a standard; fix one's aim. 〜を付ける ❶ set a standard; fix one's aim. ❷ submit a petition; lodge a complaint.

面 a mask; a (sur)face ▶ 面 ▶ 面
[が] 〜が割れる be unmasked; be identified; be exposed.
[と] 〜と向かう come face to face; meet face to face.
[を] 〜を打つ make a mask. 〜を被る ❶ put on a mask. ❷ disguise oneself. ❸ hide one's face (in shame). 〜を刻む cut a facet (on a stone). 〜を付ける put on a mask. 〜を取る ❶ take off one's mask; remove one's mask. ❷ take the corners off *sth*; plane off the corners of *sth*. ❸ [*kendō*] strike the mask of one's opponent; score a point. Ⓐ 〜を脱ぐ take off one's mask; remove one's mask. 〜を外す take off one's mask; remove one's mask.

面倒 trouble; difficulty; care
[を] 〜を掛ける cause trouble to *sb*; trouble *sb*. 〜を見る take care of *sb/sth*; look after *sb/sth*.

面目 honor; face; dignity
[が] 〜が立つ save one's honor; maintain one's dignity; ⓘ save one's face; ⓘ stand proud. 〜が無い be ashamed of oneself.

め

に 〜に関わる concern one's honor; reflect on one's dignity; be a matter of honor. 〜に掛ける do *sth* for one's honor; be bound in honor.

を 〜を失う disgrace oneself; ⓔ ⓘ lose countenance; ⓘ lose face. ⓐ 〜を凌ぐ bear the shame; suffer ignominy; ⓔ endure ignominy. 〜を保つ uphold one's honor; preserve one's honor; maintain one's dignity; ⓘ save one's face; ⓢ keep one's cool. 〜を立てる save *sb's* honor; ⓔ keep *sb* in countenance. 〜を潰す injure *sb's* dignity; cause *sb* to lose face; ⓔ blight *sb's* honor. 〜を施す gain honor; get credit for *sth*; ⓘ do oneself proud.

モ

妄言 ⒠ reckless words
を ⓔ 〜を吐く utter reckless words.

毛氈 a rug; a carpet
を ⓐ 〜を被る ❶ make an error; ⓔ commit a blunder; make a mess of *sth*; ⓒ bungle *sth*. ❷ be disowned; be disinherited; ⓒ be cut off (without a shilling). ❸ spend one's money on prostitutes; ⓘ live a fast life; run out of money. 〜を敷く spread a rug; lay a carpet.

目的 a purpose; a goal; an aim
に 〜に適う answer a purpose; serve a purpose; meet a goal.
を 〜を抱く have a purpose. 〜を推

し進める advance a cause. 〜を定める set (oneself) a purpose. 〜を達する accomplish an aim; ⓔ attain one's object; ⓒ gain one's end. 〜を遂げる reach a goal; achieve one's aim; ⓒ do the trick. 〜を持つ have a purpose; have a goal.

餅 a rice cake
に ⓐ 〜に搗く be at a loss (about what to do); be too much for one; be beyond one's control. ⓐ 〜に成る ❶ form a group; stick together; cling together. ❷ curl up (in one's futon).
を 〜を搗く ❶ pound steamed rice into cakes; make rice cakes. ⓒ ❷ make love; have sexual intercourse; have sex; ⓒ make whoopee.

畚 Ⓐ a straw basket
に ⓐ 〜に乗る be executed; be put to death; ⓔ receive the death sentence; ⓢ ⓘ kick the bucket.

勿体 pretensions; ostentation
を 〜を付ける ❶ give oneself airs; be pompous; ⓔ be ostentatious; ⓘ put on airs. ❷ give *sth* too much weight; attach undue importance to *sth*; overestimate *sth*.

髻 Ⓐ a topknot
を ⓐ 〜を切る ❶ become a Buddhist priest; take the tonsure; ⓔ retire into religion. ❷ go into seclusion; become a hermit; ⓔ retire from the world; renounce the world. 〜を掴

む seize *sb* by the topknot. Ⓐ 〜を
放つ wear one's topknot openly.

物 a thing; an object; goods

図 〜が無い be insubstantial; be of
no consequence; be insignificant.
〜が分かる understand the world;
be worldly wise.

図 Ⓐ 〜に当たる get flustered; be
confused; fidget over *sth*. Ⓐ 〜に掛
かる interfere with everything;
meddle with everything; Ⓘ have a
finger in every pie. 〜にする ❶ take
possession of *sth*; make *sth* one's
own. ❷ master a craft/skill/lan-
guage. ❸ win *sb's* heart; make a
conquest; Ⓒ Ⓘ chat a girl up. 〜にな
る ❶ turn *sth* into *sth*; amount to
sth; be of consequence. ❷ come
off; pass muster; be a success.

図 〜を言う ❶ say *sth*; address *sb*.
❷ count for *sth*; be important; go a
long way. ❸ speak for itself; be
self-evident; Ⓘ speak volumes. 〜
を言わす let *sth* speak for itself;
utilize *sth*; make use of *sth*.

物言い speech; a protest

図 〜を付ける protest against *sth*;
object to *sth*; contest a verdict.

喪服 a mourning dress

図 〜を着ける take to mourning;
put on mourning; mourn *sb's* death.

紅葉 a Japanese maple

図 (顔に) Ⓐ 〜を散らす blush shyly;
have a flush in one's cheeks.

門 a gate; an entrance ▶ 門

に 〜に入る ❶ pass through a gate;
enter (a building). ❷ become *sb's*
pupil; become a follower. 〜に立つ
stand at the gate. 〜に学ぶ study
under *sb*; Ⓔ be under *sb's* tutelage.

図 〜を開ける open the gate(s). Ⓞ
〜を出る ❶ leave home; go out into
the world; enter the real world.
❷ become a Buddhist priest; enter a
Buddhist monastery. Ⓐ 〜を打つ
close the gate(s). 〜を潜る pass
through a gate. 〜を閉める close
the gate(s). 〜を叩く ❶ knock at
the gate; call on *sb*. ❷ apply to
become *sb's* pupil; Ⓔ seek *sb's* tutelage. 〜を閉じる close the gate(s).

文句 Ⓒ a remark; a complaint

図 Ⓒ 〜を言う make a complaint;
complain to *sb* (about *sth*); raise
objections. Ⓒ 〜を付ける criticize
sb; make a complaint; object to
sth; Ⓒ grumble about *sth*.

門戸 Ⓔ the door

図 Ⓔ 〜を構える set up house;
start housekeeping. Ⓔ 〜を閉ざす
❶ shut the door (on *sb*); close the
door (on *sb*). ❷ exclude *sb*; keep *sb*
out. Ⓐ Ⓔ 〜を成す ❶ set up house;
start housekeeping. ❷ found a
school (of thought). Ⓞ Ⓔ 〜を張る
❶ live in a fine house; keep an
establishment. ❷ put up a (good)
front. ❸ found a school (of
thought). Ⓔ 〜を開く ❶ open the
door (to *sb*). ❷ give free access to

も

sb; lift restrictions. ❸ open up relations (with a country).

ヤ

矢 an arrow; a bolt; a spoke
が Ⓐ ～が入る be criticized; Ⓔ be the subject of criticism; be blamed; be reproached; Ⓐ come under fire.
を Ⓐ ～を刺す fix an arrow to the bowstring. Ⓐ ～を番える fix an arrow to the bowstring. Ⓐ ～を突く be quick; be expedient. Ⓐ ～を矧ぐ ❶ feather an arrow; prepare an arrow. ❷ prepare for battle; make oneself ready for combat; Ⓘ gird up one's loins; Ⓘ clear the decks. ～を放つ ❶ discharge a volley; open fire; take sb under fire. ❷ (質問の) fire (questions) at sb. ～を向ける fix one's aim; aim for (a target); Ⓘ set one's sights on sb/sth.

野 Ⓔ a plain; a field
に ⓄⒺ ～に居る be out of office; be in opposition. Ⓔ ～に下る step down from office; Ⓔ retire from public office; leave government service.

刃 a blade; a sword ▸ 刃
に ～に掛かる die by the sword. ～に掛ける put sb to the sword; knife sb; strike sb down. ⒶⒺ ～に伏す throw oneself on one's sword; kill oneself by the sword.

八百長 Ⓢ a rigged affair; a fix
で Ⓢ ～で負ける [sumō] lose a match on purpose; throw a match.
を Ⓢ ～を遣る [sumō] fix a match; © rig a fight.

矢面 Ⓔ the brunt of an attack
に Ⓔ ～に立つ ❶ bear the brunt of an attack; Ⓘ throw oneself into the breach. ❷ become the target of criticism; Ⓐ bear the brunt of an attack; Ⓘ step into the breach.

薬缶 a kettle; a tea kettle
を ～を掛ける put a kettle on (the fire). Ⓐ ～を被る conceal one's real personality; feign ignorance; play the hypocrite; simulate modesty. Ⓔ ～を脱ぐ be straightforward; come out strong; Ⓘ call a spade a spade.

焼き Ⓢ baking; pottery; temper
が ～が回る ❶ [forging] be fired for too long. Ⓢ ❷ become decrepit; grow senile. Ⓢ ❸ become antiquated; go out of fashion.
を ～を入れる ❶ [forging] forge a sword; temper a sword. Ⓢ ❷ inflict corporal punishment; punish sb; harden sb. Ⓢ ❸ torture sb; Ⓔ put sb to torture; lynch sb. Ⓢ ❹ reprimand sb; Ⓘ haul sb over the coals; Ⓘ teach sb a lesson. ⓄⓈ ～を掛ける drink away one's hangover.

焼餅 toasted rice cake
を ～を焼く be jealous (of one's wife); display signs of jealousy.

や

役 a post; a duty; a role

に ～に立つ be useful; be of help; serve a purpose.

を ～を演じる play a role. ～を退く resign a post; quit one's post; ⓔ retire from office. ～を勤める hold an office; perform a duty; play a role. ～を振る assign duties; allocate roles.

約束 a promise; an engagement

と ⓞ (前世からの)～と諦める come to terms with one's fate; resign oneself to one's karma.

に ～に縛られる be bound by a promise; be under a promise. ～に背く break one's promise; renege on one's promise.

を ～を交わす exchange promises; become engaged. ～をする make an appointment (with *sb*). ～を解く release *sb* from a promise. ～を取り消す withdraw one's promise; call off an engagement. ～を果たす ❶ fulfill one's promise; live up to one's promise. ❷ keep an appointment; ⓔ meet one's engagement. ～を守る ❶ keep one's promise; ⓔ honor one's promise; be true to one's word. ❷ keep an appointment; ⓔ meet one's engagement. ❸ observe the rules; abide by the rules; ⓒ stick to the rules. ～を破る break one's promise; renege on one's promise.

自棄 S self-abandonment

に ⓢ ～になる become desperate; be driven to despair; grow reckless.

を ⓢ ～を起こす abandon oneself; become desperate; ⓔ give oneself up to despair; go mad with despair.

野次 S booing; jeering; hooting

を ⓢ ～を飛ばす hoot at *sb*; jeer at *sb*; ⓒ ⓘ give *sb* the bird.

鏃 an arrowhead; a flinthead

を ⓐ ～を争う fight a battle; do battle. ⓐ ～を噛む engage an enemy; come to blows.

柳 a willow tree

に ～に受ける handle *sth* with resilience; tackle (a problem) in a flexible way; ⓔ bend without yielding; be pliable. ⓐ ～に出る comply without protest; be obedient; be docile; ⓒ be tractable. ⓐ ～に遭る handle *sth* with resilience; tackle *sth* in a flexible way; ⓔ bend without yielding; be pliable.

を ⓐ ～を折る see *sb* off; give *sb* a send-off.

脂 resin; gum; nicotine; tar

を ～を下げる give oneself airs; be self-complacent; ⓢ ⓘ be stuck-up.

藪蛇 S a snake in the thicket

に ⓢ ～になる produce the opposite result; go against one; backfire.

山 a mountain; a mine; a gamble

が ～が当たる guess right; get it

right; ⓘ be on the the mark. ～が
外<ruby>はず<rt></rt></ruby>れる guess wrong; get it wrong;
ⓘ be beside the mark. ⓞ ～が見<ruby>み<rt></rt></ruby>え
る have renewed hope; the
prospects brighten; ⓘ see light at
the end of the tunnel.

に ～にする pile *sth* up; gather *sth*
into a heap. ～に登<ruby>のぼ<rt></rt></ruby>る climb a
mountain; ⓔ ascend a mountain.

を ～を当てる ❶ ⓛ strike a vein (of
gold). ❷ make a fortune; ⓢ ⓘ make
it big time. Ⓐ ～を入<ruby>い<rt></rt></ruby>れる sell one's
day's worth of goods; close shop;
ⓒ wind up business. ～を下<ruby>お<rt></rt></ruby>りる
descend a mountain; come down a
mountain. ⓞ ～を買<ruby>か<rt></rt></ruby>う invest in
mines. ～を掛<ruby>か<rt></rt></ruby>ける ❶ speculate (in
stocks); venture on *sth*; take a
chance on *sth*. ❷ take chances on
getting the right answer; guess at
the right answer (in an exam). ～を
越<ruby>こ<rt></rt></ruby>す ❶ cross the mountains. ❷ pass
the critical point; ⓘ turn the cor-
ner; ⓒ ⓘ be over the hump. ❸ be
beyond one's prime. Ⓐ ～を止<ruby>と<rt></rt></ruby>める
❶ stop in the middle of one's work.
❷ close for the day; close shop; put
up the shutters; ⓒ wind up business. ～を成す pile *sth* up; gather
sth into a heap. ～ を 張<ruby>は<rt></rt></ruby>る
❶ speculate (in stocks); venture on
sth; take a chance on *sth*. ❷ take
chances on getting the right
answer; guess at the right answer
(in an exam). ～を盛り上<ruby>あ<rt></rt></ruby>げる build
up suspense (in a story). ⓞ ～を遣<ruby>や<rt></rt></ruby>る
speculate (in stocks); venture on
sth; take a chance on *sth*.

病 <ruby>やまい<rt></rt></ruby> Ⓔ an illness; a disease

に Ⓔ ～に犯<ruby>おか<rt></rt></ruby>される fall ill; be taken
ill; contract a disease. Ⓔ ～に掛<ruby>か<rt></rt></ruby>か
る fall ill; be taken ill; contract a
disease. Ⓔ ～に沈<ruby>しず<rt></rt></ruby>む contract a
grave disease; fall dangerously ill.

を Ⓔ ～を癒<ruby>いや<rt></rt></ruby>す cure an illness. Ⓔ ～
を養<ruby>やしな<rt></rt></ruby>う undergo medical treatment.

闇 <ruby>やみ<rt></rt></ruby> darkness; the black market

で ～で売<ruby>う<rt></rt></ruby>る sell *sth* on the black
market. ～で買<ruby>か<rt></rt></ruby>う buy *sth* on the
black market.

に ～に消<ruby>き<rt></rt></ruby>える vanish into the
night; Ⓔ be swallowed up by the
dark. Ⓐ ～に暮<ruby>く<rt></rt></ruby>れる ❶ go dark;
Ⓔ descend into darkness. ❷ lose
one's mind; go mad (with grief). ～
に流<ruby>なが<rt></rt></ruby>す channel (goods) to the
black market. ～に葬<ruby>ほうむ<rt></rt></ruby>る cover *sth*
up; ⓒ hush *sth* up. ～に惑<ruby>まど<rt></rt></ruby>う ❶ lose
one's way in the darkness. ❷ lose
one's mind; go mad (with grief).

を ⓞ ～を遣<ruby>や<rt></rt></ruby>る trade in the black
market; be a blackmarketeer; be
an off-the-books dealer.

槍 <ruby>やり<rt></rt></ruby> a spear; a lance; a javelin

が ～が入<ruby>はい<rt></rt></ruby>る be interrupted. ⓞ ～が
出<ruby>で<rt></rt></ruby>る be interrupted. Ⓐ ～が曲<ruby>ま<rt></rt></ruby>がる
fall short of one's expectations;
Ⓔ belie one's expectations.

を ～を入<ruby>い<rt></rt></ruby>れる ❶ attack *sb* with a
spear. ❷ jeer at *sb*; hoot at *sb*;
heckle *sb*; ⓒ ⓘ give *sb* the bird.
❸ interrupt *sb*; interfere in *sb's*
affairs; meddle in *sb's* affairs;
ⓢ butt in; ⓘ put one's oar in. ⓞ ～

や

を受ける ❶ be attacked with a spear. ❷ be jeered at; be heckled; ⓒ ⓘ be given the bird. ⓢ ～を食う ❶ be attacked with a spear. ❷ be jeered at; be heckled; ⓒ ⓘ be given the bird. ⓞ ～を出す ❶ thrust out one's spear. ❷ jut out; stick out; ⓔ protrude. ❸ criticize *sb*; make a complaint; raise objections; object to *sth*; ⓒ grumble about *sth*. ❹ [*nōraku*] sing before one's turn; be out of harmony.

ユ

湯 hot water; a hot spring
に ～に行く go to the bathhouse; visit a public bath. ～に漬かる have a dip in the bathtub; ⓒ have a good soak.
を ～を立てる ❶ heat water; boil water. ❷ get the bath ready; heat the bath. ～を使う take a bath. ～を使わせる give *sb* a bath. ⓐ ～を引く take a bath; wash oneself. ～を沸かす ❶ boil water. ❷ heat the bath; get the bath ready.

勇 ⓔ bravery; courage; pluck
を ⓐ ⓔ ～を鼓す pluck up courage; ⓔ muster up courage; ⓘ pull oneself together; ⓘ gird up one's loins.

優位 ⓔ superiority; ascendancy
に ⓔ ～に立つ have an advantage over *sb*; ⓔ be in the ascendant; ⓒ ⓘ have the drop on *sb*.

を ⓔ ～を与える give *sb* the lead. ⓔ ～を占める have an advantage over *sb*; ⓘ have the upper hand over *sb*; ⓒ ⓘ have the drop on *sb*.

輸贏 ⓔ victory or defeat
を ⓐ ⓔ ～を争う contend for victory; ⓔ vie for supremacy.

雪 snow; a snowfall
が ～が降る snow falls; it snows.
に ～に埋もれる be buried in the snow; be snowed under. ～に閉ざされる be snowbound; be snowed up; be snowed in.
を ⓞ ～を欺く be snow-white; be startlingly white. ～を戴く ❶ be covered with snow; be snow-crested. ❷ have (snow-)white hair. ⓞ ～を冒す brave the snow. ～をかく clear away snow. ⓐ ～を廻らす blow up the snow.

湯気 stream; vapor
が ⓐ ～が上がる get ahead in the world; succeed in life; rise in the world. ～が立つ ❶ give off steam. ❷ boil with rage.

指 a finger; the thumb; a toe
に ～に嵌める put (a ring/a pick for playing *koto*, etc.) on a finger.
を ～を折る turn in one's finger (when counting); count on one's fingers. ～を切る ❶ cut one's finger. ❷ make a vow; make a pledge. ⓞ ⓔ ～を屈する make a vow; pledge to do *sth*; make a

ゆ

pledge. 〜を銜える ❶ put a finger in one's mouth. ❷ covet *sth*; look enviously at *sb/sth*; watch *sb* with envy. ❸ remain an onlooker; stand by idly; Ⓓ sit on the fence. 〜を指す ❶ point to *sth*; point at *sth*; point *sth* out. ❷ talk behind *sb's* back; backbite. Ⓐ ❸ take part in *sth*; have a hand in *sth*. Ⓐ ❹ make an estimate; put *sth* down at a certain price. 〜を染める try one's hand at *sth*; take *sth* up; have a try at *sth*; get a taste of *sth*. Ⓞ 〜を尽くす make a pledge; make a vow; pledge to do *sth*. 〜を鳴らす snap one's fingers. 〜を詰める ❶ crush one's finger; catch one's finger (in the door). ❷ [*yakuza*] cut of the tip of one's finger in atonement. ❸ make a pledge; make a vow; pledge to do *sth*. 〜を曲げる bend a finger; flex one's fingers; curl one's toes.

弓 a bow; archery

Ⓓ 〜で射る shoot with bow and arrow.
Ⓦ Ⓞ 〜を加う fix an arrow to the bowstring. Ⓐ 〜を鳴らす drive out (an evil spirit); put *sb* to flight. 〜を外す ❶ loosen the bowstring; remove the bowstring. ❷ lay down one's arms; disarm; stop fighting; Ⓒ give up the struggle. 〜を引く ❶ draw a bow; shoot an arrow. ❷ drive out (an evil spirit); put *sb* to flight. ❸ rebel against (authority); rise against (an oppressor).

夢 a dream; a vision; an illusion

Ⓖ 〜が覚める ❶ be awakened; wake up; be roused from one's sleep. ❷ Ⓒ be disillusioned; come to one's senses; see reason.
Ⓣ (一生を)〜と過ごす dream one's life away.
Ⓝ 〜に欺かれる entertain false hopes; Ⓒ labor under an illusion. 〜に現れる appear in one's dream. 〜に通う appear in one's dream. 〜に見る dream about *sb/sth*; see *sth* in a dream; have a vision.
Ⓦ Ⓐ 〜を合わす interpret a dream. 〜を抱く Ⓐ have a dream; have aspirations. 〜を描く aspire to *sth*; have aspirations; Ⓐ have a dream. 〜を追う pursue a dream; live one's dream. Ⓞ 〜を誘う bring out the best in *sb*. 〜を覚ます ❶ awake *sb*; rouse *sb* from sleep. ❷ disillusion *sb*; bring *sb* to his/her senses; make *sb* see reason. 〜を托する rely on *sb/sth*; place one's hope on *sb/sth*. 〜を解く interpret a dream. 〜を見る ❶ dream about *sth*; Ⓒ have a dream. ❷ be lost in daydreams; be a dreamer. 〜を結ぶ get to sleep; have a dream.

夢路 "dream street"

Ⓦ 〜を辿る fall asleep; be fast asleep; Ⓒ nod off.

許し permission; pardon; leave

Ⓦ 〜を与える pardon *sb*; give *sb* leave; grant permission. 〜を受ける be pardoned; obtain leave; get

ゆ

permission. 〜を乞う ask for permission; request leave.

ヨ

世 the world; society; the public

に Ⓐ 〜に合う ❶ win popularity; meet the public taste. ❷ be prosperous; be fortunate; Ⓒ do well. Ⓐ 〜に出ず ❶ be born into the world; see the light of day. ❷ start in life; go out into the world. ❸ take up public office; come into office. 〜に遅れる fall behind the times. 〜に阿る truckle to the times; buy popularity. 〜に従う go with the tide; go with the flow. 〜に背く go against the tide. 〜に立つ succeed in life; go up in the world; Ⓘ make one's mark. 〜に連れる change with the world; Ⓐ be swept along with the tide. 〜に出る ❶ be born into the world; see the light of day. ❷ start in life; go out into the world. ❸ take up public office. 〜に問う make *sth* public; turn to the public; publicize *sth*. Ⓐ 〜に鳴る become famous; win fame. 〜に憚る avoid public notice; shun publicity. Ⓐ 〜に旧る ❶ grow old; become hackneyed. ❷ become rare; grow sparse. ❸ know what it is to be married; have a marital history.

を 〜を挙げる come together; be united. Ⓞ 〜を出づ ❶ escape from the madding crowd; get away from the hustle and bustle of the world. ❷ go into seclusion; Ⓔ retire from the world; become a hermit; renounce the world. ❸ become a Buddhist priest; take the tonsure; Ⓔ retire into religion. Ⓞ 〜を厭う become weary of life; get tired of life. 〜を送る go through life; make a living. 〜を驚かす create a sensation; be much talked about; Ⓐ shake the world; Ⓘ make a stir. Ⓐ 〜を籠む be young; Ⓔ be in the spring of life. 〜を去る pass away; leave this world. 〜を忍ぶ bury oneself in obscurity; live in seclusion. 〜を知る ❶ know what makes the world go round; be worldly wise. Ⓞ ❷ subdue a country; rule a country. 〜を捨てる ❶ become a hermit; go into seclusion; renounce the world; Ⓔ retire from the world. ❷ become a Buddhist priest; take the tonsure; Ⓔ retire into religion. 〜を狭める make one's circle of acquaintances smaller. Ⓞ 〜を背く ❶ go into seclusion; renounce the world; become a hermit; Ⓔ retire from the world. ❷ become a Buddhist priest; take the tonsure; Ⓔ retire into religion. Ⓐ 〜を保つ rule over a country; govern a country; Ⓒ manage the affairs of state. Ⓐ 〜を尽くす ❶ reach the end of one's life; end one's life; finish one's life. ❷ go through life; pass through life; spend one's life (doing *sth*). Ⓐ 〜を遁れる ❶ go into seclusion; renounce the world;

Ⓔ retire from the world. ❷ become a Buddhist priest; take the tonsure; Ⓔ retire into religion. 〜を儚む be tired of life; get weary of the world. 〜を離れる ❶ become a Buddhist priest; take the tonsure; Ⓔ retire into religion. ❷ go into seclusion; renounce the world; Ⓔ retire from the world. 〜を憚る fear to be seen by others; live in obscurity; be reclusive. Ⓐ 〜を張る show off; be vain; Ⓔ be ostentatious. 〜を響かす create a sensation; be much talked about; ① make a stir. Ⓐ 〜を済す save the world. 〜を渡る go through life; earn one's living; make a living.

夜 night; evening; dawn
が Ⓐ 〜が詰まる the nights grow short.

を 〜を明かす keep an all-night vigil; stay up all night. Ⓐ 〜を籠む the night is young. 〜を撤する sit up all night. 〜を更かす stay up late; keep late hours.

酔い drunkenness; intoxication
が 〜が覚める become sober; get sober; sober up. 〜が回る become inebriated; get drunk; Ⓔ be intoxicated; ① be in one's cups.

用 use; business; an errand
が 〜が足りる be useful; be of use; be of help; be competent; Ⓔ meet the requirements.

に Ⓐ 〜に立つ be useful; be of use;

serve a purpose; Ⓒ come in handy.

を 〜を済ます get through with one's business; finish one's business; do one's errand. ⓄⒺ 〜を節する save expenses; cut costs; be frugal. 〜を足す ❶ conduct one's business; go on an errand; run errands. ❷ relieve oneself; go to the toilet; Ⓔ answer the call of nature. 〜を勤める serve sb; do sb a service; Ⓔ be at sb's service. ⓄⒺ 〜を弁ずる conduct one's business; go on an errand. Ⓞ 〜を満たす cover the costs; meet the expenses.

要 Ⓔ the main point; the essence
を Ⓞ 〜を揚げる raise the main point; present the essence of one's message. 〜を得る be brief; ① be to the point. Ⓞ 〜を摘む give the main points; present the essence of one's message.

容儀 Ⓔ deportment; mien
を ⓄⒺ 〜を正す sit up straight. ⒶⒺ 〜を乱す act rudely; act without decorum; be a boor.

用心 care; heed; cation
を 〜を怠る be imprudent; ① be off one's guard.

要領 the point; the gist
を 〜を得る be relevant; ① be to the point; ① be on the mark; ① hit the nail on the head. 〜を教える give sb an outline; tell sb the gist of sth; ① teach sb the ropes.

よ

欲 greed; avarice; desire

が ～が突っ張る be greedy; ⓔ be avaricious; ① bite off more than one can chew. ～が深い be greedy; be selfish; ⓔ be avaricious.

に Ⓐ ～に耽る give oneself over to greed; indulge one's passions; be obsessed by *sth*; be a slave to love; ⓔ be ruled by avarice.

を ～を言う say what one has on one's mind; speak unreservedly. Ⓐ ～を渇く be greedy; be avaricious; ① bite off more than one can chew. ～を離れる be disinterested; be unselfish; be generous; ⓔ free oneself from greed.

横 the side; the flank; the width

と Ⓐ ～と出る become cross at *sb*; be cross-grained; be perverse.

に Ⓐ ～に行く ❶ be unreasonable; be cross-grained. ❷ [prostitution] sleep with another guest; tend to another guest. ～に置く lay *sth* on its side; put *sth* on its side. ～に切る intersect with a road; cross *sb's* path. Ⓐ ～に暮らす live a carefree life. ～にする lay *sth* down. Ⓐ ～に出る ❶ be unreasonable; be cross-grained. ❷ scare *sb* (into *sth*); threaten *sb*. ～になる ❶ lie oneself down; lie down. ⓒ ❷ be unreasonable. Ⓐ ～に寝る ❶ lie on one's side; go to sleep; turn in for the night. ❷ fail to pay off one's debts; stay in arrears. ❸ embezzle money; misappropriate money. (首を)～に振る ❶ shake one's head. ❷ reject *sth*; turn down (an offer) ～に曲げる bend sideways; bend to one side. (船が)～に揺れる roll from side to side; roll to one side. Ⓐ ～に渡る ❶ be unreasonable; be cross-grained. ❷ scare *sb* (into *sth*); threaten *sb*; bully *sb*.

へ ～へ切れる turn into a side road; turn the corner. ～へ退く move sideways; give way to *sb*.

を Ⓐ ～を言う ❶ be unreasonable; be cross-grained. ❷ scare *sb* into *sth*; intimidate *sb*; ⓒ bully *sb*. ⓞ ～を押す ram one's opinion through; force one's will on *sb*; go against all reason. Ⓐ ～を切る [prostitution] sleep with another guest; attend to another guest. ～を向く ❶ look aside; look the other way. ❷ reject *sth*; turn down (an offer).

横車 "a sideway cart"

を ～を押す force one's will on *sb*; ram one's opinion through; go against all reason.

横道 a side road; a byway

を ～に入る deviate from virtue; be led astray; ① leave the straight and narrow.

へ ～へ逸れる ❶ stray from the right way; be led astray; ① leave the straight and narrow. ❷ wander from the (main) subject; get sidetracked; be diverted.

横槍 an interruption

が ～が入る be interrupted.

よ

[を] ～を入(い)れる ❶ interfere in *sb's* affairs; pry in *sb's* affairs; Ⓒ Ⓘ poke one's nose into (the affairs of others). ❷ interrupt *sb*; Ⓢ butt in; Ⓘ put one's oar in.

誼(よし)み [L] **friendship; goodwill**
[を] Ⓔ ～を重(おも)んじる be true in one's friendship; value friendship. Ⓔ ～を通(つう)ずる enter into friendly relations with (the enemy); take *sb's* side. ～を結(むす)ぶ establish a friendship with *sb*; enter into friendly relations with *sb*.

涎(よだれ) [S] **saliva; drivel; drool**
[が] Ⓢ ～が出(で)る ❶ start to drool; begin to drivel. ❷ be delicious; be ravishing; be tempting.
[を] Ⓢ ～を垂(た)らす dribble over *sth*; lust for *sb/sth*; gloat on *sth*. Ⓢ ～を流(なが)す dribble over *sth*; lust for *sb/sth*; gloat on *sth*. Ⓐ Ⓢ ～を舐(ねぶ)る imitate *sb*; take *sb* off; Ⓢ Ⓘ take the mickey (out of *sb*).

嫁(よめ) a (young) wife; a bride
[に] ～に行(い)く marry a man (into the family); get married to a man; Ⓒ Ⓘ tie the knot. ～に遣(や)る give one's daughter away in marriage; marry one's daughter off; Ⓔ give *sb* the hand of one's daugher.
[を] ～を捜(さが)す look for a bride; search for a wife. ～を取(と)る get married; take a (a woman for one's) wife; Ⓒ Ⓘ tie the knot. ～を迎(むか)える get married; take a wife; Ⓒ Ⓘ tie the knot. ～を貰(もら)う have *sb* for a wife; marry a woman.

縒(よ)り a twist; a ply; a lay
[が] ～が戻(もど)る ❶ return to the original state; go back to the old days; become disentangled. ❷ be reconciled; make amends; make it up with *sb*. ❸ feel relieved; feel relaxed.
[を] ～を掛(か)ける ❶ twist a rope; twine a rope. ❷ exert oneself; do one's best; concentrate on *sth*. ～を戻(もど)す ❶ disentangle (a knot). ❷ return *sth* to its original state. ❸ get reconciled; make amends; make it up (with *sb*).

喜(よろこ)び joy; delight; rapture
[に] ～に湧(わ)く be delighted; be in raptures; Ⓘ be over the moon.
[を] ～を得(え)る derive pleasure from; draw joy from. ～を感(かん)じる take delight in; be happy about. ～を述(の)べる offer one's congratulations; express one's joy.

弱音(よわね) [S] **complaints**
[を] Ⓢ ～を吐(は)く make complaints; Ⓘ show the white feather; Ⓘ pull in one's horns.

ラ

来意(らいい) the purpose of one's visit
[を] ～を尋(たず)ねる ask for the reason of *sb's* call. ～を告(つ)げる state the

ら

reason of one's call; give the reason for one's visit.

楽 ease; comfort; relief

に ◎ 〜に居る stretch one's legs; make oneself at home.

埒 Ⓔ a fence; a boundary

が Ⓔ 〜が明く ❶ be settled; come to a settlement. ❷ make progress; make headway; come to an end.

を Ⓐ Ⓔ 〜を明ける ❶ explain *sth*; justify *sth*; plead an excuse. ❷ settle a matter; bring *sth* to a settlement. ◎ Ⓔ 〜を越える cross a boundary; Ⓔ go beyond bounds; Ⓘ be beyond the pale. Ⓐ Ⓔ 〜を付ける ❶ explain *sth*; justify *sth*; plead an excuse. ❷ settle a matter; bring *sth* to a settlement.

喇叭 Ⓒ a trumpet; a horn

を ◎ 〜を吹く ❶ blow a bugle. ❷ boast about *sth*; brag about *sth*; Ⓘ tell a tall tale; Ⓒ Ⓘ talk through one's hat; Ⓘ talk big; Ⓘ blow one's own horn (trumpet).

乱 Ⓔ a revolt; a rebellion; a riot

が Ⓐ 〜が入る be in turmoil; be in an uproar; be in a tumult.

を Ⓐ 〜を入れる make an uproar; make a tumult; Ⓒ Ⓘ raise the devil; Ⓢ kick up a row. 〜を起こす raise a rebellion; rise in revolt; Ⓔ raise the standard of revolt. 〜を治める suppress a rebellion; put down a revolt; crush a riot.

リ

利 benefit; profit; gains

が Ⓢ 〜が食う build up interest; run up interest.

に 〜に走る be eager to make a profit. Ⓐ 〜に耽る be engrossed in profit-making. 〜に迷う be swayed by interests; be tempted by gain.

を 〜を失う ❶ lose the advantage; be at a disadvantage; be handicapped. ❷ suffer a loss. 〜を得る ❶ have an advantage (over *sb*). ❷ make a profit; profit from *sth*. 〜をかく pay interest. Ⓢ 〜を食う yield interest; get interest.

理 reason; a principle; logic

が Ⓐ 〜が済む be sensible; be fair-minded; be down-to-earth.

に 〜に当たる be in the right; be right; be reasonable; Ⓘ be on the mark. Ⓐ 〜に落ちる be given to too much reasoning; be argumentative. Ⓐ 〜に折れる give in to reason. 〜に適う be reasonable; stand to reason. 〜に詰まる ❶ give in to reason; be won over. ❷ be given to too much reasoning; be argumentative; Ⓘ split hairs; Ⓒ Ⓘ chop logic (with *sb*). 〜に反する go against reason; be unreasonable; do not stand to reason; be in the wrong.

を Ⓐ 〜を砕く reason with *sb*; tell *sb* what is what. 〜を尽くす listen to reason; be reasonable; be down-to-earth. 〜を曲げる pervert the truth; bend the truth. Ⓐ 〜を持つ be reasonable; be in the right; Ⓘ be on the mark. ◎ 〜を破る pervert the truth; bend the truth. 〜を分ける see reason; know what is what.

裏 Ⓔ the reverse/other side ▶ 裏

Ⓝ Ⓐ 〜に入る ❶ [medical] strike inward. ❷ be depressed; be downhearted; be gloomy; feel down. Ⓐ 〜に落ちる be downhearted; be depressed; be gloomy; feel down. Ⓐ 〜に詰む be downhearted; be depressed; be gloomy; feel down.

力量 ability; capacity; capability

Ⓦ 〜を示す display one's ability. 〜を試す test sb's ability. 〜を問う question sb's ability; call sb's ability into question.

理屈 Ⓒ reason; logic; theory

Ⓖ Ⓐ ◎ 〜が下る understand sth; comprehend sth; follow sth. ◎ 〜が立つ be reasonable; be logical; stand to reason. ◎ 〜が付く resolve a situation; settle an affair. ◎ 〜が通る be sound; be reasonable; be sensible; stand to reason.

Ⓝ ◎ 〜に合う be reasonable; be logical; stand to reason. ◎ 〜に適う be logical; make sense; be rational; be sensible; be down-to-earth.

Ⓦ ◎ 〜を言う be argumentative; raise an argument; Ⓘ split hairs; ◎ Ⓘ chop logic (with sb). ◎ 〜を捏

ねる quibble over sth; argue for the sake of argument; Ⓘ put on an argument. ◎ 〜を付ける ❶ raise an argument; be argumentative; Ⓘ split hairs; ◎ Ⓘ chop logic (with sb). Ⓐ ❷ resolve a situation; settle an affair.

利子 interest

Ⓖ 〜がつく yield interest.
Ⓒ 〜で暮らす live on interest.
Ⓦ 〜を生む yield interest. 〜を取る charge interest. 〜を払う pay interest.

理性 reason; reasoning power

Ⓦ 〜を失う lose one's reason; go mad; Ⓢ Ⓘ lose one's marbles. 〜を欠く be devoid of reason. 〜を保つ maintain one's sanity; Ⓘ keep one's head. 〜を働かす use one's reason.

理想 an ideal

Ⓝ 〜に適う measure up to one's ideal; conform to one's ideal.
Ⓦ 〜を抱く cherish an ideal. 〜を追う pursue an ideal. 〜を立てる hold up an ideal.

溜飲 Ⓔ water brash

Ⓖ ◎ 〜が起こる suffer from water brash. 〜が下がる ❶ be cured of water brash. Ⓑ ❷ feel relieved; feel satisfaction over sth; be content with sth.
Ⓦ Ⓑ 〜を下げる feel satisfaction (in doing sth); satisfy oneself (by doing sth); gloat over sth.

料簡 E an idea; a thought

が Ⓔ 〜が付く ❶ have an idea; think of *sth*; hit on an idea. ❷ realize one's error; become aware of one's mistake.

に Ⓐ Ⓔ 〜に付く act in accordance with *sb's* ideas; comply with *sb*.

を Ⓔ (悪い)〜を起こす conceive a bad idea; yield to temptation; Ⓘ take *sth* into one's head. Ⓐ Ⓔ 〜を加える take measures; take steps. Ⓐ Ⓔ 〜を付ける be patient (with *sb*); put up with *sb/sth*; acquiesce in *sth*.

良心 conscience

が 〜が咎める go against one's conscience; feel guilty; have a guilty conscience; Ⓘ feel the pricks of conscience.

に 〜に訴える appeal to *sb's* conscience; address *sb's* conscience. 〜に顧みる search one's soul; Ⓔ consult one's conscience. 〜に従う follow one's conscience; listen to one's conscience; act according to one's conscience. 〜に背く go against one's conscience. 〜に問う listen to one's conscience; Ⓔ heed conscience. 〜に恥じる feel guilty; have a guilty conscience; Ⓔ weigh upon one's conscience; Ⓘ feel the pricks of conscience. 〜に反する go against one's conscience.

を 〜を傷つける wound one's conscience. 〜を慰める soothe one's conscience; Ⓔ appease one's conscience. 〜を悩ます feel guilty; Ⓔ weigh upon one's conscience; Ⓘ feel the pricks of conscience.

両刀 two swords; both swords

を 〜を遣う ❶ use two swords. ❷ be ambidextrous. ❸ be bisexual.

輪郭 contours; outlines; profile

を 〜を描く draw *sb* in outline; describe *sth* in outline. 〜を掴む grasp the general idea; get the picture; Ⓢ Ⓘ catch *sb's* drift. 〜を述べる give an outline (of a plan).

ル

累 trouble; implication

が 〜が及ぶ be negatively affected by circumstances; be troubled by circumstances; undergo a negative influence.

を 〜を及ぼす cause *sb* trouble; get *sb* into trouble; affect *sth* negatively; Ⓔ have negative repercussions.

塁 a fort; a base; a rampart

を Ⓐ 〜を摩する ❶ draw close to an enemy fort. ❷ be close rivals; be close contenders; run very closely. 〜を守る defend a fort. 〜を設ける build a fort; set up a parapet; erect a stronghold.

類 a species; a type; a sort

に 〜に属する belong to a species.

Ⓐ ～に触る check out *sb's* relations; hunt up one's connections.

留守 being away; absence

Ⓝ ～にする be absent; be out. (お)～になる neglect one's duties.
Ⓦ ～を預かる take charge of the house (while *sb* is absent); look after the house; Ⓘ hold the fort. ～を使う pretend to be out; feign absence.

レ

礼 a bow; etiquette; courtesy

Ⓝ (お)～に行く visit *sb* out of courtesy; call on *sb* to offer one's thanks.
Ⓦ ～を言う express one's thanks; make one's apologies; express one's gratitude; Ⓔ tender an apology. ～を欠く lack courtesy; be impolite. ～を差し上げる offer a reward. Ⓔ ～を失する go against etiquette. ～を知る be well-bred; be of good breeding. ～をする ❶ make a bow; bow to *sb*; salute *sb*; make a curtsy. ❷ offer a reward; remunerate *sb*; pay *sb* a fee. ～を尽くす show *sb* every courtesy; treat *sb* with honor. ～を述べる thank *sb*; express one's thanks. ～を貰う accept a reward; receive a reward; get a reward.

例 an example; a precedent

Ⓝ ～に倣う follow suit; follow an example; take example by *sth*.

Ⓦ ～を揚げる give an example; take an instance; refer to a precedent. ～を捜し出す ferret out an instance; find a precedent. ～を示す show an example; point out an instance. ～を作る establish a precedent; set a precedent. ～を引く cite an instance; draw an example; quote an instance. ～を設ける cite a case. ～を破る break the precedent.

霊 the spirit; someone's memory

Ⓦ ～を鎮める appease the souls of the deceased. ～を慰める appease the souls of the deceased. ～を祭る perform religious services for the departed souls; worship the spirits; celebrate *sb's* memory.

霊感 inspiration; a brainstorm

Ⓖ ～が働く be inspired; have a brain wave; get inspired.
Ⓦ ～を与える give *sb* inspiration. ～を受ける be inspired; have a brain wave; get inspired. ～を見出す find inspiration; get inspiration. ～を求める seek inspiration; look for inspiration.

冷気 cold; chill; cold weather

Ⓦ ～を感じる feel chilly. ～を催す the cold season has set in.

冷静 calmness; coolness

Ⓝ ～に返る regain one's presence of mind; Ⓔ recover one's composure; Ⓘ pull oneself together. ～に

構える affect composure; remain self-composed; ⓘ keep one's head.

礼節 ⓔ courtesy; etiquette
を ⓔ 〜を失う lose one's sense of decorum; be perturbed. ⓔ 〜を保つ remain calm; maintain one's sense of decorum; be unruffled; ⓘ keep one's head. ⓔ 〜を取り戻す regain one's self-possession. ⓔ 〜を磨く cultivate one's manners.

令名 ⓔ a good name; fame
を ⓔ 〜を博する win fame; become famous. ⓔ 〜を馳せる win fame; become famous. ⓔ 〜を汚す mar *sb's* name; ⓔ tarnish *sb's* reputation.

霊夢 Ⓐ an inspired dream
を Ⓐ 〜を見る have an inspired dream.

列 a row; a line; a tire
に 〜に加わる step into line; join a queue. 〜に並ぶ stand in line; line up; form a queue.
を ⓞ 〜を切る cross a line; break through a line. 〜を作る form a line; line up; form a queue; queue up. 〜を詰める close up the ranks. 〜を解く break up the ranks. 〜を整える dress to ranks. 〜を離れる fall out of line; leave the ranks. 〜を乱す break the line; jump the queue; break rank.

劣等感 an inferiority complex
を 〜を抱く feel inferior; have an inferiority complex. 〜を持つ feel inferior; have an inferiority complex.

蓮歩 ⓔ graceful steps
を Ⓐ ⓔ 〜を運ぶ walk gracefully.

連絡 contact; communications
を 〜を失う lose contact. 〜を絶つ break off communications; cut off contact. 〜を保つ maintain (radio) contact; keep in touch with *sb*. 〜を付ける establish contact; get in touch with *sb*; make contact. 〜を取る get in touch with *sb*; establish contact; make contact.

■ロ

炉 a fireplace; a hearth; a forge
に 〜に掛ける hang (a kettle/pot) over the fire.
を 〜を囲む sit around the fireplace; gather around the hearth. ⓞ 〜を切る make a fireplace in the floor.

櫓 a scull; an oar
を ⓞ 〜を押す work a scull; pull an oar. ⓞ 〜を漕ぐ work a scull; pull an oar.

労 ⓔ trouble; labor; pains
に ⓔ 〜に報いる reward *sb* for his/her services.
を 〜を惜しむ be sparing of oneself; spare oneself trouble. 〜

を取る take the trouble to do *sth*; take pains to do *sth*. 〜を省く save *sb* trouble. 〜を煩わす trouble *sb* to do *sth*.

牢 a prison; a jail; a gaol

に 〜に入る be imprisoned; be put in jail; be thrown into jail.

を 〜を出る be released from prison; come out of prison. 〜を破る escape from prison; break out of prison.

狼藉 Ⓔ disorder; mayhem; havoc

を Ⓒ 〜を極める commit all kinds of excesses. Ⓒ 〜を働く run riot; work havoc; commit excesses.

禄 Ⓐ a fief; a stipend; a ration

を Ⓐ 〜を窃む hold a sinecure. Ⓐ 〜を食む receive a stipend; become a vassal.

ワ

輪 a circle; a ring; a link

が 〜が外れる the wheel comes off.

に 〜になる sit in a circle; form a circle.

を 〜を描く form a circle; describe a circle. 〜を掛ける ❶ exaggerate *sth*; overstate *sth*; Ⓘ stretch the facts; Ⓢ Ⓘ pile it on. ❷ exacerbate *sth*; make *sth* worse; Ⓔ enhance *sth*; make *sth* more attractive. 〜を回す roll a hoop; drive a hoop.

和 peace; the sum; the total

を 〜を乞う sue for peace. ◎ 〜を求める do the sum (of); add *sth* up.

賄賂 a bribe; bribery

を 〜を受け取る accept a bribe; be bribed. 〜を贈る offer *sb* a bribe; bribe *sb*; Ⓒ Ⓘ grease *sb's* palm. 〜を使う offer *sb* a bribe; bribe *sb*; Ⓒ Ⓘ grease *sb's* palm. 〜を貰う accept a bribe; be bribed.

我が意 one's own mind

を 〜を得る meet one's wishes; be satisfactory to one; be happy to hear *sth*.

我が身 oneself

を 〜を顧みる reflect on oneself; search one's soul; Ⓔ consult one's conscience; Ⓔ exercise introspection.

我が道 one's own way

を 〜を行く go one's own way; Ⓘ plow one's own furrow.

我が物 one's own (property)

に 〜にする ❶ take possession of *sth*; make *sth* one's own. ❷ learn how to do *sth*; master a skill; learn a language/craft.

別れ parting; farewell

を 〜を告げる say good-bye; Ⓔ bid *sb* farewell; Ⓔ take one's leave. 〜を惜しむ dread parting; be sorry to part; Ⓔ be loath to part.

わ

脇 the side; another place

に ～に置く lay *sth* aside; put *sth* beside one. ～に抱える hold *sth* under one's arm. ～に立つ stand beside *sb*; stand by *sb's* side. ～になる take a backseat (to another problem). ～に呼ぶ call *sb* to one's side. ～に寄る step aside; go to one side; get out of the way.

へ ～へ退く step aside; go to one side; get out of the way. ～へ反らす change the conversation; divert *sb's* attention from *sth*; ⓔ digress from the subject. ～へ散らす take one's mind off *sth*; ⓘ wash one's hands of a matter. (人を)～へ連れ出す take *sb* aside. ～へ引き寄せる draw *sth* to one's side. ～へ回る go somewhere else. ～へ向く look aside; turn away.

を Ⓐ ～を搔く be eager to do *sth*; be proud to do *sth*; ⓘ be on one's mettle. ～を通る pass *sb* by. Ⓐ ～を塞ぐ grow up; come of age; attain manhood/womanhood. ～を見る look away; take one's eyes off *sth*.

和議 Ⓔ peace negotiations

を ⓔ ～を請う sue for peace. ～を結ぶ make peace; conclude peace. ～を申し込む make overtures for peace; ⓘ hold out the olive branch.

脇道 a byway; a byroad

に ～に反れる ❶ wander into a byroad; ⓔ stray into a sideroad. ❷ wander from the (main) subject; get sidetracked; be diverted.

へ ～へ反れる ❶ wander into a byroad; turn aside; ⓔ stray into a sideroad. ❷ wander from the (main) subject; get sidetracked; be diverted.

脇役 a supporting role

に ～に回る ❶ take a subordinate part. ❷ take a subordinate role; ⓘ take a back seat to *sb*; ⓘ take second billing to *sb*.

を ～を勤める ❶ play a subordinate part; support an actor. ❷ play a subordinate role; ⓘ take second billing to *sb*; ⓒ ⓘ play second fiddle to *sb*. ～を果たす ❶ play a subordinate part; support an actor. ❷ play a subordinate role; ⓘ take second billing to *sb*; ⓒ ⓘ play second fiddle to *sb*.

枠 a frame; a rim; a limit

に ～に入れる frame (a picture). ～に嵌まる be conventional; be hackneyed; ⓘ be the same old fare. ⓒ ～に巻く reel thread.

を ～を決める set restrictions; put a limit on *sth*. ～を越える exceed the framework; ⓘ be beyond the pale. ～を付ける frame (a picture; set a frame to (a picture). ～を嵌める impose restrictions; put restrictions on *sth*. ～を拡げる widen the scope. ～を設ける establish a framework; set a limit.

訳 a reason; a ground; a sense

が ～が有る have a reason; be with

reason. 〜が立つ ❶ see reason; be sensible. Ⓐ ❷ pay one's dues; clear off. Ⓐ ❸ have intimate relations with *sb*; have an affair; Ⓒ Ⓘ carry on with *sb*. 〜が違う be different; run counter to *sth*. Ⓐ 〜が付く ❶ give one's consent; understand *sth*. ❷ pay one's dues; clear off one's debts. 〜が分かる understand *sb/sth*; be sensible; Ⓒ know what is what.

Ⓥ 〜を言う ❶ give one's reasons; explain oneself; Ⓔ set forth one's reasons. ❷ make an excuse; give a pretext. 〜を聞く ask for a reason; ask for an explanation. 〜を尋ねる demand a reason. 〜を質す inquire into a reason for *sth*. Ⓐ 〜を立てる ❶ reason with *sb*; tell *sb* what is what; resolve a problem. ❷ have intimate relations with *sb*; have an affair; Ⓒ Ⓘ carry on with *sb*. ❸ pay one's dues; clear off one's debts. Ⓐ 〜を付ける settle a matter; get through *sth*. 〜を通す persuade *sb*; convince *sb*; win *sb* over. 〜を説く explain oneself; Ⓔ set forth one's reasons. 〜を話す give one's reasons; explain oneself; Ⓔ set forth one's reasons.

禍 a calamity; misfortune

Ⓣ 〜となる lead to one's downfall; Ⓔ be one's undoing.

Ⓥ 〜を招く invite a disaster; ask for trouble; Ⓔ bring calamity upon oneself. 〜を避ける avoid a disaster; keep out of harm's way.

話題 a topic; a subject

Ⓣ 〜に困る be lost for a topic (of conversation). 〜に富む have a broad pallet of topics at one's disposal; be *sb* of wide interest. 〜に上る become the topic of a talk; come up in conversation.

Ⓥ 〜を選ぶ choose a topic (for conversation); Ⓒ pick a subject. 〜を変える change the subject; shift the conversation; Ⓘ take a new tack. 〜を賑わす be much talked about; Ⓘ make a stir.

蟠り vexations; cares; grudges

Ⓖ 〜が有る be vexed; have *sth* on one's mind; be troubled by *sth*. 〜が出来る cause ill feelings; Ⓘ breed bad blood. 〜が解ける calm down; forget one's ill feelings towards *sb*; Ⓔ regain one's composure; Ⓐ cool down.

Ⓥ 〜を捨てる throw off reserve; forget one's ill feelings (toward *sb*). 〜を解く dispel ill feelings. 〜を持つ be vexed; have *sth* on one's mind; be troubled by *sth*.

渡り a ferry ; a passage ; transit

Ⓖ 〜が付く ❶ come into contact with *sb*; enter into relations with *sb*. ❷ come to an understanding; Ⓔ arrive at an understanding.

Ⓥ 〜を付ける ❶ get in touch with *sb*; enter into relations with *sb*; start negotiations with *sb*; Ⓔ effect a liaison with *sb*. ❷ reach an agreement; Ⓔ arrive at an understanding.

わ

罠 a snare; a trap; a gin

が ～が掛かる be caught in a trap; fall into a trap.

に ～に陥る be caught in a trap; be ensnared. ～に落ちる fall into a trap; be trapped. ～に誘い込む lure (an animal) into a trap. ～に掛かる be trapped; be ensnared; be caught in a trap; be taken in; ⓒ be conned; ⓢ be duped. ～に掛ける snare (an animal); ensnare sb (into doing sth). ～に嵌まる be caught in a trap; be ensnared.

を ～を掛ける lay a snare; set a trap; ⓒ ⓘ set sb up.

詫び an apology; an excuse

を ～を容れる accept an apology. ～を入れる offer an apology.

藁 (rice) straw; a straw

が Ⓐ ～が出る have one's faults exposed; ⓒ ⓘ show oneself up.

で ～で葺く thatch a house/roof.

を ～を敷く cover the ground with straw; litter a stall down. Ⓐ ～を焚く ❶ entice sb; put sb up (to commit a crime); egg sb on. ❷ speak ill of sb; ⓔ disparage sb; abuse sb; ⓘ run sb down. ❸ haggle over (a price); bargain for sth. Ⓐ ～を出す betray one's ignorance; ⓒ show oneself up. ～を束ねる bind straw into a sheaf; tie up straw.

笑い a laugh; a smile; a sneer

に ～に紛らす divert oneself with laughter; laugh sth away.

を ～を浮かべる wear a smile. ～を押える repress a laugh; stifle one's laughter; swallow a laugh. ～を買う be laughed at; be ridiculed; ⓘ make oneself a laughingstock. ～を噛み殺す suppress a smile. ～を含む wear a faint smile. ～を招く invite ridicule; ⓔ incur derision. ～を洩らす laugh in spite of oneself.

草鞋 straw sandals

を ～を脱ぐ end one's journey; take up lodgings; stop over (at a place). ～を履く ❶ set out on a journey. ❷ take a percentage; ⓒ take a rake-off; ⓒ take a cut. ❸ be on the run; ⓔ be at large.

割 a rate; a ratio; gain; profit

が ～が付く bear a premium; leave a surplus; remain in excess. ～が良い have a good yield; pay well. Ⓐ ～が弱い have a poor return; be unprofitable. ～が悪い have a bad yield; be unprofitable.

に ～に合う be profitable; pay for itself; ⓒ pay off. Ⓐ ～に当たる be profitable; pay for itself. ⓢ ～に返る be disadvantageous to one; be to one's disadvantage; ⓘ be a fall guy. ～に入る mediate between two parties; act as a mediator.

を Ⓐ ～を言う ❶ explain oneself; make an excuse; defend oneself. ❷ be given to too much reasoning; be argumentative; ⓘ split hairs; ⓒ ⓘ chop logic (with sb). ～を入れる employ a mediator; resort to

わ

arbitration. Ⓐ 〜を打つ ❶ drive in a wedge; wedge two things apart. ❷ mix *sth* with water; water *sth* down. ⓢ 〜を食う turn out to one's disadvantage; be disadvantageous to one. ◎ 〜をする allot (space) to *sb*; assign (money) to *sb*. ◎ 〜を付ける ❶ pay out a premium. ❷ act as a mediator; mediate between two parties.

割符 Ⓔ a tally; a check
か Ⓔ 〜が合う ❶ the tallies meet. ❷ be like-minded; get along well; Ⓔ be congenial to one; ① see eye to eye; ◎ ① hit it off.
を Ⓔ 〜を合わす make *sth* tally; compare the tallies.

割前 Ⓔ a share; one's lot
を Ⓔ 〜を出す bare one's share;

pay one's due; contribute one's quota. Ⓔ 〜を貰う get one's share; receive one's quota.

悪遊び a prank; evil pleasures
を 〜を覚える get into mischief; take to evil pleasures; take up gambling.

悪巧み wiles; an evil design
を 〜をする carry out a wicked design; conspire against *sb*; lay a plot against *sb*; ⓢ ① be in cahoots.

我 I; oneself; ego ▶我
に 〜に返る come to oneself; recover one's senses; be oneself again.
を 〜を忘れる forget oneself; be absorbed in *sth*; lose oneself (in); ① get carried away.

わ

Floating World Editions publishes books that contribute to a deeper understanding of Asian cultures. Editorial supervision: Ray Furse. Japanese text editing: Hiromi Miyagi-Lusthaus. Book and cover design: William de Lange. Production supervision: Bill Rose. Printing and binding: VonHoffmann Corporation. The typefaces used are Osaka and Trebuchet MS.